macromedia®
FLASH®
Professional 8

www.librex.co.uk

Macromedia® Flash® Professional 8
Training from the Source

Tom Green
Jordan Chilcott

macromedia PRESS Macromedia Press books are published by:

Peachpit

1249 Eighth Street
Berkeley, CA 94710
510/524-2178
800/283-9444
510/524-2221 (fax)
Find us on the World Wide Web at:
www.peachpit.com
www.macromedia.com

To report errors, please send a note to errata@peachpit.com

Printed and bound in the United States of America

ISBN 0-321-38403-2

9 8 7 6 5 4 3 2 1

Credits

Authors
Tom Green
Jordan Chilcott

Macromedia Press Editor
Angela C. Kozlowski

Editor
Susan Hobbs

Technical Editor
James Cullin

Production Coordinator
Myrna Vladic

Copy Editor
Nancy Sixsmith

Indexer
Julie Bess

Cover Production
Ellen Reilly

Compositors
Rick Gordon, Emerald Valley Graphics
Debbie Roberti, Espresso Graphics

Dedications

This one is for you Robert …. Finally!—Tom

This book is dedicated to my wife, Joelle, who never stopped believing in me, no matter the circumstances. I love you more than words can express!—Jordan

Bios

Tom Green is Professor, Interactive Media through the School of Media Studies at the Humber Institute of Technology and Applied Learning in Toronto. When not in class, Tom is a partner at CommunityMX and has written several articles for the Macromedia Developer Center. He is also a member of Team Macromedia, one of the founding members of FlashinTO, the largest Macromedia User Group in the world, a certified Macromedia Dreamweaver Developer, and has spoken at many Web development, Flash, and Distance Learning Conferences throughout the world. His Web site can be found at http://www.tomontheweb.ca.

Jordan L. Chilcott, born and raised in Toronto and now a resident of Guelph, Ontario, graduated from Radio College of Canada's Electronic Engineering Technology program in 1983, only to discover that he had a passion for computer programming. Spending his days working as a service technician, Jordan invested many sleepless nights teaching himself Assembly Language. He published his first program in 1985 and started learning higher-level languages such as C and C++.

Jordan co-founded The Computer Software Specialists, now known as Interactivity Unlimited, and eventually left the computer hardware industry to focus on his passion for programming. Today, Jordan has written various Web and kiosk applications for various industries including the automotive and airline industry and programs in various languages, including ActionScript, ColdFusion, Java/J2ee, and C/C++/Objective C. When not programming, or administering the Dreamweaver-Talk list, he spends time with his wife, Joelle, and five children, Margot, Dina, Henry, Jack, and Joshua, and has recently become a grandfather. Jordan also loves to compose, produce, and record music, helping upcoming artists as well as producing movie soundtracks; is a wedding photographer with Joelle; and now holds a Black Belt in Goju Ryu Karate.

Acknowledgements

This has been quite the trip and it started over hamburgers in Toronto when Mike Downey, the Flash Product Manager, showed a couple of us a pre-alpha version of Flash 8. Since then, Mike and his crew have helped me pull this book together with a bit of gentle prodding and guidance along the way. I would also like to acknowledge my Acquisition Editor, Angela Kozlowski, who got this project underway, and whose patience, advice, and just plain focus kept this project moving forward. I would also like to thank Sue Hobbs, our Development Editor, whose good humor and passion for clarity of language never ceases to amaze me. James Cullin, a colleague at Humber, also performed superbly as Tech Editor, and kept Jord and me on our toes with some rather interesting questions.

This is the third book where Jordan and I have worked together. Jord and I have developed a close working relationship but even more important than that we have become extremely close friends and colleagues.

I want to thank my boss at Humber, William Hanna, Dean of the School of Media Studies for his support, good humor, and patience. In many respects, my career as an author started in William's office over coffee and a conversation about the first book I was about to write. Considering this is the fifth since that conversation, I am deeply indebted to you. You also need a sounding board and my students were always ready to try out something and critique it with "I don't get it," which, in many respects, is the most valuable input I could ever expect. Most of all my family has put up with me for yet another writing session and finally my children, Lindsay and Robert, will actually get to have a rational conversation with me. To Keltie, my wife, "Thank you for putting up with me. I am now finally getting a good night's sleep".—**Tom**

To start, I would like to thank my wife, Joelle, and my kids, Margot, Dina (and her husband Wayne), Henry, Jack, and Joshua who would not only encourage me, but would also pray for me and push me onward, no matter how tough things got. I'd also like to thank the many people on the Dreamweaver-Talk list, who I look up to in many ways. They all inspire me so much when it comes to Web design that one cannot just simply hang around the list without getting better at their craft. I'd also like to thank my Sensei's for always believing in us and showing us how to be true teachers in anything we do. I also want to thank all of our editors for allowing me to once again be part of a great team. And, finally, I want to thank my co-author, Tom. Aside from being someone who's fantastic in being able to translate my geek to English and great to work with, Tom has become a great friend who's there to tell me what I need to hear and not what I want to hear. Here's to you!—**Jordan**

Table of Contents

Introduction

Macromedia Flash Professional 8 is the latest iteration of the application that has moved from being a simple Web animation tool named FutureSplash to a rich media content delivery platform that puts your Flash work on everything from desktop computers to cell phones. Along the way, developers and designers moved from creating simple animated movies of bouncing balls to media applications that used databases, video, and audio. In fact, Flash has become a powerhouse on the Internet. The Flash Player is installed on practically every computer on the planet and a specialized version of the player—FlashLite—is steadily heading in a similar direction with cell phones. As such, Flash is now considered to be a de facto standard for displaying rich content on the Web, and this book shows you many different techniques and methods for doing so.

There are two versions of the application—Flash 8 and Flash Professional 8. Flash Professional 8, the focus of this book, contains a number of features not found in Flash 8. These include features such as filters, blend effects, the Video Encoder, Video UI components, and the Data components. There is so much to the Professional version of the application that Macromedia is now focusing on two aspects of the application: Expressiveness and Development.

Expressiveness, the focus of this book, is the design aspect of the application. Expressiveness came to prominence when Macromedia realized it had started to alienate many of its core users through an emphasis on code. They recognized this almost from the moment Flash MX Professional 2004 was released, and spent the next 12 months in meetings around the world with Flash designers and developers looking for suggestions regarding bringing Flash back to its design roots. They didn't tell designers what they needed. They listened carefully to what designers wanted and then went to work with the wish list. It is no wonder that Macromedia regards Flash Professional 8 as the most significant Flash release in the history of the application. This book provides you with a firm foundation in the new focus of the application.

Prerequisites

Flash Professional 8: Training from the Source helps you establish a solid foundation with the Expressiveness features of the Professional version of this application. It is not a Flash Basics guide, and we assume you have a copy of Flash Professional 8 installed on your computer. We are also assuming you have some experience with Flash MX, MX 2004, or MX Professional 2004, and are somewhat familiar with ActionScript . If you don't fall into this category, we suggest you work your way through Jen deHaan's excellent Flash 8: Training from the Source before tackling this book. We are also steering clear of the other half of the Flash 8 equation: Development. The reason is actually quite simple—the application is so complex that to do the subject justice requires a separate volume such as Flash 8 ActionScript: Training from the Source.

Outline

You will quickly discover this book presents many important techniques and methods that give you a solid grounding in the Expressiveness features of Flash Professional 8. You learn how to create animations, incorporate video and audio into movies, use text and images, apply many of the new filters and blending modes to objects in your movies, create presentations driven by XML, design a movie for a cell phone, and much more. This Macromedia training course steps you through the projects in each lesson, presents many of the major features of the application, and guides you toward adding rich media skills to your Flash skill set.

This curriculum takes 20 to 22 hours to complete and includes the following lessons:

Lesson 1: Learning the Flash Interface

Lesson 2: ActionScript Basics

Lesson 3: Graphics in Flash

Lesson 4: Text in Flash

Lesson 5: Using Audio in Flash

Lesson 6: Creating Animation

Lesson 7: Creating Flash Video

Lesson 8: Building a Custom Flash Video Player

Lesson 9: Manipulating Video

Lesson 10: Communication Server: Audio and Video

Lesson 11: Using Dynamic Data

Lesson 12: Going Mobile with Flash Professional 8

Lesson 13: Publishing a Flash Movie

This book contains a number of individual projects, each designed to teach you a specific aspect of the Expressiveness features of Flash Professional 8. Each project is designed to give you the basics skills necessary to use the feature and, most important of all, the confidence to use many of these techniques in your workflow.

Each lesson starts with an overview of what you will learn and the lessons are structured in such a way that each one builds upon the skills from the previous lesson. In addition, each lesson features:

- **Tips**: There are any number of different ways to complete a task, and tips show you alternative ways of using the skills learned.
- **Notes**: Additional background information designed to add more context to the task at hand.
- **Bold text:** Bold text is used to identify the names of visual elements in a project such as movie clips, buttons and other content used.

- **Special font for code:** To help you easily identify ActionScript, XML, and HTML code in this book, the code has been styled in a `special` font that is unique from the fonts used throughout the book.

- **Appendix:** The two Appendices contain an overview of the Flash menus, the Accessibility features of Flash, and a list of resources you can go to for help or to further your knowledge of the application.

The accompanying CD-ROM contains all of the files necessary to complete each lesson. The files appear in a folder titled with the lesson number.

It is also strongly recommended that you copy all of the files from the CD to your computer. This way, all is not lost if you lose or damage the CD. Even more important is the fact that all files in this book require you to test them using the Test Movie command. This command creates a test file in the same directory as the lesson. If you work from the CD, Flash attempts to write the file to the CD. This results in an error because a CD is Read-Only media … the computer can't write to it.

Macromedia Training from the Source

The Macromedia Training from the Source and Advanced Training from the Source series are developed in association with Macromedia and reviewed by the product support teams. Ideal for active learners, the books in the Training from the Source series offer hands-on instruction designed to provide you with a solid grounding in the program's fundamentals. If you learn best "by doing," this is the series for you. Each Training from the Source title contains hours of instruction on Macromedia software products. They are designed to teach the techniques you need to create sophisticated professional-level projects.

Macromedia Authorized Training and Certification

This book is geared to enable you to study at your own pace with content from the source. Other training options exist through the Macromedia Authorized Training Partner program. Get up to speed in a matter of days with task-oriented courses taught by Macromedia Certified Instructors. Or learn on your own with interactive, online training from Macromedia University. All of these sources of training prepare you to become a Macromedia Certified Developer.

For more information about authorized training and certification, check out www.macromedia.com/go/training1

What You Will Learn in This Book

As you work your way through this book, you develop the skills necessary to build a rich media application that uses audio, video, and dynamic data.

By the end of this course you should be able to:

- Add metadata to a Flash Professional 8 movie
- Create a Flash project
- Use versioning to manage a project
- Use the imaging tools including gradients, filters, and blend effects
- Parse XML data to add content to your movie
- Add audio to a Flash movie and control it with ActionScript
- Use the filters in animations
- Insert video into a Flash movie
- Use the Media components
- Use ActionScript to control video playback
- Manipulate video
- Stream video through the Web and through a Flash Communication Server
- Load external data into a Flash movie
- Understand how to create a movie for Pocket PC playback
- Publish a Flash movie

Minimum System Requirements

Windows

- 800 MHZ Intel Pentium III Processor or equivalent
- Windows 2000, Windows XP, or Windows XP Service Pack 2
- 256 MB RAM (1GB recommended)
- 710 MB available disk space

Macintosh

- 600 MHZ Power PC g4 Processor
- Mac OSX 10.3, 10.4
- 256 MB RAM (1 GB recommended)
- 360 MB available disk space

Other

- Some features require QuickTime 6.3 or QuickTime Pro 6.3
- Flash Professional 8 requires product activation over the Internet or by phone
- Trial versions of Flash Communications Server and ColdFusion MX 7 Standard, used in Lessons 10 and 11, are available at http://www.macromedia.com/software/

The Studio 8 line of products is among the most feature-laden and robust upgrades in Macromedia history. We are sure you will be amazed at what you can do with them. With a strong foundation in Flash, you will be able to explore the field of rich media and expand your skill set in a very short time. As you proceed through the 13 lessons in this book, you will discover Flash is relatively easy to use and that you will be producing work incorporating audio, video, animation, and interactivity in your sites in a relatively short period of time. Most important of all, you will discover the amount of fun you can have using Flash Professional 8 should be illegal. See you in jail!

1 Learning the Flash Interface

Macromedia Flash Professional 8 is a tool designed to help you create engaging and stimulating animations, add streaming audio and video to your Web sites, and create rich Internet applications that can be used for e-learning or e-commerce purposes. You can create Flash content that plays not only through a browser on your PC but also from CDs and through Pocket PC devices such as handheld devices and even cell phones. As you move through the lessons in this book, you will discover all the features of Flash and, most important of all, just how much fun you can have with this application.

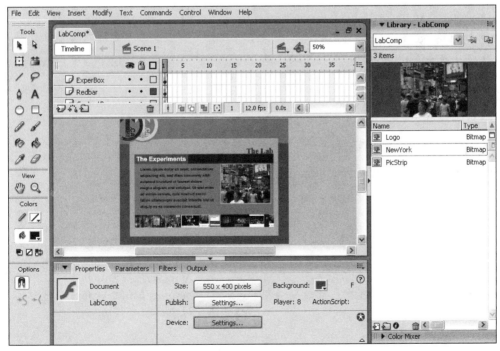

The completed interface.

In this lesson, you become familiar with many of the new features of the Flash Professional 8 interface and use those skills to create the interface for a portfolio site. If you are familiar with Flash MX Professional 2004, this chapter can either be skipped or used to review the new interface enhancements in Flash. If you are somewhat new to Flash Professional 8, this chapter is designed to get you working with the application by explaining some of the new items added to the Flash interface in this release of the application.

What You Will Learn

In this lesson you will:

- Create a Flash document
- Add metadata to Flash SWF file
- Change the Application preferences
- Rearrange Flash interface panels into tabbed groups
- Expand the Flash Pasteboard
- Use the tools in the Tools panel
- Organize content into layers
- Use the new Object Drawing mode
- Add text to the document
- Add images to a Flash document
- Test the document
- Publish the document as a SWF file
- Create a Flash project file

Approximate Time

This lesson takes about 90 minutes to complete.

Lesson Files

Media Files:

Logo.jpg
Lorem.txt
NewYork.jpg
PicStrip.jpg

Completed Files:

Lesson01/Complete/LabComp Project.flp
Lesson01/Complete/LabComp.fla
Lesson01/Complete/LabComp.html
Lesson01/Complete/LabComp.swf

Starting Files:

None

Creating a Flash Document

The first step in creating any Flash application that could be anything from a slide show of family vacation pictures to an online clothing store is a Flash document. Flash documents, which use a FLA extension, can contain text, audio, video, animations, and other material—including scripts that either can be included in the document or can be saved as external AS files linked to your Flash document through the use of ActionScript. From its early beginnings as an animation program, Flash has extended its capabilities to the point where it can deliver Web content from a wide range of media such as video, audio, and even XML documents. As such, Flash can create seven specific kinds of documents:

- **Flash Document:** This is the most common Flash document you will create. It uses the file extension "FLA" (rhymes with "Flahh") and can incorporate content such as text and images, media assets such as audio and video files, and, of course, the ActionScript code.

- **Flash Slide Presentation:** Think of a slide show with each slide in a separate screen (similar to Microsoft PowerPoint) and you will grasp the concept. Slides are not presented in this book.

- **Flash Form Application:** Similar to slides but the form content—input boxes and so on—can be placed on separate slides. Again, this feature is based on slides and, as such, will not be reviewed in this book.

- **ActionScript file:** ActionScript, Flash's coding language, can be written to a separate document in Flash and can then be linked to a FLA file. ActionScript can be used to perform a variety of tasks—from animating an object to handling user interactivity by, for example, managing what a button does when it is clicked or managing a credit card payment in an online clothing store. ActionScript can be written inside of Flash, using the Actions panel, or can be written inside an external document that is linked to the movie. These external documents, which can also be created in a text editor or Dreamweaver, use the .AS extension.

- **ActionScript Communication File:** Traditionally used for media streamed into a Flash SWF file through the Flash Communication Server MX. These files, which can be created in Flash or a text editor, are placed on the Flash Communication Server and used to deliver streaming audio and video to a Flash document in a Web page (they use the ASC extension). You do a little bit of work with the Flash Communication Server in Lesson 10.

- **Flash JavaScript file:** You can create a JavaScript file that creates customized pop-up windows from Flash, detects plug-ins, and even controls the width and height of the Flash movie from within the browser. These files, which use the JSFL extension, don't control what happens in Flash; the control happens with the Flash file in a browser. Creating JSFL files is a very advanced aspect of Flash and won't be covered in this book.

Note *ActionScript and JavaScript are sister languages. The difference is in the objects they reference. JSFL is for scripting the authoring environment; AS is for scripting the runtime objects. JSFL is beyond the scope of this book and will not be covered.*

• **Flash Project:** Available only in Flash Professional 8, a project file allows you to create an index for grouping related files and managing version control. This is an excellent feature for use by project teams. You will be creating a project file in this lesson.

In the following exercise, you create your first Flash document.

1. Copy the Lesson 1 folder from the CD to your computer's desktop.

2. Launch Flash Professional 8.

The Start page appears when you first launch Flash. This is a standard page for many of Macromedia's applications; if you want to disable it, just click the "Don't show again" check box in the lower-left corner of the Start page. If you want to re-enable it, select Edit > Preferences and click the General tab. Select "Show Start Page" and the Start page appears every time you start Flash.

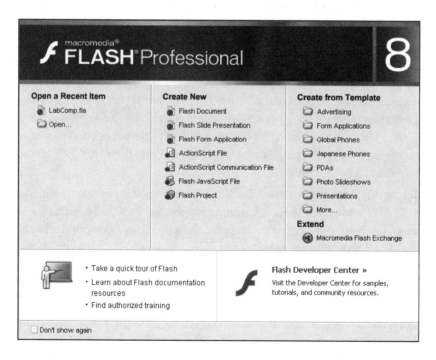

3. Select Create New > Flash Document to open the Flash Interface.

Tools panel   Main Menu   Timeline

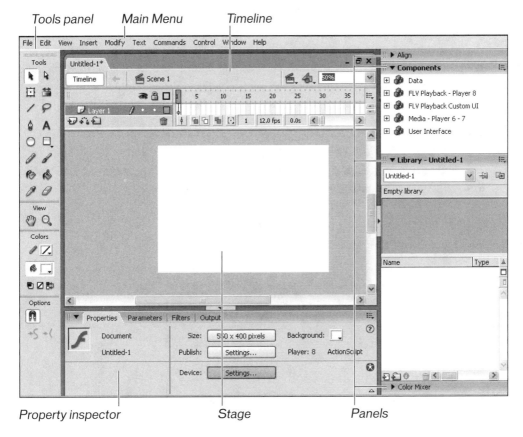

Property inspector   Stage   Panels

The interface is divided into a number of discreet areas:

- **Main Menu:** The main menu bar is the control center for the Flash interface. Here you can manipulate your Flash files and customize your working environment.

- **Stage:** This is the area the user sees when the Flash movie is playing. It contains all the visible and, in certain instances, invisible elements of the document—such as text, images, video and sound.

- **Timeline:** The Timeline contains the frames that compose a Flash movie or animation. Although Flash movies can have multiple frames, the exercises in the book rarely require more than a single frame.

- **Panels:** Panels give you access to a broad range of authoring tools. They can be open, closed, rearranged, and even grouped.

- **Tools Panel:** These are the drawing and text tools. When a tool is selected, the Property inspector changes to show the properties associated with the tool.
- **Property Inspector:** The Property inspector is actually a panel that provides you with the opportunity to modify documents and objects. The Property inspector, sometimes referred to as the PI, is context-sensitive, meaning that the properties on the PI changes to reflect those of the currently selected item. The Flash Professional 8 Property inspector is a bit different from its predecessors in that it has a tabbed interface.

Note *You can turn the Property inspector on or off by pressing Control+F3 (PC) or Command+F3 (Mac).You can also by some extra screen space by clicking the Timeline button in the upper-left corner of the Timeline area. Click the button and the Timeline disappears. Click it again and it reappears.*

4. In the Property inspector, click the Size button.

The new Document Properties dialog box opens.

In previous versions of Flash, the Document Properties dialog box did not contain the Title and Description areas. The text entered into these two new areas is now used as the metadata that search engines, such as Google, use to search your site for the title and description of the Flash SWF file. To see the metadata added to the SWF file, select Show Report in the Publish Options dialog box when you create the SWF file. When you play the SWF file, the metadata report shows you the metadata added.

```
Metadata
--------
Bytes     Value
-----     -----
  196     <rdf:RDF xmlns:rdf=
          "http://www.w3.org/1999/02/22-rdf-syntax-ns#">
          <rdf:Description rdf:about="" xmlns:dc="http://purl.org/dc/1.1/">
          <dc:title>The lab</dc:title>
          <dc:description>Flash experiments and learning</dc:description>
          </rdf:Description></rdf:RDF>
```

This addition to Flash, on the surface, could be regarded as interesting but in many respects, the addition of metadata to a Flash SWF file is a major feature. One of the biggest complaints to date about Flash sites and Flash movies was that they were virtually impossible for the search engines to locate. This situation has fundamentally changed, and your work is now accessible to the search engines.

The key to understanding how this works is that metadata is the "data about data" and the technologies that make this work in Flash—XMP (eXtensible Media Platform) and RDF (Resource Definition Framework)—are now W3C standards. In many respects, metadata labels files, but until recently there was no single standard. The result was no incentive for hardware or software vendors to include support for labels such as "Title" and "Description."

In the mid-90s, after the limitations of common labeling practices were understood, two new "languages" were developed. The first language was the *Resource Definition Framework* (RDF), which is used to structure the labels that machines can read. The RDF implementation is accomplished through the second language, *XML*, which is the language used to separate content from structure on the Web.

The RDF rules specify that the labels be composed of a series of XML statements. This is the purpose of the XMP portion of the implementation in Flash. XMP implements the XML schemas that contain the metadata entered into the Document Properties dialog box. When the browser "reads" the Flash SWF file, the XMP schemas are passed through the RDF framework inside the SWF file to the HTML page where the SWF is located and, from there, search engines are able to "find" the title and description of the document that you have entered.

5. Enter the following values into the Document Properties dialog box:
  - Title: The lab
  - Description: Flash experiments and learning
  - Width: 590
  - Height: 400
  - Background color: #676735

Click OK. The Stage shrinks to fit the dimensions shown and fills with the color chosen.

Note *You don't have to use the PI to open the Document Properties. Select Modify > Document or press Control+J (PC) or Command+J (Mac), and the dialog box opens.*

6. Save the file as Test.fla to the folder you are using on your computer.

Setting Preferences

Preferences allow you to control many aspects of the application—from how text is displayed in the ActionScript editor to the warnings you might see if a feature selected is not available in earlier versions of the Flash Player. When you open the Preferences panel, your first reaction is to wonder what happened. Nothing changed, other than the design of the panel. If you are a Dreamweaver user, the layout of the Flash Preferences panel has been moved into alignment with the design used in Dreamweaver 8.

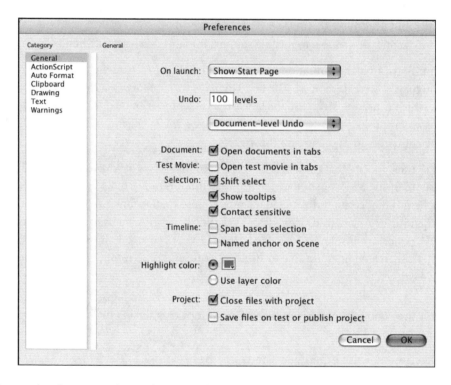

This exercise shows you the preferences added to Flash Professional 8.

1. Choose Edit › Preferences (PC) or Flash › Preferences (Mac) to open the Preferences dialog box.

There are a number of categories in this panel, and each covers a specific aspect of the application. The General category covers basic settings used to control file authoring. The ActionScript category allows you to change a number of things, ranging from the size of the font used in the ActionScript editor to class paths. The Auto Format category is new and allows you to format how the ActionScript appears in the Actions panel. The

Clipboard category controls image settings, gradient quality and how Freehand text is managed. The Drawing category, known as the "editing" preference in previous versions of Flash, contains settings for vector drawings. The Text category is new. In previous versions of Flash, this category was a part of the Editing preferences. It is now used to set the default font settings and orientation. The Warnings category allows you to choose the warnings that appear in Flash.

2. Select the Warnings category and deselect **"Warn on save for Macromedia Flash MX 2004 compatibility." Click OK** to close the Preferences dialog box.

What you have just done is to tell Flash not to check for features in your movie that won't work in previous versions of Flash.

3. Select File > Publish Settings to open the Publish Settings dialog box. When the dialog box opens, click the Flash Tab and select Flash Player 6 from the version drop-down list.

Now Flash knows it is to publish to an earlier version of the Flash Player.

4. Choose Edit > Preferences (PC) or Flash > Preferences (Mac), select the Warnings category, and select the preference deselected in Step 2.

5. To see the effect of making this choice, select the Rectangle tool and draw a rectangle on the Stage.

When the rectangle has been drawn, select it and then select Modify > Convert to Symbol. Don't bother with the name. Click the Movie Clip button in the Type area, and click OK.

6. With the box on the Stage selected, click once on the word Normal in the Blend area of the Property inspector.

A dialog box tells you that this feature, exclusive to Flash 8, is not available in the Flash Player selected. At this Stage, you can either click the Publish Setting button in the dialog box and change the player to Flash Player 8 or not add the effect.

7. Open the Preferences (Edit > Preferences) and select the Auto Format category.

This new preference determines how the ActionScript code in the Actions panel is formatted. For example, let's assume you prefer to have the command "else" appear on a separate line in your code. In previous versions of Flash, you had to do this manually.

8. Select Don't cuddle '}' and else.

You will notice the word "else" moves to separate line in sample code shown in the panel. Now every time you add an "else" statement to your ActionScript, the word "else" appears on a separate line.

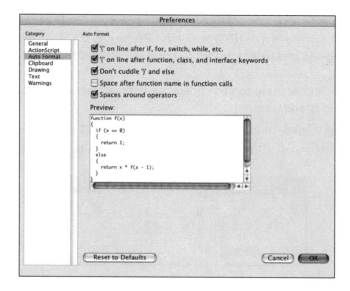

9. Click the General category to open the General preferences.

This panel is quite different from earlier versions of Flash. The "On launch" preference is now at the top of the page and is a drop-down list. For Mac users, this page presents you with a rather welcome change. On the Mac version of Flash Professional 8, there is a Document category. Select "Open documents in tabs," and all Flash documents you open will be tabbed at the top of the interface rather than a series of windows. Other changes include the ability to open a test movie in a separate window (the default) or to have it appear, as in previous versions of Flash, in a tabbed window. On the PC, you can also choose to disable PostScript when printing. This option is not available on the Mac version of Flash Professional 8.

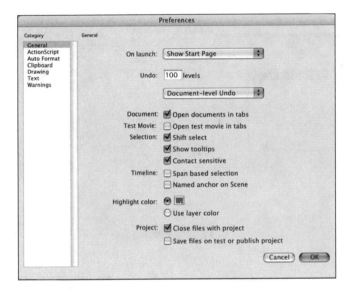

10. Click OK to close the Preferences.

Manipulating Panels

Your Flash authoring environment makes extensive use of a variety of panels that give you access to a number of tools ranging from aligning objects on the Stage to writing ActionScript. The list of panels available to you can be found in the Window menu and they are divided into three distinct groupings:

- **Design:** A collection of panels that pertain to such design tasks as choosing colors to distorting objects on the Stage.

- **Development:** A collection of panels used for such development tasks as writing ActionScript and debugging code.
- **Other:** These panels, ranging from Accessibility to Button libraries, affect the movie as a whole.

Panels can be open (the panel's contents are visible), collapsed (only the panel name is visible), and closed (the panel can be opened only through the Window menu). The position of open or collapsed panels can be changed, and the panels can also be docked in a variety of locations on the screen, including sets of panels that are docked with each other. If you don't need to see the panels, they can even by "hidden" by selecting Window > Hide Panels or by pressing F4.

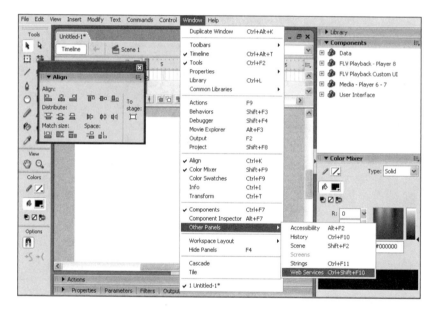

In this exercise, you move the panels and create a custom panel set.

1. Open Flash and then open the Test.fla file you created and saved in the previous exercise.

2. Select Window > Align.

The Align panel appears to float over the Stage.

The panel can actually be moved in one of two ways: You can click and drag the panel anywhere on the Stage or you can dock the panel to any side of the interface. Whether the panels "docks" or just floats depends on where the cursor is when you click and drag.

3. Place the cursor over the dots to the left of the panel name.

These dots are called the *gripper*. Notice that your cursor, if it is over the dots, changes to a compass cursor. The dots and the cursor change are your visual clues that you can dock a panel.

4. Place the cursor in the middle of the panel.

The cursor doesn't change from the selection arrow. Again, this is a visual clue that says you can move the panel but you can't dock it.

5. Dock the Align panel to the left edge of the screen by placing the cursor over the gripper. Drag the panel to the left and release the mouse when you see a black box appear.

The panel now docks to the left edge of the Stage area. To undock a panel, click and drag the panel onto the Stage. When you release, the panel "floats" over the Stage.

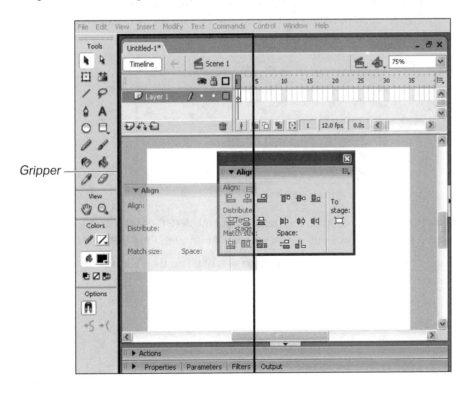

You can also align panels with each other and create panel groups using the panel's context menu. For example, assume that you want to have the Align panel become a part of the grouping of panels that make up the Property inspector instead of a separate panel located somewhere on the Stage. When you dock panels with each other, they change from the traditional look of a panel and instead become tabbed in the panel group.

6. Open the Align panel's context menu and select Group Align with > Properties & Parameters & Filters.

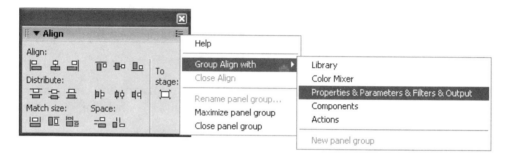

The Align panel closes and appears in the Property inspector as a tabbed panel. Simply click the tab to open the Align panel. The Align tools are now a part of the Property inspector.

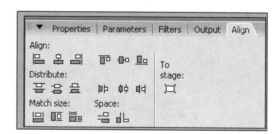

7. To remove the Align Panel from the group, right-click (PC) or Control-click (Mac) the tab to open the context menu. Select Group Align with > New Panel Group.

When you release the mouse, the panel no longer is tabbed on the Property inspector and appears to float on the screen.

Expanding the Pasteboard

Until the release of this version of Flash, there never seemed to be enough room to accommodate content that was sitting on the Pasteboard. This is now a thing of the past.

1. Select View › Magnification › 25%.

This shrinks the Stage, and the gray area surrounding the Stage is the Pasteboard. The items in the Magnification menu only make the screen larger or smaller. They have no effect on the movie.

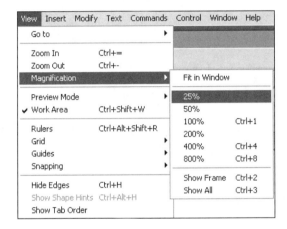

2. Select the Rectangle tool from the toolbar and draw a square on the Pasteboard.

3. Select the square using the Selection tool and drag it beyond the right edge of the Pasteboard.

When you release the mouse, the Pasteboard expands to reveal the square.

Using the Tools Panel

The Tools panel contains a number of tools used for creating text, creating vector graphics, and manipulating the content on the Stage. When you select a tool, all the properties associated with that tool display in the Property inspector. There are more than 20 tools on the Tools panel, and you use many of them as you work your way through this book. The tools used in this chapter are the Text, Rectangle, Selection, and Free Transform tools.

- **Text tool.** This is the tool used to add text to the Stage. When you click on the Stage with the Text tool, the Property inspector changes to let you adjust the width of the text, and set the font, size, alignment, and color of the text. You can also choose whether the text is static, dynamic, or entered by the user.

- **Selection tool.** There are actually two selection tools. The solid arrow tool—Direct Selection—allows you to select entire objects or groups of objects. The other selection tool is the hollow arrow or Subselection tool. As the name implies, you can use this tool to select a part of an object. Regardless of which selection tool is chosen, after an object is selected, you can click and drag the selection from one side of the Stage to the other or change its Properties, such as Fill color, in the Property inspector.

- **Rectangle tool:** Use this tool to draw squares and rectangles on the Stage.
- **Free Transform tool:** Use this tool to distort or resize a selected object on the Stage. Depending upon the object selected, you can scale, rotate, skew, and even flip an object.

Tip   *You don't have to select the tools; you can use the keyboard. To select the Direct Selection tool, press V. To select the Subselect tool, press A; to select the Free Transform Tool, press Q. The key commands are located by placing the cursor over a tool. When the tooltip appears, the key command is the letter in the brackets.*

In this exercise, you construct the Lab prototype.

1. Open the LabComp.fla file located in the Lesson01/Complete folder on your computer.

This is the document you created in the first part of this lesson.

2. Select File > Import > Import to Library.

When the Import dialog box opens, navigate to Lesson01/Complete folder, press Shift, and click on each of the three images in the folder to select them. Click the Open button, and the dialog box closes.

3. Select Window > Library or press Control+L (PC) or Command+L (Mac) to open the Library panel.

When the panel opens, you see the images you just imported. Importing content directly into the library is a good habit to develop. The reason is importing to the Stage not only puts a copy of the image on the Stage but it, too, appears in the library. If the file is complex, importing to the Stage does not allow you to control the layers where the images will be placed or where they are located on the Stage. As well, importing to the library allows you to have all your content in one place and accessible to you when you need it.

4. Drag a copy of the Logo image from the library and place it in the upper-left corner of the Stage. To ensure that it is precisely placed, set the x and the y values in the Property inspector to 0.

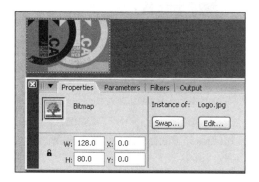

The use of the Property inspector to precisely align objects on the Stage is a good habit to develop. Attempting to do this using your eyes inevitably results in improper placement of objects on the Stage.

5. Double-click the Layer 1 name in the Timeline panel to select it, and change the layer name to Logo.

Over the years, Flash developers have learned to place all content in a separate layer and then name the layer to reflect the content it contains. Adding layers does not increase the size of your Flash movie. Instead, layers give you a means of visually locating content on the Stage. Also, the use of layers helps define the stacking order of objects when your SWF is displaying.

6. Add a new layer in the Timeline panel and name it Top. Select the layer and then select the Rectangle tool. Draw a rectangle and, set the width to 550 pixels, the height to 80 pixels, and the x and y coordinates to 0 in the Property inspector.

Notice that the shape covers the logo and has stroke and fill colors. Drag this layer under the Logo layer, and the logo becomes visible.

7. Double-click the rectangle on the Stage and click the Stroke color chip in the Property inspector to open the Color Picker. Click the No Stroke button (with the red diagonal line), and the stroke is removed.

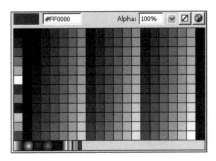

8. With the rectangle still selected, click the Fill Color chip on the Property inspector to open the Color Picker. Place the cursor in the green color on the left side of the logo. Click the mouse, and the rectangle fills with the selected color.

Note *There are three ways of selecting a color in Flash. The first, if you have the Hex color value (#989A68), is to enter it directly into the Color Picker. The second is to click a color chip in the Color Picker. The third is to select a color on the Stage.*

9. Save the file.

Object Drawing Mode

The next step in this exercise is to draw the background for the text and images that appear in the page. The issue here is drawing that background rectangle and keeping the curved cutouts that appear in the upper-left corner of the logo. In previous versions of Flash, this would involve the drawing of two or three rectangles and grouping them.

In Flash Professional 8, a new drawing mode, Object Drawing mode, has been introduced. When you select a drawing tool, the Object Drawing icon (a circle in the Options menu) appears. This feature allows you to draw separate objects that do not automatically merge together when they are overlaid.

If you are familiar with using Illustrator or Freehand, you are used to having objects overlay each other as separate objects. In previous versions of Flash, objects that overlaid each other resulted in their being merged together. If you click the Object Drawing icon when you select a drawing tool, the objects drawn do not merge with the ones they overlay.

Flash MX Professional 2004

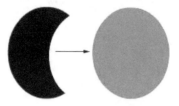

Flash Professional 8 Object Drawing

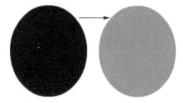

1. Select the Logo layer and select View > Rulers to turn on the rulers.

This allows you to create the guides necessary to accurately place the object you are about to draw.

2. With the Logo layer still selected, select the Rectangle tool, turn off the stroke in the toolbar, and select the Object Drawing mode by clicking the circle in the Options menu.

When the Object Drawing mode is selected, the icon has a gray background.

You will need the rectangle you will draw to be treated as a separate object.

3. Draw a rectangle in the middle of the Stage. Fill it with the light olive green color in the logo by selecting the rectangle, opening the Fill color chips on the Tools panel, and clicking the light color in the lower-right corner of the logo.

Tip *The eyedropper is a handy tool when color matching must be exact.*

4. Click the horizontal ruler and drag a guide that runs along the top of the cutout in the logo. Do the same thing for a vertical guide on the left edge of the cutout.

Guides allow for the precise positioning and alignment of objects on the Stage. You might want to zoom in on the guide locations if precision is critical. To change a guide color, select View > Guides > Edit Guides to open the Guides dialog box. Click the Color Chip in the Guides dialog box and choose a color from the color picker. Click OK to close the dialog box and the guides will now be the color selected.

5. Click the rectangle and set the width to **484** pixels and the height to **310** pixels in the Property inspector.

6. Drag the rectangle to align its upper-left corner at the intersection point of the guides. When you release the mouse, the square "merges" with the cut out.

Although it may look as if the logo and the rectangle have merged, the Object Drawing mode actually treats them as two separate objects. If you click and drag the rectangle away from the logo, you will see that it maintains its rectangular shape. If you were not to use the Object Drawing mode, the rectangle, when you moved it, would have a cutout in the corner where it intersected with the logo and also would have cut out a piece of the shape located in the Top layer.

7. Add a new layer named ContentBox and draw a rectangle in this layer. With the rectangle selected, use these values in the Property inspector: Width = 452; Height = 193; *x* = 49; *y* = 113; Fill color = #989A63.

8. Add a new layer named RedBar and draw a rectangle in this layer. With the rectangle selected, use these values in the Property inspector: Width = 452; Height = 30; *x* = 49; *y* = 113; Fill color = #730900.

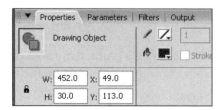

9. Add a new layer named ExperBox and draw a rectangle in this layer. With the rectangle selected, use these values in the Property inspector: Width = 175; Height = 30; *x* = 49; *y* = 113; Fill color = #676735.

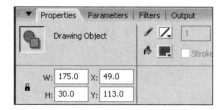

10. Add a new layer named Framer and draw a rectangle in this layer. With the rectangle selected, use these values in the Property inspector: Width = 165; Height = 129; x = 328; y = 143; Fill color = #CACC9A.

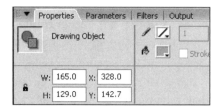

11. Save your file.

By getting into the habit of using the Object Drawing mode, the frustration of objects merging on the Stage is a thing of the past.

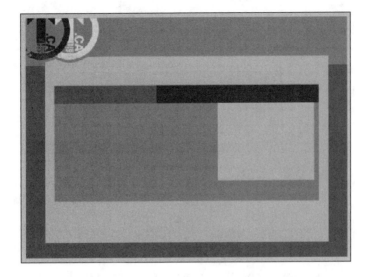

12. Add a new layer named Image, drag the NewYork.jpg image from the library into this layer, and place it over the Framer layer.

13. Select both the Image and the Framer layer and select Window > Design Panels > Align to open the Align panel. If the Align panel is in your panel group, click to open it.

Tip   *A quick way of opening the Align panel is to press Control+K (PC) or Command+K (Mac).*

14. Deselect the Align to Stage button and click the Align to Horizontal and Align to Vertical Center buttons. The image moves to the exact center of the rectangle in the Framer layer.

Selecting a layer does nothing more than select the objects on the layer. It is a handy way of selecting objects that might be difficult to otherwise select.

Tip *You can align objects relative to the Stage rather than to each other. Click the To Stage: button and then click an alignment option.*

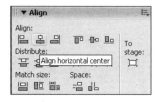

15. Add a new layer named Strip and drag the PicStrip image from the library to the layer.

16. Place the image on the Stage against the bottom of the Content box and align its left edge with the left edge of the Content box.

17. Add a new layer named Top and drag it under the Logo layer.

Draw a rectangle in this layer. With the rectangle selected, use these values in the Property inspector: Width = 550; Height = 80; x = 0; y = 0; Fill color = #989A68.

18. Save the file.

With the images and boxes in place and positioned in layers, your interface, so far, should resemble that shown in the following figure.

Text in Flash Professional 8

Having constructed the visual elements of the interface, it is time to add some text to the page. In Flash Professional 8, you have three styles of text available to you.

- **Static:** This is text that does not change. Use static text for such things as headlines, labels, or descriptive text.
- **Dynamic:** This is text that sits in a document outside of the Flash file and is added or modified, programmatically, through the use of ActionScript. These fields can also be created with ActionScript.
- **Input:** As the name implies, this is the text a user would input. You can create and modify these fields programmatically as well as capture any text that may be input by the user. You see input text frequently used in forms and login screens.

You can also change the type text field at any time by selecting the text field and changing its style through the use of the Text Style drop-down list in the Property inspector.

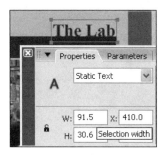

When text is added to a Flash document, you also have to decide whether the text being used will be displayed using embedded fonts device fonts.

Embedded fonts: The specified font is embedded into the SWF file. The advantage here is the ability to use any font you own in the movie. The downside is that the font adds to the size of the final file.

Device Fonts: Device fonts are the fonts on the user's computer. Using device fonts lowers the final file size but if the font chosen is not installed on the user's computer, a substitute font will be used.

> **Tip** Static text is always embedded into the SWF file. Dynamic text and Input text require you to decide whether to use embedded fonts in your movie.

In this exercise, you create and format the text used in all three methods.

1. Open the file you just saved and add a new layer named TheLabtxt.

2. Select the Text tool from the toolbar and click anywhere on the Stage to create a text field.

3. Type The Lab.

This text area is used as the headline in the interface.

4. Select the text just entered. The Property inspector changes to reflect your selection. Use the following settings:

- Font: Times New Roman
- Size: 24 points
- Style: Bold
- Color: #730900
- Alignment: Left

The text color is #730900. Also feel free to use any Serif font such as Times or Times New Roman.

Tip *A good habit to develop with documents containing a number of layers is to add the nature of the content to the layer name. For example, TheLabtxt tells you that the content in that layer is text.*

5. With the text still selected, set the x position to **410** and the y position to **90** in the Property inspector.

6. Add a new Layer named ExperimentTxt. Select the Text tool and enter the following: **The Experiments.**

Drag the text to a position over the ExperBox layer. In the Property inspector, make sure the text is Static Text and then set the font to 20 point Arial, White (#FFFFFF).

7. Open a text editor such as Notepad (PC) or TextEdit or SimpleText (Mac), open the Lorem.txt file in the Lesson folder. When the file opens, select the text and copy it to the Clipboard. Quit the text editor.

8. In your Flash file, add a new layer named DynamTxt. Select the Text tool, click once on the layer, and paste the text on the Clipboard into the text box.

You can't import text into a Flash document. The only two methods are to copy and paste the text into a text field or to bring in the text programmatically, such as using ActionScript to bring the text in from an XML document.

Lorem ipsum dolor sit amet, consectetuer adipiscing elit, sed diam nonummy nibh euismod tincidunt ut laoreet dolore magna aliquam erat volutpat. Ut wisi enim ad minim veniam, quis nostrud exerci tation ullamcorper suscipit lobortis nisl ut aliquip ex ea commodo consequat.

9. Select the text and, using the Property inspector, set the text as **12 point Arial** and the text color to Black: **#000000**.

10. With the text still selected, click the Edit Format Options button (it looks like a reverse "P") to open Format Options. Set the Line spacing to 6 points and click OK. The text spreads out.

The Property inspector does not contain a leading option. In Flash, leading—the space between lines of text—is called line spacing. Depending on how your text appears on the Stage you may or may not see this. If your text is one long line of text across the stage, you'll fix this in Step 12.

11. With the text selected, set the text property in the Property inspector to Dynamic Text and select Multiline from the Line Type drop-down list.

By formatting the text in the Dynamic text box, any text placed into it will be formatted with the text properties set in Steps 9 and 10. Selecting Multiline ensures that all the text, not a single line, appears in the interface.

Tip | *Always look for visual clues when trying to determine whether a text box you have selected on a page is static or dynamic. When you create a dynamic or input text box, the handle–the white box–is moved from the upper-right corner to the lower-right corner of the text box, as shown in the following figure. Also, dynamic text has a dotted line around it when it isn't selected on the Stage.*

12. Click the text box and resize it to fit the interface using the selection handles.

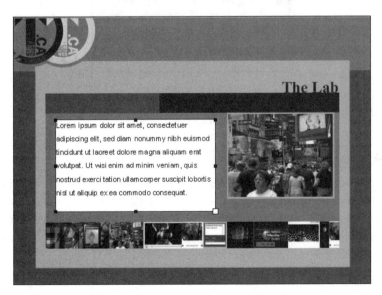

13. Select the Dynamic text box and click the Embed button in the Property inspector. When the Character Embedding dialog box opens, click Don't Embed, and click **OK** to close the dialog box.

When you see the Embed button in the Property inspector, you can decide whether or not to embed the fonts into the file. If fonts are to be embedded, select a character set from the choices presented or enter the text to be included in the Include these characters: text input box.

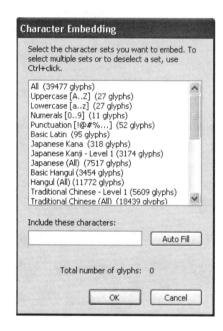

14. Save the file.

Anti-Aliasing Text

If there is one common complaint by Flash users and developers alike, it is that text, especially at sizes of less than 8 points, is difficult to read. In this version of Flash, Macromedia has addressed this issue with the addition of a new, advanced text anti-aliasing technology named FlashText. FlashText improves font rendering when the movie is playing and text, especially at the smaller sizes favored by Flash developers, is clearer and easier to read.

Aliasing is the jagged edges on curves and diagonal lines. These are commonly referred to as *jaggies* and are quite commonly seen in bitmap images. Anti-aliasing is the process of smoothing out those jaggies. The trick with antialiasing fonts to not only smooth out the jaggies but to also retain the look and feel of the font used for the text. Done poorly, and the text will appear to be "blurry" or "smudged." Done well, and the text is very distinct— legible and readable—at small point sizes.

There are two types of anti-aliasing that can be applied to your text:

- **Standard Anti-Alias** applies the default anti-aliasing settings to the selected text. If this method is applied, font smoothing will look similar to that used in earlier versions of Flash.
- **Advanced and Custom Anti-Alias** use the Saffron technology. The Advanced settings will allow you to set a new default for a variety of situations whereas permits you to change the anti-aliasing settings.

Tip *The FlashText anti-aliasing technology is only available to Flash files published for use in Flash Player 8. If you have to publish files for Flash Player 7 or lower, you will only be able to use Standard anti-aliasing on your text.*

1. Select the Text tool and click once in the Dynamic text box.

2. Apply each of the Anti-aliasing options in the Font Rendering method drop-down list in the Property inspector.

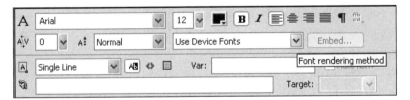

Notice that each method changes the appearance of the text.

- **Use Device Fonts:** This feature uses the anti-aliasing used in previous versions of Flash Player.
- **Bitmap Text. No Antialias:** The result of this selection is jagged text.
- **Anti-Alias for Animation:** Select this feature if the text will be moving.
- **Anti-Alias for Readability:** Apply this option if the text is fixed in place. Text in scroll boxes or on the Stage are ideal candidates for this treatment.

- **Custom Anti-Alias.** You can set your own values. Sharpness determines the smoothness of the transition between the edges of the text and the background. Thickness determines how much of the text edge blends into the background.

> - Device fonts antialiasing option
> - Bitmap text (no Anti-Alias)
> - Anti-Alias for Animation
> - Anti-Alias for readability
> - Custom Anti-Alias
>   Thickness =12
>   Sharpness = 24

Publishing a Flash Document

Documents you create in Flash use the FLA extension, which indicates that the file is the one that can be opened in Flash and changed. What you can't do is open a FLA created in a later version of the application in an earlier version. For example, you can't open FLA files created in this version of Flash in Flash MX Professional 2004.

For users to actually interact with your Flash movie, the FLA files need to be transformed (the common word for this process is *compiled*) into SWF files. SWF (pronounced "swiff") stands for Small Web Format, and these files are referred to as Flash applications. They are also called *movies* because the original purpose of Flash was for Web animations and they were called movies.

You can "play" your Flash movie by publishing the FLA file. The end result of that process is the SWF file. Your Flash application can be played in a number of ways:

- Browse a Web page that contains the SWF file embedded into the HTML. This process requires the Flash plug-in.
- Press Control+Enter (PC) or Command+Return (Mac). This tests your movie right from within Flash.
- Open the SWF file from the desktop or other location on the computer in Flash Player.
- Publish the SWF file as projector (EXE for PC and HQX for Mac), which functions as a stand-alone executable that doesn't require the user to have Flash Player installed on his or her machine.

Tip *The latest version of the Flash Player can be obtained at http://www.macromedia.com/downloads/.*

1. In Flash, open the file you have been working on.

2. Test the movie by pressing Control+Enter (PC) or Command+Return (Mac).

The movie opens in a separate window. This form of SWF file is great for development purposes. Use it to test your movie's functionality as you proceed through the production process.

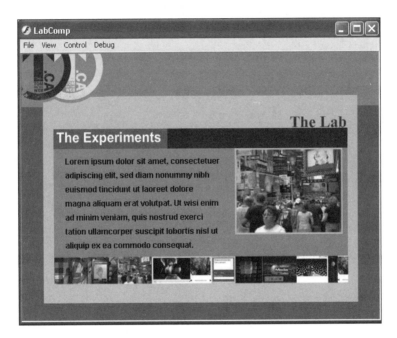

3. Close the window by clicking the Close box.

If you have used earlier versions of Flash, you may notice a change in this feature. It now opens in a separate window rather than the tabbed interface from previous versions of Flash.

4. Select File › Publish Settings.

The Publish Settings dialog box opens. Another way of opening this dialog box is to click the Settings button on the Property inspector.

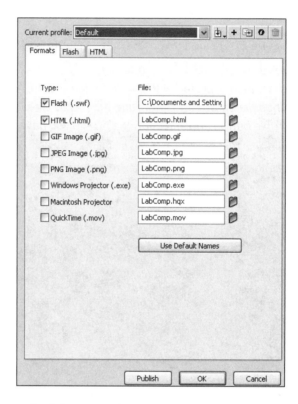

The Flash and HTML check boxes are checked by default on the Formats tab. When you publish a document, the SWF and HTML files are created in the same folder as the HTML file. You can publish the files with different names or in different locations by changing the filename and the path in the File field.

Tip *Each FLA file has a default for the Publish Settings. If you change the settings, the profile is updated for the FLA file as well. You can also create multiple publish settings profiles for a FLA. This is a handy feature to have if you publish your files to multiple locations. To create a new profile, click the New Profile button (the + sign) and give the profile a new name. You can then change the profile or switch back and forth between any profiles you may have created.*

Tip *Profiles can be reused across multiple FLA files or within work teams. To do this, click the Import/Export Profile button (the box with the arrow) and name the profile. This results in the creation of an XML file in your Flash Profiles directory. For PC users, the path is C:\Documents and Settings\Local Settings\Application Data\ Macromedia\Flash MX 200x\(language)\Configuration\Publish Profiles. For a Mac the path is Macintosh HD\Users‹username›\Library\Application Support\Macromedia\Flash MX 200x\‹language›\Configuration\Publish Profiles. After the profile has been exported, you can use it in other FLA files by opening the Publish Settings dialog box and importing the profile by clicking the Import/Export profile button and selecting the profile you have saved.*

Tip *Using the Publish Settings to save a SWF file to the folder that will ultimately be uploaded to your Web server is also a great way to test the project's function- ality. For example, if the project uses files that will be loaded into the SWF file when the movie plays, the odds are really good that if it works when tested, it will also work when uploaded or placed into an HTML page.*

5. Click the Publish button and then **OK** to close the Publish Settings dialog box. Save the file.

The SWF and HTML files that you specified in the Publish Settings dialog box is created.

Tip *If you use a graphical HTML editor–Dreamweaver or GoLive–it isn't necessary to create an HTML document in the Publish Settings dialog box. A SWF file, when inserted into a page created by these apps, also creates the* `<object>` *and* `<embed>` *tags needed to display the SWF file in a browser.*

Adding Flash Player Version Detection

It is not uncommon for a user to either not have the Flash plug-in installed or to have an earlier version of the Flash Player plug-in installed on his or computer. If the plug-in is not installed, most browsers notify the user and either go to the Macromedia Flash Player install page or display a link so the user can download the plug-in. The information used for the download is found in the `<object>` and `<embed>` tags created for your SWF file in the HTML page.

If the wrong version is detected, the content displays but does not function correctly. For example, a file created using ActionScript 2.0 plays in Flash Player 7 but loses functionality in Flash Player versions earlier than 7.

To ensure that the user has the correct version of the player, you can have Flash add the code that checks for a specific version of the Flash Player. If a user is found by the browser not to have the correct Flash Player version, he or she will be prompted to update the Player.

In this exercise, you add version detection to your SWF file.

1. Open the file you have created in this chapter.

2. Select File > Publish Settings. When the Publish Settings dialog box opens, click the HTML tab, select Detect Flash Version,

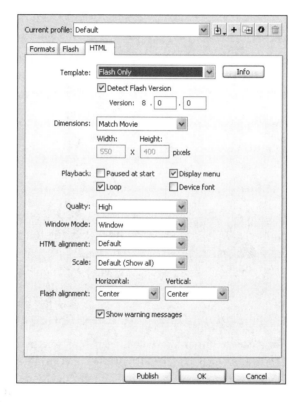

You can change the Version Detection settings to earlier versions of the Flash Player and ActionScript if you click the Flash Tab in the Publish Settings dialog box.

3. Click the Flash Tab in the Publish Settings dialog box to open the Flash settings.

4. Select the version of the Flash Player to be used from the Version drop-down list.

Your choices range from the current version of the Player, Flash Player 8 to Flash Lite 1.1, which is used primarily in devices such as cell phones and PDAs.

5. Select the version of ActionScript—Versions 1 to 3—to be used.

Keep in mind that ActionScript 2.0 works only in Flash Player 6.65, 7, and 8. Flash Player 6.5 and lower, including the Flash Lite Players, only use Actionscript 1.0.

Creating a Flash Project

An underutilized feature of Flash is the Flash Project, which helps you to organize and manage your files in a convenient location within the Flash authoring environment. A Project panel provides a quick way to view and open a file without having to use the File > Open menu.

When you create a Flash Project, a Flash FLP file is created. This file is an XML file containing the names and locations of the files to be included in your project. The information in the XML file is what populates the Project panel.

After the FLP file is created, you can add files to it from any location on your computer. The files don't have to be located in the same directory as the FLA file, which means you have the flexibility to group files in a variety of separate directories. You also have the ability to manually create folders for the Project in the Project panel. This allows you to have the Project panel reflect the directory structure you are using.

Finally, if you are in a team-based production environment, you can share a single Flash project file and use version control for the files contained in the Flash project.

To create a Flash project:

1. Select Window › Project or press Shift+F8 to open the Project panel.

When the panel opens, you will be prompted to create a new project or open an existing project.

2. Select the New Project link and name the project.

3. Select the Project and click the Add Files button to open the Add Files To Project dialog box.

The project must be selected before you add files to the Project.

4. Navigate to the files to be added, select them, and click the Open button.

The files appear in the panel.

> Tip   *The FLP file may appear in the list. Don't add it.*

5. Click the Test Project button.

You will be prompted to identify an FLA or HTML document as the default document. This actually identifies the document from which the SWF file will be created.

6. Click the Select button in the dialog box, and the Select Default Document dialog box opens. Select the document and click OK.

The dialog box closes, and Flash tests the movie in Flash Player.

7. Test the movie and close Flash Player.

When you return to Flash, notice that the icon for the FLA document in the Project panel has changed. This simply indicates that the file is the default document.

> Tip   *If you have the Project panel open and right-click (PC) or Control-click (Mac) on the Stage, you can add the document to that is currently open to the Project without going through Steps 3 and 4.*

Version Control

The Flash Professional 8 version controls are quite similar to those found in Dreamweaver 8 or earlier. In fact, the button that makes this possible looks exactly like the Put and Get buttons used in Dreamweaver's Files panel.

To use version control, you must either create a site or point to an existing site. If it is an existing site created by Dreamweaver, the site definitions you created in Dreamweaver can be shared with Flash. These site definitions can be accessed by selecting File > Edit Sites or by clicking the Project panel's Version Control button, shown previously.

Tip *Version control, with its check-in, check-out features, is more suited to a team-based workflow. If you are the only one accessing the files, you don't need to use this feature.*

After you define the site, you can check files in and out using version control from the Project panel. The following status icons will appear:

Green Check Mark: You have checked out the file and can make copies on your local computer.

Red Check Mark: Another person in the team has checked out the file, so you will not have access to the file until the person working on it has checked it back in. Like Dreamweaver, the same file cannot be checked out by two people. Attempting to check out a file that is already in use results in a dialog box asking if you want to override the other person's checkout.

Lock: The file is checked into the version control system, and it is not checked out. Your local version of the file will be locked, and no changes can be made.

No icon: If you don't see an icon, the file has been added to the project, but has yet to be uploaded to the server. To check a file into the server, if you are using a shared project file, you must first check out the project file and then add the file to the project. After you have done that, both the project file and the new file need to be checked in.

You can refresh the Project panel to ensure that you are working with the most current version of the files. When the panel is refreshed, the status of the files on the server is checked, and the icons on the Project panel are updated. What this process does not do is add new files to your Project panel, even if someone has added a new file to the shared project. The Project panel does not have the capability to automatically synch or update. To do this, you need to check out the project's FLP file from the server. Any new files in the project will appear in your Project panel and will have the missing file icon. To add the missing file, right-click (PC) or Control-click (Mac) on the file in the Project panel. When the context menu appears, select "Get file from version control."

What You Have Learned

In this lesson you have:

- Created a new Flash document (pages 3–8)
- Added metadata to a Flash movie (pages 6–7)
- Changed the movie's preferences (pages 8–11)
- Created panel sets (pages 11–14)
- Expanded and contracted the Pasteboard (pages 15–16)
- Used the Tools panel (pages 16–19)
- Added text to your movie and applied custom anti-aliasing (pages 26–32)
- Published a Flash document (pages 32–35)
- Created a Flash project with version control (pages 35–40)

2 ActionScript Basics

If you use Macromedia Flash, you will, sooner rather than later, find yourself using ActionScript. Though you can do an amazing amount of work without it, there will come a point where you need to add interactivity to your movie or move something from one location to another. That is the point where you will open the Actions panel and start writing ActionScript. As you move through this book, you encounter the use of ActionScript to do everything from navigating to a Web page to writing the code that drives a full-blown media center.

In this lesson, you are introduced to the fundamentals that drive every line of code in this book. This may, on the surface sound like a fairly tall order, but as you move through this lesson, you discover that ActionScript isn't terribly mysterious or difficult to understand. Thus, the purpose of this lesson is not to teach you how to master ActionScript but to get you comfortable with the programming concepts and terminology used in the subsequent lessons in this book.

The ActionScript Script pane showing the new Script Assist feature.

Be clear about the fact that this is not a book designed to teach you ActionScript. It is a book designed to get you using Flash Professional 8 in a very short order. If, by the time you finish this lesson and this book, you decide that understanding ActionScript is a "must have "skill, *Macromedia Flash 8 ActionScript: Training from the Source* is your next step. If you really want to start with the basics and fundamentals of the use of ActionScript in Flash, *Macromedia Flash 8: Training from the Source* is a tremendous starting point.

Many of the tasks you will apply ActionScript to are quite similar to each other, and only minor modifications to the code are what separate one task from another. The best part of all of this is that after you are comfortable with ActionScript, you will be looking at all of the code in this book and wondering, "How can I change this to fit what I need to do?"

What You Will Learn

In this lesson, you will:

- Understand common ActionScript terminology
- Learn how to use the Actions panel to write ActionScript
- Use Script Assist to write ActionScript
- Learn how to use strict data typing
- Learn the fundamentals of classes, methods, and properties
- Learn the difference between a layer and a level in Flash
- Use the LoadVars class to add text to a movie
- Create a listener for a component

Approximate Time

This lesson will require about 90 minutes to complete.

Lesson Files

Media Files:

none

Starting Files:

ScriptAssist.fla
LoadVars.fla
ButtonComponent.fla

Completed Files:

Lesson02/Complete/ButtonComponent.fla
Lesson02/Complete/LoadVars.fla
Lesson02/Complete/ScriptAssist.fla

Introducing ActionScript 2.0

ActionScript 2.0 is an object-oriented programming (OOP) language based upon the ECMA-262 scripting standards (the same standards that the JavaScript language is based on) used to add interactivity to Web pages. The major advantage to you is that OOP is designed let you reuse code when building Flash applications. OOP is a monstrous subject and trying to fully explain it is well beyond the scope of this book. The subject is covered in quite some depth in *Macromedia Flash 8 ActionScript: Training from the Source.*

If you are familiar with Flash in its MX and MX 2004 forms, you have encountered ActionScript. And if you moved from the MX version to the MX 2004 version, you encountered ActionScript 2.0. Although you can use ActionScript 1.0 in Flash Professional 8, most of the industry has adopted the use of ActionScript 2.0. In fact, Lesson 12, "Going Mobile with Flash," relies solely upon ActionScript 1.0 because of the nature of Flash Player for cell phones.

The major difference between the two versions is how the code is formatted. Strict data typing, which we get into later in this lesson, is only supported by ActionScript 2.0. Another major difference is the way *events* are generated and managed by Flash. An event is something that is initiated by a button click, a key press or the end of a video.

Another aspect of ActionScript 2.0 is the ability to write code to external files that use the .AS extension from within Flash. These files could contain custom methods and properties related to a single object such as a movie clip or a custom object. These files are referred to as classes, and classes are widely used throughout Flash Professional 8. Creating your own classes is well beyond the scope of this book, but classes are discussed later on in this lesson.

Finally, when you create a SWF file, be sure to indicate in the publishing options which version of ActionScript you are using. You need to do this in order to have the SWF file compile properly. Compile? It is a fancy word for publish. When you publish a SWF file, it is said to be "compiling."

Terminology Fundamentals

Before you start writing the code, there are some aspects of the terminology that may be foreign to you. In this section, you are introduced to some of the more common terms used in the code examples in this book. Start with variables.

A *variable* is the name for a container that holds data. When you go to the grocery store, inevitably your purchases are placed in a plastic or paper bag. Inside this bag are cans, meat, vegetables, and other items you have purchased. If anyone asks you what is in the bag the inevitable reply is, "groceries." The stuff in the bag is the data, and the term you just used to describe it—groceries—is the variable. In Flash, variables hold the value of a *data type*, which is the particular information associated with variable such as a String ("Lettuce" is a string data type because it contains a bunch of alphanumeric characters strung together—hence the data type "String") or a Number, which is another data type. The variable's name is "groceries" and when you create the name, you are said to be "declaring the variable."

> **Tip** *Do your sanity a favor when you declare variables and use a name that describes what the variable is. For example, myVideo is a lot more meaningful than coolBreakDancers. If you examine the code samples throughout this book, every variable declared relates directly to the data it contains.*

You use variables whenever you will be repeatedly using and/or modifying data. You assign a value to the variable so you can use it over and over in the ActionScript you will write. The interesting thing about variables is they can change. You see this when you go to a sporting event. The variable named score, which is a number, always starts out a 0. By the end of the game, that variable's value will have changed, but it is still known as score. This is an important concept because the last thing you need is to write 120 lines of code that track a score rising to 120. For example, you can create a variable that tracks the score by adding 1 to the current value of the score each time a goal is scored. This significantly reduces the amount of typing you must do and, most important of all, will keep the final size of the SWF file at a manageable level.

What does a variable look like? If you were to create a variable called groceries to hold the value "Lettuce" you would enter the following:

```
var groceries = "Lettuce";
```

You have just assigned the value "Lettuce" to the groceries variable using the equal (=) sign, which is called an assignment operator. The keyword var tells ActionScript that groceries is a variable meaning variables are declared as such when var is used. The semicolon at the end tells ActionScript that the end of the code line has been reached and to go to the next line in the code.

You can also assign variables to something else. In the case of the sporting event, the `score` variable would be this:

```
var score = 0;
var currentScore = score +1;
```

All this code means is that the value of the current `score` is 1, which works admirably for a game in which only one point is awarded. What about games such as baseball, in which the scores move into double digits? In this case, each time a runner crosses home plate, you simply reassess the value of score to `currentScore` before adding 1. Any code that uses the value for `score` or `currentScore` elsewhere in the script will be instantly updated to this new value.

> **Tip** A classic example of variables is the PixieDust movie you will create in Lesson 6. Little stars pour out of the cursor and fade out as they move down the screen. Considering that you could have 50 of these stars onscreen and fading at the same time, changing each one's alpha value would be a daunting task. Instead, you will create a variable for each star and use that as the starting point.

Just like any language, there are some rules that need to be followed when it comes to variables. The first is that each variable name must be unique. You can't declare two variables named `groceries` or `score` in the same function. You can declare `score` or `groceries` in different functions, however. The second is the names are *case sensitive*. The variable `Groceries` is not the same as the variable `groceries`. If, for example, you don't see the word `Lettuce` in your movie when you test it, the odds are almost 100% that you used `Groceries`.

There is more. Variables can contain only numbers, letters and underscores (_), and they cannot begin with a number or an underscore. `var score2 = 0` is legal. `var 2score = 0` is illegal. Variables cannot use any of the keywords, names, objects, or properties reserved for the use of ActionScript. These words are reserved words and when encountered by ActionScript they are treated just like the keyword or action resulting in broken code. Variables can have a name in which a keyword is present, such as `newYork` or `movieClipArray`.

The next term is *keyword*.

In ActionScript, keywords are reserved words that are used to perform a specific task. A complete listing of the ActionScript keywords is contained in the Flash Help panel.

Open it by selecting Help > Flash Help or by pressing F1. When the panel opens enter keywords into the search criteria. Each keyword has a specific meaning: var is used to create a variable.

add	and	break	case
catch	class	continue	default
delete	do	dynamic	else
eq	extends	finally	for
function	ge	get	gt
if	ifFrameLoaded	implements	import
in	instanceof	interface	intrinsic
le	lt	ne	new
not	on	onClipEvent	or
private	public	return	set
static	switch	tellTarget	this
throw	try	typeof	var
void	while	with	

Another term you will encounter on a regular basis is *Boolean value*.

When you were in school, you actually did tests based on Boolean values. These were the infamous True/False tests you wrote. The answer is an absolute value such as "True or False: A breed of dog is poodle." When you start writing ActionScript, you won't be encountering poodles, but you will be encountering absolute values.

If you draw a circle on the Stage you can see it. That means it is absolutely visible. What if you don't want the user to see it? You could set the visibility of the circle to false when the movie starts and to true when the user clicks a button.

You will also use *conditional statements* on a regular basis.

Think of one of these as being a negotiating position. You ask the boss for a raise by saying, "Boss, if I raise sales by 5 percent, I expect a 5 percent raise." The boss replies, "If you want a raise, sales will have to increase by 8 percent." Notice how the negotiation is phrased: "If this, then this." The conditions are "raise" and "percentage." The other thing you will notice is you can rephrase this negotiation in Boolean terms:

```
if a sales increase of 5% is true then my salary increases by 5%
```

The power of these statements lies in the fact that you can use both the true and false condition to initiate a series of different actions. For example, here's a script that checks for a proper password. If the password is wrong, it ends the playback to a frame labeled "Rejection". If it is correct, it goes to a frame labeled "Acceptance":

```
if (password == null) {
  gotoandStop("Rejection");
} else if (password == "Tom"){
  gotoAndPlay ("Acceptance");
}
```

The final term is *function.*

You will regularly encounter functions as you move through this book (and, for that matter, many other Flash books out there). Functions can be thought of as "a group of statements that can be referred to by name". Functions can return values and can have parameters passed into them. Parameters, sometimes referred to as arguments, allow you to pass a static value, variable, or reference to an object into a function. After they are in the function, you can manipulate them at will.

Parameters are the values that get put between the () in a line of code. For example, a common movie clip method is gotoAndPlay();.This is a common method that moves the playback head from one frame to another in a movie clip. As we have written it, ActionScript doesn't have a clue where it is to go to and play because we haven't told it where to go. It needs a parameter, such as Frame 3. Thus, the method would appear as follows:

```
gotoAndPlay(3) ;
```

When you create a custom function, the need for parameters depends on whether the function requires any further information in order to complete its task.

The power of a function lies in the fact it only needs to be written once but can be used an infinite number of times. Let's assume you have a button that when clicked increases the scale amount of a movie clip, named myClip, by 10 percent The code to do this would be:

```
on(release) {
  myClip._xscale = myClip._xscale +10;
  myClip._yscale = myClip._yscale +10;
}
```

This is ideal where there is only one button used to scale an object. What if you have five buttons that will scale the object? Are you prepared to write the same code five times? It is a waste of time and inefficient. The solution is to write a function, let's call it scaleUp, that does the scaling and is can be used by any button on the Stage. The syntax would be the following:

```
function scaleUp() {
   myClip._xscale = myClip._xscale +10;
   myClip._yscale = myClip._yscale +10;
}
```

The code attached to each button would "call" the function in this manner:

```
on(release) {
   _root.scaleUp();
}
```

In this case, when the button is pressed—on(release)—go to the main time line—_root—and execute scaleUp(). How does it know to scale the movie clip named myClip? It's name—called an *instance name*—is used in the function. Only movie clips with the instance name of myClip on the main Timeline will scale up by 10 percent.

So much for the theory. Let's dig into creating ActionScript.

Using the Actions Panel

In this exercise, you use the Actions panel as your primary tool. The Actions panel is designed for both the hard-core coder and those of you new to ActionScript and even coding. There are a variety of tools to help you check your syntax (*syntax* is a fancy term for grammar and spelling), format your scripts, and even help you along.

1. Open a new Flash document, select Frame 1, and press F9 (PC) or Option+F9 (Mac). Alternatively, select Window › Actions.

The Actions panel opens. Notice that it is broken into sections: Actions toolbox, Script pane, Script navigator, and a toolbar containing such buttons as Script Assist and a drop-down list that lets you choose the ActionScript version (*FlashLite is used for SWF files destined for cell phone playback*) to be used in the project.

Code can be placed on the main Timeline or objects on the Stage such as buttons and movie clips. The Script navigator lets you easily move through these various bits and pieces of code and change them, if necessary.

The Actions toolbox is like having an ActionScript dictionary sitting on your desk. The toolbox contains a series of "books" that can be clicked to open them. When a book is open, all the methods, actions, and properties are available. Double-click one of them and it will be added to the Script pane wherever you have clicked the mouse.

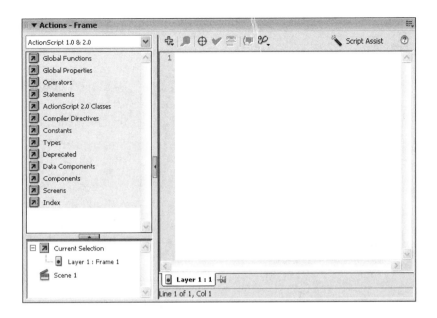

2. Click once in the Script pane.

With the "books" visible, click the Global Functions book. A series of other books will appear under it. Click the Timeline Control book to open the pages associated with Timeline control. Double-click the gotoAndPlay page. The code, with a hint telling you what goes between the brackets, will appear where you clicked in the Script Pane.

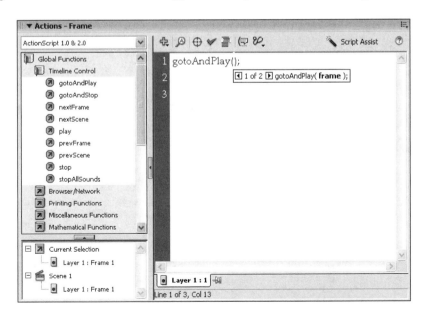

3. Press Return/Enter and type the following line of code:

```
gotoandplay();
```

The first thing you will notice is that the text is all black, whereas the same text in the line above is blue. This is a visual hint that Flash believes that you are using your own function, rather than one provided by Flash. You misspelled the keyword. Change the "a" in and to "A" and the "p" in play to "P." As soon as you change the "P", the phrase turns blue. Text that is black in ActionScript is inevitably due to a user-created variable, function, or object. Text that is blue in ActionScript is a keyword and it must be spelled properly.

Select the line you just entered and press Delete to remove it.

4. Click the Check Syntax button (it looks like a check mark) on the Actions toolbar.

Even though the code was correct, you still received a syntax error.

Click OK to close the Alert box and click the Output tab on the Property inspector to open the Output panel. The panel will give you the line of code in which the error occurred and suggest a remedy. In this case, you are being told the gotoAndPlay() event needs one or two parameters, not a 1 or a 2.

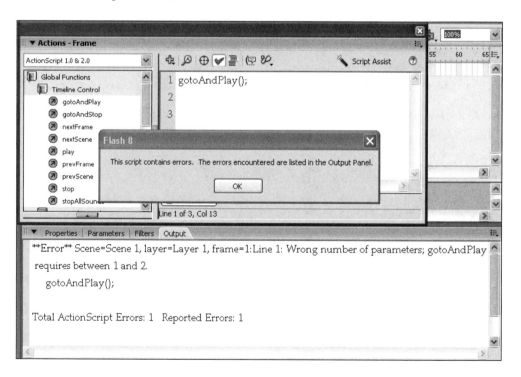

Click once between the brackets and enter the number **2**. Click the Check Syntax button, and the Alert will tell you "This script contains no errors". Click OK to close the Alert and then close the Actions panel by clicking Close.

When the Actions panel closes, you will see that a small letter "a" has been added to the frame where you entered your script. This is Flash telling you that there is ActionScript associated with the frame.

5. Select the frame on the Timeline containing your script and press F9 (PC) or Option-F9 (Mac).

The Actions panel will open and you will see your script. Delete the code and lose the Actions panel. The "a" will be removed from the frame where the script was located.

Tip | As you start working with ActionScript, a good habit to develop is to click the Check Syntax button after you write a piece of code. Although not to be regarded as a debugging tool, this feature is very good at catching such glaring errors as missing parameters, missing brackets, incorrect variables, and so on.

Tip | Throughout this book, you will see that we recommend putting all ActionScript on its own layer named Actions. This has become a standard industry practice. By keeping all the code in one place, you can quickly access the code when problems develop.

Using Script Assist Mode

Prior to the release of Flash MX 2004, there were two modes for entering ActionScript. One mode, called Expert, was designing for the hard-core ActionScript user and looked very much like the Actions panel in the current iteration of the application. There was another mode, Basic, designed for the new-to-casual coder. This interface allowed you to write ActionScript in what can best be described as a point-and-click manner. In Basic mode, you would determine what needed to be done and then select from the actions, methods, and properties that allowed you to accomplish your task.

The coders regarded Basic mode as "a toy". Their contention was that the code created in the Basic mode was more suited for extremely basic tasks than the creation of the more robust applications that could be created in Expert mode. When Flash MX 2004 was released, Basic mode was gone.

Script Assist mode resurrects Basic mode and provides those who are new to ActionScript with a rather handy little tool designed to get you working with ActionScript and to understand many of the features of ActionScript in a rather succinct manner.

In Script Assist mode, you build your script by selecting items from the Actions toolbox or by clicking the Add drop-down list (the + sign when you are in Script Assist mode). From there, constructing a script is simply a matter of double-clicking an item to add it to the code or dragging it into the Script pane.

When you click the Script Assist button, the Check Syntax, Auto Format, Show Code Hint, Debug Options buttons and menu items that are normally visible in the Actions panel are disabled because they do not apply to Script Assist mode. The Insert Target Path button is also disabled unless editing a field.

In this exercise, you will be simply exploring the features of Script Assist mode. In the next one, you will build a small movie using Script Assist mode.

1. Open a new Flash document, select the first frame of the movie, and open the Actions panel.

When the Actions panel opens, click the Script Assist button. The Script pane will actually change: The coding will move down, and a large empty area above the script will appear.

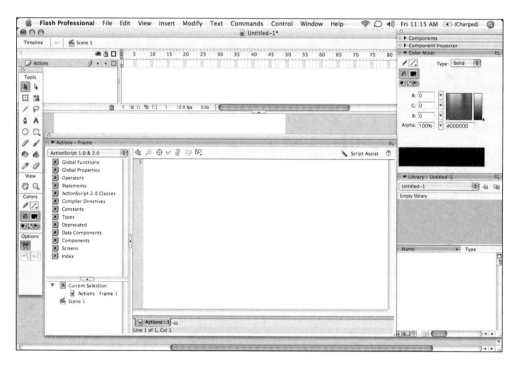

2. Open the Global Functions book in the Actions toolbox and open the Timeline Control book.

3. Select the *goto* item and drag it from the Actions toolbox to the Script pane.

The code will appear in the Script pane, and the area above the script will change to reflect the selection.

The first thing you see is a short description of the action at the top of the pane. The next item is whether the action should be gotoAndPlay or gotoAndStop. Click the radio button, and the action will change to your selection.

The next three selections answer the "Go where?" question. The drop-down lists offer you a number of choices regarding the scene to play, the frame type, and the number of the frames to go to. If you enter the number **3** in the Frame Number area and press Return/Enter, that frame number appears in the code.

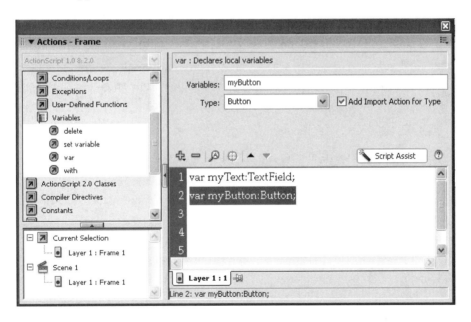

4. Select the code and click the Delete (-) button. The code will disappear.

The Add (+) button has all the choices in the Actions toolbox, but they are in a drop-down list. Select Global Functions > Timeline Control > Goto. The action is added to the script pane and the same choices as before will appear.

Double-click the stop action in the Actions toolbox. The stop action is added to the Script pane. You have just discovered the three ways of adding an action to the Script pane:

- Drag and drop the action
- Double-click the action
- Click the Add (+) button and use a drop-down list

5. **Select the stop action in the Script pane and click the Move Up button.**

The action is moved up to line 1 of the script, and the gotoAndPlay action moves to line 2. (You use the Move Up and Move Down buttons to move lines of code up and down in the window.)

> Tip | *It isn't just single lines of code that can move. If you select a multiline function, you can move that entire selection up and down in the script by clicking the Move Up and Move Down buttons.*

Using the Script Assist Mode to Create a Small Application

Now that you know how to use the various features of Script Assist, let's put this knowledge to work. In this exercise, you will create the code for a small movie. When the movie plays, you click the button and the words "I've been hit!!!" will appear on the screen.

1. Open the ScriptAssist.fla file in your Lesson 2 folder.

You will see a blue button on the Stage and a text box surrounded by dots. You will also see there are two layers in this movie—one for the stuff on the Stage and the other for the actions.

The dotted box is a dynamic text box. If you select it and open the Property inspector, you will see it has already been named myText, and that the formatting of the text that will appear in the box has been completed. Dynamic text boxes are used primarily when text is being added to a movie either directly from ActionScript or from an external document. We will be spending a bit of time in Lesson 4 exploring the power of dynamic text.

The button is actually one that is installed with Flash. If you select Window > Common Libraries > Buttons, a panel of button types will appear. This one is the blue button found in the Arcade buttons folder. It was added by dragging the button from the folder to the component layer. If you open the library (Window > Library), you will see the button is in the library. The interesting thing about these buttons is that they are fully functional buttons that just need to be coded to work and that changing them in the movie (new color, resizing, and so on) won't affect the original in the Button library.

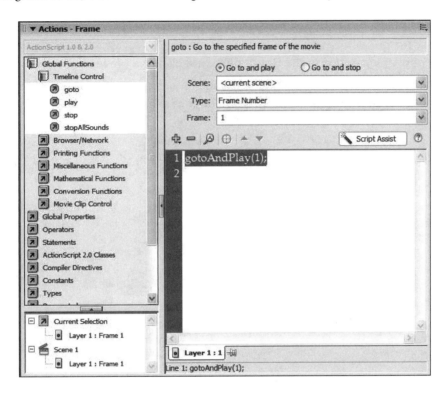

2. Select Frame 1 of the Actions layer and open the Actions panel by pressing F9 (PC) or Option+F9 (Mac).

3. Click the Script Assist button to open Script Assist mode.

Click the "+" button and select Statements > Variables > var.

The panel will change to reflect your selection. Click once in the Variables text input area and enter myText. From the Type drop-down list, select TextField.

4. Click the Add (+) button and select *Statements > Variables > var*.

Click once in the Variable text input area and enter myButton. From the Type drop-down list, select Button.

> **Tip** *If you make a mistake in Script Assist or want to change something, simply click the code line to be changed, and the Script pane will change to reflect the selection.*

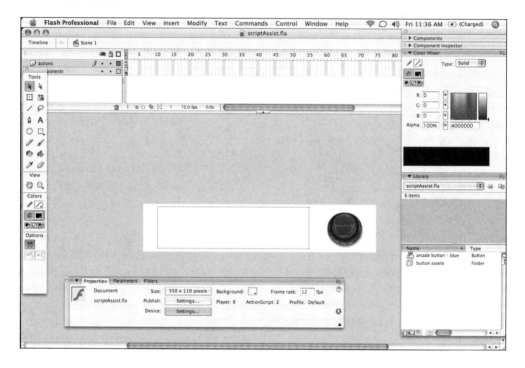

5. Click the Add (+) button and select *ActionScript 2.0 Classes > Movie > Button > Event Handlers > onRelease*.

In the Object input box of the Script pane, enter myButton.

Click the Add (+) button again and select ActionScript 2.0 Classes > Movie > TextField > Properties > text. In the Expression area of the Script pane enter myText.text = "I've been hit!!!"

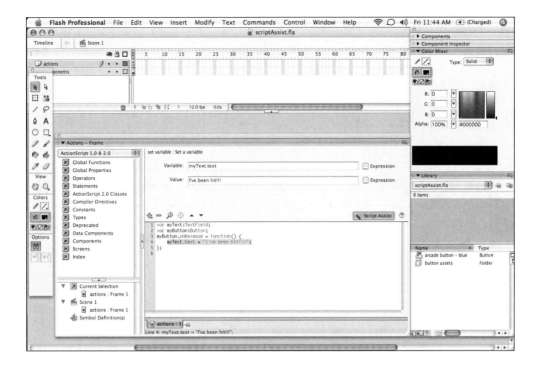

6. Close the Actions window, save the movie to your Lesson 2 folder, and test the movie by pressing Control+Enter (PC) or Command+Enter (Mac).

When the movie opens in the Flash Player, click the button and the text will appear in the dynamic text field.

Strict Data Typing and Code Hints

One of the defining features of ActionScript 2.0 is the introduction of strict data typing. All this means is that each variable you create is tied to a class. For example, `var groceries = "Lettuce";` has a problem. The variable could also use a number instead of a word, which leaves you wide open to potential errors. Strict data typing ensures that the only thing that can be associated with the `groceries` variable is a word. The other advantage of using strict data typing is that it lets you use code hinting in the Actions panel.

Using Strict Data Typing

Strict data typing tells Flash what data type is associated with a variable based on the class associated with the data type. The type of data associated with groceries will be the word "Lettuce". Lettuce is a string and there is a String class in Flash. Associate "Lettuce" with that class, and all the class' methods and properties are available to the word "Lettuce". Therefore, the variable would be declared in the following manner:

```
var groceries:String= "Lettuce";
```

Because you only have to "strict type" a variable when it is created, you no longer have to worry about what value is used for the variable. If you use the wrong value, Flash will let you know when you publish the movie. Let's look a couple of examples. Here's an example of a mistake:

```
var groceries:String= "Lettuce";
groceries = 12;
```

When the movie is published, or when you test it, you will get an error. You are getting the error because you assigned a number to the variable, and Flash is telling you that you can't do that. Flash is expecting a string such as in this code:

```
var groceries:String= "Lettuce";
groceries = "Tomato";
```

Using Code Hinting in the Actions Panel

Code hints are contained in a wonderful little drop-down list when you enter your code. The beauty of code hints is they reduce the amount of time you spend typing and reduce the number of typos and errors that might break your code.

1. Open a new Flash document, select the first frame, and press F9 (PC) or Option+F9 (Mac) to open the Actions panel.

When the Actions panel opens, click once in the Script pane and type var groceries:.

When you press the colon, a code hint drop-down list appears that lists all the classes that can be associated with a variable. Select "String" from the list. It will be entered into your code. When it appears, finish the variable declaration by entering the following:

```
Var groceries:String = "Lettuce";
```

2. Press Enter/Return and enter _groceries_ .

As soon as you type the period, all the methods and properties associated with a string will appear in the list. Double-click one of the items, and it will be added to the code.

You can turn off code hinting in the Flash ActionScript preferences. To turn it off, simply deselect Code Hinting when the panel opens.

Code hints are invaluable, especially when you are manually entering your code and can't remember which property or method is associated with the variable or action. There are two ways of having the code hints appear: Use strict data typing or add a suffix to a variable.

As you work with code throughout this book, you will encounter both methods used with variables and instance names.

Using *suffixes* is an older practice used by ActionScript 1.0 programmers. However, with strict typing, it is no longer necessary and will allow a more conventional naming practice. However, for the sake of an example, assume that you have a movie clip named myMovie on the Stage. When referring to it in your code, that name means absolutely nothing without strict typing. Give it the instance name of myMovie_mc, and ActionScript knows what it means. ActionScript will provide the methods and properties that pertain to a movie clip. Other suffixes include _btn (Button), _txt (Text Field) and _str (String).

There is another method of getting Flash to display code hints. Simply write the data type and the variable within a *comment*:

```
//MovieClip myMovie;
myMovie._x = 6;
```

Comments are messages and descriptions that you type into the code. A typical comment might be this:

```
// This code moves the movie clip 6 pixels to the right.
```

The // tells Flash that this is a comment and to ignore it. However, if you use a comment for the data type and the variable name, as soon as you type the period after the variable name, the code hints will appear.

We are fond of telling anybody that will listen; "There are 6,000 ways to do anything in the digital world. Find what works best for you." So which is the best way? Pick one.

The Basics of Classes, Methods, and Properties

Because ActionScript is an OOP language, it involves the use of classes, objects, and instances. In OOP, everything is associated with a class. Drag a movie clip from the library onto the Stage and the MovieClip class gets instantiated into that object as soon as it hits the Stage. This explains why we talk about naming an instance. All class files have two main characteristics: methods and properties.

To start understanding this section, you need to understand the concept of an *object*, which is the building block for your code and is composed of data (called *properties*) and related functions (called *methods*). Think of an object named *dog*. The things that make up a dog, its properties, could be four legs, fur, and tail. The things a dog can do, its methods, could be fetches, sleeps, and eats. Put all these things together and you have a dog object with four legs, a tail, and fur that fetches, eats, and sleeps. To differentiate one dog from another—poodle from terrier—we use the word *breed* because the properties and methods of a terrier are fundamentally different from those associated with a poodle. Instead of using the word *breed*, OOP programmers use the word *class*.

Classes are rather simple to understand. For example, let's assume that a poodle is now curled up at your feet. The poodle belongs to a class called *dog*, which in turn belongs to a class called *mammal*. For the sake of simplicity, a defining feature of the mammal class could be *four limbs as well as fur*. A mammal can also have methods called *walk* and *talk*, which are common to all mammals. The *talk* method can be used by the *dog* class to bark, and the dog can use the *walk* method to walk on all four limbs. The *fur* property would be set to *curly* in the poodle. Thus, if there is an object that walks on four feet, barks, and has curly fur, we can assume we are looking at a *poodle*.

The important point here is not the poodle. The important aspect of this is that the main methods and properties in these classes are common to these classes. The specifics of a method are handled in the subclasses (namely dog and poodle). If an animal in the dog class doesn't have curly hair, it is another class of dog, not a poodle. The other thing to notice is that poodles can use the dog methods and properties, which in turn use the animal methods and properties. If you have an animal curled up at your feet that meows and has long hair, the odds are very good that you have a long-haired cat. The interesting thing about the cat class is that shares the methods, properties, and events of the mammal class—just like the poodle.

What do dogs, cats, and ActionScript have in common? They use classes.

ActionScript contains more than 100 built-in classes, which are the predefined data types you use to make things work. To access the methods and properties associated with a class you have to create an instance of the class, except that instead of dragging an object onto the Stage, you create the instance when you declare the variable and set its data type using ActionScript.

The `MovieClip` class is a good starting point to understand how methods and properties are associated with a class. In many respects, methods can be regarded as verbs—they are the things do stuff. Two methods associated with the `MovieClip` class are `stop()` and `gotoAndPlay()`. Properties are the adjectives—they describe the movie clip. For example, if you select a movie clip on the Stage, the Property inspector tells you the height and width of the selection, as well as its x and y position on the Stage. If you can see it, another movie clip property is in play as well. It is visible. If you skip the library and create one while the movie is playing , you would do it this way:

```
Var myMovieClip:MovieClip = new MovieClip();
myMovieClip._x = 250;
myMovieClip._y = 250;
myMovieClip._width = 100;
myMovieClip._height = 150;
myMovieClip._visible = True;
```

That first line of the code is called an instantiation. In this case, you would be creating a new instance of the `MovieClip` class using a strict typed variable named `myMovieClip`. When it appears, it will be a square object of 100 × 100 pixels whose center point is located 250 pixels across the Stage and 250 pixels down.

Note *You can't create your own custom classes directly in the Actions panel; they must be created in an external file that uses the .AS extension that are subsequently compiled into the SWF file when it is published. Creating a custom class is well out of the scope of this book, which means we will be staying with the built-in classes that are included in ActionScript.*

Scope

You learned that creating a custom class is well out of the scope of this book. You understood what we were talking about because the word *scope* was used in the context of the purpose of this book, which is to teach you how to use Flash Professional 8, not to become a hard-core ActionScript programmer. When it comes to working with ActionScript, *variable scope* (how it works and how it is used) is one of those concepts that will drive you up a wall, across the ceiling, and down the other wall.

A scope is an area in your Flash file in which a variable can be referenced. If a variable is found in Frame 2 of the main Timeline, that is where it is referenced. If it is found in Frame 35 of a movie clip located on Frame 50 of the main Timeline, that is where the variable is referenced. For many people new to ActionScript, the concept of scope is not easy to grasp—it might require a high degree of patience on your part to become comfortable with this concept.

Earlier in this lesson, we explained what a variable is and how it is created, and made it very clear to you that variables cannot have the same name. Not quite. Variables can have the same name *only* if they are in a different scope. Three variable scopes are available in Flash: Local, Global, and Timeline (discussed in the following sections).

Local Variables

Local variables are local to a certain area, such as a frame or a function. They have extremely short lives that are limited only to the time that area is executing. As soon as that area finishes executing and exits that area, the local variable no longer exists. A local variable is easy to identify in a function because the variable is declared between the curly braces commonly used by a function or control statement. However, curly braces can be used within your code to simply delimit a local area.

When a local variable is declared, the variable can't be used elsewhere on the Timeline or in other bits and pieces of code in the movie outside of where it is declared. This is a good thing because you can use the variable name elsewhere in the movie and have it not conflict with the one in the function. Here's an example:

```
function myBigFatVariable() {
    var groceries:String;
}
trace(groceries);
```

If you were to run this to the Output panel, it would tell you that groceries is undefined because groceries lives only in the myBigFatVariable function and nowhere else.

Tip *Trace statements are invaluable coding aids. They are used by programmers to output test results of the code, follow variable values, and so on. The results will appear in the Output panel.*

Global Variables

Global variables are available anywhere at any time to anything. You can declare a global variable and then use it in other frames and other SWF files or movie clips that are loaded into the main SWF file without making extensive changes to your code or file structure. The major difference between a global variable declaration and a local variable declaration in ActionScript is that global variables are not defined using the var keyword. Instead, they start with _global, as shown here:

```
_global.groceries = "Lettuce";
```

Timeline Variables

Timeline variables are available only to any script within the same Timeline. If the variable is used on the main Timeline, it is available to scripts on the main Timeline. If it is used on the Timeline of a movie clip located on the main Timeline; it is available only in the movie clip Timeline. Again, because the variable is available only to a specific Timeline, you can have the same variable name used on various Timelines without running into any problems.

After a variable is declared on a Timeline, it is available to all the frames after the variable has been declared. For example, assume that groceries is declared in Frame 10. All frames from Frame 10 onward can use the groceries variable. Frames 1 to 9 won't have a clue what a "groceries" is, and it will be unavailable to those frames in the SWF file.

Moving Between Timelines and Levels

The fact that variables can exist on various timelines is good information to know. The next question is, "So, how do I get at those variables?" To answer that question, you have to understand the difference between _parent, _root, this, and level.

Let's assume that you have some code in a movie clip on the Stage and you need to access a button that is sitting on a Timeline containing that movie clip. You can use the _parent method to access the Timeline. What you can assume from this is those keywords, in one form or another, tell the SWF file where to go to access variables in the various scopes.

The keyword _parent references the parent Timeline of the current object. The parent of a movie clip sitting on the main Timeline is the main Timeline. The parent of movie clip 2 sitting on the Timeline of movie clip 1, which sits on the main Timeline, is movie clip 1. (Movie clips that are inside other movie clips are said to be *nested*.) The key word this means you are referring to the current object in the current scope. For example, if this is used on the Timeline in movie clip 2, the scope of the variable referred to would be limited to the Timeline of movie clip 2.

Still the use of the keyword this is one of those things that is difficult to understand at first. A lot of what it can do is based upon the context in which it is used. If you use this within a movie clip, it refers to the Timeline of the movie clip. However, use this with a button, and it refers to the Timeline in which the button instance is found, not the button itself.

As you go through this book, you will be using movie clips as buttons on the main Timeline to navigate to a frame. If you use the keyword this to tell the playback to go and play Frame 2, Flash will move the playback head to Frame 2 of the movie clip being used as a button. If you have the same instruction on a button on the main Timeline, the playback head will go to Frame 2 of the main Timeline.

Let's look at an example using a small piece of code that treats a movie clip like a button— a very common practice—that stops the playback head when the mouse button is released:

```
myMovie.onRelease =function(){
   this.stop();
}
```

Now let's give this code some context. Let's assume that there a sound playing on the main Timeline, and a ball is bouncing around the screen in the movie clip, which is sitting on the main Timeline. When you click the movie clip, the ball stops bouncing, but the sound keeps playing. This happens because the ActionScipt inside a function targets the movie clip's Timeline using the this keyword.

Remove the keyword, and the code becomes the following:

```
myMovie.onRelease =function(){
    stop();
}
```

In this case, the sound would stop playing and the ball would stop bouncing because buttons target the Timeline they are sitting on, and you just stopped the main Timeline from playing.

When you start cruising Flash tutorial sites or purchase books that explain Flash, you will encounter the use of _root on a very regular basis. When you see it used, it means the person developing the Flash file is directly targeting the main Timeline of the SWF file. If you understand that, you can also understand the subtle difference between _root and _parent.

There is the potential for an issue when you use _root, especially when you are loading SWF files into other SWF files. Remember that _root targets the main Timeline of the SWF file that is loading all the other SWF files into the movie. Let's assume that you have developed a Pacman game. The level maps are located in a SWF file called Levels.swf, and the controls—in a SWF file called Controls.swf—are loaded into the Levels.swf file when the movie loads into a browser. The main Timeline, therefore, is Levels.swf. Any references in Control.swf to _root will target the _root of Levels.swf and not the _root of Controls.swf. The upshot is incorrect playback and hours of unnecessary debugging and backtracking to isolate the problem. Which brings us to the keyword level.

Tip If a SWF file is going to be a self-contained unit, feel free to use _root. If other SWF files are loaded in using the loadMovie() method, use _parent in those SWF files, instead of _root. Better yet use the _lockRook property in the main Timelines of your movie clips being loaded. This will ensure that your SWF files use their intended main Timelines.

When you load new SWF files or other content into a SWF file, one of the parameters you will be asked to set is the level. Think of levels as being the stacking order of items on the Stage. For example, in Lesson 6 you will be littering the Stage with Pixie Dust that is nothing more than a movie clip in the library. That movie clip is added to the Stage using the attachMovie() method which requires three parameters be added inside the brackets-(idName, newName, depth). Depth or level determines where in the stack of clips this particular one is located. Levels have a very specific stacking order. The main Timeline is always _level0. When content is loaded in it gets placed onto new levels that are numbered in the stacking order.

> **Tip** *Don't equate Levels with Flash* layers. *Instead think of layers as being more like a stack of playing cards on the table. The table they are sitting on would be* level0 *and the last card at the top of the deck would be sitting on* layer52. *The kicker is this:* **the table and the cards could be sitting on any layer in the Flash Professional 8 interface.**

Using LoadVars() to Access External Data

During this lesson, you spent a lot of time learning how to play with data inside the Flash movie. The problem with this approach is that putting a lot of data inside a SWF file can result in a very large file size and very slow download times. The other issue is the very nature of *data*: It changes on a regular basis and you really don't need to be constantly changing the FLA file to reflect these changes.

One solution is to use an external file that can easily be edited by a text editor. When the file is saved and uploaded to the site, the changes made are instantly reflected in your SWF file. The class that "pulls" the text from the text file into the SWF file is the LoadVars() class.

There are three methods this class uses to communicate with a server:

- **send(url, method):** The data is sent to the server where it is subsequently added to a database, an XML document, or otherwise managed by a server using the POST or GET method. Here is an example:

```
//create the LoadVars instance
var someText = new LoadVars();
// create the data for the variable
someText.name = "Tom";
someText.job = "Professor";
// send the data to a ColdFusion page
someText.send ("http://www.anyserver.ca/receiveData.cfm", GET);
```

- **Load(url):** The data from the text document is loaded into the SWF file. Here is an example that would load the text of this lesson into a SWF file:

```
//create the LoadVars instance
var lessonTwo = new LoadVars();
// grab the text from the text file located in the same directory as the SWF
lessonTwo.load ("Lesson02.txt");
```

- **sendAndLoad("url",targetObject [, method])**: Think of this as being two-way communication between the server and the SWF file. An example of this is the following:

```
//create the LoadVars instance
var someText = new LoadVars();
// create the data for the variable
someText.name = "Tom";
// send and load
someText.sendAndLoad ("http://www.anyserver.ca/receiveData.cfm", someText_LV);
```

Now that you understand how it works, let's put what you have learned into practice. You are going to create a small Flash movie that loads text from a text file into a Flash SWF file.

1. Open the LoadVars.fla file located in your Lesson 2 folder.

The file is composed of two layers named Actions and Text. The "dotted box" on the Stage tells you that there is a dynamic text block on the Stage. Click the box, and the Property inspector will change to show you all of the properties associated with a text box. These properties include everything from the dimensions of the text box to the style, the size, and even the color of the text that will appear in the text box.

The text type is set to dynamic because the text will be coming into Flash and appearing in the text box. Any time text comes into Flash from an external source, it should go to a dynamic text box.

With the text box selected on the Stage, click once in the Instance Name input area on the Property inspector and enter **ourTextField**. Press Enter/Return to accept the change.

What you have just done is to "instantiate" the text box. The name can now be used by Flash to figure out where to put the text when the movie plays.

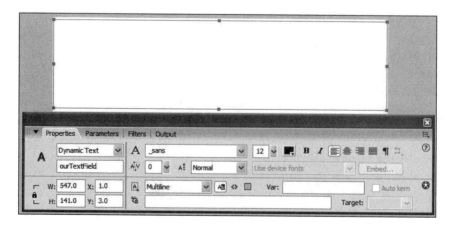

2. Select Frame 1 in the Actions layer and press F9 (PC) or Option+F9 (Mac) to open the Actions panel.

The plan of attack for this code will be rather simple:

- Create a `TextField` object and add a loading message that will appear while the text loads. You probably won't see it, but it is a great habit to develop because it lets the user know something is happening.
- Create a new `LoadVars` object that will be used to go get the text in the Lesson 2 folder.
- Write a little function that checks to make sure the text was loaded and show a message if there was a problem
- Load the text from the text file in the Lesson 2 folder—**loadvarexample.txt**—into the text field.

That plan of attack is also one of the first steps taken when writing ActionScript. Pull out a piece of paper and write down the steps the code will take as it executes using plain English or your native language. This is sometimes called *pseudo-code*.

3. Click once in the Script pane and enter the following code:

```
var ourTextField:TextField;
ourTextField.text = "Please Wait... Loading...";
```

The first line creates the variable and sets its data type to `TextField`. The next line simply says put the text between the quotes, which has the text property used by the `TextField` class into the instance named `outTextField` (which just so happens to be the instance name of the dynamic text box on the Stage).

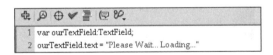

4. Press Return/Enter twice and enter the following:

```
var ourLoadVar:LoadVars = new LoadVars();
```

The second step of the plan is complete. A new `LoadVars()` object is created and given the instance name of `ourLoadVar`.

By creating this object, you are ready to deal with dynamic data.

```
1  var ourTextField:TextField;
2  ourTextField.text = "Please Wait... Loading..."
3
4  var ourLoadVar:LoadVars = new LoadVars();
```

5. Press Return/Enter twice and enter the following:

```
ourLoadVar.onLoad = function(successful) {
  if(successful) {
    ourTextField.text = ourLoadVar.exampleText;
  } else {
    ourTextField.text = "Error in loading data... "
  }
}
```

```
1   var ourTextField:TextField;
2   ourTextField.text = "Please Wait... Loading..."
3
4   var ourLoadVar:LoadVars = new LoadVars();
5
6   ourLoadVar.onLoad = function(successful) {
7     if(successful) {
8        ourTextField.text = ourLoadVar.exampleText;
9     } else {
10        ourTextField.text = "Error in loading data... "
11    }
12  }
```

This small function deals with the third step of the code.

When the LoadVars() object named ourLoadVar is loading the text, a function named successful is running. By putting the conditional statement inside the function, there are only two possible results for the function. If the text is successfully loaded into the text field named ourTextField, show the text contained in the LoadVars object named ourLoadVar.

What about the `"exampleText"` property? It wasn't a property of the LoadVar class to begin with because it wasn't declared. However, the LoadVars object is flexible enough that it will create a new property for each one it receives when executing a load command. If you open the text file for this exercise, you will see that it actually starts with `"exampleText = ..."` As soon as the LoadVars object sees a text block that starts with a word and an equal sign, it creates the exampleText property within the LoadVars object and populates it with the text that follows the equal sign. Our textfield object (called ourTextField) is assigned to our exampleText property within the LoadVars object.

6. Press Return/Enter twice and enter the following:

```
ourLoadVar.load("loadvarexample.txt");
```

The Load() method is used to load the text file into the ourLoadVar object. The complete code is shown in the following image. Note the extensive use of comments to help you understand what each piece does.

```
1  var ourTextField:TextField;
2  ourTextField.text = "Please Wait... Loading..."
3
4  var ourLoadVar:LoadVars = new LoadVars();
5
6  ourLoadVar.onLoad = function(successful) {
7    if(successful) {
8      ourTextField.text = ourLoadVar.exampleText;
9    } else {
10     ourTextField.text = "Error in loading data... "
11   }
12 }
13
14 ourLoadVar.load("loadvarexample.txt"); // LoadVars work with text files as well as dynamic solutions
15
```

7. Click the Check Syntax button to make sure you have no mistakes. If there are none, close the Actions panel.

Save the file under a different name to your folder. With the file saved, you can now test it. When you test a file, Flash will create a SWF file in the same folder as the FLA file.

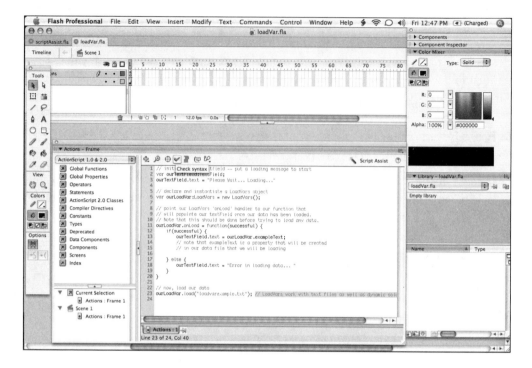

8. Press Control+Enter (PC) or Command+Return (Mac).

The first thing you will see is an Exporting Flash Movie alert box with a progress bar. When the movie has finished exporting, the movie will open in Flash Player, and you will see the text from the text file in the dynamic text box.

When you test a file, Flash will create a SWF file in the same folder as the FLA file.

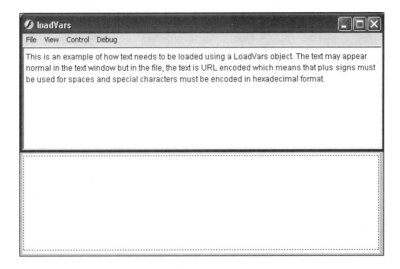

Tip | *If you have used previous versions of Flash, you will notice there has been a change in how a test SWF file is displayed. It now opens in its own window in the Flash interface, and the Output panel, used for messages and so on, is now a part of the Property inspector.*

Using Events, Handlers, and Listeners

In the previous exercise, if you carefully read the comments, you may have noticed a reference to an onLoad handler. And as you proceed through the lessons in this book, we will constantly use the terms *events* and *listeners*. These really aren't terribly mysterious, but it is still important that you be able to distinguish between the three terms.

An *event* is something that happens when the SWF file is playing. For example, being notified that a text file has finished loading or clicking a button are regarded as events. *Event handlers* and *listeners* are the actions used to manage these events when they occur. In the previous example, you used an onLoad event handler. When the text file is loaded, the onLoad event is created by Flash, and an embedded function is executed.

In Flash, there are quite a few events associated with objects you place on the Stage. When you click something on the Stage and release the mouse, an onRelease event makes things happen. In Lesson 4, you will have text appear in a text field when the mouse rolls off of an object on the Stage. This is an onRollOut event. In Lesson 5, you will have a sound load into a SWF file using a `loadSound` event. In Lesson 7 a planetoid will move across the Stage as soon as the movie starts. The planet goes in to motion because of an `onEnterFrame` event.

Listeners are a bit different. They are quite similar to event handlers in that they wait for an event to occur before doing something. Where listeners differ is that they are found in objects and they have to be told what event to "listen" for. One of the most common uses of listeners is when you use a User Interface component on the Stage.

Adding a Listener to the Button component

Using the components in Flash allows you to build rather rich applications without having to write a large amount of ActionScript. Flash Professional 8 contains 22 user components that perform a variety of tasks ranging from holding text to acting as drop-down lists. In this exercise, you will add a listener to the button component that will "listen" for the component to be clicked and then open a Web page.

1. Open a new Flash document and open the Components panel by selecting Window › Components.

When the panel opens, you will see that there are five component groupings. The Data group contains six components designed to manage communications with the server and data flow into and out of the SWF file. The two FLV groupings contain components designed to play and control video in a SWF file. (You will be making extensive use of these components in Lessons 7 and 8.) Media components are used to control video and audio playback in a movie optimized for the Flash Player 6 or Flash Player 7. The User Interface group contains a number of components that are used to construct interfaces in Flash.

Tip *Many Flash developers tend to shy away from extensive use or reliance upon Flash's ready-made components. They claim they add "unnecessary" bulk to a SWF file. They also claim they would prefer to create their own interface elements. If you are new to Flash, don't pay much attention to these claims. If you add a TextArea component to the Stage, your SWF file will grow by about 40K. Add a TextInput component and you add 25K. On the surface, a compelling argument can be made that a 65K increase is unwarranted. However, if you put both components in a movie, the increase is only 42K. This 30 percent reduction is due to Flash's capability to reuse classes and symbols.*

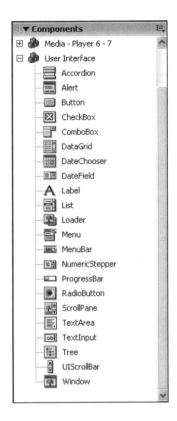

2. Open the User Interface group and drag a copy of the Button component to the Stage.

When the button is placed on the Stage you are going to need to do a couple of things: Shrink the Stage and give the button an instance name.

Obviously having a Stage that is 500 × 400 containing a single object that is 100 × 22 is a waste of space. Click once on the Stage and select Modify > Document to open the Document Properties dialog box. Click the Contents radio button in the Match area and click OK. The Stage will shrink to a more reasonable size.

> **Tip** *You don't have to use the menu to access the Document Properties dialog box. Click the Size button on the Property inspector, and the Document Properties dialog box will open.*

3. Select the button on the Stage and, in the Property inspector, give it the instance name of `myButton_cpt`.

Instance names are assigned through the Property inspector. To assign one, select the object on the Stage and click the properties tab of the Property inspector. In the upper-left corner of the Property inspector, you will see an icon of the selection and a text input box. Click once in the text input box and type the name.

4. With the button selected, click the Parameters tab of the Property inspector.

Parameters are the arguments—or options—associated with objects on the Stage such as a component. The parameter you'll change is the name of the button. It doesn't tell the user what the button does. The parameters you see when the Parameters tab is clicked are the following:

- **Icon:** You enter the name of a movie clip or graphic that would be placed in the button instance.
- **Label:** The text that will appear in the button.
- **labelPlacement:** This is the alignment for the text in the button. The locations are found in the drop-down menu that appears when you click this area in the Property inspector.
- **Selected:** If your button is set to toggle, this parameter forces the button into the selected, or On, state.
- **Toggle:** When set to `True`, your button will function as a toggle that turns things on and off on the Stage.

Select the word *button* in the label area of the Parameters tab and enter the word **Macromedia**. When you press Return/Enter, the text in the button will change.

5. Add a new layer named Actions.

To add a new layer, click the Insert Layer icon (it looks like a turned-up page) on the Timeline. When the new layer appears, double-click the layer name to select it and enter the word **Actions**.

It is a common practice, and one we use throughout this book, to have a layer devoted to ActionScript.

6. Click the first frame in the Actions layer and open the Actions panel.

The steps of creating a listener are not convoluted. You first create the object for the listener. Next, you tell the object what to do when the event occurs. Finally, you tell ActionScript which object is the one creating the event.

7. Click once in the Actions panel and enter the following:

```
var listenerObject:Object = new Object();
```

This creates the object. Now you have to create a small function that tells the object what to do when the event is detected. Press Return/Enter to go to the next line and enter the following:

```
listenerObject.click = function(){
   getURL("http://www.tomontheweb.ca");
}
```

This small function essentially says when a click event from the listenerObject is detected go to a Web page using the getURL() event.

Now all you have to do is to associate the listenerObject that will open a Web page with the button on the Stage. This is done through the addEventListener() method, which requires two parameters: the event to listen for and the ListenerObject that will "hear" the event and go to a Web page or perform some other task.

8. Press Return/Enter and add the following line of code:

```
myButton_cpt.addEventListener("click",listenerObject);
```

9. Click the syntax button and close the Actions panel if there are no code errors.

> **Tip** *You may notice that the event being listened for is "click". To see all the events associated with a component, open the Components book and select your component from the list. Open the Events book to see all the events associated with the component listed.*

10. Save the movie to your folder and test it.

When you click the button, the Web page you entered will open in a browser.

What You Have Learned

In this lesson you have:

- Been exposed to basic ActionScript terminology (pages 43–48)
- Used Script Assist mode to write a script (pages 48–57)
- Used the Script pane to enter a script (pages 48–51)
- Used code hinting to determine classes (pages 57–59)
- Used the loadVars() method to add text to a movie from a text document (pages 65–71)
- Used a listener with a User Interface component to navigate to a Web page (pages 71–75)

3 Graphics in Flash

This lesson is actually composed of two parts. In the first part of the lesson you explore the many drawing tools available to you in Flash and then manipulate them using a variety of menus and other techniques. The first part of the lesson ends with a masking exercise in which you can drag a mask around the screen.

The second part of the exercise pulls together much of what you have learned in the first part to build an interactive slide show. The first part of this lesson focuses on precision rather than technique. The slide show you build in the second part requires both precision and technique. Images and other interface elements will require precise placement on the Stage and the use of specific colors in the interface. You finish this lesson by constructing a graphic presentation that doesn't use graphics in the movie... they are sitting on a Web server.

The complete slide show.

What You Will Learn

In this lesson you will:

- Create, edit, and manipulate vector images
- Distort objects on the Stage using a variety of menus
- Create a static and an animated mask
- Learn how to add custom colors and gradients to a movie
- Import vector and bitmap images into Flash
- Learn how to create a gradient and add it to your color palette
- Use grids, guides, and rulers to precisely place objects on the Stage
- Use ActionScript to add interactivity to a slide show
- Use ActionScript to add text and images to a movie at runtime

Approximate Time

This lesson will require about 90 minutes to complete.

Lesson Files

Media Files:

Image01.jpg
Image02.jpg
Image03.jpg
Image04.jpg
Image05.jpg
TOTW.ai
TOTW.eps
TOTW.png

Starting Files:

Mask.fla
Slideshow_AS.fla

Completed Files:

Lesson03/Complete/Mask.fla
Lesson03/Complete/SlideShow.fla
Lesson03/Complete/SlideShow_AS.fla

Vectors and Bitmaps

In this lesson, you work with two main types of Macromedia Flash Professional 8 images—vector images and bitmaps. Vector images are usually created in drawing applications such as Adobe Illustrator CS2 or Macromedia Freehand MX. Vectors are also the images you draw when you use the drawing tools in Flash. Bitmap images are created in applications such as Adobe Photoshop CS2 or Macromedia Fireworks 8.

The reliance on vectors in Flash is, in many respects, its reason for being. The roots of the application—FutureSplash—were in a tool that could actually animate vector drawings and make them "Web-ready." Considering that the application arrived on the market just as broadband was arriving made this tool appealing for people who relied on a dial-up service and the ubiquitous 56K modem. In those days, size was everything, and vectors were extremely small images. Though we won't get into the technical details of vectors, one of the keys to their appeal is their relatively small file size.

In simple terms, when you draw a vector circle that is 100 pixels in diameter, the image requires very little information and computing power to be drawn onscreen. There are five points—four on the circle and one in the center—and those five points are used in a mathematical calculation of the diameter of the circle from the center. Then the computer needs to know if there is a stroke around the circle and whether color is being used for the fill. This means the circle requires seven pieces of information.

Bitmaps are treated differently. A photograph is the most common example of a bitmap. Bitmap images are fairly large because each pixel's location and color value must be remembered by the computer. A photo that is 100 x 100 pixels requires the computer to remember the location of 10,000 pixels. As well, each pixel will require three more bits of information to produce the red, green, and blue values of the pixel. This means there are about 30,000 pieces of information associated with a small image.

Which is smaller: An image that requires seven bits of information to be drawn onscreen, or one that requires 30,000 bits of information? In today's environment of wide broadband acceptance, that question is a bit dated. Still, an over-reliance on bitmaps can still have a detrimental effect on download times.

Drawing and Editing a Simple Vector Shape in Flash

All the drawing tools in the Tools panel are vector-based. If, for example, you select the Pencil tool and draw a line, anchor points become visible if you click the line with the Subselection tool. In this exercise you use the most common vector drawing tool—the

Pen tool—to draw a simple shape and then make changes to it using the Property inspector and other tools on the Tools panel. This exercise introduces some of the techniques and tools used in Flash Professional 8.

1. Open a new document in Flash. When it opens, select the Pen tool in the Tools panel.

Before you start drawing, select a fill color and a stroke color in the Tools panel.

Click and drag the Pen tool on the Stage and repeat this action a couple of times. As you click and drag, an anchor point appears that looks like a square with two handles. When you click the second time, the line drawn between the two points and the handles changes the direction or shape of the line.

To close the shape, roll the cursor over the starting point until a small circle appears under the pen. This tells you that the shape will be closed, and the starting point will join with the last point created.

When you release the mouse, the shape is created. The lines appear as the color you chose, and the interior of the shape fills with your desired fill color.

2. Select the Subselect tool and click the stroke around the shape.

The points and their handles become visible. If you click a point, you can choose a handle and move it inward or outward to change the shape of the object.

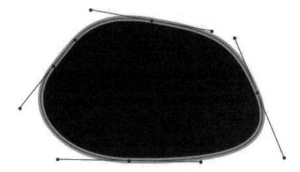

3. Select the Direct Selection tool and then click once on the stroke.

The stroke icon appears under the tool when you roll it over the stroke. If you roll the tool over the fill, you see a Compass icon. Those two icons tell you what you are about to select.

Selection Tool ———— Subselection Tool

Double-click the stroke. When the stroke is selected, it looks like it is "hashed," or composed of tiny white dots. Change the stoke color and the thickness in the Property inspector, and the thickness and color of the stroke around your shape changes.

If you select a fill color, the Property inspector changes to reflect your choice.

Filling and Manipulating Strokes and Fills

In this exercise, you draw a shape using the Pen tool and then use the features of the Property inspector and the Tools panel to change the color of the stroke and the fill.

1. Select the Pen tool; in the Property inspector, set a stroke width and color along with a fill color.

The Ink Bottle tool and the Paint Bucket tool are located beneath the Pencil and Brush tools on the Tools panel. The Ink Bottle tool is used to change the stroke color; the Paint Bucket tool is used to change the fill color of an object.

Select the Ink Bottle tool by clicking it in the Tools panel or by pressing S. Change the stroke color in the Tools panel, and click once on the stroke surrounding your object. The stroke changes to the color chosen. Now select the Paint Bucket tool by clicking it in the Tools panel, or by pressing K. Change the fill color and click once in the fill area to change the color.

2. Select the object on the Stage and select Modify > Shape > Convert Lines to Fills.

This menu item creates a rather interesting shape that essentially treats the stroke as being a part of the object's fill color. This is especially useful if, for example, the stroke is to be a gradient. When you select it, nothing really changes until you change the fill color. Change the fill color in the Property inspector, and the stroke essentially disappears. Select the object again, apply a stroke color, and the stroke reappears.

You can also blur or "feather" the edges of a nonstroked shape to have a smoother transition between shapes and colors.

3. Select the object on the Stage and turn off the stroke by selecting the No Stroke icon on the Stroke Color palette. Select Modify > Shape > Soften Fill Edges.

The Soften Fill Edges dialog box asks you to determine a distance, in pixels, for the effect. You also need to decide how many steps to use for the effect and whether you want to apply the edge outward (Expand) or inward (Inset). Make your choices and select OK.

Press Ctrl+Z (PC) or Cmd+Z (Mac) to undo the change.

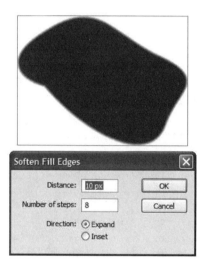

Tip *This technique works best with single shapes containing a single color. Applying it to multicolored shapes increases the file size and affects the performance of the SWF file.*

Shapes drawn on the Stage can be modified by using the Smooth and Straighten buttons on the Tools panel. When you select a shape, two buttons appear at the bottom of the Tools panel. The S is the Smooth button. Click it, and the curves and abrupt changes in direction will be rounded. Click the Straighten button, and the direction changes will be changed to straight lines.

Smooth Tool ———— ·S ·⟨ ———— Straighten Tool

4. Select the shape on the Stage and then click the Smooth and Straighten buttons.

Notice that the shape changes to reflect your choice. Clicking the buttons multiple times changes the shape without your moving the anchor point or the handles in the object. Select the object on the Stage and press Delete to remove the object from the Stage.

> **Tip** *The Smooth and Straighten buttons are also available to objects drawn using the Pencil tool.*

So far, you have seen how to draw and manipulate shapes. Flash Professional 8 also includes some serious improvements over the drawing of how lines end and join with each other.

5. Select the Line tool and then click and drag a line across the Stage.

The Property inspector changes to reflect the shape you just created. In the Property inspector, set the thickness to 10 points.

You can change the look of the line by selecting one of the choices in the Stroke Style drop-down list. The choices range from a solid stroke to a dotted stroke. Click the Cap drop-down list and select Square. The line now ends in a straight edge rather than the default style of rounded.

Click the Custom button to open the Stroke Style dialog box. This dialog box allows you to change the default value for your stroke style. Select Ragged from the Type drop-down list. Select a pattern that will be applied to the stroke from the Pattern drop-down list. Wave height allows you to adjust the waviness of the stroke, and the length allows you to choose how long the wave will be. Click the Zoom 4x button, and you can see how the edges join. Finally, you can also change the thickness of the stroke and whether the point where the lines meet or change direction is sharp—pointed—or round.

Select a solid stroke with a square cap.

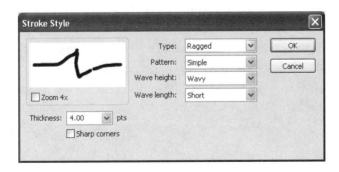

Although lines are straight, they are regarded by Flash as being vectors and can be curved.

6. Select the Direct Selection tool, roll over the line and click and drag the line up or down when you see the stroke icon appear under the cursor.

The line bends as you drag the cursor. The end points of the line are also the line's anchor points. Drag a line between the two end points to change the shape of the line.

Now that you understand the drawing fundamentals, you can build the interface for a slide show.

Tip *This is a great feature but it is also dangerous. If you want to move a line, click on it and move it only when you see the line selected on the Stage. If you don't, you will bend the line.*

Manipulating Objects on the Stage

Objects that you create in Flash or import to the library can be manipulated using many of the tools introduced in Flash Professional 8. In this series of small exercises, you explore the use of the following:

- Distort
- Envelope
- Union
- Intersect
- Punch
- Masking

If you have used Illustrator, Freehand, or Fireworks, you should be familiar with these tools. They are found in most drawing applications.

1. Open a new Flash document and draw a rectangle and a circle on the Stage.

Select the rectangle and select Modify > Transform > Distort. You will see a set of handles appear around your object. When you drag a handle, the distortion is similar to doing the same thing using the Free Transform tool. Undo the change by selecting Edit > Undo or pressing Ctrl+Z (PC) or Cmd+Z (Mac).

Select the rectangle on the Stage and select Modify > Transform > Envelope. There are a lot more handles than the ones in the Distort command. Drag a handle downward, and the line curves. This is the fundamental difference between Envelope and Distort. Distort treats all lines as lines. Envelope sees them as being curves.

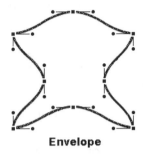

Envelope

2. Drag the circle to the right edge of the rectangle. Select Modify › Combine Objects › Union.

The circle and the rectangle are combined into one object. If you select Intersect, the topmost object is trimmed to fit onto the one below it. If you select Punch, the shape of the topmost object is cut out by the object below.

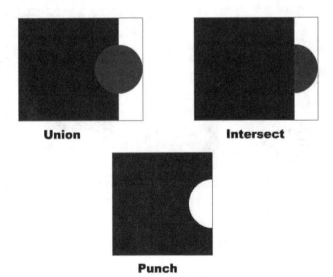

Union   **Intersect**

Punch

Applying a Mask in Flash

The ability to apply a mask in a Flash presentation is an essential Flash skill. All a mask does is hide or reveal parts of the Flash Stage. In many respects, masks are similar to stencils. You can see through the part that is transparent, and the part that isn't hides everything under it. Masks can be stationary or animated. There are many stunning Flash sites that actually use both techniques.

Masks are created by converting a layer of the Timeline to a Mask layer. The object on the Mask layer becomes the hole in the stencil, and any objects on layers below the mask that are linked to it are hidden.

In this exercise, you create both a stationary mask and an animated mask.

1. Open the Mask.fla file in your Lesson 3 folder.

When the file opens, you will see an image of the ceiling architecture for the Luxor Hotel in Las Vegas; in the library, you will see the image, the graphic symbol used for the image on the Stage, and a movie clip named Dot.

The movie clip will be used as the mask; when applied, you will only see the part of the underlying image that is directly under the Dot movie clip.

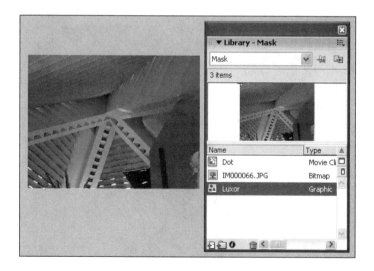

2. Add a new layer and drag the Dot movie clip from the library to this new layer.

To create the masking layer, simply right-click (PC) or Control-click (Mac) the layer containing the Dot movie clip and select Mask from the drop-down list. When you release the mouse, the mask is applied, and only the area of the image under the dot shows through.

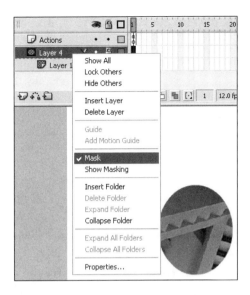

The layers also change. The layer used for the mask will change color, get a new icon, and be locked. The layer containing the object being masked also changes. The name is indented to indicate that it is linked to the mask in the layer above it, and the layer is locked as well.

To release the mask and move it to another location on the Stage, click the Lock icon in the Mask layer. Drag the Dot movie clip to a new location and click the Lock icon on the Mask layer to lock the layer and reapply the mask.

Masks don't have to be stationary; they can also be interactive.

3. **Add a new layer named Actions.**

In this exercise, you will move the dot around the screen while the movie is playing. When you have an object that will be both moveable and a mask, that object must be a movie clip.

To start, unlock the Mask layer and select the dot on the Stage. Give it the instance name of mcDot in the Property inspector and then relock the Mask layer.

4. **Select the Actions layer and open the Actions panel by selecting Window › Actions.**

The ActionScript you will write is fairly simple. The ability to click and drag an object while a movie is playing is due to a startDrag() function tied to a mouse event which, in this case, will be the mouse button being held down. When the mouse is released, the mask is no longer able to be dragged due to a stopDrag() function. Click once in the Script pane and add the following code:

```
mcDot.onPress = function() {
    this.startDrag();
}
mcDot.onRelease = function () {
    this.stopDrag();
}
```

There are two functions that depend on whether the mouse is being held down (onPress) over the movie clip or whether the mouse is released (onRelease). When the mouse is pressed the startDrag() function is applied to the movie clip (this) that has been clicked. The opposite function—stopDrag()—is applied when you let go of the mouse.

5. Save the movie and press Ctrl+Enter (PC) or Cmd+Return (Mac) to test the movie.

When you place the cursor over the mask, it changes to indicate that the object can be dragged or clicked. Drag the mask around the picture.

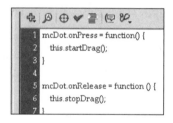

Aligning Graphics to the Stage and to Each Other

You will eventually encounter a situation in which an object on the Stage needs to be precisely aligned with the center of the Stage or a number of objects must be precisely aligned with each other. This is the purpose of the Align panel. You open the panel by choosing Window > Align or by pressing the Ctrl+K (PC) or Cmd+K (Mac) keys.

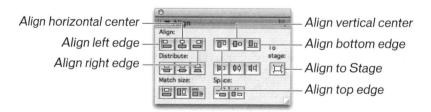

1. Open a new Flash document, draw a circle on the Stage and convert it to a graphic symbol.

2. Open the Align panel.

The Align panel enables you to align objects to each other and to the Stage. Select the symbol on the Stage and click the To Stage button on the Align panel. Clicking this button means anything selected on the Stage will be aligned relative to the dimensions of the stage. Now click the Align Vertical Center and the Align Horizontal buttons in the Align panel. The circle will align itself with the center of the Stage. Clicking any of the buttons in the top row will move the circle to an appropriate position on the Stage. Click the To Stage button to turn off this aspect of the Align panel.

3. Drag two more instances of the circle to the Stage and select all three.

This time you will align objects with each other. Click the Align Vertical Center button, and the circles will move into a perfect row across the center of the Stage.

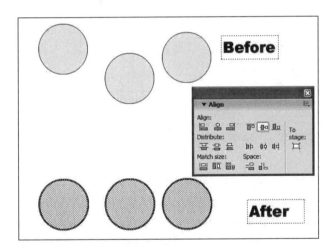

Building a Slide Show Interface

This project is fairly typical of the type of work that can be done in Flash. Your client, a local college, approaches you with an idea. They have a creative photography program and they want to give their students the opportunity to display their work through the Web. Being typical clients, they have very little understanding of how this can be done but are clear on the fact that it should be a simple solution.

This tells you two things:

- The project must be consistent in look and feel, and meet the college's design standards for the Web.
- There must be a rigid adherence to both the physical size of the images and how they are named.

After a couple of weeks of trading sketches and ideas you settle on a design, and the time has arrived to construct a prototype, called a comprehensive design, which can be presented to the client.

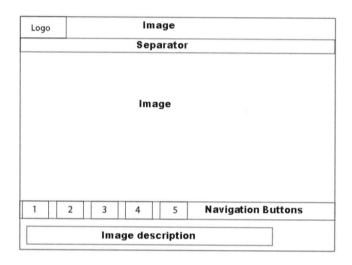

Adding Custom Colors to Flash

The first step in the process is to build a color palette. Although this may seem like a relatively simple task, it is actually a bit trickier than you may first assume. Most clients use Pantone—a print-based, color-naming system—for their corporate work. Unfortunately, print color and Web color are two separate models. You will also discover that, more often than not, when you ask a client for hexadecimal Web colors, you will see a blank look. In this case, you got lucky. The client told you the colors are these:

Dark Blue: #000034

Medium Blue: #046399

Light Blue: #D5D7E2

Gold: #C99B00

1. Open a new Flash document and select Insert › New Symbol (Ctrl+F8 for a PC or Cmd+F8 for a Mac) to open the New Symbol dialog box.

Name the symbol **Swatches** and select graphic as its property. Click OK to close the dialog box. The Symbol Editor opens, in which you can create a palette of swatches.

If you open the library, you will see that the Swatches symbol you just created is now in the library.

Symbols are the building blocks of Flash movies. In many respects, you can think of symbols as reusable assets. When a symbol is on the Stage, it is called an *instance*. An instance is simply a copy of the original artwork in the library. You can manipulate and distort the instance without affecting the original item in the library.

There are three types of symbols that you can build: *movie clips, buttons*, and *graphics*. *Graphic symbols* usually contain a bitmap, a vector image, or artwork you can draw on the Stage. Buttons are simply four-frame movie clips that control how the button looks and works, depending on its relation to the mouse. *Buttons* are used for navigation, rollovers, and hot spots on the Stage.

A *movie clip* is the most commonly used symbol in the Flash authoring environment. In many respects, you can regard it as being a miniature Flash document. It can have actions; can have a Timeline with as many frames as needed; and can contain other movie clips, buttons, sounds, and practically anything that can be added to a Flash movie.

Symbols are always located in the Flash library. The advantage of using symbols is they keep the SWF file size manageable because Flash is able to use multiple copies of the same symbol. This is why instances are so important. A great way of regarding an instance of a symbol on the Stage is to think of it in terms of a shortcut or alias on your desktop. These files are about 1K in size and can point to files that are 1G in size or larger. Imagine how quickly you would run out of hard drive space if you had 40 references to the file but couldn't use a shortcut or an alias. It is the same in Flash. The original content sits in the library and *instances* of the content point to the original content found in a symbol.

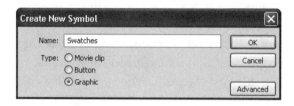

Tip *Keep in mind that when you import such assets as sounds, video clips, bitmaps fonts and so on, they, too, are added to the library.*

2. Select the Rectangle tool and draw a rectangle in the open window.

The shape fills with whatever stroke and fill color are currently chosen in the Tools panel.

Click once on the Stroke color chip in the Tools panel and select the No Stroke (the color chip with a red line through it) option. You don't need a stroke on the rectangle because you are more concerned with the fill color.

Click once on the Fill color chip and enter the value for the Dark Blue color (**#000034**) in the input area of the swatches that open. When you press the Enter (PC) or Return (Mac) key, the selection will fill with the chosen color. Repeat this step three more times to create three more rectangles and fill the rectangles with the Medium Blue (**#046399**), Light Blue (**#D5D7E2**), and Gold (**#C99B00**) colors.

Tip *A faster way of creating the chips is to draw one, select the object, and with Alt+Shift (PC) or Option+Shift (Mac) held down, click and drag a copy of the selection to a position under the original object. Simply select each copy and fill it with the color needed.*

Now that the chips are created, you have the colors identified in Flash. The problem is that these colors will be used quite a bit, and either sampling them or entering their values into the Color palette can be a time-consuming process. One of the features of Flash is the capability to add custom colors to the swatches.

3. Select the Medium Blue swatch on the Stage and select Window > Color Mixer (Shift+F9) to open the Color Mixer panel.

The Color Mixer is where you create colors for subsequent use in the movie. Colors you create here can have a single usage or be added to the Color Swatches panel for multiple usage.

When the Color Mixer panel opens, you will notice that there are a few ways of creating a color. You can enter the RGB values, enter the hexadecimal values or click on a color in the Color Picker and use the Hue slider to pick the exact "shade" of the color needed. Regardless of the method chosen, your color will appear in the swatch at the bottom of the Color mixer. The "type" drop-down list allows you to choose how the color is added to the selection. Your choices are these:

- Solid: The color will be a solid color.
- Linear: A linear gradient will be used.
- Radial: A radial gradient will be used.
- Bitmap: Uses an image on your computer as the fill. When you choose Bitmap, a dialog box lets you select a bitmap image on your local computer and add it to the library. If the object is larger than the bitmap, the bitmap will be tiled in the object.

In this case, enter the hexadecimal value of Medium Blue into the entry area of the Color Mixer. The blue will appear at the bottom of the Mixer as a large swatch. Now that the color has been created, select Add Swatch from the Color Mixer Options drop-down list.

Open the Color Swatches panel by pressing Ctrl+F9 (PC) or Cmd+F9 (Mac). Medium Blue now appears at the bottom of the swatches. Add the remaining three colors and close the Color Mixer. Click the Scene 1 link on the Timeline to close the Swatches symbol and return to the main Timeline.

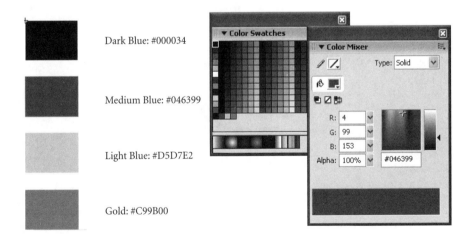

Dark Blue: #000034

Medium Blue: #046399

Light Blue: #D5D7E2

Gold: #C99B00

Importing Vectors and Bitmaps into Flash

Having created the color swatches to be used in the project, the next step is to assemble the assets. In this case, the assets are the images used in the slide show and the logo. There are two good habits to develop when working with media in Flash:

- Import everything into the library. Although you can import directly to the Stage, anything imported to the Stage is also placed in the library.
- Keep similar media together in folders in the library.

The logo is the first piece of artwork placed in Flash. It is an Illustrator CS2 image.

Note *The file you import in this exercise should be opened in Illustrator CS2. If you don't have Illustrator CS2 or if you have an earlier version of Illustrator or Freehand, use the TOTW.eps file found in the Lesson 3 folder. If you don't have a vector-editing application, we have included a file, TOTW.png, which can be used instead of the vector graphic.*

1. Open the TOTW.ai file found in the Lesson 3 folder in Illustrator CS2.

When the document opens, choose Select > All or press the Ctrl+A (PC) or Cmd+A (Mac) keys.

With the objects on the page selected, you have two methods of quickly getting the file into your Flash document. The first is to copy the selection using Edit > Copy. Open the Flash document, create a new Graphic symbol named Logo, and select Edit > Paste when the Symbol editor opens.

The second method is to create a new graphic symbol named Logo in the Flash document and then drag and drop the selection from Illustrator into the Symbol editor.

Quit Illustrator and return to your Flash document.

Note *The "official" method of importing an Illustrator or Freehand document into Flash is to select File > Import > Import to Library and then make a number of choices in the resulting Import Options dialog box. The problem with this method is the Illustrator file must be saved as an Illustrator 10 or lower for the import to work properly. Full details regarding using the Import dialog box for Illustrator files can be found by choosing Window > Help and entering* **illustrator** *into the search criteria.*

2. Open the Library panel by choosing Ctrl+L (PC) or Cmd+L (Mac) and click the New Folder icon at the bottom of the Library panel.

A folder named "untitled folder 1" appears in the library. Select the folder name and enter Logos. Press Enter (PC) or Return (Mac), and a named folder will appear in the library. Drag the Logo symbol into this new folder. Double-clicking a folder opens the folder or closes it.

Create two more folders named Images and Button_Images. If they appear in the Logos folder, drag them out of the folder.

3. Select File > Import > Import to Library to open the Import to Library dialog box. Navigate to the *Images* folder found in your Lesson 3 folder.

There are five images—***Image01.jpg*** to ***Image05.jpg***—that will be imported. Though you can import each one individually, there is a way to bring them all into the library at once. Press Shift and click all five images. With the images selected, click the Open button or press the Enter (PC) or Return (Mac) key. The dialog box will close, and all five images will appear in the library.

With the Library panel open, select the five images you just imported and drag them into the Images folder.

The first thing you should notice is that the icon for an image, which looks like a tree, is different from that used for a graphic symbol in the library. Although you can place bitmaps on the Stage, there really isn't much you can do with them. This is why Flash artists inevitably place bitmaps into Graphic or Movie Clip symbols.

4. Check the optimization settings for each of the images in the *Images* folder.

Flash allows you to optimize the images—a bit—when they are imported into the library. Select Image01 and click the Properties icon at the bottom of the Library panel to open the Bitmap Properties dialog box.

Click the Test button to see how much of a file size reduction there will be compared with the original bitmap.

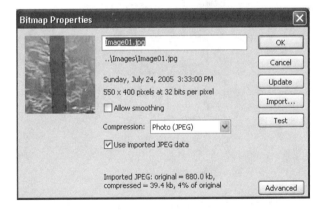

You can also choose to apply either Photo (JPG) or Lossless (PNG/GIF) compression to the image by selecting a method in the Compression drop-down list. If you are already using JPG images, select the Use Imported JPEG data radio button to use the compression in the image in Flash as well. Use the Lossless option for images using fewer colors and simple shapes such as logos or illustrations.

Click the Allow Smoothing check box to apply anti-aliasing to smooth the edges of the bitmap.

Tip *The JPEG compression amount is set when the SWF file is created, not in the Bitmap Properties dialog box. Select File > Publish Settings to open the Publish Settings dialog box. Click the Flash tab and use the JPEG Quality slider to set the compression amount. A value of 100% is no compression and a value of 0 is full compression. When working with JPG images, a setting between 80% and 100% is best.*

Tip *You can import Photoshop (.psd) documents into Flash. If you right-click or Control-click (Mac) the image in the library, you can choose to edit the file in Photoshop. Any changes made in Photoshop are automatically updated in Flash when you save the PSD file.*

5. Import the images in the `ButtonImages` folder in the Lesson 3 folder into the Flash library.

When the images appear in the library, move them to the `Button_Images` folder in the library.

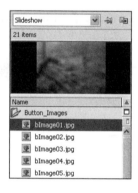

6. Save the Flash file.

Constructing the Slide Show Interface

With the assets for the slide show in place, you can now concentrate on the interface. This will involve using the tools in the Tools panel to build the interface and then converting the images to symbols. To add a bit of "zip" to the interface, the separator will use a gradient fill to give it a 3D look.

1. Open the file you have been working on, if you have closed it, and add six layers to the Timeline.

To add a layer, click the Add Layers button on the Timeline.

Your Timeline now has seven layers. From the top layer down, name them as follows:

- Actions
- Text
- Images
- Buttons
- Separator
- Title
- Logo

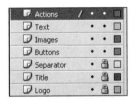

Adding layers to a movie has no effect on the final file size. The advantage of using layers is they can be used to hold individual pieces of content. This makes access to content on the Stage a lot easier because you can see where it is. It is also a common practice to include an Actions layer if ActionScript will be used in the movie.

Finally, click the Size button on the Property inspector to open the Document Properties dialog box. Set the Stage width to 550 pixels and the height to 575 pixels. Set the Stage color to Dark Blue by clicking on the Background color chip in the Document Properties dialog box and clicking the Dark Blue chip at the bottom of the Color Picker. Click OK. The Stage resizes, and the background appears dark blue.

2. Select the Logo layer and drag a copy of the Logo symbol to the Stage.

Obviously, the logo needs to be resized. Select the logo and in the Property inspector, set its x and y positions to 0,0. When you press Enter (PC) or Return (Mac), the logo moves to the upper-left corner of the Stage. Using the Property inspector is a great way to precisely position objects on the Stage.

With the logo selected on the Stage, select the Free Transform tool. When you select this tool, the logo will be surrounded with a solid box with handles. You will also notice a white dot in the center of the selection. That white dot is the object's center point, and any transform done with this tool will be done using the center point. If you were to scale the logo, it would expand or contract inward or outward from that center point.

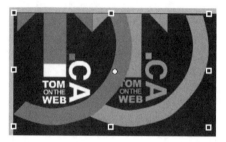

Drag the center point until it is over the handle in the upper-left corner of the selection. Place the cursor on the lower-right corner and watch for the Scale icon to replace the cursor.

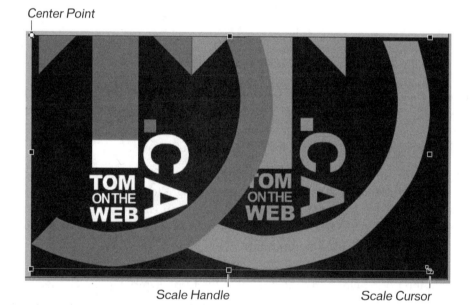

Center Point

Scale Handle　　　　　*Scale Cursor*

Press Shift and drag the selected corner diagonally upward toward the center point. As you drag, the width and height numbers in the Property inspector change. When the width value equals 77, release the mouse.

Lock the Logo layer by clicking the dot in the Logo layer that is located under the Lock icon. By locking a layer, you are ensuring that you don't accidentally select the logo and move it out of position.

3. Select the Title layer, click the Text tool, and click once on the Stage.

The text you will be adding is the slide show title, meaning that it will appear on every screen. In this case, the text won't be coming from an external source or moving around. In this situation, select Static Text from the Text Type drop-down list on the Property inspector.

Enter the words **The British Columbia rain forest**.

The text will appear onscreen and reflect the default text format for Flash in the Property inspector. Select the text with the Text tool and use these formatting settings in the Property inspector:

- Font: Times
- Style: Bold
- Size: 20 points
- Color: White (#FFFFFF)
- Alignment: Left.
- Width: 326
- Height: 27
- X: 210
- Y:11

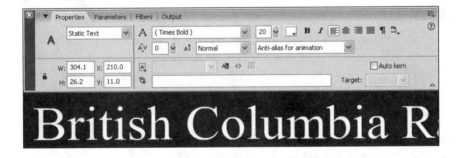

Using Gradients

Filling shapes with *gradients* can be used to give the object a 3D effect. A gradient is simply a gradual transition between colors. In Flash Professional 8, you can create gradients containing up to 16 colors. The two types of gradients available in Flash are *radial* and *linear*. A radial gradient does the color transition using a circular pattern; a linear gradient makes the transition in a straight line.

In this exercise, you create a linear gradient for the bar that will separate the logo and title from the image in the slide show.

1. Select the Rectangle tool and draw a rectangle that is 550 pixels wide and 15 pixels high. Apply a solid fill with no stroke. Open the Color Mixer panel by pressing Shift+F9.

When the Color Mixer opens, select the fill color chip and select Linear from the drop-down list. The Color Mixer changes to indicate a gradient has been selected.

Black and white is the default gradient that appears in both the Fill color chip and in the gradient bar in the Color Mixer. This won't work with our design. The plan is to have a gradient that transitions from the Dark Blue #000034 to the Light Blue #D5D7E2 used in the color palette for the project.

Click on one of the arrows to change its color. You can do this change by entering the color value directly into the input box, clicking on the Color Picker to choose the color, or clicking once on the arrow to open the Color Palette and choosing one from there.

Click and hold on the selected arrow and then release the mouse. When the Color Palette opens, select the Dark Blue color chip added earlier in this lesson. The gradient will change to reflect your choice. Select the other arrow and enter the value into the Hexadecimal input area. The gradient now transitions from dark blue to light blue.

To give the separator a bit of a rounded 3D effect, the gradient should transition from light to dark back to light. Move the dark blue slider to the middle of the gradient bar. Click once under the bar, to the right of the dark blue. When you release the mouse, a pointer has been added. Select it and set its color to Light Blue. Close the Color Mixer.

Tip *Custom colors aren't the only colors that can be saved. If you have a gradient you will be using on a regular basis, save the swatch, and every time you open the Fill Color Picker it will be grouped with the gradients at the bottom.*

2. Select the bar with the gradient and select the Gradient Transform tool.

The Gradient Transform tool is located directly under the Subselection tool on the Tools panel. When you select the Gradient tool, you will notice the selection changes on the Stage. The icons you see are identified in the following image.

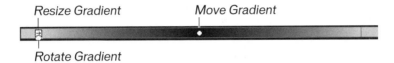

Resize Gradient   **Move Gradient**

Rotate Gradient

Mouse over the rotation handle and then click and drag the handle in a circular motion to rotate the gradient 90 degrees. The gradient might seem to disappear because of the narrowness of the shape it is filling. To make the gradient visible in the bar, the gradient needs to be resized. Click and drag the Resize Gradient handle until it touches the bottom of the bar. Release the mouse, and the gradient transitions through the bar.

3. Switch to the Selection tool and move the bar to an *x* value of 0 and a *y* value of 50 in the Property inspector.

With the bar selected, right-click (PC) or Control -click (Mac) and select Convert to Symbol from the context menu. When the Convert to Symbol dialog box opens, name the symbol **Gradient** and select the Graphic radio button. When you click OK, the symbol will appear in the library, and the outline for the symbol turns blue. This change in color tells you the object is now a symbol.

4. Select the Separator layer and draw a box filled with the medium blue color and no stroke that is 550 pixels wide by 40 pixels high.

This bar will be used as a background for the navigation buttons and will serve to separate the content from the text that will describe the image. In the Property inspector, set the *x* and *y* coordinates for this bar to 0 and 465, respectively. Lock the *Separator* and *Title* layers and save the document.

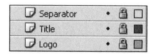

Tip *Sometimes you will place an image or symbol in the wrong layer, only to discover this fact after you have precisely placed it into position. If that happens to you, select the object and select Edit › Cut. Click on the layer where the object is supposed to be and select Edit › Paste in Place. The object on the Clipboard will be pasted into the same location on the Stage as that from where it was cut. The keyboard command is Ctrl+Shift+V (PC) or Cmd+Shift+V (Mac)*

Using Grids, Guides, Rulers and Snapping in Flash

As you may have noticed in this lesson, there is a lot of precision placement of objects in a Flash movie. The *x* and *y* coordinates in the Property inspector are used to precisely position objects on the stage. In fact, you will be using ActionScript in Lesson 6 that uses an object's *x* and *y* coordinates to move that object from one location on the Stage to another. The 0,0 point for the Stage is the upper-left corner and for am object in a symbol, the 0,0 point is the + sign you see in the center of the Stage when you are in symbol-editing mode.

Guides, grids, rulers, and snapping also help with the precise positioning of objects on the Stage. These tools are available to assist you to manually place objects on the Stage with a degree of precision that is simply unavailable when dragging an object from the library onto the Stage. When you use guides or the grid on the Stage, they are visible only while you are creating the movie. They will not appear when the SWF file is created.

You can turn on the grid by selecting View > Grid > Show Grid. When the grid appears, the Stage will look like it has been overlaid with graph paper. You can change the size of the squares in the grid by selecting View > Grid > Edit Grid to open the Edit Grid dialog box. In this dialog box, you can change the size of the squares in the grid, the color of the grid lines, whether objects snap to the grid lines, and even how accurate the "snapping" will be. To turn off the grid, select View > Grid > Show Grid.

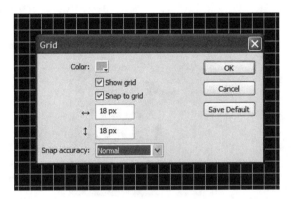

Guides are simply lines on the Stage used for object placement. Guides are created by selecting View > Rulers and dragging a guide from either the horizontal or vertical rulers that appear. You can see the guides by selecting View > Guides > Show Guides. You can also change the guide settings by selecting View > Guides > Edit Guides.

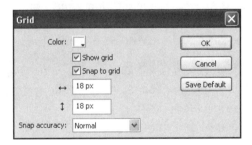

As you can see, the Edit Guides dialog box allows you to change the color of the guides, whether they are visible or not, have objects snap to them, and even lock them so they can't be accidentally moved. Like the Edit Grid dialog box, you can also choose how close an object is to a guide before the object snaps to it.

1. Turn on the rulers and select the Buttons layer.

Select the magnifying glass and zoom in on the left edge of the Medium Blue bar at the bottom of the Stage. Drag a horizontal ruler from the top ruler and place it at the 500-pixel mark. Place another guide at the 10-pixel mark on the vertical ruler. These guides will be used to align the buttons used for the navigation in the movie.

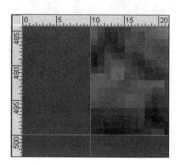

When you zoom in on an object, you don't necessarily need to use the scroll bars to move around the Stage. If you hold down the spacebar, the magnifying glass cursor will change to a grabber hand. If you click the mouse and drag, you can move around the Stage. When you release the spacebar, the grabber hand will be replaced with the magnifying glass. If you need to zoom out, press Alt (PC) or Option (Mac) and a minus sign will appear in the magnifying glass. Click the mouse, and the screen will zoom out. If no cursor appears in the magnifying glass, you have reached maximum magnification, which is 2000%.

Tip *If you want to quickly return to the 100% view of the Stage, double-click the Magnifying Glass tool in the Tools panel. Another handy magnifying glass trick is to "marquee" the area in which you want to zoom in by clicking and dragging the magnifying glass over it. When you release the mouse, the area will be in the center of the screen.*

Tip *You can also set the screen magnification by the numbers. Enter a value into the Stage View percentage located in the upper-right corner of the Timeline and press Enter (PC) or Return (Mac).*

2. Drag a copy of *bImage01.jpg* from the *Button_Images* folder in the library and place the lower corner of the image where the guides intersect.

The buttons will be spaced 10 pixels apart from each other. Drag a vertical guide from the ruler and place it against the left edge of the image. Note the value on the horizontal ruler and place another guide 10 pixels from that value. Drag the bImage02.jpg file from the

Button_Images folder and place it against the new guide. Repeat this for the remaining images in the folder. When the images are in place, turn off the guides and the rulers.

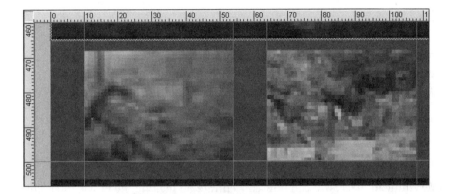

3. Click the first image and press F8 to open the Convert to Symbol dialog box.

Name the symbol Button1 and set its type to Movie Clip. With the button selected, give the instance name of Button01. Repeat this for the remaining four symbols. When you finish, each of the buttons will appear as a movie clip in the library.

You could have just as easily selected the Button type, but it is now becoming a common practice to use movie clips in place of buttons when ActionScript is involved.

4. Save the file and select the Images layer.

Open the Images folder in the library and drag a copy of Image01.jpg to the Stage. Use the Property inspector to place it at 0 on the *x* axis and 65 on the *y* axis. Convert the image to a Graphic symbol named Image1.

5. Select the text layer and add a text box under the button bar.

Enter the following text:

"The coastal rain forest on the West Coast of Vancouver Island is an amazing place."

With the text box selected, use the following settings in the Property inspector:

- Text type: Static text
- X: 9
- Y: 531
- Font: _sans. You can choose your own font. We chose _sans because it is available to everybody.
- Size: 12 points
- Color: White #FFFFFF
- Style: Bold
- Alignment: Left

With everything in place, you can now concentrate on making the movie interactive. Save the file.

Adding Interactivity to the Slide Show

With the interface constructed, you can now turn your attention to making the movie interactive. The plan is rather simple: Click one of the thumbnails on the Button layer and the image and text will change.

In this exercise, we will use the five images in the Images folder in the library and put each one on a different frame. This means when you click a button, the playhead will move to the frame containing the image and descriptive text. This will be accomplished by adding both frames and keyframes to the Timeline. Being able to distinguish the difference between a frame and a keyframe is important.

Frames are added to layers where content doesn't change. For example if you were to add a frame to Frame 10 of the Logo layer, the logo will appear in Frames 1 to 10. The Timeline will have a dot in Frame 1 (a keyframe indicator), and Frames 2 to 9 will appear to be blank. Frame 10 will contain a square that tells you where the last frame is located.

Keyframes are used where things change on the Stage. You would put a keyframe in Frame 2 of this movie because the image and the text will be different from that in Frame 1. Keyframes on the Timeline are indicated with a solid dot.

There is another type of keyframe called a blank keyframe. Blank keyframes are used when objects in a layer need to be visible for a specific number of frames. Let's assume that the logo in Frame 1 only needs to be visible in Frame 1. If you add a blank keyframe in Frame 2 of the Logo layer, the logo won't be visible in Frames 2 to 10. The icon for a blank keyframe is a hollow dot in the frame.

After the keyframes and the extra frames have been created, you can then add the ActionScript that will drive the movie.

1. Open the slide show and add a frame to Frame 5 of the Logo layer.

There are three ways to do this. The first is to click on Frame 5 and press F5. The second is to select Insert > Timeline > Frame. The third is to right-click (PC) or Control-click (Mac) on Frame 5 and select Insert Frame from the context menu. Insert a frame at Frame 5 of each of the remaining layers.

> **Tip** *Doing that last step six more times is a bit tedious. A faster way is to click Frame 5 of the Actions layer and Shift-click Frame 5 of the Title layer. With all these frames selected, press F5, and the frame is added to all of the layers.*

2. Add keyframes in Frames 2, 3, 4, and 5 of the Image and Text layers.

A keyframe is added by selecting the frame and pressing F5. In this case, you can select Frame 2 of the Images layer and with the Shift key held down, select Frame 5 of the Text layer. If you press the F5 key, keyframes are added to all of the selected frames.

3. Select Frame 2 of the Images layer, delete the image, and replace it with *Image02.jpg* **from the** *Images* **folder in the library.**

The image in the frame is located in a keyframe, so deleting the image won't delete the one in Frame 1. When you replace the image, it is critical that it have the same Stage coordinates (x:0, y:65) as the image being replaced. If it is not exact, the image will appear to jump as you move from frame to frame.

Replace the images in Frames 3, 4, and 5 with their counterparts in the Images folder. Save the file.

4. Select the text in Frame 2 and replace it with the following text:

> The regular rainfall results in a lush growth of the vegetation in the forest.

Again, the keyframe makes this possible. Changing this text won't change the text in the previous frame. Replace the text in the remaining frames with the following:

Frame 3: The moisture in the rain forest is also due to the regular fog that rolls in from the Pacific Ocean.

Frame 4: The fog makes for a sense of mystery on the beach.

Frame 5: Trees grow to amazing heights and sizes in the rain forest.

The text in Frame 3 is fairly long and will wrap to a second line. If this happens, reduce the width of text box by selecting the text box and dragging a handle to the left. As the edge of the box touches a word, the word will move down to the next line.

Save the file.

Tip An alternate method of reducing the size of a text box is to click inside the Text Box with the Text tool. A white handle will appear in the upper-right corner of the text box. Drag that handle to the left.

Text Box Handle

Coding the Navigation

The series of little movie clips above the text will be used as buttons designed to give the user control of the slide show. If the user, for example, clicks on the thumbnail in the middle, the playhead will be sent to Frame 3 of the movie and remain on Frame 3 until the user clicks another button.

Although you can create a Button symbol for this purpose—and a lot of developers would—buttons are slowly falling out of vogue with the Flash community. The reason has more to do with manageability of the code than it has to do with buttons themselves. By having all the code in one place—in this case, a frame in the Actions layer—changes to the code can be made in a rather efficient manner. If a button doesn't do what it is supposed to do, the developer doesn't have to look in two places (code attached to a button and code on the Timeline) to isolate and correct the problem.

Movie clips can be used as buttons because event handlers such as onPress, onRelease, and onMouseUp can be attached to the movie clip instance. From there, the actions that will occur can be placed in a function. In this way, the action is confined strictly to that movie clip when the mouse button is pressed. The syntax will be in the following form:

```
instanceName.EventHandler = function(){
    do_something;
}
```

1. Select the first frame of the Actions layer and press the F9 (PC) or Option+F9 (Mac) keys to open the Actions panel.

Open the Actions panel option menu and select Line Numbers from the drop-down list. This is another good habit to develop. Having the line numbers visible on the left side of the Script pane allows you to find the line in question if the Output panel informs you there is an error in your code. When this happens, it will always tell you the line number where the error was found.

2. Click once in Line 1 of the Script pane and enter this:

```
stop();
```

This is actually more important than the code that will follow. When a movie plays, the playback kicks into gear and moves across the Timeline at the frame rate set in the Document Properties dialog box. This command stops the playback head on Frame 1.

3. Press Enter (PC) or Return (Mac) twice and enter the following function:

```
Button01.onRelease = function(){
    gotoAndStop(1);
}
```

As you can see, this code follows the syntax presented earlier. The do_something is replaced with a gotoAndStop(1); function. The number between the brackets is the parameter. In this case, it is the number of the frame the playhead is to go to when the mouse button is released.

In this movie, the Timeline is very short, and you can get away with using frame numbers. This is regarded by many developers as being a huge mistake. Using frame numbers "hard codes" the value into the function. By doing that, you essentially put yourself into a development box. If you have to add five frames between Frames 1 and 2, the buttons are now broken and you will have to go through the code searching for all references to Frames 2 to 5 in the code and change them. If the code is complex, you are in for a very long session.

The solution, in this case, is to use labels. Labels associate a frame with a name, not a number. If you do use labels, the first thing to do is to create a layer named Labels. The labels will now all be in one place and easily accessible. When you select a frame on the Timeline, the Property inspector will prompt you to add a frame label. Frame labels, by the way, can be added only to keyframes in the layer. Adding keyframes in the Label layer will have no effect upon the movie. You enter the label name into the Property inspector, and when you press Enter (PC) or Return (Mac) a little red gold flag with the name just entered will appear on the selected keyframe in the Labels layer.

To navigate to the label instead of a frame number, you simply enter the name of the label as the parameter in the gotoAndStop(); function. In the case of our movie, if we have a label over Frame 3 named "Fog" the code would be the following:

```
gotoAndStop("Fog");
```

Click the button when the movie is playing and the playhead goes to the label named "Fog". Add five frames in front of it, and it will still go to "Fog" when the mouse button is released. Move the "Fog" label to another frame on the Timeline, and the playhead will go there when the mouse is released.

4. Select the function in lines 3, 4, and 5 of the Script pane and press Ctrl+C (PC) or Cmd+C (Mac) to copy the code to the Clipboard.

One of the best lessons around digital media is: *Let the software do the work.* This code on the Clipboard will be the same for each of the buttons. The only change will be the frame number and button number in the instance name. Which is faster: entering the same code four more times or changing a frame number?

Press Enter (PC) or Return (Mac) twice and press Ctrl+V (PC) or Cmd+V (Mac). When the code is pasted into place. change the code to this:

```
Button02.onRelease = function(){
   gotoAndStop(2);
}
```

Do this for the remaining three buttons. When you finish, click the Check Syntax button to make sure that there are no errors and close the Actions panel.

5. Save and test the movie.

When you click a button, you will navigate to the frame associated with the button and see the picture and text in that frame.

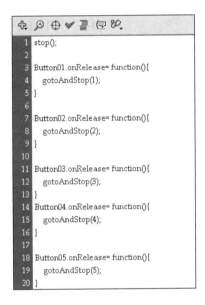

Using ActionScript to Create the Slide Show

Movie clips are more than small, self-contained animations. Over the years, movie clips have become the building blocks of Flash movies. In this exercise, you will build the same slide show as the previous exercise, only this time the movie will consist of a single frame and the five images used for the slides won't be added to the library. Instead, the images and their descriptive text will load into the movie from the server, when it is playing. As you will discover, the advantage to this technique is a surprisingly small SWF file.

The key to this is the creation of an emptyMovieClip when the movie starts. Each time a button is clicked; the image associated with the button is pulled from the server and placed into this empty movie clip. You create a new empty movie clip instance by using the createEmptyMovieClip() method. This new instance, which can be placed on the main Timeline (root) or nested in another movie clip on the Stage, requires two parameters: the name and the depth of the new instance.

What can be loaded into an empty movie clip? You can load another SWF file or a JPG image into the instance. In this exercise, you will load the JPG images used in the previous exercise.

Tip | *If you are loading JPG images into an empty movie clip, they can't be progressive JPG images. If you do use one, you will discover that nothing will load.*

If you do load a JPG image into an empty movie clip, just be aware that once the image data loads into the movie clip, the Timeline data is replaced with the JPG data. The implication here is that the object can no longer be treated as a movie clip object. Instead, it is treated by Flash as more of an instance of a graphic symbol than a movie clip symbol.

1. Open the *Slideshow_AS.fla* file in your Lesson 3 folder.

When you open this file, the first thing you will notice is that the Timeline consists of one frame. You will also notice that the image and the text are missing from the Stage. If you open the library, the images aren't in the library. If you click on the text box, you will also notice that its Type has changed from Static to Dynamic.

The text box type has changed because the text will be added to it when the button is clicked. Whenever text is added to a movie, either through ActionScript or contained in an external source such as an XML document, the text type should be set to Dynamic. When the text type is Dynamic, the Line Type drop-down list in the Property inspector becomes available. The type chosen here is Multiline, which ensures that text that is too long for the text area wraps.

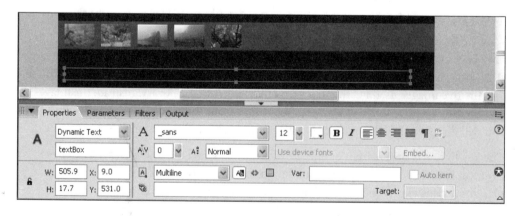

2. Select Frame 1 of the Actions layer, press F9 (PC) or Option+F9 (Mac) to open the ActionScript panel. When the panel opens, enter the following code:

```
_root.createEmptyMovieClip("mcImageHolder",1);
mcImageHolder._x = 0;
mcImageHolder._y = 65;
```

The first line creates the empty movie clip on the main Timeline: _root. The first parameter is the instance name for the empty movie clip, and the second parameter places the clip on Level 1 on the Stage.

The next two lines tell Flash where the emptyMovieClip is placed on the Stage. In the previous exercise, we used the Property inspector to place the image at those *x* and *y* coordinates. In this case, because the clip is being created at runtime, you have to enter them.

> **Tip** If you are using an emptyMovieClip and are unsure of its coordinates on the Stage, use the Rectangle tool to draw a placeholder for the movie clip. After it is in position, write down its x and y coordinates from the Property inspector. If you are putting a JPG image into the emptyMovieClip, match the size of the rectangle to the size of the image. This way, you can see if the image will interfere with any other content on the Stage. If the images are different sizes, use the size of the largest image.

3. Press Enter (PC) or Return (Mac) twice and enter the following function:

```
Button01.onRelease = function(){
    mcImageHolder.loadMovie("Image01.jpg");
    textBox.text = " The Coastal rain forest on the West Coast of Vancouver
        Island is an amazing place.";
}
```

```
5  Button01.onRelease = function() {
6      mcImageHolder.loadMovie("Image01.jpg");
7      textBox.text = " The Coastal rain forest on the West Coast of Vancouver Island is an amazing place.";
8  }
```

The first thing to notice about this code is that the function is remarkably similar to that from the previous exercise. JPEG images are loaded into emptyMovieClips using the loadMovie() method. The parameter for the method is the name of the image. Keep in mind that ActionScript 2.0 is case sensitive, and the main reason an image won't appear in the emptyMovieClip will be due to a spelling error. There are two ways of pointing to the JPEG image. This example, using just the name of the image, requires the SWF file to be in the same folder as the images. This is the second most common reason why an image won't appear when the movie plays. If the images are kept in another location on the server, an absolute path—.../Images/Image01.jpg—must be used. If you do use this method, the path must be enclosed in quotation marks as well.

> **Tip** One of the authors is a teacher, and his students are used to being presented with a never-ending series of Teacher Tricks. One Teacher Trick involves getting the correct name of an image. Locate the image on your hard drive, select the image, and copy the name to the Clipboard. Paste that name, between quotation marks, into the loadMovie() parameter.

Click the Check Syntax button and if there are no errors, close the Actions panel. Save the movie and test it, keeping in mind that only the first button works. When the movie starts, the image and the text are missing. Click the button and the image will appear where you positioned the emptyMovieClip:

```
_root.createEmptyMovieClip("mcImageHolder",1);
    mcImageHolder._x = 0;
    mcImageHolder._y = 65;
```

and the text

```
textBox.text = " The Coastal rain forest on the West Coast of Vancouver
    Island is an amazing place.";
```

will appear in the dynamic text box.

> **Tip** Testing the movie at this stage is a good habit to develop. The code for the remaining buttons, as you saw in the previous exercise, is exactly the same as that for *Button01*. If it works for one button, it will work for them all.

4. Close the SWF file and reopen the Actions panels. Enter the following code to complete the exercise:

```
Button02.onRelease = function(){
    mcImageHolder.loadMovie("Image02.jpg");
    textBox.text = "The regular rainfall results in a lush growth of the
        vegetation in the forest.";
}
```

```
Button03.onRelease = function(){
  mcImageHolder.loadMovie("Image03.jpg");
  textBox.text = "The moisture in the rain forest is also due to the
    regular fog that rolls in from the Pacific Ocean.";
}
Button04.onRelease = function(){
  mcImageHolder.loadMovie("Image04.jpg");
  textBox.text = "The fog makes for a sense of mystery on the beach.";
}
Button05.onRelease = function(){
  mcImageHolder.loadMovie("Image05.jpg");
  textBox.text = "Trees grow to amazing heights and sizes in the rain
    forest.";
}
```

5. Save and test the movie.

Why do it in one frame when you can do it in five? As we said at the start of this section, the SWF file is really small. The file size for this SWF file is 13K. The file size for the one created in the previous exercise is a hefty 530K thanks to the inclusion of the bitmaps in the SWF file . On top of that, this SWF file only requires the browser to download a file that is 13K in size. The other one will take much longer to open in a browser.

What You Have Learned

In this lesson you have:

- Learned how to add, create, and manipulate graphics in Flash (pages 79–85)
- Created a static and an animated mask (pages 86–88)
- Created a multiframe slide show and used ActionScript to control the navigation (pages 89–112)
- Created, manipulated, and saved a gradient (pages 101–104)
- Used guides, rulers, and the Align panel for precise placement of objects on the Stage (pages 104–108)
- Created a single-frame slide show that loaded images and text at runtime (pages 113–118)

4 Text in Flash

When you get right down to it, the primary way to convey information on your Web site is through text. Macromedia Flash gives you control not only over the type of text you can add to a document but also over the properties of the text. Text can be loaded into a Flash document from a Web server or can be added directly to the Stage. After the text is in place, the kerning, character spacing, leading, font style, font size color, justification, and even anti-aliasing can all be controlled in the Property inspector. Because Flash is both an interactive tool and an animation tool, you can add text effects to a Web page that are simply unavailable through HTML or Cascading Style Sheets (CSS).

In this lesson, you learn how to add and format text. You learn how to embed fonts for consistent branding identity. You create a couple of text-based animations and other special effects designed to introduce you to the creative aspects of text use in Flash. You also learn how to add text to the TextArea component, use a dynamic text field, and spell check a document. By the end of this lesson, you will have a solid grounding in the way Flash works with text and fonts and, most important of all; you will discover that text "is not the gray stuff on a page."

The new Flash Professional 8 Filters can be applied to text as well.

What You Will Learn

In this lesson you will:

- Learn the difference between static text and device fonts
- Add and format text in a Flash Professional 8 document
- Create a text-based motion graphic
- Apply the Blur and Drop Shadow filters to text
- Spell check a document
- Create a text mask
- Use Distribute to Layers to prepare letters for animation
- Use ActionScript to add dynamic text to a Flash movie
- Use the TextArea component to display text in a Flash movie

Approximate Time

This lesson will require about 90 minutes to complete.

Lesson Files

Media Files:

None

Starting Files:

Caught.fla
Title.fla
Effects.fla
Dynamic.fla
FontStyle.fla
Spell.txt

Completed Files:

Lesson04/Complete/Caught.fla
Lesson04/Complete/Title.fla
Lesson04/Complete/Dynamic.fla
Lesson04/Complete/TextArea.fla
Lesson04/Complete/FontStyle.fla

Using the Text Tool

There are several types of text that can be used in Flash. The three main text types are static, dynamic, and input, and each has a specific purpose. Static text (the text does not change or can be changed while the SWF file is playing) is located on the Flash Stage. Dynamic text is the exact opposite—it can change based. for example, on which button a user clicks, which then loads the text into Flash from the server where the text document is located. Dynamic text traditionally uses ActionScript to load the text into the SWF file or to change the text in a text field on the Stage. Input text allows the user to input keyboard data when the SWF file is playing in a Web page. A common example of this would be a login sequence in which the user must enter a user name and/or password into an input text field. ActionScript is then used to capture this text.

After the text or the text field is on the Stage, it can be subsequently formatted using the Property inspector. The Property inspector gives you control over the font, color, size, kerning (the space between letters), alignment, style (Regular, Italic or Bold), alignment (Flush Right, Flush Left, Justified), spacing position, and even the orientation of text fields.

Tip *When selecting a font, pay close attention to the name of the font in the Property inspector. For example, the font Times also has versions named Times Italic, Times Bold, and Times Bold Italic. These are the fonts that should be used if, for example, you need an Italic version of Times. If you do not have these type fonts in your font list, select them by clicking the Bold or Italic buttons on the Property inspector.*

To see the Text properties, select the Text tool and click once on the Stage. The Property inspector changes to that shown in the following figure.

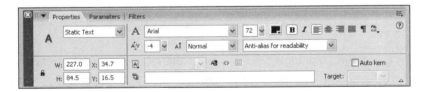

The options shown in the Property inspector change depending upon the type of text selected from the Text Type drop-down list.

Choosing between Static Text and Device Fonts

Regardless of whether a font is a Postscript or TrueType font and the text is Static or Dynamic, the actual characters you see on your computer are drawn from outlines or drawings of each character in the font. Flash uses these outlines to display the text so the font always looks the same, regardless of user. These outlines are included when the SWF file is created, and add to the size of the final SWF file. If file size is an issue, there is a solution: *device fonts.*

Device fonts are essentially generic font bitmaps that reside in the computer's system and are best used for horizontal lines of text. If you don't need to embed the font outlines into the SWF file, a device font is a good choice because these fonts are resident on Mac and PC computers. There are three device fonts that are used by Flash. They are: _sans, _serif, and _typewriter. The _serif font closely resembles Times or Times New Roman. The _sans font is similar to Arial or Helvetica, and _typewriter is a close cousin of Courier.

> **_Sans**
>
> **_Serif**
>
> **_Typewriter**

There is a caveat to using device fonts. They will display differently on each system, depending on what the user is using as a device font. What you see on the Flash Stage may not necessarily be what the user sees on his or her computer through Flash Player. When a SWF file plays, Flash uses the first device font it finds on the user's system that is a close match to the device font you use. The formatting that you apply to the text is preserved and applied to the font selected by Flash Player from the viewer's system to render the text in the SWF file.

Keep in mind that although device fonts leave a small file size footprint, they cannot be rotated. Another major difference between a font embedded in the SWF file and a device font is that embedded fonts are anti-aliased, or smoothed, whereas device fonts are aliased, or jagged. You might be wondering, "If device fonts are so bad, why use them?" Device fonts are ideal for small type, such as under 9 points, used for captions or menu items. Anti-aliasing, especially at small point sizes, tends to make the text fuzzy and hard to read.

> **Tip** *If you are using Macintosh OS X, you might not see much of a difference between aliased and anti-aliased text because the system applies automatic smoothing to any text, including that in menus, appearing on the Macintosh screen. This feature can't be turned off, but it can be reduced by selecting Appearance in the System Preferences found in the Apple drop-down list. At the bottom of the Appearance window, you can choose between five Font Smoothing Styles and to turn smoothing off for point sizes lower than 12, 10, 9, 8, 6, or 4 points.*

Adding Text to a Document

The easiest way to learn how to work with text is to add to some text to a movie. In this exercise, you add a couple of lines of static text to a FLA file. This file and the one used in the next exercise use effects based on those used for the DVD of the Steven Spielberg movie, *Catch Me If You Can.*

This first exercise re-creates one of the screens used on the Bonus Features disc. It essentially introduces each feature of the DVD by using text that slides onto the screen from either side of the Stage.

 **Tip** *The titling sequences from movies are a tremendous source of inspiration regarding the use of text in motion graphics. Many of today's top Flash artists carefully study the work of Kyle Cooper and Saul Bass and bring what they learn from those two masters into their work.*

If you've not already done so, copy the Lesson 4 folder to your desktop. Now you're ready to begin!

1. Open *Caught.fla* from the Lesson 4 folder.

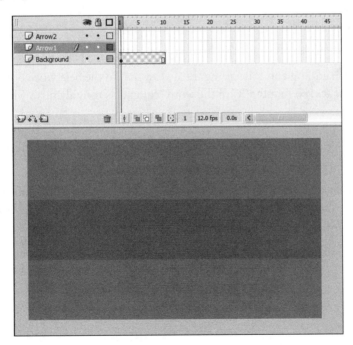

2. Open the library and double-click the Arrow1 symbol to open the Symbol editor. Select the Text tool, click once on the Stage, and type the words **Frank Gets Caught**.

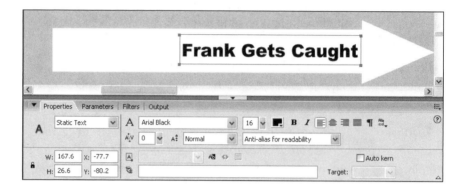

3. Select the text you just entered and change the font properties in the Property inspector to the following:

- **Font:** Arial Black (if you don't have Arial Black, use Arial and click the Bold button)
- **Size:** 16 points
- **Color:** Black
- **Alignment:** Flush Left

When you finish adding and formatting the text, switch to the Selection tool by pressing **V**; then drag the text so that the "t" in the word "caught" is roughly flush with the base of the arrow head.

4. Open your Library panel if you closed it previously and double-click on the Arrow2 symbol to open it and select the Text tool.

Enter the words **and Turns His**. Press Enter/Return and type the words **Life Around**. Notice that you don't need to format the text. The Property inspector applies the formatting of the previous text block.

With the Text tool still selected click in front of the word "life." Use the spacebar to move the line until the "L" is under the letter "u" in the word "turns". Drag the text onto the arrow and move it into position close to the end of the arrowhead.

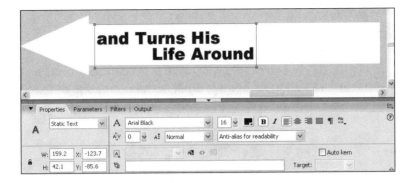

5. Select the text and click the Edit Format Options button on the Property inspector.

The two lines are a bit far apart and need to be brought closer to each other. This is accomplished by using a typographic technique called *negative leading*. Leading, in very basic terms, is the space between lines of text. It is traditionally two points larger than the point size for the text. In Flash, the leading is called Line Spacing, and there is an input area for this in the Format Options dialog box. Select the default value of 2 and enter -7. When you click OK, the two lines of text move closer to each other. Be careful with this technique because you run a very real risk of having lines of text bump into each other.

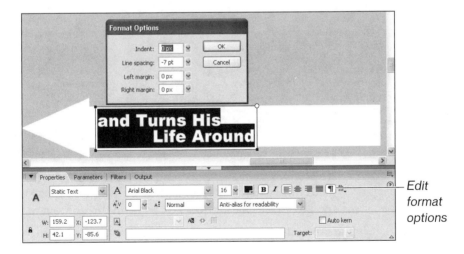

Edit format options

6. Click the Scene 1 link above the Timeline to be returned to the Stage.

You will now construct a short animation using the arrows. To start, select the Arrow1 layer. Drag a copy of the Arrow1 symbol onto the Stage from the Library panel. Place the arrow so the base is against the left edge of the Stage and the top edge of the shaft is flush with the top edge of the brown box.

7. Select the Arrow2 layer and drag the Arrow2 symbol from the library onto the Stage. Place the arrow so that its point is against the right edge of the Stage and the bottom of the shaft is flush with the bottom of the brown box.

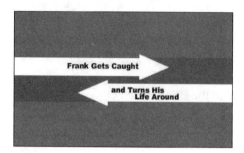

8. Add keyframes in Frame 10 of both the Arrow1 and Arrow2 layers.

With keyframes in place, select the keyframe in Frame 1 of the Arrow1 layer and move the top arrow off of the Stage by pressing the left arrow key. Do the same thing for the Arrow2 layer.

9. Right-click (PC) or Control-click (Mac) anywhere between the two keyframes in the Arrow1 layer and select Create Motion Tween from the context menu.

The arrow that appears indicates a motion tween. Also apply a motion tween to the Arrow2 layer.

10. Save and test the movie.

The arrows move across the screen and stop. The two text blocks will actually be read by the viewer as one block of text.

> **Tip** | *To use this technique in your work, add a stop(); action on the last frame of the movie to prevent it from constantly looping. You can add this action by clicking on the last frame in the Timeline and opening up the Actions window and entering your action there.*

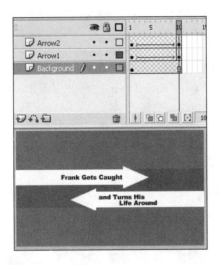

Creating Text-based Motion Graphics

Flash artists have discovered that the careful yet creative use of animated text is an effective method of drawing a viewer's attention to the message. This has given rise to a form of Flash movie called a *motion graphic*. The key to understanding motion graphics is that the motion cannot be gratuitous. If it doesn't have a specific communication purpose, it shouldn't be there. If text moves quickly across the screen, it conveys that the message is immediate. If it moves slowly across the screen, it conveys calm. If the font chosen is distressed, it conveys a message of chaos, whereas a sans serif font such as Arial or Helvetica conveys order.

In this exercise, you explore motion graphics by creating a variation of the titling sequence from the movie, *Catch Me If You Can*. In the movie, the protagonist, Frank Abignale, assumes the identity of an airline pilot. The title of the movie conveys this by having the ascenders and arms of a couple of the letters rise or fall offscreen. This technique serves to divide the Stage into discrete graphical areas and follows the style of the entire opening sequence. A small stylized jet airliner moves from the bottom left to the top right of the screen. The word "me" moves from the top of the Stage, at the same time, to its final position in the text block. As the airliner passes the word "me," the word turns into a cloud. Depth is conveyed by the airliner passing behind and then in front of the words onscreen.

Apart from the motion, careful attention should also be paid to the text. Most designers are not satisfied with the default spacing between the words (tracking) and the letters in the words (kerning). By making subtle adjustments to the tracking and kerning, the words on the Stage become both a communications tool as well as graphic objects.

Note An ascender is the long line in the letter "h," and an arm is the line that the curve in the letter "u" runs into.

1. Open *Title.fla* **from the Lesson 4 folder.**

The background has already been added to the Stage as well as the symbols you will be using in the movie to the library.

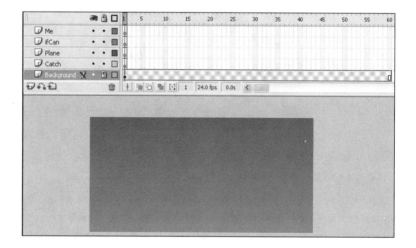

2. Select the Catch layer, select the Text tool, and click once on the Stage. Enter the word Catch.

Apply the following styles to the text:

- Font: Arial
- Size: 72
- Color: Black
- Style: Bold
- Alignment: Left

If you look at the word just formatted you will notice the "C" and the "a" seem to have a rather large space between them. These spaces become more noticeable at larger point sizes. Click once between those two letters and change the Letter Spacing value in the Property inspector to -4. The letters move closer toward each other. The purpose of kerning is to strengthen the relationship between pairs of letters. The real great danger of this technique is having the letters too close to each other. In that situation, the reader will have a hard time understanding the word.

3. Select the ifCan layer, select the Text tool, click on the Stage, and enter **if you can**.

The text automatically formats to the settings used in the previous step. Still, there is a bit of a problem. The space between the words "if" and "you" should be reduced. Click once between the two words and set the Letter Spacing value to -8 to move the two words closer together.

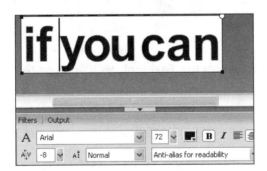

Note   *Removing space between words is called* tracking.

The word "you" is also a bit too spread out. Select the word and set its Letter Spacing value to -4.

Finally, click once between the words "you" and "can" and set the Letter Spacing value to -12.

> **Tip** *When you are adjusting the tracking and kerning values, keep an eye on the text as you make the change. There are no hard and fast rules about which values to use. The decision is a personal one. A great way of seeing the effect of a change in either of these values is to use the Letter Spacing slider in the Property inspector. As you move it up–increasing the spacing–or down–decreasing the spacing–the change will occur on the Stage.*

4. Select View > Rulers to turn on the rulers. Drag a vertical guide from the vertical ruler and place it on the left edge of the letter "h" in the word "Catch."

This guide is used to ensure the rising ascenders, and arms will be aligned with each other. The effect you are creating is to have the ascender in the letter "h" rise to the top of the screen. At the same time, the arm in the letter "u" will be moving downward.

Drag the "if you can" text block to a point where the left edge of the arm in the letter "u" is aligned with the guide.

5. Select the Me layer, select the Text tool, click once on the Stage, and enter the word **me**.

The only change you need to make here is to set the color to white in the Property inspector. Drag the text to a position above the Stage.

6. Select the word "me" and click the Free Transform tool on the Tools panel.

The whole story revolves around Frank, so the word "me" is the most critical. It needs to stand out.

Place the cursor along the top edge of the selection and click and drag to the left. The word will also slant in that direction. This is opposite of the slant of an italic character— the word will definitely get noticed.

7. Select the Plane layer and drag a copy of the Plane symbol to point on the pasteboard that is just a bit to the left of the lower-left corner of the Stage.

The plane moves diagonally to the upper-right corner of the Stage. By placing it between the two text layers, it appears to move behind the "if you can" text and then in front of the word "Catch." This gives the illusion of depth.

8. Save the movie.

The first stage of the process is complete.

Putting Things "In Motion"

With the assets in place, you can now turn your attention to the "motion" aspect of motion graphics. The plan here is the following:

- Have the ascenders and arms grow up or down to the top or bottom of the Stage.
- Have the plane move from the lower-left corner to the upper-right corner of the Stage.
- Have the word "me" move into position.
- When the plane touches the word "me," have the word soften into a cloud.

1. Right-click (PC) or Control-click (Mac) in Frame 60 of the Catch layer and select Insert Frame from the context menu.

Repeat this step for the ifCan layer. When the frame has been added, click the lock icon for both of these layers. When objects on the Stage will remain unchanged, you need to add a frame only at the end of its duration. Locking the layer ensures that the content is not moved or otherwise disturbed when you are finished with it.

2. Select Frame 60 of the Plane layer and add a keyframe to this layer.

After the keyframe is created, select the frame and drag the plane to just off of the upper-right corner of the Stage. Right-click (PC) or Control-click (Mac) between the two layers and select Create Motion Tween from the context menu. The arrow indicates a motion tween is in place and you can test it by dragging the playhead across the Timeline.

The Me layer will be treated a bit differently.

Add a keyframe at Frame 25 of the Me layer and drag the word "me" down to its final position, taking care to ensure that the bottom of the letter "m" is aligned with the bottom of the word "Catch." Also move the word far enough from the word "Catch" so it doesn't appear as if it is a part of "Catch." When the word is in its final position, click/drag the first keyframe in the Me layer to Frame 15. By shortening the span of the animation to 10 frames, the word moves into position fairly quickly. Add a motion tween between the keyframes in Frames 15 and 25.

Click/drag the keyframe in Frame 1 of the Plane layer to Frame 25. This ensures the plane starts to move across the screen when the word me finishes its movement.

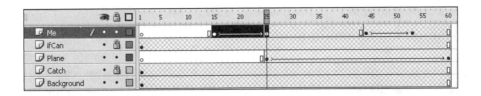

3. Add three new layers named u, t, and f.

These three layers will each contain a small animation. This animation takes place before the word "me" moves into place.

4. Select the u layer and drag a copy of the box symbol from the library onto the Stage.

This symbol is used to create the effect of the growing letters. Drag the symbol to the top edge of the letter "u." Select the Magnifying Glass tool and click and drag a marquee around the box and the top of the letter. Using the arrow keys on your keyboard, nudge the symbol into place so that its left edge is flush against the guide. After the symbol is in place, you still need to make one more adjustment to it. Select the Free Transform tool, click the symbol, and drag the white centerpoint dot down to the middle handle at the bottom of the symbol.

This is the object that grows upward, over the ascender in the letter "h" and off the Stage. If you don't adjust the center point, when you distort the symbol it will grow both upward and downward.

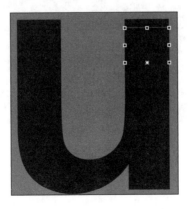

5. Click once in Frame 15 of the u layer and add a keyframe.

When the keyframe is added, click on Frame 60 of the layer and add a frame.

6. Zoom out to a magnification of 400%. Select the Free Transform tool, click the top middle handle of the Box symbol, and drag that handle to the top of the Stage.

The edge covers the ascender of the "h" directly above it as it moves upward. Add a motion tween between the two keyframes. Repeat Steps 4 to 6 for the t and f layers. The only difference is the animation in the f layer moves to the bottom of the Stage.

7. Drag the playhead to the right and note the frame where the nose of the plane touches the word "me." Select the previous frame in the Me layer and add a keyframe.

In the completed file, the frame where the plane touches the word is Frame 45. The keyframe was added to Frame 44. Drag the playhead to the right and add another keyframe to the Me layer at the point where the plane moves off of the word.

8. Select the keyframe you just added and click the word "me."

With the word selected, you can now add the effect of the word turning into a cloud.

9. Click the Filters tab in the Property inspector; then click the Add Filter icon and select Blur from the filter drop-down list.

Add the following values to the Blur filter:

- Blur X: 25
- Blur Y: 25
- Quality: Medium

The word "me" becomes a cloud. Add a motion tween; if you drag the playhead across this sequence, the word morphs into a cloud.

10. Save the file and test the animation.

As you can see, the use of motion graphics is a powerful communications tool that can be used for everything from intro pages to banner ads.

This exercise has shown you how the type tools, filters, and animation tools can be combined to create some rather interesting visual effects with nothing more than a few words and an image of a jet.

Spell Checking a Document

Flash contains a spell-checking tool that checks all the text in a Flash document. Needless to say, doing a spell check before you publish the document to the Web is a good habit to develop. The spell checker in Flash is a surprisingly robust tool. It allows you to check not only the spelling of text in text fields but also the layer names in Flash. In this exercise, you import a paragraph into Flash and then run a spell check.

1. Open a new Flash document and open the Spelling Setup dialog box by choosing Text › Spelling Setup.

Set your spelling preferences from the choices shown in the dialog box.

If you have never used the spelling features of Flash, you need to open this dialog box before you can do your first spell check. This feature is surprisingly comprehensive. You can, for example, check the spelling of scene or layer names in the "Document options" section. You can choose one of multiple dictionaries. The options found in the "Checking options" area allow you to decide what words or types of words are included or omitted during the spell-check process. In the Spelling Setup dialog box, change your settings, which are the application default settings, to the selections made in the following figure.

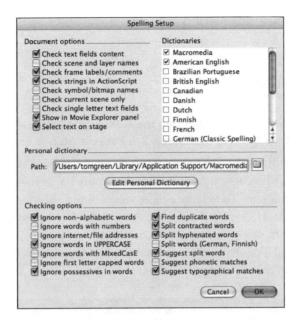

When did Macromedia become a language? The Macromedia dictionary will check the spelling of words that are pertinent to Macromedia products. For example, a normal spell checker would point out that the word "ColdFusion" is spelled improperly.

2. Open the spell.txt document in the Lesson 4 folder in a word processor.

Flash does not have a feature that allows you to import text directly into the application. Instead you must open the text document in a word processor—Microsoft Word, SimpleText (Mac), Notepad (PC)—and then copy and paste the text directly into Flash.

Select the text in the word processor and copy it to the Clipboard. You can exit from the Word processor without saving any changes.

3. Select the Text tool, click once on the Stage, and paste the text into place.

When the text appears on the Stage, use the following formatting in the Property inspector:

- Font: Times, Times New Roman
- Size: 16 points
- Color: Black
- Alignment: Flush left

4. Select Text › Check Spelling to open the Check Spelling dialog box and check the document's spelling using the Check Spelling dialog box.

If a word is not recognized, you see the correct spelling of the word as well as a list of alternatives. If the word is correct, you can click the Ignore button to ignore this one instance of the word, Ignore All to ignore all instances in the document, Change to choose a word from the list and change this one instance, Change All to choose a word from the list and change all instances in the document, or Add to Personal to add the unrecognized word to your personal dictionary. When the process is complete, an alert box appears. Click OK to exit the Check Spelling dialog box.

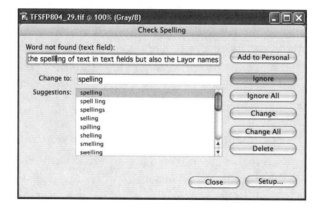

Text Effects in Flash

As you saw with the motion graphics exercise earlier in this chapter, text can be used effectively in animations or banner ads. There are times, however, when a headline or other piece of text needs similar attention but should remain fixed in place. In this exercise you explore three common techniques that can be used to make static text stand out.

The first technique is the addition of a simple drop shadow to text. *Drop shadows* are added through the application of the Drop Shadow filter, which is new to Flash Professional 8. The second method uses text to mask an image. And the third technique prepares a word so that each letter in the word can then be animated.

Adding a Filter to Text

1. Open the *Effects.fla* file in your Lesson 4 folder.

2. Select the text with the Selection tool and then click the Filters tab on the Property inspector.

Filters can be applied only to symbols and text. Click the plus sign (+) to open the Filters list and select Drop Shadow. The shadow is applied to the selected text and the settings appear in the Property inspector. Use these settings:

- Blur X: 10
- Blur Y: 10
- Strength: 100%
- Quality: Medium
- Angle: 45 degrees
- Distance: 5

As you change the settings, note that the selection updates to reflect the changes you made.

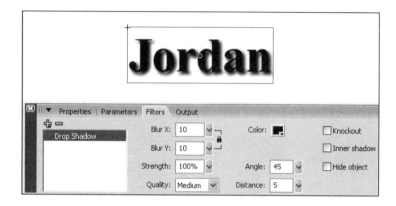

The three selections on the right side of the Property inspector are also versatile. If you select "knockout," the text turns white and is surrounded by the shadow. In actual fact, you have punched a hole in the shadow and if you were to place an image under the text, it would show through the knockout area. If you select Inner Shadow, the shadow filter is applied inside the text, and the shading gives the text an almost 3D look. Select Hide Object—the text disappears, but the shadow remains visible. Select both Knockout and Inner Shadow, and the text takes on the texture of marble.

3. Click the minus (-) sign to remove the filter.

Now that you know how to add and remove a filter, let's explore how a drop shadow can be manipulated.

4. Add a new layer to the *Effects.fla* file.

Choose the Selection too, click once on the text on the Stage and copy it.

Select the new layer and select Edit > Paste In Place to place a copy of the selection in the same position as the original selection. You will manipulate the image in the layer below. Click the layer visibility icon on the new layer to turn it off.

5. **Select the text on Layer 1 and apply a Drop Shadow filter to the selection.**

After you have the desired shadow effect, click the Hide Object checkbox in the Property inspector. The word disappears, and only the shadow will be visible.

6. **With the shadow selected on the Stage, select the Free Transform tool.**

Skew the shadow selection by dragging the skew cursor to the right or the left. When you get the effect you need, turn on the visibility of the second layer by clicking the Visibility dot on the Layer name.

7. **Select the text in Layer 2. Use the arrow keys to nudge the words into place.**

Use Hide Object to access the shadow and manipulate it. If you were to turn off the visibility of Layer 2 and deselect Hide Object, you would see the original word matches the skew applied to the Drop Shadow.

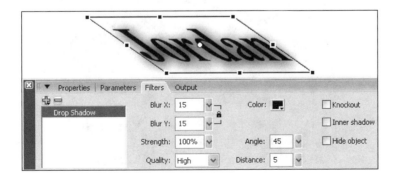

8. Select File > Revert to return to the state of the original document.

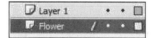

Creating a Text Mask

Text doesn't always have to be filled with a solid color. You can also use it as a mask.

1. If it isn't already open, open the *Effects.fla* file in the Lesson 4 folder.

2. Add a new layer to the document and name it **Flower**.

Drag this layer under the text layer.

3. Open the library and drag the flower image into the Flower layer.

The image is rather large and you will notice that the text is over the image.

4. Right-click the top layer and select Mask from the Layer option menu that appears.

The flower disappears, and the text fills with the area of the image that it covered. If you want to change the fill, simply click the lock in the Text layer. The image reappears, and you can reposition the text over the image. If the position of the text is critical, unlock the Flower layer and move the image instead. When you are finished, lock the layer, and the mask is reapplied.

Tip   *Don't forget that when working with Mask layers, both the Mask layer and the masked layer (the layer name that is indented is called the* masked layer) *must be locked for the effect to be visible.*

5. Before moving to the next exercise, select File › Revert.

Preparing Letters for Animation

If you have ever seen a Flash movie in which the individual letters of a word scatter and reform to recompose the word, you have also seen one of the fundamental rules of Flash at work. The rule is: Let the software do the work.

1. If it isn't already open, open the *Effects.fla* file in the Exercise folder.

If you have the last exercise open and didn't save the file, select File > Revert to open the Revert dialog box. Click OK, and the file returns to its original state.

2. Select the text on the Stage and press Ctrl+B (PC) or Cmd+B (Mac).

This key combination has the same effect as selecting Modify > Break Apart. This command functions very much as a deconstruction tool for text and bitmaps. In the case of text, you have to keep pressing the keys until each letter in the word is in its own box.

3. With each of the letters selected, select Modify › Timeline › Distribute to Layers.

What Ctrl+Shift+D (PC) or Cmd+Shift+D (Mac) does is to move each shape to its own layer. In the case of text, not only is each letter moved to a layer but the layer name is also changed to the letter name. By moving each letter to its own layer, without moving its position on the Stage, you can animate the layers or otherwise manipulate the letters.

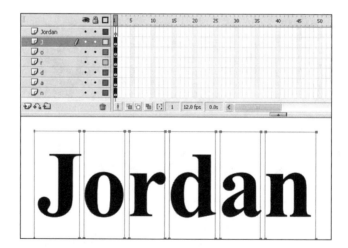

Tip   When you distribute text to layers, the original layer is maintained. You can either delete it or hide it by turning off its visibility.

Tip   Images and bitmaps can be broken apart and used as a fill color. Select the image and repeatedly press the Break Apart key combination until the image is a collection of pixels. Select the Eyedropper tool and click the image. The Fill Color chip on the Tools panel fills with the image.

Adding Text using ActionScript

Throughout this lesson, you have worked with static text. Static text doesn't change based upon an event. In this exercise you create a small movie that uses dynamic text. When you roll over one of the buttons on the Stage the text changes to describe the object you just rolled over. That is dynamic text.

Dynamic text can be added to a page by adding the text to an ActionScript-driven event or can be called into a dynamic text field through the use of an external XML document. Dynamic text fields can also "understand" HTML-formatted text, so you can use HTML tags and CSS styles within the text you enter or load into a dynamic text field. In this case, Flash reads the styling information and formats it accordingly. For example you can enter <b> tags to create bold text and Flash applies a bold style to the text between the tags. You can also place URLs, images, and large text blocks into a dynamic text field using the HTML tags. You explore this technique in greater detail in Lesson 11.

In this exercise, the text is contained in the ActionScript attached to each button on the Stage.

1. Open the *Dynamic.fla* file contained in the Lesson 4 folder.

When the document opens, notice that three graphics have been placed on the Stage: the buttons you use to change the text. If you open the library, notice that each of the buttons is nothing more than a graphic that has been converted into a Movie Clip symbol. As well, each of the buttons has been given an instance name in the Property inspector.

2. Select the Text tool and set the text type to Dynamic Text in the Property inspector.

Text that is called in from an external source such as ActionScript or an XML document is always placed into a dynamic text field.

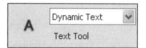

3. Select the Text layer and then draw a text box.

A dynamic text box always has its resize handle in the lower-right corner of the text box. With the text box selected give it the instance name of Text_txt. In the Property inspector, click on the Line Type pop-up menu and change it from Single Line to **Multiline**.

Tip *Simply naming an instance can result in confusion when there are a number of named instances on the Flash Stage. Develop the habit of adding an identifier at the end of the instance name that tells you the type of object you have selected. In this case, the _txt identifier lets you know the object is a text box. Other identifiers could be _mc for a movie clip, _btn for a button, and _cpt for a component. Another approach, which is quite common, is to put the identifier at the beginning of the instance name such mcMyMovie.*

4. Select the Actions layer and then press F9 to open the ActionScript editor.

Enter the following code:

```
Button1_mc.onRollOver =function(){
  Text_txt.text = "What happens when the viewer is placed into a movie
    title? An interesting example of the Flash/Freehand connection.";
}

Button1_mc.onRollOut =function(){
  Text_txt.text="";
}

Button2_mc.onRollOver =function(){
  Text_txt.text="Was recently asked how they did this. Then they added,
    'Must have been a lot of Photoshop work?' Not quite. Did the whole
    thing using the Studio. Click the image to preview.
";
}
Button2_mc.onRollOut =function(){
  Text_txt.text="";
}

Button3_mc.onRollOver =function(){
  Text_txt.text= "Was in New York recently and wondered what would happen
    if I used a combination of recorded video and a web cam to let the
    user interact. Attach a web cam and click the image to see the result.";
}

Button3_mc.onRollOut =function(){
  Text_txt.text="";
}
```

The code is the same for all three buttons, so let's examine what happens with button 1.

The neat thing about movie clips is they can use button actions. In this case, when the Button1_mc is rolled over by the mouse, a function is initiated. The function simply puts the text between the quotes into the object named Text_txt that is located on the Stage.

The next function says that when the mouse rolls off of the movie clip, remove the text from the text field. This is done by putting nothing between the quotation marks.

```
Button3_mc.onRollOut =function(){
  Text_txt.text=""
}
```

5. Save the movie and test it.

When you roll over a button, the text appears on the Stage, and when you roll off, it disappears.

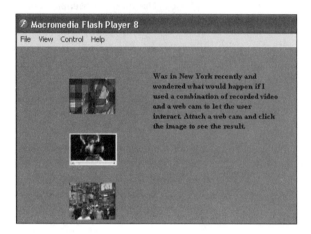

Using the TextArea Component

Flash Professional 8 ships with a fairly extensive collection of prebuilt interface elements called *components*. These are the buttons, sliders, media widgets, and text boxes that are located in the Components panel. You can open this panel by selecting Window > Components or by pressing Ctrl+F7 (PC) or Cmd+F7 (Mac). All components have drag-and-drop functionality, meaning that they can be dragged from the panel to the Stage and with a little bit of ActionScript, you have added some fairly complex interactive elements to your movie.

For all intents and purposes, think of a component as being nothing more than a movie clip designed for a specific purpose. In the case of this exercise, the TextArea component is used to manage the presentation of text in a Flash movie.

The TextArea component is simply a text field that includes scroll bars. It can manage blocks of text, ranging from a single line to multiple paragraphs, and if you want, the user can edit the text in the component. You can load plain or formatted text into the component; if the amount of text exceeds the width and height of the component, scroll bars are automatically added.

1. Open a new Flash document and add two new layers.

Name the Layers, starting from the bottom to the top: **Components**, **Buttons**, and **Actions**.

In this exercise you learn how to add text to the component. When the movie plays, a large amount of text is visible, and the scroll bars allow the viewer to read the text. The buttons are used to teach you how you can use interface elements to change the text in the component when a button is rolled over. When you roll off of the button, the text is either replaced with the large block of text or else the text is completely cleared out of the component.

2. Select the Components layer. Open the Components panel, open the User Interface components, and drag a copy of the TextArea component from the Components panel to the Stage.

The TextArea component on the Stage is nothing more than a box with a gray line around it. The text area is the white area inside the component. If you want to change the size or shape of the component, select it with the Free Transform tool and drag the handles.

Select the component on the Stage and, give it the instance name of ourTextArea in the Property inspector.

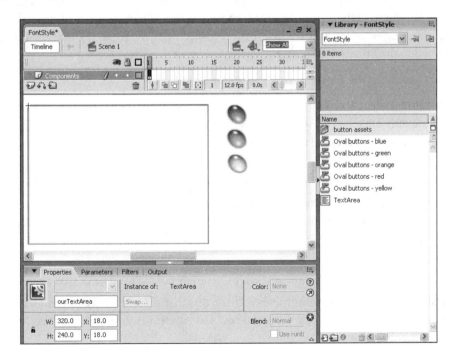

3. Select the `TextArea` component on the Stage and click the Parameters tab in the Property inspector to open the `TextArea` component's parameters.

Select the editable parameter and select false from the drop-down list.

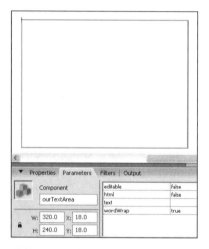

The parameters you see in the Property inspector are just a few of the parameters that can be changed for this component. Select Window > Component Inspector or press Alt+F7 (PC) or Option+F7 (Mac) to open the Component inspector. When the inspector opens, click the Parameters tab to view the `TextArea` parameters. If you compare those in the Component inspector to those in the Property inspector, there are six parameters that are not shown in the Property inspector.

The parameters for the `TextArea` component are as follows:

- **editable** indicates whether the `TextArea` component is editable (true) or not (false). The default value is true, which means the user can change the text. If the text is meant to be read, set the value to `false`.

- **html** indicates whether the text is formatted with HTML (true) or not (false). If HTML is set to true, you can format the text using the font tag. The default value is false.

- **text** indicates the contents of the `TextArea` component. You cannot enter carriage returns in the Property inspector or the Component inspector. The default value is "" (an empty string), which means the TextArea will be blank when viewed through a browser.

- **wordWrap** indicates whether the text wraps (true) or not (false). The default value is true.

- **maxChars** is the maximum number of characters that the TextArea can contain. The default value is null, which means you could, theoretically, add the entire text for *War and Peace* into this area.

- **restrict** indicates the set of characters that a user can enter in the TextArea. The default value is undefined. For example, the default value means that anything can be typed into the TextArea. If you decide to restrict the string to containing only the letters in the name "Jordan", any entry containing these letters can only be entered. If the user tried entering **"Tom"**, the entry would be unacceptable because the "T" and "m" are not part of the restriction parameter string. However, if the user entered "darn" or "adorn", they would be an acceptable entry. A more appropriate use of the restrict parameter is to check a range of characters such as "a-z", indicating that only lower case alpha characters are acceptable. If any upper case characters are entered, the entry would be unacceptable. You can also use it for a numeric only fields by using the string "0-9" in the restrict parameter.

- **enabled** is a Boolean value that indicates whether the component can receive focus and input. The default value is true, which means that when the TextArea is visible in the browser, it is available and can have text entered into it if you allow it.

- **password** is a Boolean value that indicates whether the input is a password or other text that should be hidden from view as it is typed. Flash hides the input characters with asterisks. The default value is false, which means it isn't being used for password entry.

- **visible** is a Boolean value that indicates whether the object is visible (true) or not (false). The default value is true, which means the TextArea component is seen by the user in the browser.

- **minHeight** is a value, in pixels, for the minimum height of the component in the browser. The default value is 0.

- **minWidth** is a value, in pixels, for the minimum width of the component in the browser. The default value is 0.

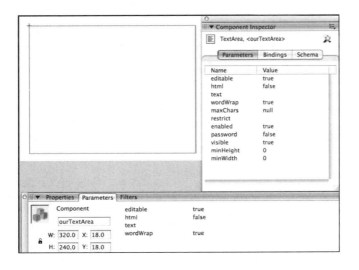

4. Select the Buttons layer and then select Window > Common Libraries > Buttons to open the Buttons panel.

Open the Ovals buttons folder in the Buttons panel. Drag a copy of Oval buttons-blue, Oval buttons-orange and Oval buttons-yellow to the Stage.

Select the blue button and, in the Property inspector, give it the instance name of Button1_mc. Select the orange button and give it the instance name of Button2_mc. Select the yellow button and give it the instance name of Button3_mc.

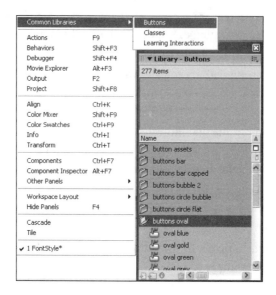

5. Select the Actions layer and press F9 to open the Actions panel.

When the panel opens, enter the following code:

```
ourTextArea.text = "Text, when you get right down to it, is where a
  site's information can be located. Flash gives you quite a lot of
  control not only over the type of text that can be added to a document
  but also over the properties of the text. It can be loaded into a
  Flash document from a web server or even added directly to the stage.
  Once the text is in place the kerning, character spacing, leading, font
  style, font size color, justification and even anti-aliasing can all be
  controlled in the Property inspector. Naturally, because Flash is both
  an interactive tool and an animation tool, you can add text effects to
  a web page that are simply unavailable through HTML or Cascading Style
  Sheets (CSS).In this lesson you will add and format text. You will learn
  how to embed fonts for consistent branding identity. You will also
```

create a couple of text-based animations and other special effects designed to introduce you to the creative aspects of text use in Flash. You will also learn how to add text to the TextArea component, use a Dynamic text field and how to spell check a document. By the end of this lesson you will have received a solid grounding in the way Flash works with text and fonts and, most important of all; you will discover text is not the grey stuff on a page.";
;

```
Button1_mc.onRollOver = function() {
  ourTextArea.text = "What happens when the viewer is placed into a movie
    title? An interesting example of the Flash/Freehand connection.";
};
```

```
Button1_mc.onRollOut = function() {
  ourTextArea.text = "Text, when you get right down to it, is where a
    site's information can be located. Flash gives you quite a lot of
    control not only over the type of text that can be added to a
    document but also over the properties of the text. It can be loaded
    into a Flash document from a web server or even added directly to
    the stage. Once the text is in place the kerning, character spacing,
    leading, font style, font size color, justification and even anti-
    aliasing can all be controlled in the Property inspector. Naturally,
    because Flash is both an interactive tool and an animation tool, you
    can add text effects to a web page that are simply unavailable through
    HTML or Cascading Style Sheets (CSS).In this lesson you will add and
    format text. You will learn how to embed fonts for consistent branding
    identity. You will also create a couple of text-based animations and
    other special effects designed to introduce you to the creative aspects
    of text use in Flash. You will also learn how to add text to the
    TextArea component , use a Dynamic text field and how to spell check
    a document. By the end of this lesson you will have received a solid
    grounding in the way Flash works with text and fonts and, most
    important of all; you will discover text is not the grey stuff on a
    page.";
};
```

```
Button2_mc.onRollOver = function() {
  ourTextArea.text = "Was recently asked how they did this. Then they
    added,'Must have been a lot of Photoshop work?' Not quite. Did the
    whole thing using the Studio. Click the image to preview. ";
};
```

continues on next page

```
Button2_mc.onRollOut = function() {
  ourTextArea.text = "Text, when you get right down to it, is where a
    site's information can be located. Flash gives you quite a lot of
    control not only over the type of text that can be added to a document
    but also over the properties of the text. It can be loaded into a
    Flash document from a web server or even added directly to the stage.
    Once the text is in place the kerning, character spacing, leading,
    font style, font size color, justification and even anti-aliasing can
    all be controlled in the Property inspector. Naturally, because Flash
    is both an interactive tool and an animation tool, you can add text
    effects to a web page that are simply unavailable through HTML or
    Cascading Style Sheets (CSS).In this lesson you will add and format
    text. You will learn how to embed fonts for consistent branding
    identity. You will also create a couple of text-based animations and
    other special effects designed to introduce you to the creative
    aspects of text use in Flash. You will also learn how to add text to
    the TextArea component, use a Dynamic text field and how to spell check
    a document. By the end of this lesson you will have received a solid
    grounding in the way Flash works with text and fonts and, most
    important of all; you will discover text is not the grey stuff on a
    page.";
};

Button3_mc.onRollOver = function() {
  ourTextArea.text = "Was in New York recently and wondered what would
    happen if I used a combination of recorded video and a web cam to let
    the user interact. Attach a web cam and click the image to see the
    result.";
};

Button3_mc.onRollOut = function() {
  ourTextArea.text = "";
};
```

Notice that all the text entered into the component is between quotation marks. Their purpose is to let Flash know that the content between them is to be treated as a string. Where you see quotation marks with no text, you are clearing out the text in the TextArea component.

The first line of the code simply says, "Put all the text between the quotation marks into the TextArea component named ourTextArea." By using the text property, you are ensuring that the only thing that can be placed in the component is text.

Buttons 1 and 2 simply swap out the text in the component with their own text. Button 3 clears out all text in the TextArea when the mouse rolls off of the button.

> **Tip** *If you have a large block of text in the TextArea component, you can break it into paragraph by using /n in the string or putting the paragraphs between <p> and </P> tags. If you do use quotation marks around words, place them in "\" sequences such as <\>"Jord"<\>.*

6. Save and test the movie.

Take note of the large amount of text in the TextArea component and the scroll bar. Also notice that the text changes when you roll over the first two buttons, and disappears when you roll off of the third button.

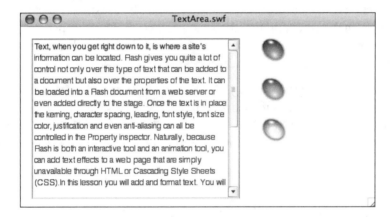

Styling Text in the TextArea Component

In the previous exercise, you placed text into the TextArea component, swapped the text, and even cleared the text out of the component. In this exercise you add even more control to the process by controlling the font, size, and even text color in the component.

1. Open the file you saved from the previous exercise, or open *FontStyle.fla* in the **Lesson 4 folder.**

Select the buttons layer and add the Green and Red Oval buttons from the button library. Move them close to the bottom of the Stage. Select the Text tool, click once, and enter **Text Style #1**. Click the Text tool beside the bottom button and enter **Text Style #2**.

Select the first style button on the Stage and give it the instance name of **FontButton1_mc**. Select the second style button and give it the instance name of **FontButton2_mc**.

2. Select the keyframe in the Actions layer and press F9 to open the ActionScript editor.

The editor is open because you can use ActionScript to format the text in the component.

The setStyle() method of the TextField.StyleSheet class in ActionScript determines how the text is to be styled. This class lets you create a style sheet object containing text formatting such as font, size, and color. You can then apply the styles you define to a TextField object such as the TextArea component that contains HTML- or XML-formatted text. In the case of the component, you use the HTML <p> tag.

The style sheet is created through the parameters set in the setStyle() method. There are two parameters in the setStyle() method: name and style. The name parameter is nothing more than a string that specifies the name of the new style to be added to the style sheet. The style parameter is an object that describes the style or has a null value.

Although you can create a style and use it in Flash using the TextFieldStyleSheet class, you can also use this same class to load an external CSS style sheet that was created using Dreamweaver 8 or another text editor. The syntax is TextField.StyleSheet.load(). For example, assume that you have an external style sheet named myStyles.css. In this case, the code would be the following:

```
TextField.StyleSheet.load("myStyles.css");
```

If you do use the load method to style text, the CSS style sheet must be in the same root directory of the site as the SWF file.

3. Click once in front of the code in line 1 of the ActionScript editor and then press the Enter (PC) or Return (Mac) key twice to move the code down to line 3.

Click once in line 1 and enter the following code:

```
var ourStylesheet = new TextField.StyleSheet();
ourStylesheet.setStyle("p",{fontFamily:'Times,serif',fontSize:'12 px',
color:'#CC6699'});
ourTextArea.styleSheet = ourStylesheet;
ourTextArea.html = true;
```

The first line of the code creates the StyleSheet object and names it ourStyleSheet. The next line creates the styles that are going to be applied to the text in the TextArea component. The fontFamily property uses two fonts: Times and Serif. Serif is the machine font used if the user doesn't have Times installed on his or her computer.

The third line of code attaches the style sheet to the TextArea component, and the last line tells Flash to use HTML values in the component.

With the style sheet defined, created, and attached to the component, you now have to change all the text to be added to the component from a simple string to an HTML format. This is accomplished by placing all the text going into the TextArea component between the <p></p> tags. For example, the text for the Button1_mc would now be the following:

4. Press the Return/Enter key twice and enter the following code:

```
Button1_mc.onRollOver = function() {
    ourTextArea.text = "<p>What happens when the viewer is placed into a
        movie title? An interesting example of the Flash/Freehand connection.</p>";
};
```

```
Button1_mc.onRollOver = function() {
    ourTextArea.text = "<p>What happens when the viewer is placed into a movie title? An interesting
};
```

5. Save the movie and test it by pressing Ctrl+Enter (PC) or Cmd+Return (Mac).

Notice that the text is now formatted using a serif font and is a "pinkish" color.

Styles can also be changed while the movie is playing. This is a great technique to use if certain text blocks are to be perceived by the user as being different from each other.

6. Close the SWF file. When you return to Flash, select the keyframe in the Actions layer and press F9 to open the ActionScript editor.

Click once on the right hand side of the brace in the last line of code and press Enter (PC) or Return (Mac) twice.

Enter the following code:

```
FontButton1_mc.onPress = function() {
  var ourStylesheet = new TextField.StyleSheet();
  ourStylesheet.setStyle("p",    {fontFamily:'Arial,Helvetica,sans-serif',
    fontSize:'12px',color:'#CC6699'});
  ourTextArea.styleSheet = ourStylesheet;
  ourTextArea.html = true;
  ourTextArea.text = ourTextArea.text;
  }

FontButton2_mc.onPress = function() {
  var ourStylesheet = new TextField.StyleSheet();
  ourStylesheet.setStyle("p", {fontFamily:'Georgia,Times,serif',
    fontSize:'12px', color:'#CC6699'});
  ourTextArea.styleSheet = ourStylesheet;
  ourTextArea.html = true;
  ourTextArea.text = ourTextArea.text;
}
```

Other than the use of different styles, the two functions are exactly the same. What they do is to assign a new style sheet to the TextArea component. The last line of the function is a little trick you can use to swap the style and change the text in real time. The trick simply redraws the component on the Stage.

```
34  FontButton1_mc.onPress = function() {
35    var ourStylesheet = new TextField.StyleSheet();
36    ourStylesheet.setStyle("p", {fontFamily:'Arial,Helvetica,sans-serif',fontSize:'12px', color:'#CC6699'});
37    ourTextArea.styleSheet = ourStylesheet;
38    ourTextArea.html = true;
39
40    ourTextArea.text = ourTextArea.text;
41  }
42
43  FontButton2_mc.onPress = function() {
44    var ourStylesheet = new TextField.StyleSheet();
45    ourStylesheet.setStyle("p", {fontFamily:'Georgia,Times,serif',fontSize:'14px', color:'#990000'});
46    ourTextArea.styleSheet = ourStylesheet;
47    ourTextArea.html = true;
48
49    ourTextArea.text = ourTextArea.text;
50  }
```

7. Save the movie and test it.

When you click the buttons, the text in the component is reformatted based upon the style within the function.

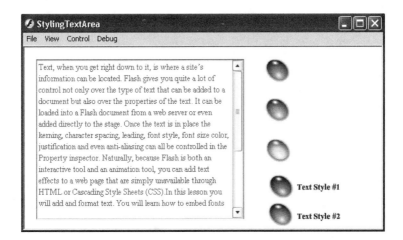

What You Have Learned

In this lesson you have:

- Learned about static and device fonts (pages 121–123)
- Used the Text tool to add and format text (pages 121–127)
- Created a text-based motion graphic (pages 127–136)
- Applied filters to text (pages 139–142)
- Prepared a block of text for animation (pages 142–145)
- Used ActionScript to add dynamic text to a text field (pages 145–148)
- Used the TextArea component instead of a text field (pages 148–155)
- Formatted text inside of a TextArea component (pages 155–160)

5 Using Audio in Flash

In many respects, Macromedia Flash developers tend to regard audio as the red-headed kid in a family of brunettes. That statement may be seen by some as being a sweeping generalization, but audio is rarely the focus of a Flash presentation. More often than not, it is simply there. This is understandable because most designers have a graphic background and working with a medium that is nonvisual moves them out of their comfort zone.

Sound, whether in the form of music or a sound effect, is an important addition to a SWF file. It enhances the user experience by adding an aural dimension to the presentation and, if done properly, will have a profound effect upon how the audience receives your work. Sound can also be a key aspect of the accessibility to your Flash movie. If part of your audience is visually impaired, audio prompts for key presses or descriptions of the screen will be appreciated.

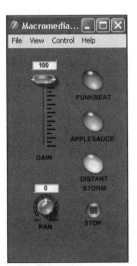

An MP3 Player constructed using the buttons installed with Flash Professional 8.

What You Will Learn

In this lesson you will:

- Learn the basics of sound in Flash
- Learn to add an audio file to a Flash movie
- Understand the difference between an event and streaming sound
- Add playback controls to manage audio playback
- Use ActionScript to create a Sound object
- Add and manage volume and pan controls for sound in a Flash movie
- Stream sound into a SWF file
- Use ActionScript to manage and stream multiple sounds
- Use ActionScript to react to what the user is doing
- Synchronize sound to an animation
- Use the Audio Envelope controls

Approximate Time

This lesson will require about 2 hours to complete.

Lesson Files

Media Files:

Crickets.mp3
AppleSauce.mp3
funkbeat.mp3
DistantStorm.mp3

Starting Files:

Sound1.fla
Object.fla
AnimateSound.fla
SliderMulti.fla

Completed Files:

Lesson05/Complete/AnimateSound.fla
Lesson05/Complete/Feedback.fla
Lesson05/Complete/Object.fla
Lesson05/Complete/Slider.fla
Lesson05/Complete/SliderMulti.fla
Lesson05/Complete/Sound1.fla

Flash and the Import Formats

When it comes to sound, Macromedia Flash is a robust application. Regardless of whether you are using a Mac or PC version of the application, you can import most of the major sound formats into Flash. The more common formats are these:

- **MP3** (Moving Pictures Expert Group Level-2 Layer-3 Audio): This cross-platform format has become the de facto standard for Web audio. Fueled by the popularity of the iPod and other portable devices, this format uses an efficient compression algorithm and is easy to create. These files allow you to output in stereo and, if you are creating MP3 files, pay more attention to the bandwidth rather than the sample rate.

- **WAV:** For the longest time, WAV was the sound king on the PC, although its popularity decrease has somewhat matched the rise of the MP3 standard. If you use a PC to record a voiceover or other sound, the odds are almost 100% that the resulting file will be a WAV file. This robust format offers you sample rates ranging from 8 kHZ (the quality of your phone) up to 48 kHz (DAT tapes) and beyond. These files are also available with Bit Depths ranging from 8 bits right up to 32 bits.

- **AIFF** (Audio Interchange File Format): AIFF is the standard for the Macintosh and offers the same sample rates and bit depths as a WAV file. Many purists will argue that the AIFF format is better than the WAV format, but to the average person, the difference is almost inaudible. There is one slight difference with the AIFF format that will win you serious kudos at a trivia contest. AIFF also has a sample rate of 22,254.54 kHz. This was the original Macintosh sample rate and was based on the horizontal scan rate of the monitor in a 128K Mac.

- **QuickTime:** These files show extensions of .qta or .mov, and can contain audio in many formats. If you do create a QuickTime audio file you need to make the movie self contained in QuickTime Pro.

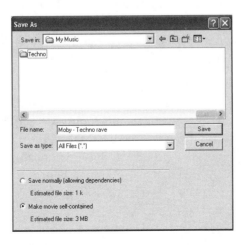

- **Sun AU:** This format was developed by Sun Microsystems and is more commonly found buried in Java applets on the Internet. The audio quality of these files is not very good.
- **SoundDesigner II:** This format (.sd2) is proprietary and created by Digidesign for its audio suite: Pro Tools. These files can be placed only in the Macintosh version of Flash. If you don't have access to a Mac, convert the file using QuickTime 4 or later.

Bit Depth and Sample Rates

We traditionally visualize sound as a sine wave—when the wave rises above the vertical, the sound gets "higher"; where it runs below the vertical, the sound gets "lower." These waves are called the *waveform*.

For the sound to be digitized, like a color image in Fireworks or Photoshop, the wave needs to be sampled.

A sample is nothing more than a snapshot of a waveform at any given time. This snapshot is a digital number representing where, on the waveform, this snapshot was taken. How often the waveform is sampled is called the *sample rate*.

Bit depth is the resolution of the sample. 8 bits means the snapshot is represented as a number ranging from -127 to 128. 16 bits means that the number is between -32,767 to 32,768. If you do the math, you see that an 8-bit snapshot has 256 potential samples, whereas its 16-bit counterpart has just over 65,000 potential samples. The greater the number of potential samples, the more accurate the sound. The downside is that the number of samples has a direct impact on file size.

These numbers represent where each sample is located on the waveform. When the numbers are played back in the order in which they were sampled and at the frequency they were sampled, they represent a sound's waveform. Obviously, a larger bit depth and higher sample rate means that the waveform is played back with greater accuracy because more snapshots are taken of the waveform, which results in a more accurate representation of the waveform.

One wave cycle in one second is known as a *hertz* which can't be heard by the human ear, except possibly as a series of clicks. Audio traditionally uses thousands of these waves and they are crammed into a one-second time span. A thousand waveform cycles in one second is called a kilohertz, and if you listen to a CD the audio rate is sampled at the frequency of 44 thousand waves per second, which is traditionally identified as 44 kHz. These waves are also commonly referred to as the *sample rate*.

The inference you can draw from this is the more samples per wave and the more accurate the samples, the larger the sound file. Toss a stereo sound into the mix and you have essentially doubled the file size. Obviously, the potential for huge sound files is there, which is a not a good situation when dealing with Flash. The sound takes an awfully long time to load into the browser.

One way of dealing with this is to reduce the sample rate or number of waves per second. The three most common sample rates used are 11 kHz, 22 kHz, and 44 kHz. If you reduce the sample rate from 44 kHz to 22 kHz, you achieve a significant reduction in file size. You obtain an even more significant reduction if the rate is reduced to 11 kHz. The problem is that reducing the sample rate has a profound effect on sound quality. Listening to your favorite CD (16-bit, 44 kHz stereo) at 11 kHz results in the song sounding as if it were recorded in a tin can.

Thus, there is a "dance" you must do when working with sound. The objective is to obtain the best quality sound with the smallest file size. Though many Flash developers tell you that 16-bit, 44 kHz stereo is the way to go, you'll quickly realize this is not necessarily true if you fall in love with the user and not the technology. For example, a 16-bit, 44 kHz stereo sound of a mouse click or a sound lasting less than a couple of seconds—such as a whoosh as an object zips across the screen—is a waste of bandwidth. The duration is so short that average users won't notice that the click sound is an 8-bit, 22 kHz mono sound. They hear the click and move on. The same holds true for music files. The average user is most likely using the cheap speakers (and maybe a subwoofer) that were tossed in as an inducement to seal the sale of the PC. In this case, a 16-bit, 22 kHz sound track will sound as good as its CD-quality rich cousin.

Audio Codecs and Compression

The most common sound files you use are WAV and AIFF. Both formats share a common starting point—they are both based on the Interchange File Format proposal written in 1985 by Electronic Arts to help standardize transfer issues on the Commodore Amiga. Like video, sound contains a huge amount of data and must be compressed before it is used. This is the purpose of a codec. Codec is an acronym for enCOder/DEcoder.

Here is a list of the more common audio codecs used for AIFF and WAV files:

- **PCM (Pulse Code Modulation):** Most professionals use this codec. The downside is that a large file but the CPU hit on playback is minimal.
- **ADPCM (Adaptive Differential Pulse Code Modulation):** This format makes the PCM file smaller. This is accomplished by simply noting the differences between the samples on the waveform rather than noting each sample as is done with PCM.

- **A-law:** This is the European telephone standard.
- **Mu-law:** These are the Japanese and American telephone standards.
- **LPC (Laser Predictive Coding):** If you are into computer voices, this one is for you. LPC takes recorded speech and makes a best guess based on a model of the human voice; then tosses out the speech and only keeps the triggers for the vocal changes. Playback sounds like a computer-generated voice.
- **CELP (Code Excited Linear Prediction):** This one is optimized for human speech and is defined by the U.S. Department of Defense. This standard is very much like the LPC version without tossing out the actual speech. The differences are saved in a code book that is stored with the file and the differences are used to excite the linear prediction tables, which sort of explains the odd name.

When you get right down to it, PCM and ADPCM are really the only two you need to be aware of.

The MP3 Format

From your perspective, the need to compress audio for Web delivery makes the use of AIFF or WAV files redundant. The MP3 format is the standard rather than the compression offered in AIFF or WAV files, which explains why WAV and AIFF files can be imported into Flash but are then subsequently converted to MP3 files on playback. If you are working with an audio production facility, the odds are you will be handed an AIFF or WAV file. Even if they give you the option of receiving an MP3, you are better off with the AIFF or WAV file for the same reason that you wouldn't want to recompress a JPEG file because they are both lossy compression schemes. An obvious question is this: Why are MP3 files are so small but still sound so good? The answer lies in the fact that the MP3 standard uses perceptual encoding.

All Internet audio formats toss a ton of audio information into the trash. When information gets tossed,, there is a corresponding decrease in file size. What gets tossed when an MP3 file is created are sound frequencies your dog may be able to hear, but you can't. In short, you hear only the sound a human can perceive.

All perceptual encoders allow you to choose how much audio is unimportant. Most encoders produce excellent quality files using no more than 16 Kbps to voice recordings. When you create an MP3, you have to pay attention to the bandwidth. The format is fine, but if the bandwidth is not optimized for its intended use, your results will be unacceptable, which is why applications that create MP3 files ask you to set the bandwidth along with the sample rate.

Audio In/Audio Out

Knowing that you can bring all of these formats into Flash and that MP3 is the output format for Flash is all well and good. But what about when you publish the SWF file in Flash?

Double-click an audio file in the Flash library to open the file's Sound properties dialog box. In this dialog box, you are first asked to pick a codec. In Flash, the default is to export all sound in the MP3 format. Still, the ability to individually compress each sound in the library is an option that shouldn't be disregarded.

Your choices are as follows:

- **ADPCM:** The sound file is best-suited for very short clips and looped sound. This format was the original sound output format in older versions of Flash. If, for example, you are outputting for use in Flash Player 2 or 3, ADPCM is required.

- **MP3:** Use this for Flash Player versions 4 or higher. This format is not compatible with Flash Player 4 for Pocket PC. It is compatible with the FlashLite player. MP3s are also not suited for looping sounds because the end of a file is often padded.

- **Raw:** No compression is applied, and it is somewhat useless if sound is being delivered over the Web. If you are creating Flash Player for use on a DVD or CD or a Flash movie for incorporation into a video, this format is acceptable.

- **Speech:** Introduced in Flash MX, this codec (licensed by Macromedia from Nellymoser) is ideal for voiceover narrations.

- **Device Sound:** This is available only if you are using Flash MX 2004 Professional. Click the folder to link to a device sound file used in such mobile devices as PocketPC.

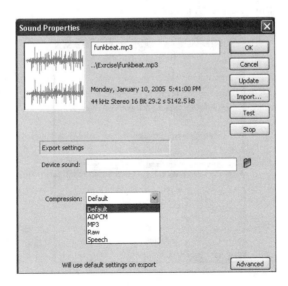

Importing Sound into Flash

There are two methods of adding sound to a Flash file. Both methods result in the sound file being added directly to the library.

1. Open a new Flash document.

When the document opens, you can make a choice regarding which sound file to import. You can choose your own sound file, or use `funkbeat.mp3`, which is available in the Lesson 5 folder. If you use your own file, copy it to the Lesson 5 folder.

2. Select File › Import to Library. You can also press Ctrl+R (PC) or Cmd+R (Mac).

When the Import dialog box opens, navigate to the folder that contains the sound file you want to place in Flash. Open the folder and either double-click the sound file or click it once and then click the Open button. The sound is imported into Flash and placed in the Flash library. You can open the library by selecting Window > Library or pressing Ctrl+L (PC) or Cmd+L (Mac).

Tip *There is a menu item in the Import dialog box named Files of Type. If you have a lot of files in the Flash content folder, selecting this option and then All Sound Formats from the drop-down list will show only the sound files. If you are a Mac OS X user, be aware that it is a bit different. When you select Import, you will not see Files of Type. The All Sound Formats selection is in the Enable drop-down list.*

Note *When it comes to importing sound, there is no difference between Import to Stage and Import to Library. Regardless of which you choose, the file will be imported directly into the Flash library.*

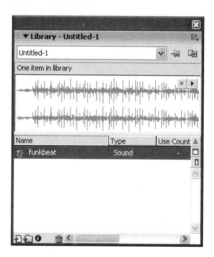

There is an alternative method for bringing a sound into Flash—drag and drop—which works in both the Mac and PC versions of Flash and is a handy thing to know.

Drag and drop on the PC functions a bit differently than on a Mac.

To drag and drop on the PC requires you to do the following:

- Locate the sound file to be added.
- Drag the PC sound file onto the Flash Stage and then release the mouse.

When you release the mouse, the sound will open in a separate PC document. What you can then do is to drag the sound from the new document's Library panel to the target document's library.

To drag and drop on the Mac simply drag the sound file from the folder on the desktop or elsewhere onto the Flash stage. When you release the mouse, the sound will appear in the Library.

Event versus Streaming Sound

Before you start playing with the sound you have just added to the Flash library, it is important to understand what happens when a sound moves from the library into your Flash movie.

First, your FLA file size just increased by the size of the sound placed into the library. If you are using the sound file included with this exercise, your FLA just increased by 1.22 megabytes. Still, Flash does have some rather significant things that it does with sound.

When a sound is added to your movie's Timeline, the sound isn't placed on the Timeline. What goes on the Timeline is a reference to the file in the library. This reference is called an *instance*. If you get deeper into Flash you will encounter this term quite frequently. An instance refers to the original or master file in your library, which can be a vector image, a bitmap, or a sound. In this case, the instance is referring to the sound file "funkbeat.mp3" which was imported earlier.

When you publish the SWF file, the sound is compressed and stored only once in the movie. If you have four instances of the file on the Stage, your SWF file won't grow by 4.88 MB. Those instances refer to the master compressed version of the sound in the SWF file. That is the good news.

What we just talked about is an *event sound*, which is tied to an event such as a mouse click or the playback head entering a frame.

Sometimes the sound simply plays in the background and is not associated with any event whatsoever. This is a *stream sound*. Stream sounds are stored in the Flash movie each time they are encountered on the Timeline. If the file you just imported is a stream sound that is used four times, the SWF files increases by 4.88 MB.

1. Drag the sound from the library to the Stage.

Notice that Frame 1 has a line in it. This is the waveform for the sound. Also notice that there is nothing on the Stage indicating where you placed the sound.

2. Add a keyframe in Frame 30 of the Timeline.

The waveform now becomes visible. Click once on the waveform on the Timeline. The Property inspector changes to indicate you have selected a sound.

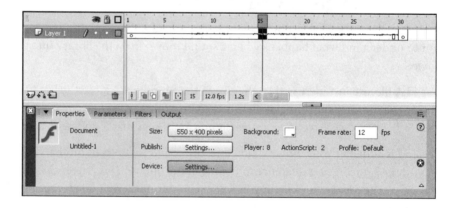

3. To preview your sound, drag the playhead to Frame 1 and press Enter (PC) or Return (Mac).

The sound plays and there really is no way to stop it from playing. In fact, if you press Enter/Return a second time, the result will be the sound playing again. What you learn from this is that an event sound plays until the sound is finished. Event sounds are great for short sounds, but unless you plan to give the user the ability to turn them off, longer sounds such as your favorite tune might be annoying to your user. If you drag the playhead to the middle of the sound on the Timeline and press Enter/Return, nothing happens because of the very nature of the sound. If you check the Property inspector, you will notice that the sound's synch is set to event. The event is the start of the movie in Frame 1.

4. Select the sound in the Timeline and select Stream in the Property inspector's Synch drop-down list.

Drag the playhead to the middle of the sound and press Return/Enter. The sound plays from the beginning and stops when it reaches the keyframe.

What you have just experienced is the fundamental difference between an event sound and a stream sound. A stream sound is somewhat independent of the Timeline and plays regardless of events such as the first frame of the sound.

Another interesting feature of stream is the ability to scrub the sound on the Timeline. If you drag the playhead across the Timeline, you hear the sound. Dragging the playhead to preview sections of an audio or video track is called *scrubbing*.

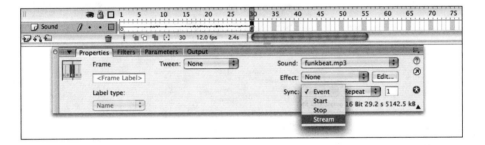

Controlling Audio

If you put sound in a Flash movie you have a couple of choices when it comes to controlling it. The first is to add no control. In this situation, the sound is integral to the action. For example, the screeching sound you hear when Fred Flintstone applies the brakes to his car is integral to the action. It gives an audible clue that the car is stopping.

The other is to add controls to the audio. A common feature of many Flash sites these days is a button that switches the audio on or off. A great example of this is a site that uses a Mungo Jerry song as the background music. An on/off switch allows the users who aren't Mungo Jerry fans or others who simply don't like the music to turn it off.

1. Open the *Sound1.fla* file located in the Lesson 5 folder.

When the movie opens, it is composed of two frames and two buttons on a Stage that is not much larger than the buttons. If you open the library you will also see a folder named Fireworks Objects. If your copy of Flash Professional 8 was a part of the Studio 8 CD, you already own Fireworks 8. The buttons were created as button symbols in Fireworks 8, and the slice over the Fireworks 8 button was dragged from Fireworks to the Flash Professional 8 Stage. When you release the mouse, a bitmap containing the button is placed on the Flash Stage, and a movie clip and a Button symbol are placed in the Flash library.

Tip *The Fireworks 8/Flash Professional 8 combination is an unbeatable work flow aid. Being able to drag and drop Fireworks symbols into Flash without using the Import menu seriously reduces the import process into Flash.*

2. Select the Play button on Frame 1 and give it the instance name of *play_mc*.

Do the same thing with the button in Frame 2, only this time give it the instance name of "stop_mc".

3. Select Frame 2 of the sounds layer and drag *funkbeat.mp3* to the Stage.

When you release the mouse, the sound's waveform appears in the frame. Select the frame containing the waveform in the Timeline and, in the Property Inspector, set the Sync Sound pop-up menu to Event.

Tip *You can't simply delete a sound by selecting the frame and pressing Delete. To remove a sound, select the frame containing the sound. In the Property inspector, select None in the Sound drop-down list. When you release the mouse, the sound will be removed from the frame.*

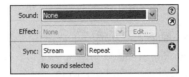

4. Select Frame 1 of the Actions layer and press F9 to open the ActionScript editor.

Enter the following code:

```
Stop();
stopAllSounds();

play_mc.onPress= function() {
   gotoAndPlay(2);
}
```

```
1  stop();
2  stopAllSounds();
3
4  play_mc.onPress= function () {
5     gotoAndPlay(2);
6  }
7
```

This code is fairly self-explanatory. The playhead waits—stop();—for a mouse action, and if a sound is playing, turns it off: stopAllSounds();. When the button named play_mc is pressed, scoot the playhead to Frame 2 of the movie: gotoAndPlay(2); .

Stopping all sounds in Frame 1 is important. The sound being used is an event sound, and event sounds will play in their entirety after they are triggered.

5. Select the Actions layer in Frame 2 and open the ActionScript editor.

Enter the following code:

```
stop();
stop_mc.onPress= function() {
   gotoAndPlay(1);
}
```

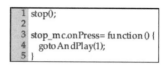

```
1  stop();
2
3  stop_mc.onPress= function () {
4      gotoAndPlay(1);
5  }
```

All this code does is stop the playhead in Frame 2 and wait for the user to press the Stop button.

The `stop();` action actually has a second purpose. When the playhead arrives in the frame, the music starts playing. If you didn't have a `stop();` action on this frame the user would briefly stay on Frame 2 and go right back to Frame 1. In this scenario, the user is denied access to the Stop button and is in for a very unpleasant experience if he or she keeps clicking the Play button.

6. **Save the movie and test it by pressing Control+Enter (PC) or Command+Return (Mac).**

The sound starts and stops as you click the buttons.

Controlling Sound through the Use of a Sound Object

Although the term *Sound object* might appear to be a relatively intimidating term on the surface, it is quite simple to understand. In very simplistic terms, you tell Flash where the sound is located in the library, give it a name, and from that point on Flash remembers both the sound and its location. What this does is to make sound interactive. Instead of a linear sound chained to the Timeline, a sound is now responsive to mouse location, clicks, object collisions, and a host of other events controlled by ActionScript.

The key to this is the Sound object. The beauty of this object is that it can refer to a sound in the library, a sound in a movie clip, or even an MP3 file located on a server. In this case, the sound can either stream into the Flash movie through the Flash Communication Server or Progressively Download much like a FLV file sitting on a server.

The Sound object is created in the Actions frame. When the Play button is clicked, there is a call to the object, the sound is found, and the movie plays. When you click the Stop button, you tell Flash to stop all sounds. That's all that needs to be done. Another interesting aspect of this object is that in Flash animations in which a number of sounds can be used, each sound can now be contained in a Sound object and separately managed. This, for example, is how MP3 players created in Flash allow you to play a number of songs. Each one is contained in its own Sound object.

1. Open the *Object.fla* file in your Lesson 5 folder.

The file is exactly the same as the one used in the previous exercise. The major difference is that this file does not contain a Sounds layer. The sounds used won't need to be placed on the Timeline. To start this process, the first thing you need to do is to give ActionScript a pointer to the Sound object via the Linkage properties.

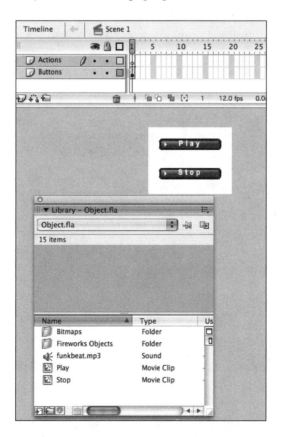

2. Open the library, and either right-click (PC) or Control-click (Mac) the file named *funkbeat.mp3*.

The context menu opens. Select Linkage to open the Linkage Properties dialog box. If the Identifier text box is blank or grayed-out, click the Export for ActionScript box. Doing this tells Flash that ActionScript can access the sound.

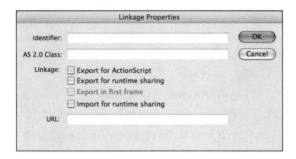

3. Enter a name in the Identifier area.

I chose **funk** to avoid confusion. I could just as easily have used the file's name, funkbeat, but I prefer to keep these terms unique so I can tell what I am working with. Click OK to close the Linkage Properties dialog box.

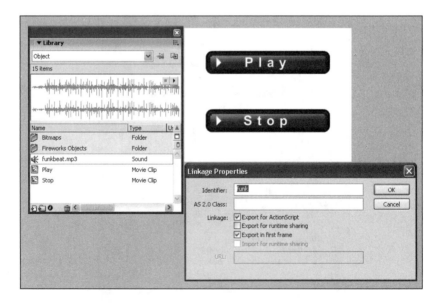

4. Select the keyframe in Frame 1 of the Actions layer.

Open the ActionScript editor and enter the following script:

```
var tune:Sound = new Sound();
tune.attachSound ("funk");
stop();
```

The first two lines create the Sound object. In fact, the purists argue that it is the first line. Either way the first line simply creates a variable named tune that Flash recognizes as the name for a new sound. Flash has to be told which sound gets used. The attachSound does that, and the name of the sound from the Linkage Properties is the one to be used.

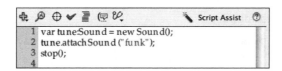

5. Still in Frame 1 of the Actions layer, add the following code:

```
play_mc.onPress = function() {
   tune.start();
}
```

All this does is tell Flash, when the Start button is pressed to start playing a thing named tune. That thing is the Sound object pointing to the sound in the library.

6. Again, in Frame 1 of the Actions layer, Add the following code:

```
stop_mc.onPress = function() {
   tune.stop();
}
```

Alternatively, if you have a number of sounds playing, you can stop all of them by changing the second line to tune.stopAllSounds ();.

```
8
9  stop_mc.onPress = function () {
10     tune.stop();
11 }
```

7. Save and test the movie.

Clicking the buttons stops and starts the sounds.

Controlling the Pan and Volume of a Sound Using the Flash Buttons

In this exercise, you create a small controller that turns sound on and off, adjusts the volume, changes the sound, and pans the sound across channels. The controllers that make all of this possible are already prepackaged with Flash. All you have to do is to wire them up.

The other important concept in this exercise: instead of the sound being embedded into the SWF, it sits on the server and is loaded into the movie using a `loadSound();` method when the SWF plays. The advantage to you is a very small SWF file.

1. Open a new Flash document.

Set the Stage size to 90 pixels wide by 325 pixels high and set the Stage color to #666666. Add two layers to the Timeline. Name the layers, from the top to the bottom, as follows:

- Actions
- Buttons
- Sliders

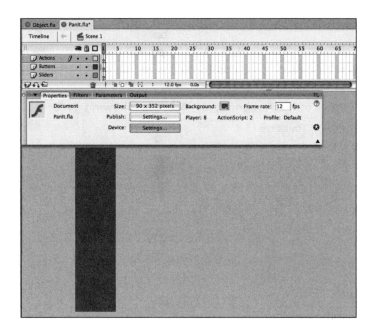

2. Select Window > Common Libraries > Buttons > classic buttons and open the Knobs and Faders folder.

3. From the folder, drag copies of the fader-gain symbol and the knob-pan symbol to the Sliders layer.

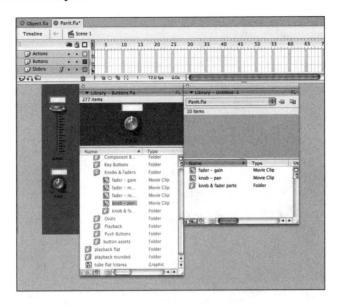

4. Select the Buttons layer and open classic buttons folder in the library. Drag copies of the playback-play and playback-stop buttons from the Playback folder to the Stage.

As you add these various controls to the Stage they are also placed into the movie's library.

5. Select the two buttons on the Stage and give them the following Instance names in the Property inspector:

- Play: play_btn
- Stop: stop_btn

Save the document to your project folder containing the sound file used in this exercise.

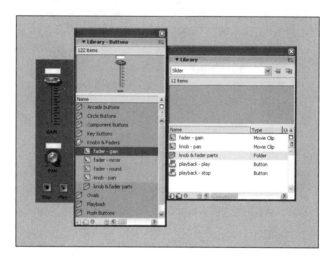

6. Double-click the slider on your Stage to open the Symbol.

Double-click it again to open the gain details movie clip. Select the Text tool and click once on the text in the open movie clip. Select the Text and change it to Volume. Set the font to Arial, 10 points, bold. Return to the main Timeline by clicking the Scene 1 button.

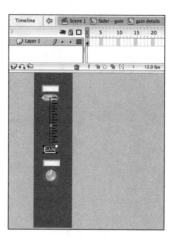

7. Select the Buttons layer and add the words Play and Stop under the buttons. Set the text property for these two buttons to Static.

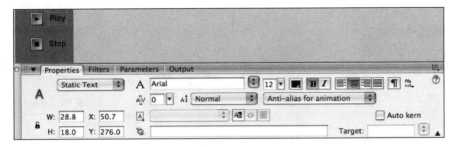

8. Select the Actions layer and open the ActionScript editor.

With the assets in place, you can now concentrate on having the objects do what they were designed to do: control a sound. When the ActionScript editor opens, enter the following code:

```
var dynamic_sound:Sound= new Sound();
dynamic_sound.loadSound("funkbeat.mp3" , false);
dynamic_sound.onLoad = function() {
  dynamic_sound.stop()
}
```

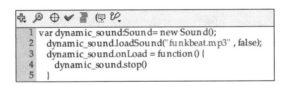

This code is rather easy to follow:

Create a Sound object named `dynamic_sound: new Sound()`. Load the sound—`funkbeat.mp3`—into the object from the server using the `loadSound ()` method and don't stream it just yet—`false`. Create a function that makes sure the sound doesn't play when the Flash movie loads—`stop()`.

With the Sound object created, you can now concentrate on tying it to the Pan and Volume sliders.

9. Double-click the Volume slider to open the slider's movie clip.

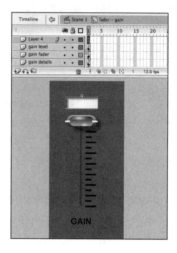

10. Select the frame and open the ActionScript editor.

The code for the slider is prewritten. What needs to be done is to connect the slider to the Sound object.

Scroll down to the bottom of the code and select the last line of code:

```
sound.setVolume(level);
```

You connect the slider to the Sound object by changing the line to this:

```
root.dynamic_sound.setVolume(level);
```

```
15  vol.onReleaseOutside = function() {
16      dragging = false;
17  };
18  //
19  this.onEnterFrame = function() {
20      if (dragging) {
21          level = 100-(vol._y-top);
22      } else {
23          if (level>100) {
24              level = 100;
25          } else if (level<0) {
26              level = 0;
27          } else {
28              vol._y = -level+100+top;
29          }
30      }
31      _root.dynamic_sound.setVolume(level);
32  };
33
```

With the Volume slider connected to the funkbeat.mp3 sound, you can now connect the Pan control to the sound as well.

11. Return to the main Timeline and double-click the Pan movie clip to open the movie clip.

Open the ActionScript layer and change this last line of code:

```
sound.setPan(level);
```

to this:

```
root.dynamic_sound.setPan(level);
```

Close the ActionScript editor and return to the main Timeline by clicking the Scene 1 link.

> **Tip** *These last two examples are a great way to discover that symbols can be edited in place right on the Stage. Instead of opening the symbol in the library, simply double-click a symbol that is on the Stage to open the Symbol editor.*

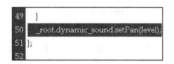

12. Open the ActionScript in the Actions layer of the main Timeline.

Add the following code to the script:

```
play_btn.onRelease = function() {
   dynamic_sound.start(0,1);
}
```

The important concept here is this:

```
dynamic_sound.start(0,1);
```

This says start the object right at the beginning of the sound—0—and loop it once—1. The first parameter is an offset value, measured in seconds. For example, if you want to start the sound one minute into the track, the offset value will be 60. If you want to loop the sound 3 times and then finish, the value for the second parameter would be 3.

In the ActionScript editor press Return/Enter and add the following code for the Stop button:

```
stop_btn.onRelease = function() {
   dynamic_sound.stop();
}
```

13. Save and test the movie.

As you move the slider up and down, the volume changes. Moving the Pan knob plays the sound on the right or the left speaker and clicking the Stop and Start buttons stops or starts the sound.

Using Buttons to Play Multiple Sounds

Now that you understand the fundamentals of adding and controlling a dynamic sound, you can apply these same principals to the control multiple sounds. For example, you may want to create an MP3 player that allows the user to listen to a variety of sounds that you have created.

1. Open the *SliderMulti.fla* file in your Lesson 5 folder.

When the file opens, the interface is somewhat similar to the one created earlier. The major difference is that the Play button has been replaced by three buttons. Each button loads a sound and the Volume and Pan controls control the volume and pan properties of the sound associated with the button.

2. Select the keyframe in the Actions layer and press F9 to open the ActionScript editor.

When the Editor opens, enter the following code:

```
var dynamic_sound:Sound = new Sound();
dynamic_sound.onLoad = function() {
  dynamic_sound.start(0,1);
};

funkbeat_btn.onRelease = function() {
  dynamic_sound.loadSound("funkbeat.mp3",false);
};

applesauce_btn.onRelease = function() {
  dynamic_sound.loadSound("Applesauce.mp3",false);
};

distantStorm_btn.onRelease = function() {
  dynamic_sound.loadSound("DistantStorm.mp3",false);
};

stop_btn.onRelease = function() {
  dynamic_sound.stop();
}
```

The new concept here is the `loadSound()` method, which has only two parameters: `dynamic_sound.loadSound("url",isStreaming)`. The first parameter is the location of the sound. In the case of this example, the location is a relative path. This means the sound is in the same root directory as the SWF file. If the sound were located elsewhere, the URL would be `http://www.mysite/funkbeat.mp3`.

The second parameter—`isStreaming`—is a Boolean value that is either `True` or `False`. If the value is `True`, Flash knows to treat the sound as a streaming sound. If the value is `False`, Flash treats the sound as an event sound.

3. **Close the Editor, save the file, and test your movie.**

When you click a button, the sound will change and you can use the Volume and Pan controllers to control the sound's properties. Click the Stop button and the sound will stop playing.

Using Sound to Provide User Feedback

Throughout this lesson you have been using sound as a means of providing user interactivity. There is another important aspect of this subject: using sound to provide the user with feedback. If you have ever played a computer game you have experienced this concept. Depending on where you move the mouse or the object onscreen the sound gets louder or fainter or, in many instances, completely changes. In this exercise, you use ActionScript for this precise purpose. As the mouse is moved around the Stage, the sound gets louder and softer.

1. Open _Feedback.fla_.

The movie clip on the Stage with the instance name Bug_mc is what will be used to provide the feedback. The user will drag the clip, which is a blinking light, around the Stage and—depending on where the clip is—the sound's volume and pan values will change. The sound, Crickets.mp3, is embedded into the movie clip.

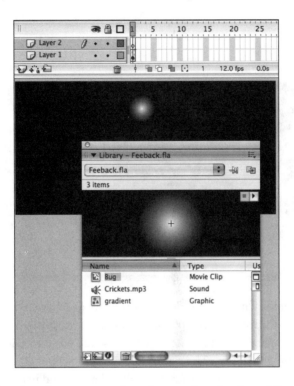

Before you get going, it makes sense to plan what needs to be done. The first consideration is the movement of the movie clip. You don't want the user to drag it off of the Stage. This means it will have to be constrained to the Stage.

The Stage has four coordinates that will be used to constrain the movie clip. They are the Top, Bottom, Left, and Right sides of the Stage. If you look at the dimensions of the Stage in the Property inspector, you can see that the values for the boundaries are these:

Top = 0

Bottom = 100

Left = 0

Right = 200

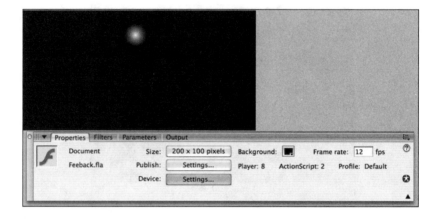

To ensure that the movie clip stays visible at all times, we also have to take the width and height dimensions of the movie clip into consideration. If we stay with those values, you can still move the clip partially off of the Stage because the position calculation is from the center point of the movie clip. The circumference of the clip is 20 pixels, meaning that if the clip is sitting on any edge of the Stage, it will be half on and half off of the Stage. Thus the boundaries have to be these:

Top = 10

Bottom = 90

Left = 10

Right = 190

Because the clip is being moved around the Stage, we'll have to be sure that the pointer is actually within the Stage boundaries before the movie clip can be dragged. If the clip is being dragged and the pointer moves outside of the boundaries; then stop dragging.

To do this, you have to constantly monitor the mouse's position using an onMouseMove event handler.

2. Select the keyframe in the Actions layer and press F9 to open the ActionScript editor and add the following script:

```
var bug: Sound = new Sound(Bug_mc);
var leftSide:Number = 10;
var rightSide:Number = 190;
var topSide : Number = 10;
var bottomSide: Number = 90;
```

These variables contain the maximum *x* and *y* coordinates for the Stage.

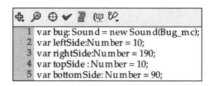

The next step is to create a series of variables that track the mouse's position at any location on the Stage.

3. Add the following code at the end of the current script:

```
var topBoundary: Number = bottomSide - topSide;
var widthBoundary: Number = rightSide - leftSide;
var areaSize : Number = widthBoundary/2;
var stageCenter : Number =rightSide - areaSize;
```

The four variables actually set the boundaries for mouse movement. The topBoundary variable simply says the movie clip can only move up or down by a maximum of 80 pixels. The widthBoundry variable constrains the movement from left to right to 180 pixels. The values for areaSize and stageCenter will be used to set the volume and pan values of the cricket sound as the movie clip is moved around the Stage.

With these variables in place, you can concentrate on setting the volume of the sound based upon the position of the movie clip on the Stage.

```
1  var bug: Sound = new Sound(Bug_mc);
2  var leftSide:Number = 10;
3  var rightSide:Number = 190;
4  var topSide : Number = 10;
5  var bottomSide: Number = 90;
6  var topBoundary: Number = bottomSide - topSide;
7  var widthBoundary: Number = rightSide - leftSide;
8  var areaSize : Number = widthBoundary/2;
9  var stageCenter : Number =rightSide - areaSize;
```

4. Insert the following lines of script after the last line:

```
this.onMouseMove = function() {
    if (_xmouse > leftSide && _ymouse > topSide && _xmouse <
      rightSide && _ymouse < bottomSide) {
    Bug_mc.startDrag(true);
    var heightPercent = (((_ymouse - topSide)/ topBoundary) * 100);
    bug.setVolume(heightPercent);
```

```
11  this.onMouseMove = function() {
12      if (_xmouse > leftSide && _ymouse > topSide && _xmouse < rightSide && _ymouse < bottomSide) {
13      Bug_mc.startDrag(true);
14      var heightPercent = (((_ymouse - topSide)/ topBoundary) * 100) ;
15      bug.setVolume(heightPercent);
```

The first thing this function does is to check whether the mouse is within the limits set earlier. If it is within the boundaries, the movie clip can be dragged—Bug_mc.startDrag(true). If the cursor is outside of the boundaries, the drag value will be false.

Once the movie clip starts moving, the sound volume is tied to the distance, expressed as a percentage, of the movie clip on the *y* axis. To do this you need three values. The first is the _ymouse (the vertical position of the mouse's pointer), the topSide which is the minimum value—10 pixels—allowed for vertical movement. The final value—topBoundary—is the height of the vertical movement.

A useful exercise is to "follow the numbers" and manually do the calculations in the code to see if they work. In this code heightPercent is being used to also set the volume level of the sound. The only number you don't know is the _ymouse position.

Let's assume that the _ymouse position is 70. Knowing that, you can calculate a value for heightPercent.

```
var heightPercent = (((70 - 10)/ 80) * 100);
var heightPercent = ((60/80) * 100);
var heightPercent = (.75 * 100);
var heightPercent = 75;
```

Now that you know the percentage value, that number is used to set the sound volume as well.

```
bug.setVolume(heightPercent);
```

Having determined the sound volume, you can also use that number to give the usual a visual clue as well by using that number to resize the movie clip as it moves around the Stage.

5. Insert the following lines of script after the last line:

```
Bug_mc._xscale = heightPercent;
Bug_mc._yscale= heightPercent;
```

All objects have properties that can be changed. One of the more effective is the ability to scale objects to give the illusion of depth. This is accomplished by using the _xscale and _yscale property value of the object. If it never changes size, both values remain constant at 100. In this case, the value will be the one determined when the heightPercent calculation is done.

Now that the sound volume and the movie clip scaling are done, you can turn your attention to the pan value.

```
10
11  this.onMouseMove = function() {
12    if (_xmouse > leftSide && _ymouse > topSide && _xmouse < rightSide && _ymouse < bottomSide) {
13      Bug_mc.startDrag(true);
14      var heightPercent = (((_ymouse - topSide)/ topBoundary) * 100) ;
15      bug.setVolume(heightPercent);
16      Bug_mc._xscale = heightPercent;
17      Bug_mc._yscale= heightPercent;
```

6. Insert the following lines of script after the lines added in Step 5:

```
var panValue = (( _xmouse - stageCenter) / areaSize) * 100;
bug.setPan(panValue);
```

Just as you did with the volume calculation, you are determining a percentage value for the pan.

There is one fundamental difference. Panning moves the sound from the right to the left or vice versa. This means the Stage has to be divided into a left half and a right half. The point where they split is the center of the Stage and its value is stageCenter.

Again, let's *follow the numbers* to see how this works using an _xmouse position of 150 pixels from the left edge of the Stage.

xmouse = 150

stageCenter = 100

areaSize = 50

If you put those numbers into the calculation, you can determine a percentage value of how far along the mouse is on either side of the Stage.

```
var panValue = (( _xmouse - stageCenter) / areaSize) * 100;
var panValue = (( 150 - 100) / 90) * 100;
var panValue = (.55) * 100;
var panValue =  55;
```

That value is then used as the value for the setPan method. This method uses a range of values from -100 to 100, where -100 uses only the left channel, and 100 uses only the right channel. A value of 0 balances the two channels.

Having dealt with the volume, pan, and size issues, you can now deal with what happens if the mouse is not within the boundaries of the Stage.

7. Insert the following lines of script after the lines added in Step 6:

```
else {
   stopDrag();
   }
}
```

```
1  var bug: Sound = new Sound(Bug_mc);
2  var leftSide:Number = 10;
3  var rightSide:Number = 190;
4  var topSide : Number = 10;
5  var bottomSide: Number = 90;
6  var topBoundary: Number = bottomSide - topSide;
7  var widthBoundary: Number = rightSide - leftSide;
8  var areaSize : Number = widthBoundary/2;
9  var stageCenter : Number =rightSide - areaSize;
10
11 this.onMouseMove = function() {
12    if (_xmouse > leftSide && _ymouse > topSide && _xmouse < rightSide && _ymouse < bottomSide) {
13    Bug_mc.startDrag(true);
14    var heightPercent = (((_ymouse - topSide)/ topBoundary) * 100) ;
15    bug.setVolume(heightPercent);
16    Bug_mc._xscale = heightPercent;
17    Bug_mc._yscale= heightPercent;
18    var panValue = (( _xmouse - stageCenter) / areaSize) * 100;
19    bug.setPan(panValue);
20    } else {
21       stopDrag();
22    }
```

The entire function is a classic conditional statement. All the code so far has answered the question "Is the mouse within the boundaries?" You can't ask that sort of question in ActionScript, so you essentially say, "If the mouse is within the boundaries, adjust the volume, scale the movie clip, and change the pan value." Using the word "if" sets a condition that is either true or false. Should the value result in False, you can't write "Then stop dragging the movie clip". Instead, you use the keyword else. When the condition is False, the entire function skips to else and does whatever is between the brackets after else.

8. Close the ActionScript editor; then save and test the movie.

When the movie opens in the player, move your mouse around the screen. As the pulsing light is moved towards the top of the screen the movie clip will shrink in size and the volume of the crickets will lower. As the movie clip is dragged lower, the sound increases in volume, and the movie clip gets larger. Move the mouse to the left and the right, and the sound will move across your speakers.

Adding Sound to an Animation

Using sound to provide user feedback is one use for audio. Sound used in this manner can provide the user with a deeper and richer interactive experience. Animations that use sound also provide the user with a deeper experience.

In this exercise you will start with an animated character pushing a broom across the screen as he sweeps the floor. If you play the animation, you will see him sweeping the floor and, on the surface, you could get away with simply using the animation. What's missing is that little extra that moves the animation from interesting to engaging. The extra? Audio. When a person pushes a broom you hear a sweeping sound and footsteps. Add those two sounds to the animation and the user experience expands from the visual into both the visual and aural realms.

1. Open the *AnimateSound.fla* file in your Lesson 5 folder.

When the file opens, drag the playhead across the animation or press Enter/Return to start it playing. If you open the Sounds folder in the library you will see two sounds: `brush.aif` and `footsteps.mp3`.

Double-click each sound in the library and when the Properties dialog box opens, click the Test button to preview the sound.

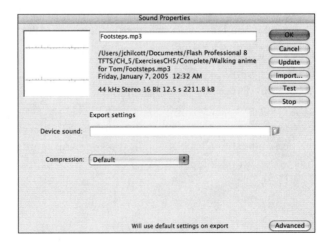

When it comes to sound creation, necessity truly is the mother of invention. Finding a sweeping sound in an audio collection is not exactly the easiest task. So, we created our own sound. We sampled a brush rubbing on a snare drum. This technique, known as foley, is how footsteps and other sound effects are created for the movies.

2. Add two new layers to the Timeline and name them Sweeping and Footsteps. Move the two layers to the bottom of the Timeline layering order,

There are two purposes for the layers: The first is to separate the sounds so you can easily see where the sounds are located. The second is so the sounds will be used in two different manners.

The sweeping sound is very short, meaning that it can be an event sound. The footsteps sound is much longer, meaning that there is a very real risk of it continuing to play when the animation is finished. In this case the sound can't be an event sound. It must be a streaming sound, which can be made to end at a specific time in the animation.

3. Select the Footsteps layer and drag a copy of the *footsteps.mp3* file to the Stage.

Select the sound in the Timeline and set its Synch property to Stream in the Property inspector.

Click the Edit button in the Effect area of the Property inspector to open the Edit Envelope dialog box.

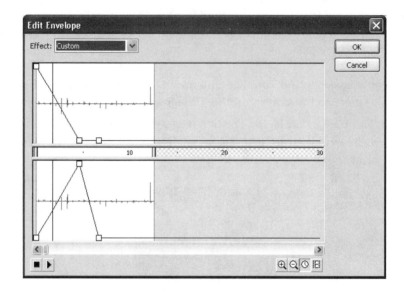

Edit Envelope is a rudimentary sound editor built into Flash. Click the Effect drop-down list, and you can choose from a selection of fades and pans that are preset. The Custom option allows you to create your own effects. The sound in the graph is quite easy to read. Lines that move to the top indicate an increase in volume, and the flat lines along the bottom indicate no volume.

The first thing to notice is that the footsteps use two channels, and that one channel increases in volume as the other decreases. This simulates the sound footsteps walking from the left side of the screen to the right side of the screen. The white squares on the lines are called handles, and they can be dragged up or down to increase or decrease the volume. To add a handle, click once on the line. To remove a handle, select it and drag it off of the line.

The controls along the bottom are the following:

- **Start/Stop:** Click either one to play or pause the audio.
- **Zoom In/Out:** Clicking either of these will zoom in on the Timeline or make it smaller. As you zoom in, the waveform of the sound becomes more distinct.
- **Seconds:** Click this button, and the measurement on the Timeline is in seconds.

- **Frames:** Click this button, and the duration of the sound is measured in frames.

- **In/Out Points:** The double lines on the Timeline between the graphs can be used to set the In and the Out points of an audio file. The one on the left is the *In* point and the one on the right is the *Out* point. Use this feature to remove unwanted portions of the sound file.

4. Select the last frame of the Footsteps layer, right-click (PC) or Control-click (Mac) and select Insert Blank keyframe from the context menu.

Adding the blank keyframe ensures that the walking sound stops when the animation ends. If you move the playhead back and forth on the Timeline, you hear the walking sound.

5. Select the Sweeping layer and add keyframes at Frames 3, 7, 9, 11, 14, 16, 18, and 20.

If you scrub the playhead across the Timeline you will see that those frames are the start of the sweep action. There should be a sound associated with each push of the broom.

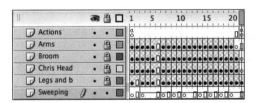

6. Select the keyframe in Frame 3 and drag the *brush.aif* file from the library to the Stage.

When you release the mouse, you see the sound appear only in Frames 3 and 4. Select the sound on the Timeline and ensure that the Synch properties are Event, Repeat, and 1. What you have done is to tell Flash that the brush.aif file is an event sound that will repeat only once.

Select each of the remaining keyframes and drag the brush.aif file from the library to the Stage. Make sure that the Synch settings match those of the first instance of the sound placed on the Timeline.

7. Save the file and test it in the Flash Player by pressing Ctrl+Enter (PC) or Cmd+Return (Mac).

What You Have Learned

In this lesson you have:

- Used streaming and event sounds (pages 169–171)
- Managed audio playback (pages 171–174)
- Created a Sound object to manage multiple sounds (pages 174–178)
- Loaded sounds dynamically at runtime (pages 178–193)
- Used controls that manage the volume and pan properties of a sound (pages 178–193)
- Used ActionScript to control the volume and pan of a sound (pages 178–193)
- Synchronized event and streaming sounds with animation (pages 193–198)
- Used Audio Envelope to edit sound (pages 196–197)

6 Creating Animation

Macromedia Flash's reputation as an animation application was established right from its inception. The reason Flash is so commonly used for Web animation is because, if done right, you can have a complex animation and a relatively small file size. This hasn't gone unnoticed by animators, and Flash animations are now appearing on television, cell phones, and other devices. One of the great features of animation in Flash is how easy it is for amateurs and professionals alike to move objects on the Stage. With Flash 8, animations can take on new dimensions through the use of tweens, filters, and blend effects within the FLA file.

Animations in movie clips can have the Filters, such as Drop Shadow, applied to them.

What You Will Learn

In this lesson you will:

- Create a video object on the Flash Professional 8 Stage
- Use the `netConnection` and `NetStream` classes to play a video from a server
- Add playback controls to a video
- Use ActionScript to control the playback of multiple FLV files
- See how the FLVPlayback component uses Listeners to trigger events
- Learn the ten transitions found in the `Transition` class
- See how to manage those transitions through the use of the `TransitionManager` class
- Learn how to access the transitions using the `Import` key word

Approximate Time

This lesson will require about 90 minutes to complete.

Lesson Files

Media Files:

GlassBreak.mp3
SkidScreech.mp3
BigNose.png
Racecar.FH11

Starting Files:

Bball.fla
Bball2.fla
FilterTween.fla
Hinge.fla
StreetType.fla
Sweep.fla

Completed Files:

Lesson06/Complete/Bball.fla
Lesson06/Complete/Bball2.fla
Lesson06/Complete/PixieDust.fla
Lesson06/Complete/FilterTween.fla
Lesson06/Complete/Hinge.fla
Lesson06/Complete/MotionBlur.fla
Lesson06/Complete/StreetType.fla
Lesson06/Complete/Sweep.fla
Lesson06/Complete/Tweening.fla

Tweening: The Basics of Motion

The first thing that catches an animators' attention is Flash's capability to tween objects. Essentially, a tween is Flash automatically drawing the changes in shape or location of objects on the Stage. Done properly, tweening will be a huge timesaver. If done incorrectly, you will find yourself contending with choppy animation and rather large file sizes. There are three types of tweens you construct in this exercise:

- Shape tween
- Motion tween
- Hinge tween

Shape Tweening

Shape tweening allows you morph shapes between keyframes. The simpler you keep the shape, such as from a square to circle, the cleaner the animation appears.

1. Open a new Flash document, select the Line tool, and draw a line that crosses the Stage.

The line should be no more than two pixels thick and should have a black stroke.

This line will be the start point of a shape tween. All tweens have a start point and an end point, and they are always between two key frames.

2. Add a keyframe at Frame 5 and another at Frame 10.

In this animation, the line acts much like the surface of a trampoline. When an object is dropped onto it, the surface bends downward and then bends back upward to its start position. The end of the bend downward will be located at Frame 5.

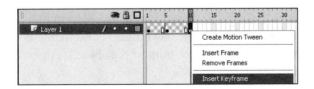

3. Move the playhead to Frame 5 and place the cursor over the line. When you see the stroke cursor, click and drag the line downward.

The line bends as you drag the mouse. Drag the line down to a point just above the bottom of the Stage. Release the mouse. The line curves between the line's two anchor points.

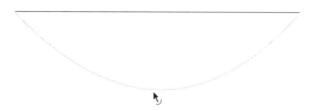

4. Hold down the Shift key and click the keyframes at Frames 1 and 10.

When the entire line is selected, select Shape from the Tween drop-down list in the Property inspector.

If you look at the Timeline, you see arrows between Frames 1 and 5 and between Frames 5 and 10. The frames also have a green color that indicates a Shape tween. If you drag the playhead across the Timeline, you see the line bend downward and then spring back into position.

Tip *Shape tweens can be applied only to objects drawn on the Stage. You can't apply a shape tween to a symbol or a grouped object.*

5. Save your file and leave it open for use in the next exercise.

Motion Tweening

Motion tweening creates the in-between positions of an object in motion. Like a Shape tween, a Motion tween occurs between two keyframes. The differences is that Flash automatically creates the intermediate positions of the object set in motion between the two keyframes.

1. Add a new layer to your animation. With the new layer selected, draw a ball on the Stage.

Drag this ball to a position to the middle of the line and position the ball so the bottom of the ball is just touching the line.

2. Add keyframes at Frames 5 and 10 of the new layer.

The effect you will create is the ball pushing the line down and then being pushed back up as the line springs back to its original shape. The ball needs to follow the line as the line curves downward.

3. Drag the playhead to Frame 5, select the ball, and move it downward until it just touches the bottom of the curve.

With the ball in its final position, you can now add a Motion tween. Right-click (PC) or Control-click (Mac) anywhere on the Timeline in Layer 2 between Frames 1 and 5. When the context menu appears, select Create Motion Tween. Notice that an arrow appears between the two keyframes. Do the same thing between Frames 5 and 10. Drag the playhead between the frames, and the ball appears to bounce on the line.

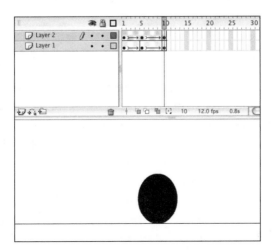

This animation is a bit fast. A quick way to slow it down is to select the keyframes in Frame 10 and drag them to Frame 36. Next, drag the keyframes in Frame 5 to Frame 18. What you have essentially done is to increase the duration of the animation from about 1 second to 3 seconds.

4. Select Control › Loop Playback and press Enter/Return.

The animation plays. This is a great little technique for testing an animated sequence without creating a test SWF file. It can also be used to test an animation in a movie clip.

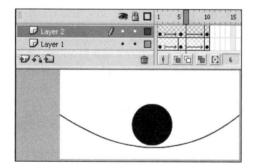

Hinge Animation

All animations and tweens need a single reference point. In Flash, that reference point is the object's or symbols' center point. In many cases, the use of the center point is more a hindrance than a help because the default location of any object or symbol's center point, especially for rotation, is the physical center of the object. In this case, the center point needs to be moved to where the pivot will occur.

1. Open the *Hinge.fla* folder in your Lesson 6 folder.

In this exercise, you create two animations using the same object—a glove. The animation is a simple wave of the glove to either welcome or wave goodbye.

Change the name of Layer 1 to Rotate. Add a new layer and name it Wave.

2. Open the library and drag an instance of the glove symbol to Frame 1 of the *Rotate* layer.

The glove was created in Adobe Illustrator CS2 and was imported directly to the library. When postscript artwork created in Illustrator is imported into Flash, the Illustrator Import dialog box opens and asks you how the object will be treated upon import. Layers maintains any layering that may be present in the file. Key Frames prepare the object for animation by placing the drawing in a movie clip containing two keyframes. Flatten essentially converts the image to a bitmap. Include Invisible Layers in the Options section of the dialog box imports any layers in the Illustrator document that may have been turned off.

3. Add a keyframe in Frame 10 of the *Rotate* layer.

Now that the keyframes have been added, you can concentrate on the animation.

4. Select the Free Transform tool in the Tools panel and click once on the glove in Frame 10.

When you click on the glove, a bounding box with handles appears. Depending on where you place the cursor, it changes to a Skew cursor that looks like two arrows pointing in opposite directions, a Rotate cursor that looks like a circular arrow, or a Scale cursor that is a double arrow.

5. Rotate the glove 90 degrees clockwise and add a motion tween between the keyframes.

If you press Enter/Return, the glove will look like it is waving. The problem with this animation is that it is not natural. We wave using our wrist, not the center of our palm as the pivot point.

6. Select the Wave layer and drag an instance of the glove from the library to the Stage.

7. Select the glove with the Free Transform tool.

The white dot in the center of the glove is the center point of the object. Drag the center point to the lower-right corner of the bounding box and release the mouse. This process just set the pivot point for the animation. Add a keyframe in Frame 10 of the Wave layer.

8. Select the Free Transform tool, click once on the glove in Frame 10 of the Wave layer, and rotate the glove 90 degrees in a clockwise direction.

Add a motion tween between the keyframes and press Return/Enter. The wave is much more realistic.

The animation is good, but a good Flash artist pays attention to the details. In this case, you created only half a wave. The glove seems to pop back to its start position at the end of the animation. When we wave at somebody, it is actually a two-part process. The first half is the hand moving from right to left and the second is the hand moving back from left to right. Add a keyframe at Frame 20 and, using the Free Transform tool, select the glove in Frame 20. Rotate the glove 90 degrees in a counterclockwise direction. Add a motion tween between Frames 10 and 20 and press Return/Enter.

Easing In and Easing Out

The best way of understanding Ease In and Ease Out is to think of gravity. When you drop an object, it accelerates on its way to the floor, which is Ease In. When the object hits the floor and bounces up, it decelerates as it moves upward, which is Ease Out.

As in the Hinge tween example, the key here is to pay attention to the details. A normal tween in Flash will have an object move at a uniform speed when it hits and bounce up at the same speed. In many respects, Ease In/Ease Out lets you add gravity into your animations.

1. Open the *Bball.fla* folder in your Lesson 6 folder and press Enter/Return to watch the animation.

The basketball bounces, but the speed is uniform.

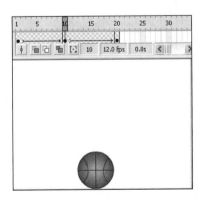

2. Double-click between Frames 1 and 10 to select the range.

3. When the frames are selected, click the Ease slider and move it down to a value of -100.

If you press Return/Enter, you will notice that the ball speeds up (Ease In) as it heads to the bottom of the Stage.

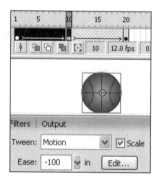

4. Double-click between Frames 10 and 20 and set the Ease value in the Property inspector to 100.

If you press Return/Enter, you will see the ball decelerate (Ease Out) as it moves upward.

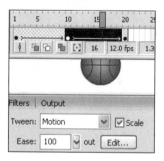

The animation is still not quite right. When a ball hits a solid surface, it tends to flatten when it hits the floor and then regains its shape when it bounces off the floor. This distortion technique is called *Squash and Stretch*.

5. Add keyframes at Frames 5 and 15 of the Bball animation.

Select the object in Frame 10 with the Free Transform tool. Move the center point to the bottom of the selection and drag the top center handle downward to flatten the ball. If you play the animation, the ball will appear to flatten as it hits the floor and springs back to its normal shape on the way back upward.

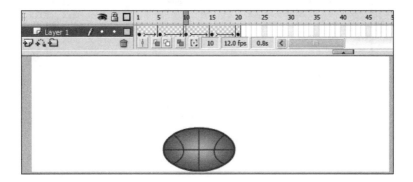

Using Custom Ease In and Ease Out

Although the Ease In and Ease Out sliders do a good job, the ability to control the velocity of the objects using this method is quite limited. For example, in the previous exercise you created a ball that bounced, but the laws of physics are such that an object that bounces loses energy with each bounce until it comes to rest. To accomplish a couple of bounces that decrease in height and speed until the bounce is finished would require a lot of extra work on your part. It also means a lot of keyframes and minor adjustments to get the movement just right. In this exercise, you will use the Custom Ease feature of Flash to accomplish this task in relatively short order.

1. Open the *Bball2.fla* file in your Lesson 6 folder.

Notice that the motion tween has already been done. If you will be using the Custom Ease In/Ease Out feature, you need nothing more than a motion tween to get started.

2. Click once between the keyframes and then click the Edit button in the Ease area of the Property inspector.

The Custom Ease In/Ease Out dialog box opens. The graph in this dialog box represents the animation. The start point is at the bottom of the diagonal line, and the end point is at the top. This line is called the velocity curve. Each square in the curve represents a frame in the animation. The straight line represents constant speed throughout the animation.

The Property drop-down menu allows to you to change the individual properties of the object. The Play and Stop control, located in the lower-left corner, preview your settings on the Stage.

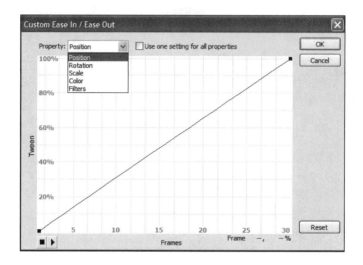

3. Click once on the curve to add a control point.

When a control point is clicked, hollow handles, called tangent points, appear on either side of the control point. Moving or dragging a tangent point creates a curve in the velocity curve. Also, if you click a control point, the coordinates of the control point appear in the lower-left corner of the dialog box.

The coordinates are expressed as a number (the *x* value) and a percentage (the *y* value). Let's assume that an object is moving from pixel 100 to pixel 200 on the *x* axis of the Stage. If the *y* scale shows 90%, the object will be at pixel 190, or 90% of its total tween.

Tip *Pay attention to the cursor when selecting a control point or a tangent point. If the cursor is over a control point, a solid box appears beside the cursor. If it is over a tangent point, a hollow box appears. Place the cursor over a curve; an arrow appears. If the cursor is over nothing, only the arrow point appears.*

4. Drag the control point to an *x* value of about 8 and a *y* value of about 97%.

Click the Play button, and the ball appears to bounce a couple of times after it hits the floor. Those two bounces are indicated by the curve between the new control point and the one at the end of the graph.

Tip *Use the arrow keys to move selected control points on the velocity graph. They add a higher degree of precision than dragging.*

5. Add three more control points, for a total of six points, to the velocity graph.

Use the following *x,y* values for all six of the points starting with the lower-left point:

- Point 1: $x=1$, $y=0$
- Point 2: $x= 9$, $y= 100\%$
- Point 3: $x =14$, $y = 77\%$
- Point 4: $x = 20$, $y = 100\%$
- Point 5: $x =26$, $y = 90\%$
- Point 6: $x = 30$, $y =100\%$

Tip *Click the Play button to preview the animation and see a more natural bounce sequence.*

Tip *The tangent handles indicate the velocity of the motion. If there are no tangent points, the velocity is constant. A curve shows acceleration toward the point and deceleration as the line moves to the next control point.*

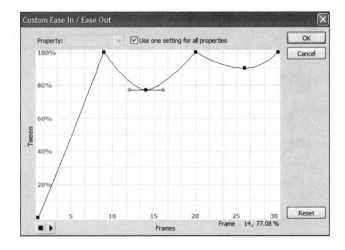

Creating Motion Using the Blur Filter

One of the more common questions asked of Flash artists is, "How do you do a motion blur with a static image?" Although there are about as many techniques as there are Flash developers, one of the more common techniques uses an optical illusion to create the effect. You use this technique in the exercise.

1. Open a new Flash movie and change the Stage size to **430** pixels wide by **180** pixels high.

With the Stage the proper size, import the `BigNose.png` image in your Lesson 6 folder into the library. Flash now has the capability to work with a PNG image without altering it. This type of image, created in either Fireworks 8 or Photoshop CS2, can contain an alpha channel used for transparency.

2. Add a new layer to the file.

Name the bottom layer `Blur` and the top layer `Nose`.

3. Select Insert > New Symbol. When the New Symbol dialog box opens, name the symbol **Nose** and set the property of the symbol to Movie Clip.

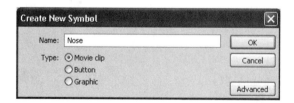

When you close the dialog box the movie clip opens in the Symbol editor. Drag a copy of the BigNose.png image into the movie clip and set the image's x and y coordinates to 0,0 in the Property inspector. Click the Scene 1 link to return to the main Timeline.

Tip *If you want to see how an alpha channel works in a PNG image, change the Stage color. The Nose symbol shows you the Stage color. Regular images in the JPG format sit on a white background that hides the section of the Stage it is covering.*

4. Add a keyframe in Frame 3 of the *Blur* layer and drag a copy of the movie clip to this keyframe.

There will be two frames of this movie where there will be no content. The plan is to present the illusion of the image zipping into place. Two empty frames won't be noticeable and present just enough of a pause to create the illusion of speed.

5. Select the image on the Stage and then select the Filters tab in the Property inspector.

Filters can be applied to movie clips and text.

6. Click the plus (+) sign to open the Filters drop-down list and select Blur.

The image immediately appears to blur because of the preset values in the Property inspector. The value in the *x* area applies a blur across the selection, and the value in the *y* area applies a blur from the top to the bottom of the selection. The Low, Medium, and High Quality selections determine the fineness of the blur.

The lock with the lines between the *x* and *y* values ensures the blur value is applied equally on both axes. To create a custom blur, click the lock. The lines disappear, so you can enter different values for the blur across either axis.

7. Click the lock and set the *Blur* values to x= 25, y= 0, Quality = High.

The blur might result in a piece of the image hanging off of the Stage. Select the blurred image and move it onto the Stage using the arrow keys.

8. Add a keyframe in Frame 4 of the *Blur* layer.

Click the image in Frame 4 and move it until the right side of the image is touching the right side of the Stage. With the two blurred images in place, add a frame in Frame 10 of the Blur layer by pressing the F5 key. To clear the blurred image out of Frames 5 to 10, select Frame 5 of the Blur layer, right-click (PC) or Control-click (Mac) and select Insert Blank keyframe from the context menu.

Tip *Always add a blank keyframe when you don't want the content in a keyframe to persist for the duration of the movie.*

9. Add a keyframe in Frame 5 of the *Nose* layer and drag a copy of the Nose movie clip to this keyframe.

Place this image at the lower center of the Stage. Add a keyframe in Frame 6.

To make this animation a little more realistic, select the image in Frame 5 with the Free Transform tool. Move the center point to the center-right point of the image. Click and drag the middle point on the left side of the image to the right to squash the image. This actually makes sense. The Big Nose guy comes zooming across the Stage and then suddenly stops. When objects come to an abrupt stop, they tend to compress.

10. Press Return/Enter to preview the animation.

The Big Nose guy zips across the Stage, squashes, and then bounces out to his final size.

This exercise is notable for its lack of tweening. Many animators use a tween when it is necessary, but they are also quite sensitive to the optical illusions created by abrupt changes. Your eye adds the tween. Starting with a blur that moves across the Stage you immediately give the illusion of speed. When the blur stops, and the Big Nose guy appears to expand, you have given the illusion of a squash and stretch without the use of a tween.

Creating an Animated Drop Shadow

The addition of filters in Flash Professional 8 is one of the major changes to the application. For example, the creation of the blur effect in the previous exercise prior to Flash Professional 8 required the application of a blur in Fireworks 8 or Photoshop CS2 before the image could be placed in Flash. This is no longer the case.

In Lesson 4, you learned how to apply a drop shadow to a static object. In this exercise, you learn just how powerful filters can be when applied to movie clips.

1. Open the *Sweep.fla* folder in your Lesson 6 folder.

Open the library; you will see a movie clip named Sweep. Select the movie clip in the library and press the Play button. An animation of a character who suspiciously resembles one of the authors is pushing a broom.

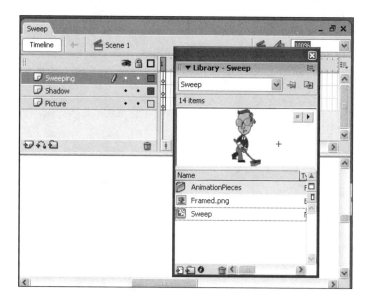

2. Select the first frame of the *Sweeping* layer and drag the movie clip from the library onto the Stage.

Drag the movie clip to the left edge of the Stage and, with the movie clip still selected, click the Filters tab in the Property inspector.

If you are familiar with Fireworks 8 or Photoshop CS2, you are also familiar with filters. The six that are installed with Flash Professional 8 are the following:

- **Drop Shadow:** Adds an offset shadow behind the selected text or movie clip. Used to mimic depth.

- **Blur:** Blurs an image. Can be used to create depth or speed, or to call attention to an object.

- **Glow:** Adds a solid color feather-like effect around the outside edge of the selected object.

- **Bevel:** Adds a beveled edge around the selected movie clip or text. Used subtly, it can result in a 3D-like effect.

- **Gradient Glow:** Adds a halo-like gradient around the selected object.

- **Gradient Bevel:** Adds a gradient to a beveled edge.
- **Adjust Color:** Allows you to change the Brightness, Contrast, Saturation, and Hue properties of the selected object. It can be used for subtle color changes or adjustments.

The filters can be used individually or in combination with other filters.

3. With the Filters tab active in the Property inspector, click the plus (+) sign and select Drop Shadow from the Filters drop-down list.

The Property inspector changes to show the properties for the Drop Shadow filter and the default values are applied to the movie clip on the Stage. The properties are:

- **Blur X:** The distance, in pixels, in which the shadow is applied on the horizontal axis. Higher values result in larger shadows.
- **Blur Y:** The distance, in pixels, in which the shadow is applied on the vertical axis. Higher values result in larger shadows.
- **Strength:** Sets the intensity of the color used for the shadow. Values range from 0 to 1000. The default value is 100.
- **Quality:** The three values—Low, Medium, and High—determine how fine the shadow will be rendered.
- **Color:** Opens the Color chips and allows you to change the shadow color.
- **Angle:** Select this and a knob allows you to change the angle of the shadow behind the selected object.
- **Distance:** This slider allows you to move the shadow's location behind the selected object.
- **Knockout:** Select this and the selected object is knockout of the shadow.
- **Inner shadow:** Select this and the shadow is placed on the inside edge of the selection, not the outside edge.
- **Hide Object:** Select this and only the shadow is visible.

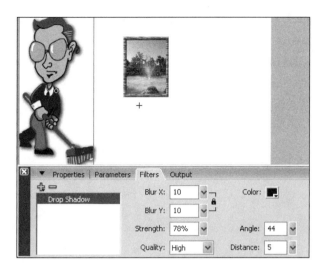

4. Save the movie and test it by pressing Ctrl+Enter (PC) or Cmd+Return (Mac).

Notice that the shadow keeps pace with the character as he pushes the broom and moves across the screen.

In Lesson 4, you discovered that you could manipulate the shadow of a text object independently of the original object. You can do the same thing with an animation in a movie clip.

5. Close the Flash Player and add two new layers to the Timeline named *Shadow* and *Picture*.

The true power of these filters is how they can be manipulated to mimic real life. In this part of the exercise, the character will move across the screen, but his shadow will pass over a picture hanging on the wall.

To get started, move the Picture layer under the Sweeping layer, and move the Shadow layer between them. Select the first frame of the Picture layer and drag a copy of the Framed.png symbol from the library to the Stage.

6. Select the movie clip on the Stage and copy it to the Clipboard. Select the *Shadow* layer and select Edit > Paste In Place.

A copy of the symbol is placed in the same position as the original symbol. Turn off the visibility of the Sweeping layer and select the movie clip on the Stage.

This movie clip acts as the shadow for this effect. Apply a Drop Shadow filter to the selection and use the following settings:

Blur X: +20

Blur Y: 20

Strength: 48%

Quality: High

Hide Object: Selected

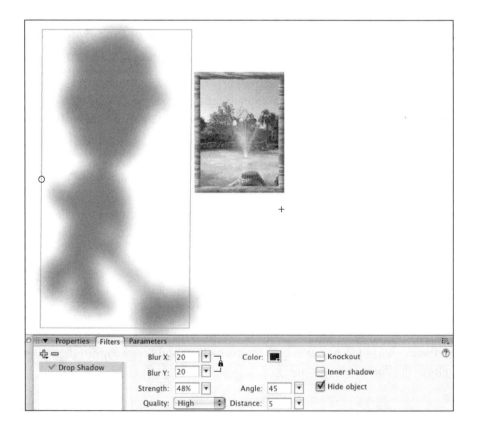

7. Select the Free Transform tool and skew the shadow.

You can apply the Free Transform tool because, as far as Flash is concerned, there is a selected object on the Stage.

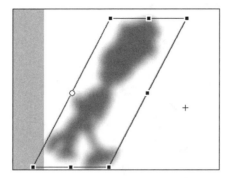

Tip *Don't forget that you can create an interesting skew by moving the center point on the selected object.*

8. Turn on the visibility of the *Sweeping* layer and line up the character's feet with those in the shadow.

9. Save the movie and test it.

Notice that the shadow animates with the sweeping character and watch the shadow pass over the picture on the wall.

Tip *If you really want to add a dose of realism to this animation, add the sweeping and walking sounds used for this movie clip in Lesson 4. Simply open the animation from Lesson 4, select the two sounds in the library, and copy and paste them into the library for this movie.*

Tweening Filter Effects

One of the really interesting features of the filters installed with Flash Professional 8 is that because they affect the properties of the object to which they are attached, they can be tweened, which opens the use of filters to a variety of creative possibilities. In this exercise, you create a small animation of a racing car that hits a wall. As it hits the wall, it decelerates, and the Blur filter applied to the animation is tweened from 100% blur to 0% blur to give the illusion of rapid deceleration.

1. Open the *FilterTween.fla* file in your Lesson 6 folder.

All the elements you need for this exercise can be found in the library. There is a movie clip of a racing car and two small sound files.

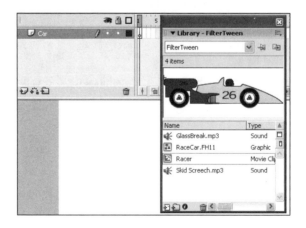

2. Add a new layer to the Timeline. Name the layers *Car* and *Sounds*.

3. Select the *Car* layer and drag the Racer movie clip from the library to the Stage.

Place the car on the left edge of the Stage so that just the nose of the car is visible.

4. Add a keyframe at Frame 10 of the *car* layer and move the car across the Stage so the nose of the car is just touching the right edge of the Stage.

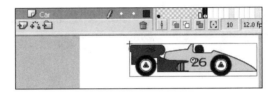

5. Add two more keyframes at Frames 15 and 20.

The first ten frames involve the car hitting the wall, and the next ten frames use a Squash and Stretch to show the accident.

6. Right-click (PC) or Command-click (Mac) Frame 25 of the *Racer* layer and select Insert Frame from the context menu.

By adding that frame at Frame 25, the car will be stationary for five frames.

7. Select the car in Frame 1, click the Filters tab in the Property inspector, and select Blur from the filter list.

Because the car is moving horizontally, you don't need to apply the Blur to both axes. Use the following settings for the Blur filter:

Blur X = 82

Blur Y = 0

Quality = Medium

8. Move the playback head to the keyframe in Frame 10. Select the car on the Stage and change the Blur setting as follows:

Blur X = 50

Blur Y = 0

Quality = Medium

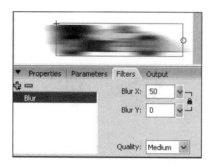

9. Move the playhead to the keyframe in Frame 20. Select the car on the Stage and change the Blur setting to the following:

Blur X = 0

Blur Y = 0

Quality = Medium

> **Tip** If a Filter is applied to an object on the Stage, select the object, not the frame, to access the Filter settings.

10. Move the playhead over the keyframe at Frame 15, select the Free Transform tool and click on the car on the Stage.

Move the center point of the object to the middle handle on the right side of the bounding box. Click and drag the left handle inward to squash the car.

With the Free Transform tool still selected, move the center point to the bottom center handle. Drag the top center handle upward to stretch the car.

11. Add motion tweens between the keyframes and test the movie.

The car comes zooming across the Stage, hits the wall, squashes inward and upward, and then bounces back into position. Note that the blur changes as the car decelerates.

There is still a problem with this animation. The car tends to bounce back to the middle of the screen and then to the wall between Frames 15 and 20. The bounce is a little too pronounced. This can be corrected by turning the motion tween between Frames 15 and 20 into a frame-by-frame animation.

Creating a Frame-by-Frame Animation

There is no way around it. A frame-by-frame animation is an exacting and time-consuming process because each frame in the animation must be individually created, manipulated, and tweaked if the final result is to be of a high quality. In many cases, each frame of the animation requires the use of a separate illustration.

This technique is suited to complex animations such as matching mouth movements to a voice or, as you saw in the previous exercise, creating a walk sequence. Most animators attempt to keep this type of animation to a minimum because it tends to increase the final size of the SWF file.

In the following example, you fix the car bouncing off the wall.

1. Press Shift and click Frames 16 to 19 in the *Car* layer.

Right-click (PC) or Command-click (Mac) and select Convert to Keyframes from the context menu. The four frames are now treated as separate frames in the sequence.

2. With the sequence of frames selected turn on onion skinning by clicking the Onion Skin Outlines button in the Timeline.

Onion Skin Outlines

Onion Skin

Onion skinning is a powerful tool to use when creating a frame-by-frame animation. It allows you to not only view the content of the frame you are currently working on but to also see the contents of the frames on either side of that frame. Being able to see the animation allows you ensure that the animation drawings are lined up and that the final animation is smooth. When you select a frame and turn on onion skinning, a full-color image of the content in the frame appears, whereas the frames on either side of it appear to be either washed-out as aresult of clicking the Onion Skin button) or composed of outlines because you clicked the Onion Skin Outline button. The default is to allow you to edit only the current frame, and you can expand the view on either side of the selected frame by dragging the onion skin markers on the Timeline inward or outward.

3. Select Frame 16 on the Timeline.

When onion skinning is turned on and you select a frame, two things happen. The content in that frame is selected, and the onion skinning brackets on the Timeline move to show you the content on either side of the selection.

4. Select the car in the frame and move it to the right.

The objective is to keep the nose of the car in line with that of the car in the previous frame. Repeat this for Frames 17, 18, and 19.

5. Select the *Sound* layer and add a keyframe at Frame 10.

Select Frame 1 of the Sound layer and drag a copy of the SkidScreech.mp3 file onto the Stage. In the Property inspector set the Synch to Stream and the Repeat to 1.The car now sounds like it is skidding into the side of the Stage, and the sound stops when it hits the side of the Stage.

6. Select Frame 11 of the *Sound* layer and drag a copy of the *GlassBreak.mp3* file to the Stage.

The car sounds like it is breaking up as it squashes, stretches, and comes back to rest.

7. Save and test the file.

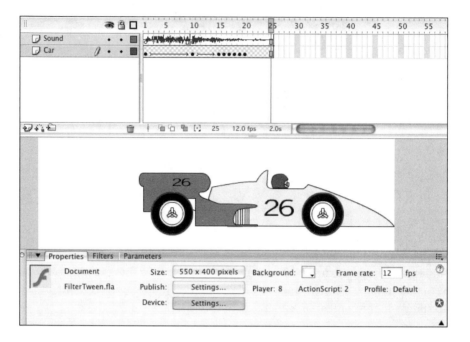

Animating Color Changes

One of the more interesting features of Flash animations is the ability to change the color of an object while it is in motion. These color changes can range from fades, where the object gets fainter and fainter as it moves from one position to the next, to a color change, where an object in motion changes from red to blue. Prior to the release of Flash Professional 8, Flash artists devised a number of clever ways to create special effects using animated color. These techniques are still valid, but the introduction of filters and blend modes to Flash Professional 8 opens up a world of creative possibilities.

This exercise starts with a basic color tween and a fade using objects on the Stage. You will then explore some of the interesting effects that can be created using the Filter and Blend features of Flash Professional 8. Just keep in mind that color tweens, fades, and other effects can be memory-intensive processes that affect playback performance. Flash artists tend to keep the use of these effects to a minimum and usually apply them to relatively small-sized objects on the Stage.

1. Open a new Flash movie by selecting File > New. Select the Type tool, and type your name on the Stage.

Use a fairly large point size, such as 48 to 60 points, and fill the text with a dark gray such as #666666. If you have a font on your system that has a bold version such as Arial Black or Franklin Gothic Heavy, use that font; otherwise, click the Bold button on the Property inspector.

2. Right-click (PC) or Cmd-click (Mac) on your name and select Convert to Symbol from the context menu to open the Convert to Symbol dialog box.

Name the symbol and select Graphic from the Type choices. Click OK. The symbol appears in your library.

> **Note** *One of the nuances of Flash is that you can't simply draw an object on the Stage and expect to tween its color or fade it out. These effects can be applied only to symbols.*

> **Tip** *If you have a shape or text on stage, and create a Motion Tween, Flash Professional 8 will automatically convert your shape to a movie clip so that the tween is not broken. The movie clip is named Tween, or Tween 1, Tween 2, etc. The reason for the movie clip is to accommodate the tweening of filters because filters cannot be applied on a Graphic symbol.*

3. Select Frame 20 on the Timeline and press F6 to insert a keyframe.

In Frame 20, select your name on the Stage and move it to new location. Right-click (PC) or Command-click (Mac) between the keyframes and select Create Motion Tween. If you scrub the playhead across the Timeline, your name moves across the Stage.

One of the great things about working with keyframes is any change applied to either keyframe in the sequence affects the entire tween. Move the playhead to Frame 20 and select your name on the Stage.

The Property inspector changes to reflect your selection. Click the Color drop-down list to open the Color effects. Select alpha and set the value to 0.

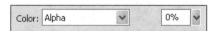

When you open the Color menu, you are presented with a number of choices:

- **None:** No effect is applied, or if an effect has been applied, it will be removed.
- **Brightness:** Adjusts the brightness or darkness of the symbol instance. The values range from 100% (white) to -100% (black). The default value is 0, which means there is no change. You can either use the slider or input a value into the entry field.

- **Tint:** Shifts the color in the selected instance. You can either choose the color from the Color Picker or enter the desired RGB values. Then you select saturation (Tint value) by using the slider or entering a value. The values range from 0% (no saturation, and the color doesn't change) to 100% (completely saturated). If you change the color from a blue to a red, the 0 value will be the blue and the 100% value will be the red. As the slider moves, the color changes,

- **Alpha:** Modifies the transparency of the instance. You can change the transparency percentage by either entering a value into the entry area or by using the slider. The percentage values range from 0 (totally transparent) to 100 (no transparency).

- **Advanced:** When you select this choice, the Setting button will appear on the Property inspector. Clicking the button opens the Advanced Effect dialog box, which allows you to change the Tint and alpha settings of the selected instance. The sliders on the left of the dialog box reduce the Tint and alpha settings by percentages. The controls on the right increase or decrease the Tint and Alpha settings by a constant value.

4. Press Enter/Return to see the fade.

This is a classic fade called an alpha tween. The issue with an alpha tween is that the effect requires processing power. Another approach, which has a lower processor demand, is to tween the color, not the alpha.

The text color used for your name is a shade of gray. You can get the same effect as the alpha fade by changing the color in Frame 20.

5. Select the instance in Frame 20 and select Tint in the Color drop-down list on the Property inspector.

Click once on the Color Picker and choose white. Move the Tint slider to 100%. The color will change to white, and because the Stage color is white, it will seem to disappear.

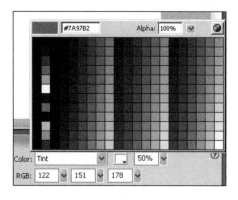

Press Enter/Return to preview the color tween. Change the color of the instance in Frame 20 to a Red. When you press Return/Enter, your name will subtly change color as it moves across the Stage.

6. Insert a keyframe in Frame 10 of the Timeline and select the instance on the Stage in Frame 10.

7. Place the playhead over the keyframe in Frame 10 and click your name on the Stage.

8. Open the Transform panel by selecting Window > Panels > Transform or by pressing Ctrl+T (PC) or Cmd+T (Mac).

The Transform panel can be used to resize, scale, skew, and rotate objects you select on the Stage. The major advantage this panel offers over the Free Transform tool is the ability to do-it-by-the-numbers rather than by eye. Another major benefit is that this panel allows you to constrain your transformations so you can maintain the same ratio for the selected object. Enter the following values:

X Scale= 36%

Y Scale = 36%

Rotate = 40 degrees

The input areas in the Transform panel are as follows:

- **Scale:** Enter an amount to resize the object by the percentage value entered. You can scale both the height and the width of the selected object or, by clicking the Constrain button, you can scale both the weight and width by the same value. When you enter your value, press Return/Enter to scale the object. If the effect is not the one you are looking for or is incorrect, click the Reset button in the lower-right corner of the panel. If you have deselected the object and want to remove the change, select Edit > Undo or press Ctrl+Z (PC) or Cmd+Z (Mac).

- **Rotate:** Click the Radio button to apply a rotation amount to the selected object. Press Return/Enter to apply the rotation value. The rotation uses the selected object's center point for the rotation. To rotate objects in a clockwise manner, enter a positive number. To rotate in a counterclockwise manner, enter a negative number.

- **Skew:** The selected item will be sheared or slanted in either a horizontal or vertical direction. Click the radio button, enter a value, and press Return/Enter to apply the effect.

- **Copy and Apply Transform button:** Click this button, and Flash will make a copy of the selected item (including shapes and lines) and apply the transform values entered to the copy, not the original. The copy is pasted in the same location as the original and can be moved to a new location on the Stage. The original selection will not be affected.

- **Reset button:** Click the button in the lower-right corner of the dialog box to remove all transformation settings applied to the selected object. When the button is clicked, the object will revert to its original shape. This button works only when an object is selected.

Tip *You can only go so far when using the Property inspector to resize a selection based on pixel values. When you select an object on the Stage, a small black lock icon appears between the selection's Width and Height values in the Property inspector. Two lines will run from the lock to the Width and the Height input areas. If you change one value, the other will change automatically. Deselect the lock, and each value can be changed independent of the other.*

W: 66.0	X: 29.0
H: 66.0	Y: 194.0

9. Drag the playhead across the screen or press Return/Enter to preview the animation.

By placing a transformation between keyframes, you can create some rather interesting effects.

Tweening Filters and Blends

Earlier in this lesson you explored how the Shadow and Blur filters can be used to enhance an animation. Though they are extremely powerful features, a combination of the filters and blend modes can result in some quite striking color changes.

The blend modes, which are available only in Flash Professional 8, allow you to manipulate the colors in a movie clip by comparing the color pixels of the foreground object and the object immediately below it and then changing the color values of the foreground and background pixels. For example, there may be a red pixel (the Blend color) in the foreground object that is above a blue pixel (the Base color). One of the filters will add the color values of the red pixel and the blue pixel and divide the value by 256. The result (Result color) is inevitably a darker pixel value for the red pixel.

1. Open the *StreetType.fla* file in your Lesson 6 folder.

We placed all the elements on the Stage for you. In this exercise, the word *Type* moves to the bottom of the Stage and—through using a blend tween and a filter tween—results in a rather striking finish. As the word type moves down the Stage, it reappears by fading in. While everything is moving the phrase "on the street" moves from one side of the screen to the other and changes color.

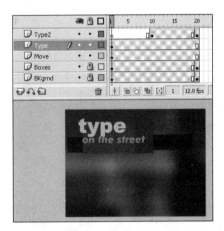

2. Select the word *Type* on the Stage and click the Blend drop-down list.

Select Hard Light from the Blend drop-down list. The word turns somewhat opaque and shows the color of the objects below the letter.

If you are familiar with Photoshop CS2 or Fireworks 8, you are familiar with the various choices available to you:

- **Normal:** No blend will be applied, and the selection is unaffected. Use this setting to remove a blend.
- **Layer:** Allows you to stack movie clips on top of each other with no effect upon their color.
- **Darken:** Compares the foreground and background colors and keeps the darkest one.
- **Multiply:** Multiplies the base color by the blend color and divides the result by 256. The result color is inevitably a darker color.

- **Lighten:** The opposite of darken. The result color is always the lightest color.
- **Screen:** The inverse of the blend color is multiplied by the base color. In many respects, it is the opposite of Multiply. The result is a lighter color.
- **Overlay:** Multiplies or screens the colors, depending on the base color. The base color is not replaced; it is mixed with the blend color to reflect the lightness or darkness of the original color.
- **Hard Light:** Mimics the effect of shining a very bright light through the selection. If the blend color is darker than 50% gray, the image is darkened as if it were multiplied. This is useful for adding shadows to an image.
- **Add:** The blend and the base colors are added together. The result color is a lighter color.
- **Subtract:** The blend and the base colors are subtracted from each other. The result is usually a darker color.
- **Difference:** Based upon their brightness values, either the base color value is subtracted from the blend value, or vice versa. The end result is similar to a color negative image.
- **Invert:** Inverts the base color.
- **Alpha:** The blend color is converted to an alpha channel. The blend area, essentially, turns transparent.
- **Erase:** The base color pixels, including those of the background image, are erased.

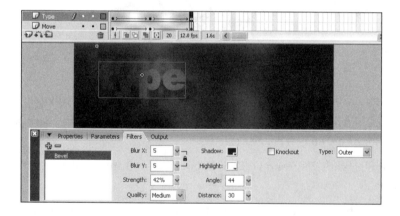

3. Add a keyframe to Frame 20 of the *Type* and *Move* layers.

Move the playhead to Frame 20 and drag the word *Type* to the bottom of the screen. Add a motion tween between the two frames and drag the playhead across the Timeline. Notice that the word *Type* changes color as it moves across the various colors beneath it as the blend effect interacts with the colors in the image.

The words *on the street* will work a little differently. They will move across the screen, change color using a blend mode and the Advanced color panel and then move back to their original position.

Add a keyframe in Frame 10 of the Move layer. With the playhead over Frame 10, select the phrase on the Stage and drag it to the right edge of the screen. With the phrase selected in Frame 10, select difference in the blend modes. The various letters change their tint based upon the colored block they are in front of. The strongest change should be in the letters overlaying the image.

Select the Advanced color effect from the Property inspector and click the settings button. Use the following values:

Red = 53%   xR) +121

Green= 53%   xG) +24

Blue = 53%   xB) +12

Alpha - 100%   xA +0

Add motion tweens between the keyframes and press Enter/Return to preview the animation. Notice that the color changes based upon the difference mode and the dark orange color set in the Color effects.

4. **Select the object in Frame 10 of the *Type 2* layer.**

Select Brightness from the Color effects drop-down list and set the value to -32%. Apply a hard light blend to the selection. Select the word in Frame 20, set the Brightness value to 0, and add a motion tween between the keyframes. When you press Enter/Shift, the word will fade into view. Pay close attention to the way the hard light blend affects the text as the brightness values tween.

5. Move the playhead to Frame 1, select the word *type*, and change the blend mode to overlay.

The filters mode can also be used to add some rather stunning effects to the objects to which they are applied. With the word *Type* selected at the type of the Stage, apply a Bevel filter using these settings:

Blur X: 0

Blur Y: 0

Strength: 0%

Quality: Low

Angle: 45

Distance: 0

Type: Inner

6. Move the playhead to Frame 10 and select the word *Type* on the Stage. Open the Bevel setting and change the settings to the following:

Blur X: 2.5

Blur Y: 2.5

Strength: 19%

Quality: Low

Angle: 189

Distance: -31

Type: Inner

7. Move the playhead to Frame 20 and select the word *Type* at the bottom of the Stage. Open the Bevel setting and change the settings to the following:

Blur X: 5

Blur Y: 5

Strength: 42%

Quality: Medium

Angle: 44

Distance: 30

Type: Outer

As the word moves down the page, it takes on texture as the angle and distance values of the Bevel filter change. The effect at the end is a result of the distance values changing. As well, you can see how a bevel is actually composed of three images that when spread apart can be used in ways for which they were never conceived.

Bitmap Caching Movie Clip and Button Symbols

You may have noticed that under the blend modes in the Property inspector there is a radio button that says Use runtime bitmap caching. If you select the keyframe in Frame 1 of the Type layer, you will notice this radio button has been selected.

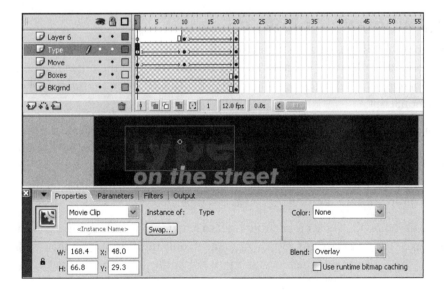

Runtime bitmap caching, introduced in Flash Professional 8, lets you optimize playback performance by specifying that a static movie clip (for example, a background image) or button symbol be cached as a bitmap when the movie is playing in a browser. Caching a movie clip as a bitmap prevents Flash Player from constantly redrawing the stationary image, which provides a significant improvement in playback performance.

The key word is "stationary." Bitmap caching works best when the content in the object does not move. Caching an object with moving content defeats the purpose because objects in motion are continually being redrawn. If the background image in this exercise were placed in a movie clip and you moved the movie clip around the Stage, you could still apply bitmap caching to the image. If you were to create a movie clip in which objects are moving over the background image, bitmap caching wouldn't work.

In the next exercise, the background image is rendered as a bitmap stored at the current screen depth. It can be drawn very quickly, letting the Flash animation play both faster and more smoothly, because the background doesn't need to continually be redrawn. If the movie clip were not cached, there is a real risk of slow playback as the image is constantly redrawn as the playhead moves.

In many respects, bitmap caching lets you use a movie clip and "freeze" it in place. If a region changes, Flash uses vector data to update the bitmap cache, which minimizes the number of redraws that Flash Player must perform and provides smoother, faster playback performance.

Programmatic Animation

Throughout this lesson, you have been physically moving objects on the Stage from one location to another using tweens. There is another way: "Let the software do the work." *Programmatic animation* is nothing more than a fancy term for movement using ActionScript.

Anything on the Stage (for example, objects, movie clips, and graphic symbols) that have instance names can be manipulated by ActionScript. Properties that can be manipulated include the *x* and *y* position of the object on the Stage, its scale value, its opacity, and even its rotation value. The common factor between the properties of all objects on the Stage is that these properties are always expressed as a number.

When an object on the Stage moves from right to left, it is in fact changing its position on the *x* axis. The same goes for vertical movement, only this time it is on the *y* axis. The properties are `._x` and `._y`. When an object is to follow the mouse on the Stage, it is simply instructed to move to the `._xmouse` or `._ymouse` positions. In fact, you can use either one or both to determine how an object moves on the Stage. Let's assume, for example, that you want an object to move 10 pixels to the right and down 10 pixels. Flash already knows its *x* and *y* coordinates, so the move would be expressed as `._x +10` and `._y-10`. If you want to move in the opposite direction, the calculation would be `._x -10` and `._y +10`.

Another property of objects on the Stage is their physical dimension. To mimic movement, objects get larger as they move forward and smaller as they move backward. Instead of moving the object, scaling it, and then adding a tween between the keyframes, you can move it using ActionScript and then reduce or increase the `._xscale` and `._yscale` values of the object. An alpha fade of 10% would be expressed as `.alpha-10`.

In this final exercise, you explore several aspects of programmatic animation. In the first exercise, you explore inertia and movement by moving a planet across the screen. In the second, you create a small movie that sprinkles pixie dust from the tip of the cursor as it moves around the screen. The little specks of dust appear to spring out of the tip of the cursor and disappear as they fall toward the bottom of the screen.

Simulating Movement

Let's do a small exercise that pays attention to movement in the real world. All objects have *mass* This is the thing that makes them heavy and makes it hard to start or stop them from moving. When you toss a bowling ball down the alley, you have to pick up a heavy object and give it a real push down the lane. Use a ping pong ball and there is less effort to exert on your part. Now imagine that you are one of the pins. Which would be easier to stop: a ping pong ball rolling at you at top speed or a bowling ball rolling toward you at top speed? Obviously, it's the ping pong ball because of its lower mass.

What does this have to do with Flash? All the top Flash artists pay very close attention to real life, and some even break out the physics books.

1. Open the *movement.fla* file in your Lesson **6** folder.

The first thing you will want to do is to change the frame rate from 12 frames per second (fps) to 20 fps. Open the Document properties by selecting Modify > Document or double-clicking the frame rate box at the bottom of the Timeline.

Tip *There is a school of thought that claims 12 fps is an acceptable frame rate for a Flash movie. This was true when computers weren't terribly powerful. In today's computing environment, fast processors are the norm, and a frame rate of between 18 and 20 fps is now regarded as a standard.*

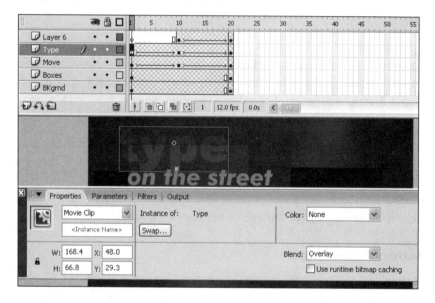

2. Click once on the keyframe in the Actions layer and press F9 to open the Actions panel.

Enter the following code:

```
planet_mc.onEnterFrame = function() {
  if(this._x<500) {
    this._x +=4;
  }
}
```

If you save and test the movie, you will see the little planet move across the screen and stop when it touches the right edge of the screen.

The code is rather simple to follow. To start, you must first imagine the playhead moving through Frame 1. When it leaves the frame, it sees nothing in Frame 2 and comes back to Frame 1. The first thing it does is to enter Frame 1 and check the .x position of the planet_mc instance on the Stage.

If the position has a value of less than 500 pixels—if (this._x<500)—move it four pixels to the right—this._x += 4. The playhead leaves Frame 1, and the process starts all over again until the planet is touching the right side of the Stage.

The number 500 is not arbitrary. The planet symbol is 50 pixels wide, and the Stage is 550 pixels wide. Subtract the width of the planet from the width of the Stage, and it will come to rest at the 500-pixel mark.

Now that you understand how it moves, you should notice that the movement isn't natural. First, the speed across the Stage is uniform. The second aspect of this animation is that the object stops abruptly. Objects in motion tend to decelerate before they come to rest.

Obviously, the code needs to be reworked.

3. **Close the SWF file and open the Actions panel. Select the code and delete it. Replace it with these two lines:**

```
var speed:Number = 0
var distance:Number = 500
```

When values constantly change, it makes sense to use a variable to "hold" the changing numbers. In the case of this movie, we need two variables.

The first is a value for speed. The choice of 0 is the object's speed when it comes to rest against the right side of the Stage. What will happen, though, is that this number will start large and steadily decrease to 0. This decrease in speed will occur over the distance the object moves, which in this case is 500 pixels.

An obvious question is, "What large number?" We will use the distance and continually subtract the planet's ._x position from the distance to determine the speed number. As it moves across the Stage, the distance will steadily decrease as will the speed value until it reaches 0.

4. **Press Return/Enter in the Actions panel and enter the following function:**

```
planet_mc.onEnterFrame = function() {
  speed = (distance-this._x);
    this._x += speed;
}
```

The calculation constantly sets the speed value by subtracting the planet's location on the Stage from the distance it will travel. Everything will stop when the speed value eventually reaches 0. If you save and test the movie at this point you will see this code at work.

```
▼ Actions - Frame

1  var speed:Number = 0
2  var distance:Number = 500
3
4  planet_mc.onEnterFrame = function() {
5      speed = (distance-this._x)/5;
6          this._x += speed;
7  }
8
```

5. Open the Actions panels and change the code in line **6** to the following:

```
speed = (distance-this._x)/5;
```

When you tested the movie, the planet simply shot over to the end of the Stage. Line 6 was the culprit. The planet moves across the Stage in 50-pixel increments. Do the math:

Start position (`this._x`) = 50

Distance = 500

On the first pass through the code *speed = 450* (500-50). In the second pass, *speed= 400* (500-100), and so on. If the movie is playing back at 20 fps, it takes only about one-half second for the planet to get to its final position.

Dividing the speed by 5 slows things down by moving the planet by one-fifth the distance and giving it a more natural deceleration as it approaches the right side of the Stage.

6. Save and test the movie.

The planet zooms across the Stage and steadily slows until it comes to rest against the right edge of the Stage.

The duration of the deceleration or time it takes a moving object to come to a complete stop is called *inertia*. The number you used in line 6 of the code is what simulates inertia. This also shows a keen attention to detail on your part. In the first part of this exercise, the planet moved across the screen at a constant rate and simply stopped when it reached the right edge of the Stage. This isn't natural. As well, if you compare the movement between the two, the movement with deceleration actually seems smoother than the constant speed example.

This little exercise might, on the surface, appear to be relatively insignificant. In fact, it is one of the more important exercises in this lesson. When designing anything with movement from games to menus that fly out of the interface, always use movement with inertia.

Tip *Try changing the inertia value in this example to a number between 1 and 2, such as 1.5. You will see the planet move in an even more natural manner as it comes to rest.*

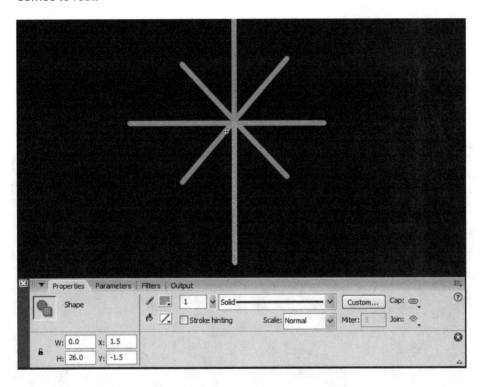

Cursor-based Animations

In Lesson 5, you created a small movie that used sound to provide user feedback. As you moved the cursor across the Stage, a movie clip followed the cursor and, depending upon the position of the cursor on the Stage, the volume and pan of a sound changed. This exercise builds upon what you learned in that lesson.

In Lesson 5 the object simply followed the cursor. In this one, as the cursor moves, a movie clip will be created and set in motion. As the cursor moves around the Stage, pixie dust appears to flow out of the tip of the cursor and disappears as it gently falls toward the bottom of the Stage.

1. Open a new Flash document, change the screen color to black, and save the file to the Lesson 6 folder on your computer.

To do this animation you need to create a speck of pixie dust.

2. Press F6 to open the New Symbol dialog box.

Name the symbol **Pixie Dust Speck**.

3. Select the graphic property and click OK.

The Symbol editor opens, and you can create the object. In our case, we selected the Line tool and drew a vertical line 26 pixels high and 1 pixel thick. The line color selected was FF9900, which is an orange color.

The line was then copied, pasted, and rotated several times to create the object.

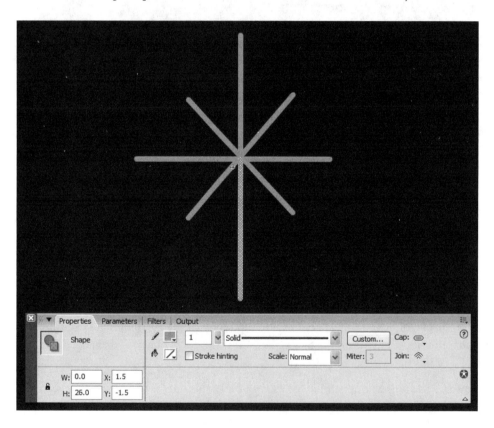

You don't need to draw a star. You can use a circle with a radial gradient as the fill, a piece of clip art, text, or anything else you can image.

4. Select Insert > New Symbol to open the New Symbol dialog box and create a new symbol.

Name the new symbol **Pixie Dust**, set the movie clip property, and click OK. The movie clip appears in the library.

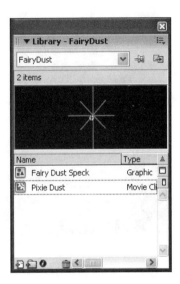

5. Open the movie clip in the library and drag a copy of the Pixie Dust Speck graphic symbol to the Stage.

6. Open the Align Panel by pressing Ctrl+K (PC) or Cmd+K (Mac) and align the selected object to the center of the Stage.

With the image of pixie dust still selected, click the Properties tab in the Property inspector and click the lock beside the width and height values on the Property inspector. A line joining them appears. Change the width value of the object to between 6 and 8 pixels. Press Return/Enter, and the image shrinks to the selected size but still maintain its aspect ratio. Click the Scene 1 link at the top of the Timeline to return to the main Timeline.

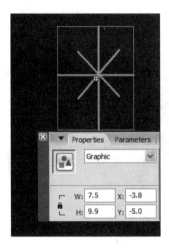

7. Select the Movie Clip symbol in the library and select Linkage from the panel options menu.

When the Linkage Properties dialog box opens, enter **Pixie Dust** into the Identifier input area and select both Export for ActionScript and Export in first frame. Click OK to accept the values and close the dialog box.

This movie will create a number of instances of the movie clip and shower the Stage with them. Unfortunately, Flash is not as smart as you may think. You simply can't say to Flash, "Grab copies of the Pixie Dust movie clip in the library and shoot them out of the tip of the cursor."

When you name a symbol, in many respects, that name is simply there to tell you what it is. As far as ActionScript is concerned, the name doesn't exist. To have ActionScript pull a symbol out of the library, you need to give the symbol a name that ActionScript can see. The text you entered, **Pixie Dust**, is that name and is referred to as the *linkage identifier*. Selecting Export for ActionScript ensures that the movie clip gets exported with the SWF file.

> **Tip** As soon as you click the Export for ActionScript radio button, the Export in first frame button will also be selected, which ensures that everything loads up and works properly as soon as the movie starts. Don't deselect this option.

8. Select Frame 1 of the movie and press F9 to open the Actions panel.

When the Actions panel opens, enter these three lines of code:

```
var speckCount:Number = 0;
var numberOfSpecks:Number = 50;
var cleanUpArray:Array = new Array();
```

```
1  var specCount:Number = 0;
2  var numberOfSpecs:Number = 50;
3
4  var cleanUpArray:Array = new Array();
```

There will be a lot of copies of the movie clip pouring out of the tip of the cursor, so we need a way to remember them and store them. The first two variables, speckCount and numberOfSpecks, simply create a counter for the movie clip on the screen—speckCount— and how many will be on the screen—numberOfSpecks.

The third variable, cleanUpArray, creates a container used to clean up any old and unused specks onscreen by creating an Array object. The easiest way of understanding the purpose of an array is to think of it as being a container, like a filing cabinet or grocery bag, for a collection of variables that is accessed using a single name. In the case of this movie, each speck that is at the end of its life will be added to this array when its alpha value reaches 2. The movie clip is then added to the array and removed. This way, if there are 50 specks of pixie dust on the screen, only the four, for example, whose alpha value is less than two will be affected. The 46 specks with higher alpha values will still be visible.

9. In the Actions panel, press Enter/Return to move the cursor to line 5 and enter the following function:

```
var pixieDust:Function = function() {
  if( numberOfSpecks ) {
    var ourNewMovie:MovieClip = _root.attachMovie( "Pixie Dust",
      "pixieDust" + speckCount, 100 + speckCount );
    ourNewMovie._x = _root._xmouse + (Math.random() * 10) - 5;
    ourNewMovie._y = _root._ymouse;
    ourNewMovie._alpha = 100;
    if( speckCount++ > 10000 ) {
      speckCount = 0;
    }
```

This part of our function, named `pixieDust`, pulls the Pixie Dust movie clip out of the library and sends it shooting out of the tip of the cursor.

```
7   var pixieDust:Function = function() {
8     if( numberOfSpecs ) {
9       var ourNewMovie:MovieClip = _root.attachMovie( "Pixie Dust", "pixieDust" + specCount, 100 + specCount );
10      ourNewMovie._x = _root._xmouse + (Math.random() * 10) - 5;
11      ourNewMovie._y = _root._ymouse;
12      ourNewMovie._alpha = 100;
13      if( specCount++ > 10000 ) {
14        specCount = 0;
15      }
```

The second line of the function gets things started by making sure that the number of specks is greater than 0. If it is, the rest of the statement is executed. In many respects, this number is being used as a counter.

The next line of code simply creates a new movie clip named `ourNewMovie` and attaches the Pixie Dust movie clip in the library to it. The new movie clip is placed on the main Timeline: `_root` .

When using the `attachMovie()` method, you need to add a couple of parameters. The first is the `idName` of the movie clip symbol that is being attached. The name used here is the linkage identifier used in Step 3. The next parameter is a unique instance name—`pixieDust`—for the movie clip being attached to the movie clip—`ourNewMovie`. The problem is that because there will be so many of them, they really can't all have the same name if they are to be managed by ActionScript. Otherwise, what will happen is that we will overwrite one movie clip 50 times, meaning there will be only one movie clip on the Stage at a time. In this case, each new instance created will have a unique name depending on what number it is given in the `speckCount` order. The first one will be named `pixieDust0`. The second one will be named `pixieDust1`, and so on. All these names will eventually be handed over to the array.

The third parameter sets what is known as the z-level for the new movie clip. When movie clips are placed dynamically on the Stage, they need to be placed either in front of or behind each other. This is the `level` parameter, which essentially sets the stacking order of the movie clips appearing on the Stage. Movie clips with lower numbers are essentially placed under those with higher numbers. In the case of this function, the first instance of the movie clip is placed at level 100. The second is placed at 101, and so on. In many respects, adding a level is a virtual way of adding a layer to the Flash Timeline.

The next three lines set the clip's .x and .y positions on the main Timeline to the location of the mouse as well as give it an alpha value of 100. The calculation for the _x position simply says "pick a random number between -5 and 4.999—(math.random() * 10)-5. The effect is to push the movie clip to the right or left by about 5 pixels at most.

The `math.random()` method picks an arbitrary nonrepeating number between 0 and 1, but not including 1. This means the potential values are between 0 and 0.9999999. So how do we get the range from -5 to 4.9999999? If the number picked is 0, the maximum number will be -5. If the number picked is .9999999, the value will be multiplied by 10. This number 9.999999 will have 5 subtracted from it, meaning that the maximum value will be 4.999999.

The effect is to have the movie clip smoothly appear in a variety of positions as the cursor is moved.

The final condition adds a degree of sanity to the process. It keeps increasing (++) the `speckCount` number up to 10,000. The last line says that if there are more than 10,000 copies of the clip on the Stage, start the count over again at 0.

10. In the Actions panel, press Return/Enter key and add the following line of code:

```
numberOfSpecks--;
```

Because the cursor is moving, there will be copies of the movie clip constantly appearing, which could overwhelm the movie. This line is executed after the function creates the movie clip and so on, and reduces the number used for the numberofSpecks variable by one, thereby reducing the available number of movie clips that can be placed on the Stage.

17	numberOfSpecs—;

11. In the Actions panel, press Return/Enter twice and add the following embedded function along with the rest of the function:

```
ourNewMovie.onEnterFrame = function() {
    this._y += 2;
    this._alpha -= (Math.random() * 7);
    if( this._alpha < 2 ) {
        cleanUpArray.push(this);
    }
};
}

while( cleanUpArray.length > 0 ) {
    var ourMovie:MovieClip = MovieClip(cleanUpArray.pop());
    ourMovie.removeMovieClip();
    numberOfSpecks++;
}
}
```

```
ourNewMovie.onEnterFrame = function() {
    this._y += 2;
    this._alpha -= (Math.random() * 7);
    if( this._alpha < 2 ) {
        cleanUpArray.push(this);
    }
};
}

while( cleanUpArray.length > 0 ) {
    var ourMovie:MovieClip = MovieClip(cleanUpArray.pop());
    ourMovie.removeMovieClip();
    numberOfSpecks++;
}
}
```

The embedded function is the engine that animates the pixieDust function. The outer part of the pixieDust function created the movie clip, named it, and put it on the Stage. It then assigns our new movie clip's enterFrame handler a function that essentially says what happens to that movie clip every time the playhead advances a frame.

The first line moves it downward by two pixels and reduces its alpha value by a number between 0 and 6.9999999. It then constantly checks the alpha of the movie clip as it moves down the screen. When the alpha value is less than 2 (virtually transparent), the movie clip is added to the cleanUp array—.push(this)—and forgotten. How is it forgotten? It is forgotten by the next conditional statement.

The next conditional statement is constantly checking how many items are in the cleanup array. As long as the number of items in the array is greater than 0, the movie clip is removed from the stack of clips being watched (.pop();) and the movie clip, named ourMovie in the first function, is removed from the Stage (removeMovieClip();). As soon as that movie clip is removed, the number of specks that can placed on the Stage will increase by 1- numberOfSpecks++.

12. In the Actions panel, press Return/Enter and enter the following line of code:

```
_root.onEnterFrame = pixieDust;
```

This line simply says, when the playhead on the main Timeline comes back into the frame, execute the pixieDust function from Step 5 and create a new instance of the movie clip.

13. Save and test the movie by pressing Ctrl+Enter (PC) or Cmd+Return (Mac).

When you place the cursor onscreen and move it, the Pixie Dust movie clip pops out of the tip of the cursor and, as it gently falls to the bottom of the screen, it fades out of existence. The code you just wrote drives each speck of pixie dust on the Stage.

What You Have Learned

In this lesson you have:

- Created tweened animations (pages 201–212)
- Used Ease In/Ease Out to simulate gravity (pages 206–211)
- Animated the Filters and the Blend modes (pages 212–216)
- Used blurs, sound, and other effects to add realism to animations (pages 216–228)
- Tweened colors and opacity (pages 228–232)
- Created animations driven by ActionScript (pages 228–251)

7 Creating Flash video

In 2004, Macromedia started popping up at conferences showing off some of the really interesting things one could do with video using the Flash Player. Prior to that, developers were quietly discovering that Flash Player 7 was a serious media player that required no extra software to play. About that same time, Jeremy Allaire, one of the inventors of ColdFusion, told anybody who would listen that Flash Player was a Trojan Horse and "people are just now turning it on."

What makes this technology so popular is the ubiquity of Flash Player. None of the video player solutions—from QuickTime to Real—have the market penetration nor have experienced the rapid adoption of Flash Player. Flash Professional 8 builds upon the success of the past and puts video creation and delivery squarely into your hands.

This lesson will begin with the use of the new video encoder tool and gives you the knowledge necessary to professionally produce video that meets the needs of the users. It will end with your creating a Flash video using the new video PlayBack component.

The video and the controls used in this lesson.

What You Will Learn

In this lesson you will:

- Use the Video Wizard to create a FLV file
- Choose a skin for a Flash 8 video component
- Use the Advanced Encoding settings in the Flash 8 video encoder
- Customize the data and audio rates and set the keyframes in a Flash video
- Learn the difference between streaming video and a progressive download
- Attach a FLV file to the FLVPlayback-Player 8 component
- Use the Component inspector to set a video component's parameters
- Buffer video for optimized Web playback
- Attach video to a Flash 6-7 MediaPlayback component
- Prepare a Flash video for playback through Flash Player 7
- Test a video
- Use the FLV UI components to control video playback

Approximate Time

This lesson will require about one hour to complete.

Lesson Files

Media Files:

MAMMAAND.MOV

Starting Files:

None

Completed Files:

Lesson07/Complete/Wizard.fla
Lesson07/Complete/Component.fla
Lesson07/Complete/ComponentV7.fla

Using Video in Flash

The inclusion of video into your Flash projects will result in experiences that are compelling and engaging. You can add video to a Flash movie or simply create a Flash movie containing nothing more than the video for inclusion in a Web page. However, keep in mind that creating video involves more than deciding to add a video to a Web page or Flash movie.

The first thing to keep in mind is the user. Video is *rich media*—it enriches the user experience…if it is done right. Though Flash might be a cool technology and video—even cooler, if a user has to wait for an inordinate amount of time for the video to load—the rich experience will turn sour in a very short order. Never forget that your video is being delivered through the Internet, and a key factor is the user's bandwidth. If you create a FLV file for broadband playback, you can bet that users with a dial-up connection are in for a long wait!

Apart from keeping an eye on the pipe, you should also pay close attention to the user, who might not be interested in the video—so the inclusion of an on/off control is an important consideration. Give users control of the entire experience by letting them make the decision whether or not to play the video by not having the video play when it loads. If it is a large video, include a progress bar that shows the user that the video is indeed loading. Controls such as a volume control and a scrub bar that advances the video as you drag it are other techniques you can use to let the user control the process.

Using the Flash Video Encoder Wizard

The first thing you have to understand about the use of video in Flash is the original video must be converted to a format Flash can read. This format is FLV (Flash Video) and you can either use Flash, the Flash Video Encoder, or third-party software to create the FLV file. If you use video-editing software such as Adobe After Effects, you can also export the file as a FLV file. If you are a Dreamweaver user, the current version of Dreamweaver—Dreamweaver 8—contains a feature that allows you to add an FLV at the click of a button. The purpose of the Encoder, therefore, is to convert the video file to the FLV format.

When you installed Flash Professional 8, the Flash Video Encoder application was also installed on your machine. If you also have QuickTime, Adobe After Effects, Avid Studio, or Final Cut Pro installed on your machine, they, too, were given the capability to use the Encoder when it was installed.

If you will be converting a video to the FLV format, the video must be in one of these formats:

AVI—Audio Video Interleave

MOV—QuickTime 4 or later

MPEG—Motion Picture Experts Group

DV—Digital video, the format used by most commercial camcorders

WMF/ASF—Windows Media

> **Note** *Don't be terribly surprised if, in certain instances, Flash imports the video but not the audio. For example, audio is not supported in MPG/MPEG files imported with QuickTime 4. In such cases, Flash displays a warning indicating that the audio portion of the file cannot be imported or the audio section will be dimmed in the Encoder.*

For this exercise, you will use Flash's Video Wizard to import a video and format a video that will be placed in a Web page.

1. Copy the Lesson 7 files to your hard drive or create a folder on your hard drive and copy *MOMMAAND.MOV* **to this folder.**

The wizard will be creating a FLV file for you and saving it to the same folder as the source video. If you try to work from the CD, you will get an error.

2. Create a new file called *video.fla* **and save it anywhere on your hard drive.**

When you create this file use the default dimensions for the Stage, which are 550 by 400.

3. Change the frame rate of your Flash movie to 15 fps.

When creating video, a good habit to develop is to have the frame rate of the video and the Flash movie in which it will be placed match. Thus, you avoid having the video finish before the sound and other nasty issues that tend to crop up when there is no match. The frame rate can be changed in the Property inspector.

4. Choose File > Import > Import Video to open the Video Import Wizard.

From here, you can navigate to MOMMAAND.MOV on your hard drive. The Video Import Wizard leads you through the import and conversion process. When the Select Video page of the wizard opens, click the Browse button and navigate to the folder containing the video. Select the file and click the Open button. The path appears, and you can click the Next button to open the Deployment page.

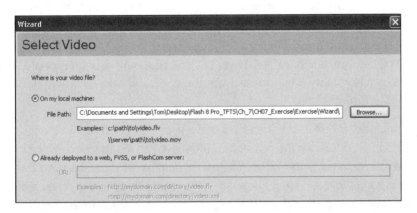

Note | *The other option—Already deployed to a Web, FVS,S or Flash Comm server— assumes that the FLV file has already been created and is sitting on your Web server, a Flash Video Streaming Service server, or a Flash Communication Server.*

5. Select Progressive download from a standard Web server and click Next.

A progressive download is a standard for Flash video being played from a Web server. In very simple terms, this means that as soon as enough of the video has downloaded into the SWF file on the Web page, the video plays. Depending on the length and quality of the video, this delay ranges from almost instantly to a few seconds.

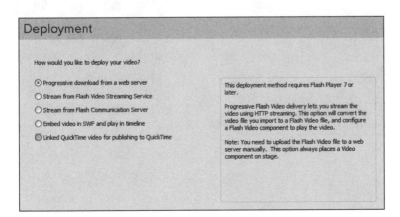

6. When the Encoding page appears, select Flash 8 - Medium Quality (400kbps) from the encoding profile drop-down list and click Next to move to the Skinning page.

The list of quality options in the encoding profiles allows you to choose both the version of Flash Player to be used and a bit rate. Bit rate determines how fast the video data streams into the SWF file embedded in a Web page. The one chosen here is appropriate for broadband delivery. Low quality is best for dial-up situations, and high quality is ideal for high-speed and LAN connections.

Tip *The three sliders under the video preview can be used to trim the video. The top slider simply shows the position of the playhead in the video. Move it back and forth to scrub through the video. The two sliders under it can be used to set the in and out points for the video. For example, assume that the video has a couple of seconds of black before it starts. Drag the in point to the frame; when the video is encoded, that first couple of seconds of black screen will not appear. The slider on the right is the out point. Drag it to the left, and any video beyond this point will be ignored.*

Note *We'll deal with the advanced settings later on in this lesson.*

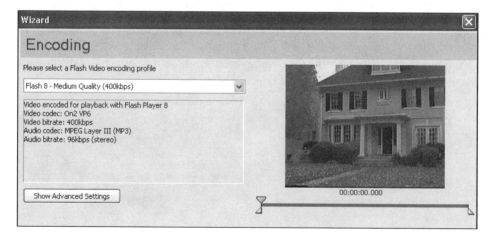

7. In the Skinning page, select *SteelExternalAll.swf* from the choices in the Skin drop-down list and click Next to move onto the Finish Video Import page.

The skins, for all intents and purposes, are nothing more than a collection of 32 custom controller styles for the video. The one chosen places the controls under the video and makes them visible to the user. Pay close attention to their names. Each of the styles allows you to place the controller over the video—SteelOverAll.swf. In this case, the video appears on the Web page, and the controls appear only when the user rolls the mouse over the video. Other styles, such as SteelOverNoVol.swf, remove controls such as a volume slider from the controller. When you choose a skin, a preview of your selection appears in the page.

Note *The Custom style is ideal for those situations in which you want to create your own controller. For example, you might want to add your client's logo to the controller and use a different style from those offered. This can be done, but the technique is out of the scope of this book.*

Tip *Note the minimum width in the Skinning page, which tells you the minimum Stage width required for the controller. This value can be set in the Property inspector. If the video is wider than the minimum value, you can ignore this direction.*

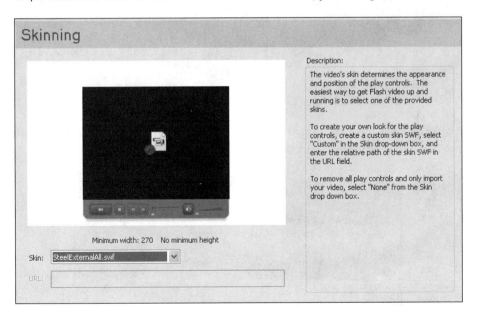

8. Examine the Finish Video Import page. When you're sure that all the information on this page is correct, click Finish.

The Finish Video Import page of the wizard gives you all the information you need regarding what happens next. It also tells you where the files it creates will be placed, how to link the video to the SWF file, and even allows you to access the Help file when the import is finished. If you make a mistake or need to change a setting, click the Back button.

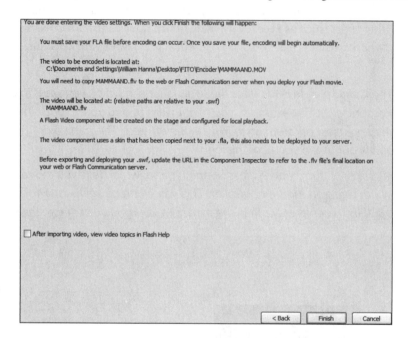

When you click the Finish button, the FLV Encode Progress page appears, showing you the progress of the encoding process.

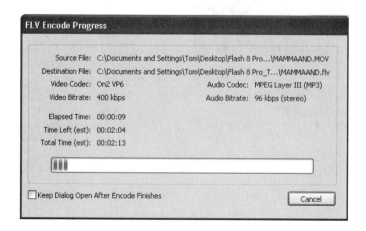

9. Click the Stage; in the Property inspector, set the Stage dimension to 320 x 270.

If a video is destined for a Web page, always set the Stage size to match that of the video. The unused portion of the Stage is nothing more than excess bandwidth. This video is 320 × 240, but the extra 30 pixels will accommodate the height of the controller under the video.

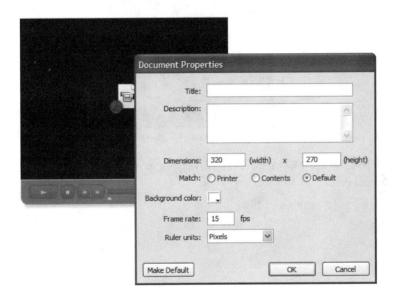

10. Click the video and set the *x* and *y* coordinates to 0,0.

11. Save the movie and test it.

12. Publish the movie. Minimize Flash and open the folder where you have saved this Flash project.

Inside the folder are a number of files:

- `video.swf`
- `SteelExternalAll.swf`
- `MAMMAND.FLV`
- `Video.fla`
- `MAMMAND.MOV`

The first three files—`video.swf`, `SteelExternalAll.swf` and `MAMMAND.FLV`—are the ones that have to be uploaded to the Web server. The one that gets placed in the Web page is `Video.swf`.

Using the Flash 8 Video Encoder and the Advanced Settings

Although the wizard is an extremely useful tool, especially for rapid prototyping, the true power of Flash video is realized by the capability to create a FLV file that is optimized for the user's bandwidth. The video you created in the previous exercise, for example, is ideal for playback through a cable modem, but will give the users of dial-up services a less-than-satisfactory experience.

The Flash 8 Video Encoder asks you to answer some very specific questions as you move through the process of encoding the video. Among them are these:

- Which codec do you want to use?
- At what data rate do you want the video to stream?
- What is the data rate for the Audio?
- Is the video to be resized?
- How often will keyframes be added?

The encoder, like the wizard, creates a stand-alone FLV file that can be uploaded to a variety of servers.

In this exercise, you create the same video player as that from the previous exercise, but there are a couple of differences. You manually add the FLVPlayback-Player 8 component and connect the FLV file to it in Flash. You also custom-optimize the FLV file for broadband playback rather than use a preset.

Before you start, be sure that you have copied the Lesson 7 folder from your CD to your hard drive.

1. Open the Flash 8 Video Encoder.

If you are on a PC, you can access this application by opening the application located at C:\Program Files\Macromedia\Flash 8 Video Encoder. Mac users can find the application at Macintosh HD\ Applications\ Macromedia\ Macr Flash 8 Video Encoder.

2. Drag the *MOMMAND.MOV* file from your Lesson Folder to the files area of the Encoder. Alternatively, you can click the Add button and navigate to the folder and select the video.

When you add a video, the path to the file is shown in the Files area. As well, the default encoding settings are applied to the video file.

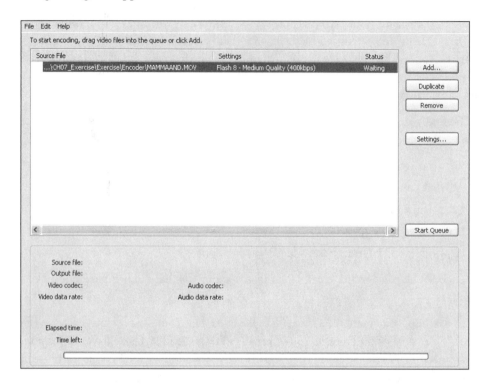

3. Click the Settings button to open the Encoding Settings window.

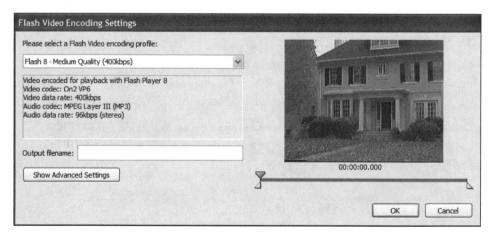

4. Click the Advanced Settings button.

The Advanced Encoding Settings are divided into three distinct areas that can be reached by clicking the appropriate tab. The Encoding tab is where the video is optimized for output. The Cue Points tab is where you can set the timing for other events in the Flash movie based upon a specific point in time in the video (you use the Cue Points in Chapter 9). The Crop and Trim tab allows you to crop a video and set the in and out points by the numbers.

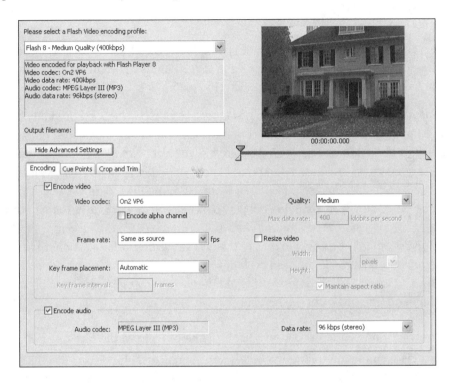

5. On the Encoding tab, select the On2 VP6 codec to choose the codec to be used for the encoding.

The term codec is an acronym for en**CO**der/**DEC**oder. The codecs used for Flash video are the On2 VP6 codec and Sorenson Spark, which is a lite version of the Sorenson Squeeze codec. The On2 VP6 codec is a new addition to Flash Professional, and if the digital video being encoded contains an alpha channel, it is the one to use. Your choice of codec is up to you because they both produce high-quality video.

These two codecs are the real workhorses of the video-creation process. They can compress a QuickTime video that is 45 MB and create an FLV file that weighs in around 13 MB or lower. This happens because the codecs see the video as being nothing more than a series of pictures on a Timeline. The frames where the picture is uncompressed are called keyframes and the frames between the keyframes—called difference or delta frames—are where the compression occurs. The more frames there are between the keyframes, the greater the reduction in file size during the compression process. In regular video production, keyframes are usually found on every 15th or 30th frame. These two codecs are designed to produce excellent results for keyframes spread out to every 48th frame, example, which results in a smaller file size.

Another feature of these two codecs that is critical to the use of Flash video. They add metadata, such as the video's width and height, to the FLV file. This metadata is accessible to Flash Player and can be used by ActionScript to manipulate the video.

> **Tip** *If you are working with a video producer or video production company, try to have them give you a digital video file that is uncompressed. If it must be compressed, specify it to be compressed using either the video or animation codec. These two video codecs are lossless, meaning the information in the video remains intact. The two codecs in Flash Professional 8 are lossy, meaning data will be lost during the compression process. The best way of understanding this is to think of JPG image compression. If you recompress a JPG image using the JPG format, the image will actually be lower in quality than what you started with (look for banding in gradients, square blocks, and artifacts in your images). The same principle applies to video. If you compress a video that is already compressed–Sorenson or Cinepac–the quality of the FLV file is lower.*

6. **Open the Frame Rate drop-down list and select 15 from the choices.**

Although Flash animations play quite well at a frame rate of 24 fps, Flash video has its problems at that speed. You also have to understand that frame rate is independent of the host SWF file. If the video has a frame rate of 12 fps and the SWF file where the FLV file is placed has a frame rate of 24 fps, the Flash movie in the Web page will play back at 24 fps, whereas the video in that movie will play back at 12 fps. The most common bit of advice around frame rate is to have the two of them equal to or multiples of each other.

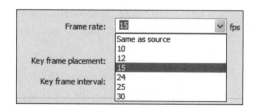

7. Select Custom in the Key Frame Interval drop-down list and enter 30 in the Key Frame Interval input box.

When setting the number of keyframes, pay attention to the video. If there is a lot of motion in the video, such as cars moving, people walking, or moving scenery, use a lower keyframe number. If the video is nothing more than your dog running in a field, a higher keyframe number will work. Keep in mind that if you have a controller that allows the users to move forward or backward in the video (the official term is *seeking*), what the user sees when they seek is the keyframes.

8. Set the Quality to Custom and enter 460 into the Max data rate input box.

If there is one theme running through this part of the lesson, it is this: Data rate controls quality. Bandwidth controls the user experience.

Regardless of the platform used, bandwidth, or the pipe, is the critical consideration. In fact, when deciding to use video you should have a bandwidth strategy in place for the user, the server, and the video. The server bandwidth strategy must revolve around the maximum or total number of users accessing the video. The last thing you need is to have users hanging around waiting for their turn in the line to download and play the video. When it comes to the user, the bandwidth required has to have enough room for the stream and other Internet activities. For example, a user with a 56K dial-up connection can connect and process data at an ideal rate of 56.6 Kbps. In fact, the target data rate for a video in this situation is about 40 Kbps, which leaves some room for other activities on the browser.

A low data rate reduces the number of bits per second shot down the pipe. The result is a lower-quality product that is ideally suited for low bandwidth (dial-up) connections and has a much smaller file size. A higher data rate, such as the traditional target of 350 Kbps for most DSL connections, will result in a great-looking, fast-loading file on a cable modem, but will choke a dial-up connection.

Note *Data rate is simply the amount of data transferred, per second, to the user's computer. This, in turn, determines the bandwidth required to play the video. The data rate calculation is this:*

Data rate= w x h x color depth x frames per second/ compression

The video for this exercise is 320 x 240 and it uses 24-bit color. If you plug in the numbers and use 60:1 compression, the benchmark for the Spark and On2 VP6 codecs, the data rate for the video at 15 fps is 460,800 bits/sec or 460 kilobits per second, which explains the data rate value you entered.

If you do the calculation for the uncompressed video–no compression number– the calculation gives you a result of 27,648,000 bits per second. To deliver that kind of file, you would need an Internet pipe that is the diameter of a railroad tunnel. Also Flash Player supports a maximum data rate of 4 MB per second; anything over that and you have problems. Toss the compression ratio into the equation and you have a video whose data rate is very comfortably within Player's range.

9. Don't resize the video.

If you must resize a video, resize to a lower size. Don't resize to a higher size. What many people tend to forget is that a video is composed of a number of images. If you resize an image, it tends to get fuzzy because an image is composed of a set number of pixels. If you double the size of the image, all you do is make the pixels bigger—the same number of pixels in a larger space—and the result is a fuzzy image.

The standard sizes for video are these:

- 320 x 240
- 240 x 180
- 160 x 120

The first number is easily divisible by 4, and the second is easily divisible by 3. The measurements indicate that the height is 3/4 the width. If you divide the height by the width, you will get 1-1/3 or 4/3. That is the 4:3 ratio. The 4:3 ratio is the standard aspect ratio for digital video and, if you must resize the video, make sure that the Maintain Aspect Ratio radio button is clicked.

10. Click the Encode Audio radio button and select **64 Kbps (mono) from the Data Rate drop-down list.**

There are actually two compressor used for FLV file creation: one for audio and another for video.

The choice you make here is rather uncomplicated. These settings will compress the sound portion of the video to the FLV file format, which is an MP3 format. The bit rates presented to you essentially optimize the audio track for FLV file playback. The number chosen has a direct effect upon quality. Higher numbers mean higher quality and less compression. Lower numbers mean lower quality and greater compression.

11. Click OK to return to the Video Encoder window; then click the Start Queue button.

The interesting aspect of this window is that you can use it to encode one or a dozen videos. As well, each of the videos can have its own settings.

When the video encodes, you will see a progress bar, and the video will appear during the process. When the video is finished encoding, the resulting FLV file will be placed in the folder containing the original video.

All videos that you have compressed will be listed in the Encoder dialog box. If you want to redo the compression, simply select the video in the list and click the setting button. To clear the list, select the videos and click the Remove button.

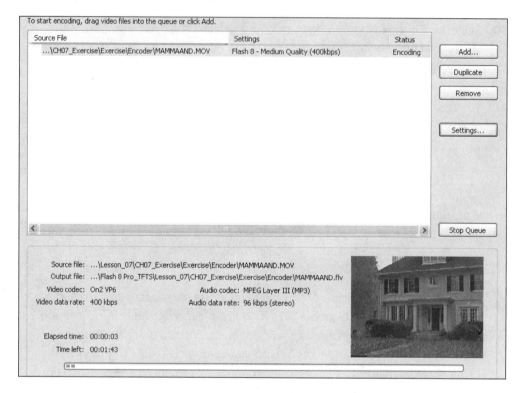

12. When the video finishes encoding, close the Flash 8 Video Encoder dialog box.

If you want, compare the file size of the FLV file just created to that of the original QuickTime video.

MAMMAAND
QuickTime Movie
9,518 KB

MAMMAAND
Flash Video File
4,137 KB

Creating a Video using the FLVPlayback Component

In the first part of this lesson, you created an FLV file that automatically played through the FLVPlayback component. In this exercise, you link the component to the FLV file.

As you become more comfortable with creating Flash video and adding it to your Web pages, you will see the creation process as essentially involving these two steps:

- Creating the FLV file using the Flash 8 Video Encoder
- Linking the FLV file to a video object, in this case the Player, on the Flash Stage

By linking a FLV file to an object, you can reuse the player as the videos change; at the same time you can also customize the Player's properties to enrich the video experience and give the user an even greater degree of control over the video.

1. Open a new Flash document and open the Components panel.

If your Components panel isn't open, you can open it by selecting Window > Components or by pressing the Control+F7 (PC) or Command+F7 (Mac).

2. Double-click the FLVPlayback-Player 8 component and drag a copy of the FLVPlayback component onto the Stage.

This component is the one automatically added to your movie when you use the Video Import Wizard.

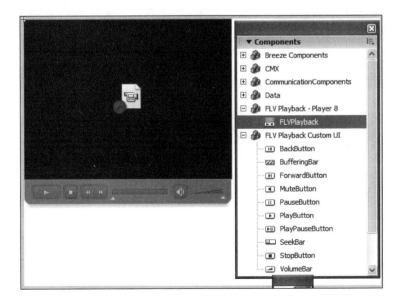

3. Select the component on the Stage, click the Properties tab of the Property inspector, click once in the Instance Name area of the Property inspector, and name the component mcMyVid.

> **Tip** *Although you won't be using the instance name in this exercise, giving components instance names is a good habit to develop.*

4. With the component selected on the Stage, in the Property inspector, set the width to **320**, the height to **240** and the *x* and *y* coordinates to **0**.

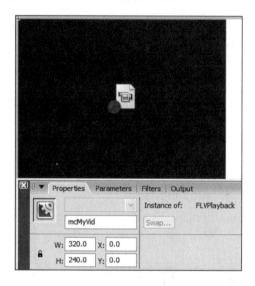

The default value for this component is a lot smaller than the dimensions of the FLV file you have created. As well, this will be a video placed into a Web page. Placing the component in the upper-left corner of the Stage ensures that the SWF file will not contain wasted space on the Stage.

5. Click the Stage and then click the Size button on the Property inspector. When the Document Properties dialog box opens, set the Stage dimensions to **320 x 275** and the Frame Rate to **15 fps**. Click OK.

The white space under the video area will be used by the Controller you will add to the Component. It requires about 30 pixels of space under the video or there is a risk of it getting "trimmed off" upon playback. The change in the frame is to ensure that the frame rate for the SWF file holding the video has the same frame rate as the FLV file.

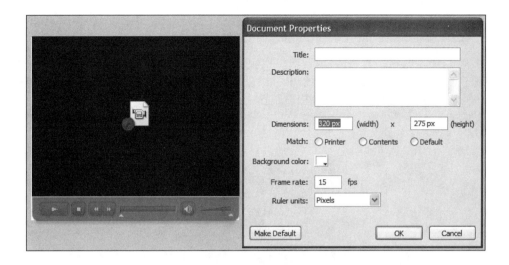

6. Click once on the video component on the Stage and click the Parameters tab in the Property inspector.

All components, this one included, use customizable values that determine how the component looks and often functions. When you select a component, the parameters will appear in two places: the Parameters tab of the Property inspector or in the Parameters window of the Component inspector.

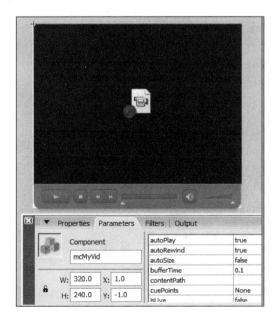

7. Open the Component inspector and click the Parameters tab to view the full list of parameters for this component.

Although you can use the Property inspector, most Flash developers tend to use this panel instead of the Property inspector. To open the Component inspector, you can either select Window > Component Inspector or press Alt+F7 (PC) or Option+F7 (Mac). If you don't see the parameters when you click the Parameters tab in the inspector, select the component on the Stage.

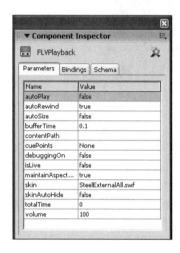

8. Click the Value area for autoPlay and select False from the drop-down list.

This selection means the user will have to click the Play button in the controller when the video loads into the browser to play the video.

9. Click once in the *bufferTime* value and enter .5.

autoSize	false
bufferTime	0.5
contentPath	
cuePoints	None

The value you just entered tells Flash to store one-half second of video in a buffer. This is especially useful when a video streams because a buffer minimizes dropped video frames. When a video plays, the frames must be shown at specific times. If there is a delay, the frames between where the playback head is currently located and where it should be are dropped. The result is a "jerky" video. Creating a buffer and storing frames in the buffer is a great habit to develop. You can use any value you wish but the more common values are between .5 and 2 seconds. Remember the more you buffer, the longer the wait for the video to start.

10. Click once in the *contentPath* value area and enter the name of the FLV file.

Values for the path can be either Absolute or Relative. For example, if the final SWF file and FLV file are to be located in the same directory on the server, a relative path—the name of the FLV file—will suffice. If you have the FLV files located in a separate folder, you would enter ./flvFolderName/VideoName.flv.

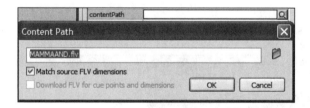

Tip *You can double click the Browse Button in the content Path and navigate to the folder containing the FLV.*

11. Click once on the Skin value and then click on the magnifying glass in the value input area to open the Select Skin dialog box.

This is the same dialog box used in the wizard.

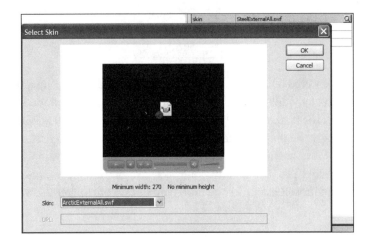

12. Select `ArcticExternalAll.swf` from the list of skins and click OK.

The skin selected will appear in the Component inspector.

13. Close the Component inspector.

If you click the Parameters tab of the Property inspector, the values chosen in the Component inspector appear here as well.

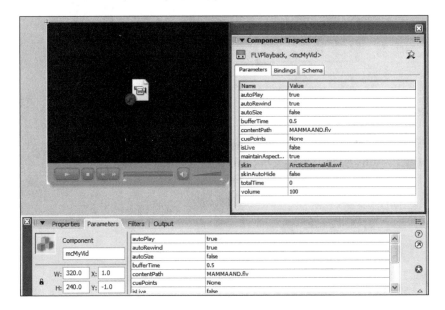

14. Save the Flash file to the same folder as the FLV file and test the movie.

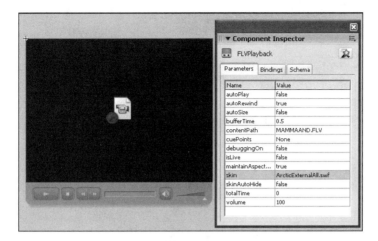

Creating a Video using the MediaPlayback Component for Flash Player 6/7

The inclusion of the MediaPlayback component in Flash Professional 8 is an acknowledgment that at least for the first year of its existence, not all Web users will have the Flash Player 8 installed on their computers. This could be because of corporate IT policies, where users are not permitted to add or upgrade software on their company computer.

In this case, a previous version of Flash Player, version 6 or version 7, will have to be used for playback. This will be accomplished through the use of the MediaPlayback component that was included in Flash MX 2004 Professional and is also a part of the Component panel in Flash Professional 8.

1. Open a new Flash movie by choosing File › New and then save it to the same location as your FLV file.

This ensures that the FLV file will be found when it is needed at playback.

2. Select File › Publish Settings. Click the Flash tab and select Flash Player 7 from the Version drop-down menu. Click OK to close Publish Settings.

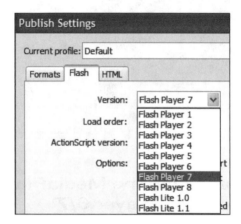

By selecting the Player even before the file is constructed, you ensure that the file will play properly in Flash Player 7.

> **Tip** *The Flash Player 8 video components are clearly named as such in the Component panel for a reason. They are not compatible with earlier versions of Flash Player. Thankfully, you don't discover this fact when the video is uploaded to the server and played through a browser. You will be notified of this, through a warning box, when you test the movie.*

3. Open the Components panel and drag a copy of the MediaPlayback component from the Media-Player 6-7 Component group to the Stage.

The MediaPlayback component is a composite of the two other components in the group: MediaDisplay and MediaController.

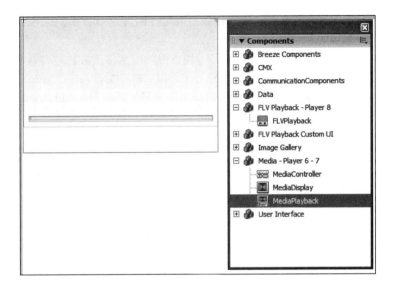

4. With the component selected on the Stage, set the width and height of the component to **320 x 240** set the X and Y locations to **0,0**. Click the **Parameters** tab and click the **Launch Component Inspector** button.

When you drag the component onto the Stage and click the Parameters tab in the Property inspector, the parameters are replaced with a Launch Component Inspector button. This difference is the way the media Component parameters were determined in previous versions of Flash.

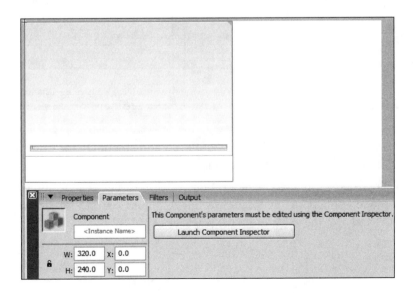

5. When the Component inspector opens, select FLV, enter the name of the FLV file, and deselect Automatically Play.

This tells the component that you are using a FLV file. As in the previous exercise, the name of the component is actually the path to the FLV file. Deselecting Automatically Play lets the user decide whether or not to view the video. The MP3 button is used in Flash MX 2004 for MP3 files.

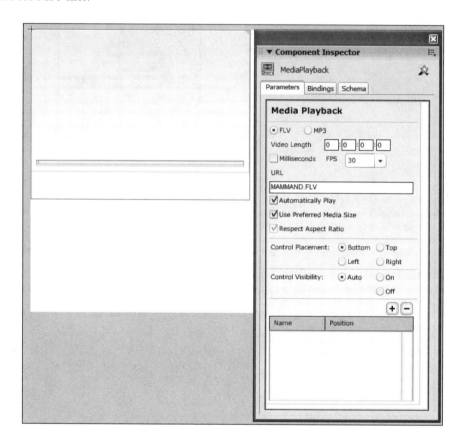

6. Select Bottom in the Control Placement area and select On for Control Visibility. Close the Component inspector.

When you choose a Control Placement location, the choice made will be immediately reflected in the component on the Stage. Selecting Auto for Control Visibility means the user has to roll over the video to see the playback controls.

Tip *If you deselect Autoplay and turn off Control Visibility in this component or the Flash Player 8 components, be aware that the user won't be able to play the video. The video will be there, but the user will have no way of playing it.*

7. Save and test the movie.

Using the FLV Custom UI Components to Control the FLVPlayback Component

There will be occasions when the user will be given limited control over video playback. This could include, for example, the use of a video in an e-learning situation, in which the student simply has to watch a video. In this scenario, the only two controls needed would be a play button to start the video and a pause button to stop it from playing. This is the purpose of the FLV Custom UI components.

This collection of 10 components, new to Flash Professional 8, lets you build your own video controller and wire it up using ActionScript. In essence, each one is a movie clip or button and, as such, they can be customized.

When one of these components is added to the Stage, not only is the component added to the library but the component is also added to the FLVPlayback Skins folder. You could, for example, change the color of the gradient used in the Play button or even change the green in the PlayButtonOver to blue. Best of all, these changes don't affect the original component in the Component panel.

1. Open a new Flash movie by choosing File › New and then add two new layers above the existing layer Name your three layers Video, Buttons, and Actions.

2. Select the Video layer and drag a copy of the FLVPlayback component to the Stage.

Select the Playback component and, in the Property inspector, add these values:

- Instance name: myVideo
- W: 320
- H: 240
- X: 0
- Y: 0

3. Select the Buttons layer and open the FLV Custom UI-Player 8 components. Drag a copy of the PlayButton and the PauseButton components to the Stage.

With buttons on the Stage, select the Pause button and add these values in the Property inspector:

- Instance Name: btnPause
- X: 50
- Y: 245

Select the Play button and add the following values in the Property inspector:

- Instance Name: btnPlay
- X: 195
- Y: 245

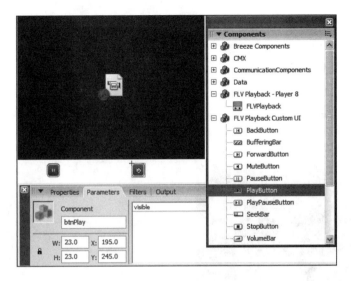

Tip *You don't necessarily have to drag components onto the Stage to get them to appear in the library. You can drag them from the Components panel directly into the Library panel.*

4. Click once on the Stage and, in the Property inspector, click the Size button.

When the Document Properties dialog box opens, change the Stage size to 320 pixels wide by 275 pixels high. Click OK to accept the change and close the Document Properties dialog box.

5. Select the FLVPlayback component and click the Parameters tab in the Property inspector.

Use the following values in the Parameters area:

- autoPlay: False
- contentPath: MAMMAAND.FLV
- Skin: None

The Play button will control the playback of the movie and because you have two buttons, there is no need for a skin.

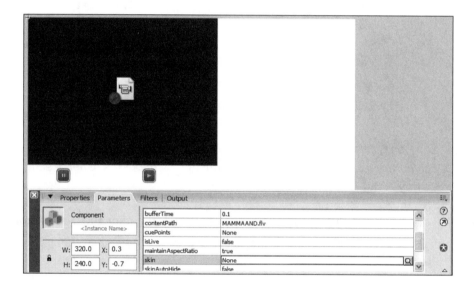

6. Select the Actions layer and press F9 to open the Actions panel. Enter the following code into the panel:

```
myVid.playButton = Play btn;
myVid.pauseButton = btnPause;
```

By setting the autoStart parameter of the FLVPlayback component to false, you have essentially stopped the movie from playing. The FLV file is streamed into the FLVPlayback component, which means it can be controlled by the play() and pause() methods contained in the button components. In this case, when the Play button is released the stream starts because of the play() method.

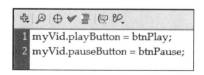

The play and pause buttons are simple buttons and nothing more. Because they inherit the component architecture, the video component knows all it needs to know about a button.

Once it finds out there is a button attached to it (the myVid.playButton), it latches on to it by adding itself to the button's list of listeners. Once the button is clicked, the FLVPlayback component is notified and will take action based on where you assigned the button (playButton, pauseButton, and so on). The button itself doesn't have any function; it simply tells the FLVPlayback component that it has been clicked. The component does the rest of the work.

7. Drag a copy of the VolumeBar component onto the Stage and give it the instance name *cVolumeBar*.

The volume bar is treated in exactly the same manner as the two buttons on the Stage. It is a component with methods, properties, and events that are accessed by the FLVPlayBack component.

8. Open the Actions panel and add the following line of code:

```
myVid.volumeBar = cVolumeBar;
```

9. Save the movie and test it.

The movie shows you only the first frame of the video. If you click the Play button, the video plays. Click the Pause button, and it stops. If you click the Play button once more, the video resumes playing. Drag the volume controller, and the volume of the sound playing from the video increases or decreases depending on which direction you dragged the mouse.

Note *Now that you understand how to add the UI components to a movie and control the video play back, here is how the rest of them are connected. The syntax is:*

```
Instancenameof FLVPlaybackcomponent.UIcomponentName =
instancenameofUIcomponent
```

In the following examples, the instance name for the FLVPlayback component is "myFLVPLayback".

```
myFLVPlayback.playButton = myPlayButton;

myFLVPlayback.pauseButton = myPauseButton;

myFLVPlayback.playPauseButton = myPlayPauseButton;

myFLVPlayback.stopButton = myStopButton;

myFLVPlayback.backButton = myBackButton;

myFLVPlayback.forwardButton = myForwardButton;

myFLVPlayback.muteButton = myMuteButton;

myFLVPlayback.volumeBar = myVolumeBar;

myFLVPlayback.bufferingBar = myBufferingBar;

myFLVPlayback.seekBar = mySeekgBar;
```

What You Have Learned

In this lesson you have:

- Created an FLV file using the Video Wizard (pages 255–263)
- Created an FLV file using the Flash 8 Video Encoder (pages 263–271)
- Optimized a video for Web playback using the advanced settings of the Video Encoder (pages 263–271)
- Added a skin to a Flash Professional 8 FLVPlayBack component (pages 271–277)
- Linked an FLV file to a component (pages 271–277)
- Set the parameters of the FLVPlayBack component (pages 271–277)
- Used the Flash 6/7 MediaPlayback component to play a video through a previous version of Flash Player (pages 277–281)
- Used the FLV UI components to control the video playing in the FLVPlayback component (pages 281–286)

8 Building a Custom Flash Video Player

In Lesson 7, you learned how to use a video component to create a video player. In this lesson, you will build your own video player that doesn't use components. An obvious question is, "Why bother if I have the components?"

Most Macromedia Flash pros avoid using components because they tend to add "weight" to a SWF file. For example, the player you constructed in the previous lesson had a file size of 34K, plus the skin came in at 15K. In this lesson, you will construct a player with simple Start and Stop buttons that weigh in at 1K. Obviously, one SWF file will load a lot faster than the other and because you are constructing the player, customization is a lot easier to accomplish.

The other factor is control. You might need to use only a Start and a Pause button in your project. To do this, you simply add a Video object to the Stage and use your two buttons to control the video playing through the object. This control is available through ActionScript.

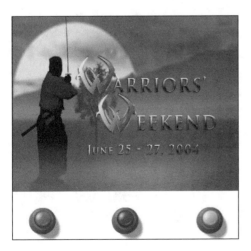

You don't have to use the components to control video; you can create your own controllers.

This lesson is divided into three sections. The first section shows you how to stream video using ActionScript and a Video object. The next section shows you how to add button controls that allow the user to control the playback of a video. The final section of this lesson explores the power of ActionScript to control video playing through the FLVPlayback component, which involves the creation of two projects. The first shows you how to play multiple FLV files so that you create the illusion of one large video file. The second explores the TransitionManager class in ActionScript. This project shows you how to fade in a video at the click of a button.

What You Will Learn

In this lesson you will:

- Create a Video object on the Flash Professional 8 Stage
- Use the NetConnection and NetStream classes to play a video from a server
- Add playback controls to a video
- Use ActionScript to control the playback of multiple FLV files
- Understand how the FLVPlayback component uses Listeners to trigger events
- Learn about the ten transitions found in the Transition class
- Learn how to manage those transitions through the use of the TransitionManager class
- Learn how to access the transitions using the Import keyword

Approximate Time

This lesson will require about 90 minutes to complete.

Lesson Files

Media Files:
Converge.flv

Starting Files:
Player.fla

Completed Files:
Lesson08/Complete/Player.fla

Streaming Video

The first thing to understand about streaming, especially when it involves Flash video, is that your Web server will more often than not be used as the streaming server. There are other solutions, such as a Flash Video Streaming Service provider or a Flash Communication server (see Chapter 10), but the most common method for streaming video is to use your Web server to deliver the video as a progressive download. Regardless of method, the ActionScript required to stream video is the same.

You will use two types of classes of ActionScript. The first type of class is the Connection class, which communicates with your server. The second type of class is composed of the User Interface classes used to display the video in the SWF file.

The way this works is fairly simple. The file will be loaded into the Flash Player using the NetStream and NetConnection classes, which in turn will feed the video into an embedded Video object on the Stage. That object will use the Video and Sound classes to display the video and to control its volume.

The NetConnection class manages the connection between Flash and the server. The NetStream class manages and controls the stream, allowing you to play, stop, pause, and even "jog" through the video stream. A great way of visualizing how this works is to think of the cable at the back of your television. The cable is your connection to the company providing the service. The actual programming fed into the cable and into your television is your stream.

Although it all sounds rather mysterious and technical, here is the absolute minimum code required to connect to a server and play a video:

```
new NetConnection();
NetConnection.connect(null);
New NetStream(NetConnection);
NetStream.play("myVideo.flv");
Video.attachVideo(NetStream);
createEmptyMovieClip("newMovie",this.getNextHighestDepth());
newMovie.attachAudio(NetStream);
Sound soundObj = new Sound(newMovie);
```

As you can see, it is a three-step process: *connect, stream, play*. The last few lines of the code simply attach the video stream to the Video object and connect to the video's sound.

Creating a Video Object

The key to successfully streaming video is to have the FLV file play almost as soon as the Web page opens. The data from the FLV file will flow through the `NetStream` into the SWF file. That data is then sent to a Video object on the Stage.

There are some serious advantages of using a Video object:

- **There is no need to embed a video into the SWF file.** This avoids the resulting massive SWF file that makes the user experience a bad one in dial-up situations.

- **There is no frame limit.** If you embed a video into a Flash SWF file, it is placed on a Timeline; depending on the length of the video, you might actually exceed the 16,000-frame limit on a Flash Timeline. More often than not, you will be creating single-frame video player.

- **Play means play.** As soon as the connection is made and the stream starts, the video also starts to play. With a progressive download, there will be a very short delay between connection and play. If you use a streaming server, playback is virtually instantaneous.

- **The SWF file is miniscule.** As you saw in the previous lesson, using components results in a SWF file that weighs in at around 70K. Use a Video object and a couple of buttons, and the SWF file shrinks to under 10K.

- **Videos can be as long as you want.** Whether a video is 1 minute long or 10 minutes in duration is irrelevant when you stream video.

1. Copy the Lesson 8 folder from your CD to your computer. Open the *Player.fla* file.

You will be saving this file and testing it as you proceed through this lesson.

2. Open the library and select New Video from the Library Options drop-down list.

This selection will create the Video object into which the FLV file is streamed. The Video Properties dialog box will open up, allowing you to choose the type of video object you wish to use, either an embedded video that will play directly on the Timeline, or an external video hooked up using ActionScript.

3. When the Video Properties dialog box opens, name the symbol Converge and select Video (ActionScript controlled). Click OK.

Notice that a small camera with the Video object's name appears in your library. This is the Video object.

Video object

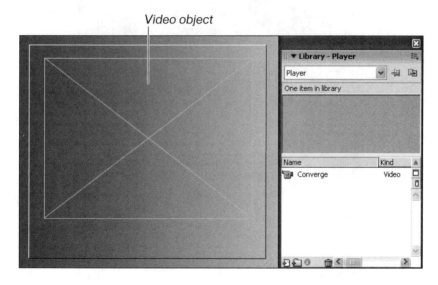

A Video object is where the video appears on the Stage. It remains invisible until a video is played in the movie. This Video object is rather unique in that it can use only the Video class, which has methods and properties but no events. This object can be sized, rotated, moved, masked, and even put into a movie clip. What it does not do is control the video playback. It acts very much like a television in that it hooks up to a stream and displays whatever the stream offers up. Those controls will be added later in the lesson. Finally, you can attach a sound to the Video object, but it is rarely done because most video already contains a sound track.

4. Select the *mVideo* layer and drag the Video object onto the Stage. In the Property inspector, give it the instance name of *myVid*, set the dimensions to 320 W by 240 H, and set the *x,y* coordinates to 40,35. Save the file.

The Video object is nothing more than a box with a big "X" through it when it is placed on the Stage. You can also place a Video object in a movie clip and because it is an object on the Stage, you can mask a Video object.

Tip   *You don't have to stream an FLV file into a Video object; you can attach a Web cam to your computer and stream the video signal from the camera into the Video object.*

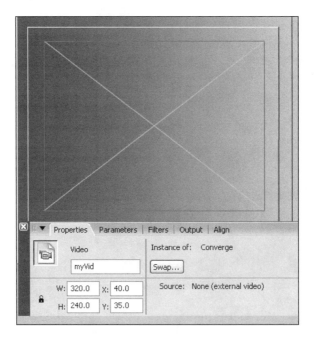

The Video object is added to the library and instantiated, resized, and placed on the Stage using the Property inspector.

Connecting Flash Player 8 to a Web Server

The connection process is managed by the NetConnection class. When this code is added to a movie containing a Flash Video object, the NetConnection class manages the communication between the user's computer and the server. Introduced in Flash Player 6, the NetConnection class can support multiple streams over a single connection.

The NetConnection class has three methods, two of which are available only if you are using a Flash Communication Server or a Flash Video Streaming Service:

- **NetConnection.connect()**: This makes the connection request with the server where the FLV file is located.
- **NetConnection.close()**: Used with streaming servers only, this method turns off the connection with the server.
- **NetConnection.call()**: Used with streaming servers only, this method can be used to call remote methods from the Flash Player.

After the connection is made, the stream can be established, NetStream, and the Video object can then be attached to the stream.

1. Select the *actions* layer and press F9 to open the ActionScript editor.

2. Add the following ActionScript into the Actions panel:

```
var nc:NetConnection = new NetConnection();
nc.connect(null);
```

The first line of code defines and instantiates a connection object and gives it the name nc. The second line is the connect method—connect—used to establish the connection. The Null parameter is used to establish the connection between a local Web server or a disk.

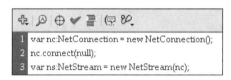

3. Press Return/Enter and add the following ActionScript:

```
var ns:NetStream = new NetStream(nc);
```

This line of code defines and instantiates a NetStream object using the NetConnection object defined previously. Flash movies must use both a NetConnection and a NetStream object to direct a stream to a Flash movie.

```
3   var ns:NetStream = new NetStream(nc);
```

Note *Audio and video data is transferred to the user's computer by attaching it to a stream. A movie that creates a stream in a network connection and uses that stream to send data to your user is said to be* publishing, *while the movie that creates a stream to receive data (this Lesson is an example of this) is said to be a* subscriber. *Just be aware that a stream can contain only one audio and one video file at any one time. If you have five videos, they all can't use the same stream. When you want another video to play, either the current playing video must be removed from the stream before the new video can be added, or a new stream must be instantiated and our Video object must be attached to the new stream.*

4. **Press Return/Enter and add the following ActionScript.**

```
var myVid: Video;
myVid.attachVideo(ns);
ns.play("Converge.flv");
```

With the NetConnection made and the NetStream established, the Video object is given a name—myVid—which matches the instance name of the object on the Stage. The Video object is then attached to the NetStream object through the attachVideo() method. Now that the stream and the Video object are talking to each other, the last line of code uses the play method to load the Converge.flv file to the NetStream and stream it to the Video object.

Note *If you are using code hinting to select the data types for the variables, the Video class is not included in the drop-down list. This class is restricted to Video objects and does not have a wide application in Flash, which explains its omission from the list.*

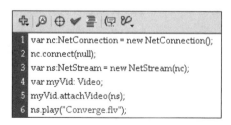

5. Save and test the file.

The video starts to play in the Video object on the Stage.

Leave this file open for the following exercise.

Note *The code does not exactly follow a common coding practice, which is to list the variables at the start of the script. The variables declarations are done in line, simply to help you understand what is going on behind the scenes. If we follow common coding practices, the code still works and would be entered this way:*

```
var nc:NetConnection = new NetConnection();
var ns:NetStream = new NetStream(nc);
var myVid: Video;

nc.connect(null);
myVid.attachVideo(ns);
ns.play("Converge.flv");
```

Adding Playback Controls

The components in the FLV Custom UI-Flash 8 panel don't work with a Video object. On the surface, this fact may appear to be a negative. In fact, it is a positive because the components add to the file size of the final SWF file. If you create your own controls, you will discover that the final SWF file size is smaller.

In this exercise, you use a couple of the buttons that ship with Flash Professional 8. If you find they don't fit your design, buttons can also be created in a number of imaging and drawing applications such as Illustrator CS2 and Photoshop CS2 from Adobe or through Freehand MX or Fireworks 8 from Macromedia. In a pinch, they can even be created in Flash Professional 8.

What you have to understand about buttons is they don't control the video. They are used to control the NetStream. When a Pause button is clicked, the message isn't "Stop the video." When the button is clicked, a message is sent to the server that says, in essence, "Turn off the faucet."

1. Use the file you saved and left open in the previous exercise.

If you didn't save the file, open the Buttons.fla file located in the Lesson 8 folder named Buttons. Add a new layer to the file named buttons.

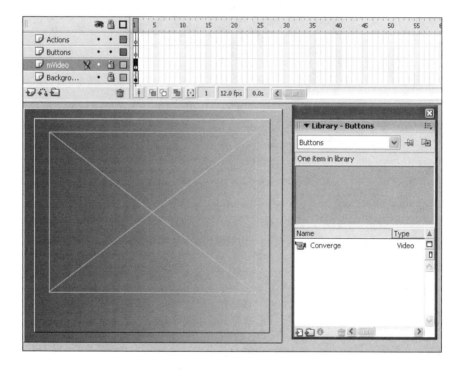

2. Select Window > Common Libraries > Buttons.

The Library-Buttons panel opens. Both versions of Flash—Flash 8 and Flash Professional 8—contain a wide variety of buttons that are designed for a variety of purposes, ranging from navigation to video control.

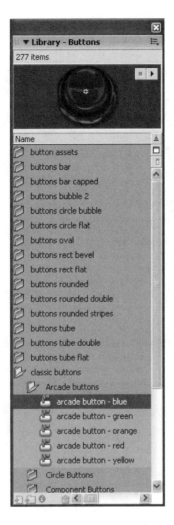

These buttons are contained in a number of folders in the Button library. When you add a button from this panel to your Stage, you can manipulate the button without harming the original.

3. Open the Circle Buttons folder located in the classic buttons folder in the Library-Buttons panel. Select the *buttons* layer in the Timeline and drag a copy of the Play and Stop buttons to the Stage.

When you drag a button from the Buttons panel, a copy of the button appears in the movie's library.

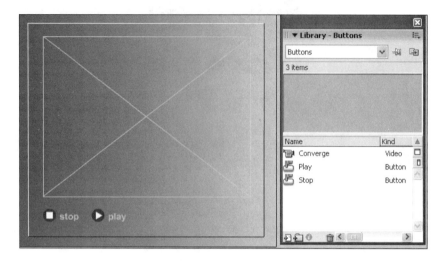

4. Select the Play button and give it the instance name *playButton* in the Property inspector.

5. Select the Stop button and give it the instance name of *stopButton* in the Property inspector.

Now that the buttons have been instantiated, they can be used in the movie's ActionScript to control video playback.

6. Select the first frame of the *actions* layer and press F9 to open the ActionScript panel.

When the panel opens, delete the code from the previous example and add the following code starting with line 1:

```
var myVid:Video;
var playButton:Button;
var stopButton:Button;
```

By creating variables and assigning a data type to a variable, you ensure that only the code that pertains to a video or a button can be applied to those variables.

```
var myNetConnection:NetConnection = new NetConnection();
myNetConnection.connect(null);
var myNetStream:NetStream = new NetStream(myNetConnection);
myVid.attachVideo(myNetStream);
myNetStream.play("Converge.flv");
myNetStream.pause(true);
```

The last line of the code—myNetStream.pause(true);—turns off the stream and holds the playback until the user clicks the Play button. Notice the use of the Boolean value true.

It's all a matter of control. Using pause without a parameter simply toggles the pause and play. There is no real control in this case. The Boolean value provides control. Passing true means that we know that we want to pause the video. By the same means, passing false indicates to start the video. Using the pause toggle is good for a single button that would go between play and pause. In a case where you want to knowingly pause a video, you should specify a Boolean.

```
 5  var myNetConnection:NetConnection = new NetConnection();
 6  myNetConnection.connect(null);
 7  var myNetStream:NetStream = new NetStream(myNetConnection);
 8  myVid.attachVideo(myNetStream);
 9  myNetStream.play("Converge.flv");
10  myNetStream.pause(true);
```

7. Press Return/Enter and add the following code.

```
playButton.onPress = function() {
  myNetStream.pause(false);
}

stopButton.onPress= function() {
  myNetStream.pause(true);
}
```

Clicking a button simply uses the pause(true) method to stop the stream and pause(false); method to start the stream.

```
1   var myVid:Video;
2   var playButton:Button;
3   var stopButton:Button;
4
5   var myNetConnection:NetConnection = new NetConnection();
6   myNetConnection.connect(null);
7   var myNetStream:NetStream = new NetStream(myNetConnection);
8   myVid.attachVideo(myNetStream);
9   myNetStream.play("Converge.flv");
10  myNetStream.pause(true);
11
12  playButton.onPress = function() {
13      myNetStream.pause(false);
14  }
15
16  stopButton.onPress= function() {
17      myNetStream.pause(true);
18  }
```

8. Save the movie and test it.

When the video starts, the screen is blank. Click the Play button, and the video starts. Click Pause to stop it, and click Play again to restart the video.

Playing Multiple Videos

The exercises in the previous chapter and this chapter focused on playing a single video. One of the more interesting aspects of the Flash Professional 8 FLVPlayback component is the ability to create a virtual playlist of videos and have them play back automatically. This is an extremely valuable technique to learn. Instead of having one "overly large" FLV file streaming through the player, a series of smaller videos is played instead. Also, a list of videos gives you the flexibility to add videos, delete videos, or even swap videos without having to spend the time creating the MOV file, converting it to a FLV file , and then loading it into the player.

In this example, you create a video player that plays two videos—Warrior.flv and MAMMAAND.flv—and puts the title of the currently playing video into a text box under the video. This is accomplished by first creating a list of the FLV files to be used and then loading the video into an instance of the FLVPlayback component that is loaded when needed.

The videos play in sequence because of a property of an FLV file: its duration. You write a small function that essentially says, "When the video ends, start playing the next instance in the lineup." You also write a small function that constantly monitors the lineup of videos, and when the end of the lineup—the last video—is reached, the process starts all over again. This is accomplished by using the "length" property of a list. When the last item in the list is reached, the video plays to the end and stop.

Tip *Though this technique uses only two video, the power of lists is at play here. It is just as easy to create a player containing two videos as it is to create one using 10 videos. All you need to do is to add the video names to the list in the code.*

1. Open Flash Professional 8, create a new document, and set the Stage size in the Property inspector to 320 × 280.

Even though the videos being used are 320 × 240, you need to leave room for the video's name on the Stage.

2. Add two more layers to the Timeline and name the layers *Actions*, *Video*, and *Text*.

By separating the elements you can easily select them on the Stage.

3. Select the *text* layer, click on the Text tool, and click/drag to create a text box on the Stage. Enter a series of random letters into the text box.

In the Property inspector, add the following:

- Text type: Dynamic text
- X: 23
- Y: 250
- Instance name: vidName
- Font: Arial

- Size: 16 points
- Color: Black (#000000)
- Style: Bold
- Aliasing: Anti-Alias for Readability

Tip *The random letters are simply there to let you see how the text will look in the text box when the video plays. The text will be replaced with the name of the currently playing video during playback.*

4. Select the *video* layer and drag an instance of the **FLVPlayBack** component to the Stage.

With the component selected, add these values in the Property inspector:

- Width: 320
- Height: 240
- X: 0
- Y: 0
- Instance name: `vidComp`

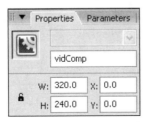

5. Save the file to the Lesson 8 folder.

It is important to save the FLA and SWF files to the same folder as the FLV files used. The movie will load them in from the directory where the FLA is saved and if the FLV files aren't in that directory, the videos won't play.

6. Select the *actions* layer and press F9 to open the ActionScript panel.

When the panel opens, enter the following code:

```
var videoLoaderIndex:Number = 0;
var videoPlayerIndex:Number = 0;
var videoList:Array = new Array("Warrior.flv","MAMMAAND.flv");


vidComp.contentPath = videoList[0];
vidName.text = vidComp.contentPath;


function eready(e:Object):Void {
  if ( videoLoaderIndex < videoList.length ) {
    videoLoaderIndex++;
    vidComp.activeVideoPlayerIndex = videoLoaderIndex;
    vidComp.load( videoList[videoLoaderIndex] );
  }
}
vidComp.addEventListener("ready", eready);
function ecomplete(e:Object):Void {
  ++videoPlayerIndex;
  if(videoPlayerIndex >= videoList.length) {
    videoPlayerIndex = 0;
  }
  vidComp.activeVideoPlayerIndex = videoPlayerIndex;
  vidComp.visibleVideoPlayerIndex = videoPlayerIndex;
  vidComp.play();
  vidName.text = e.target.contentPath;
}
vidComp.addEventListener("complete", ecomplete);
```

```
 1  var videoLoaderIndex:Number = 0;
 2  var videoPlayerIndex:Number = 0;
 3  var videoList:Array = new Array( "Warrior.flv", "MAMMAAND.flv");
 4
 5  vidComp.contentPath = videoList[0];
 6  vidName.text = vidComp.contentPath;
 7
 8  function eready(e:Object):Void {
 9    if( videoLoaderIndex < videoList.length ) {
10      videoLoaderIndex++;
11      vidComp.activeVideoPlayerIndex = videoLoaderIndex;
12      vidComp.load( videoList[videoLoaderIndex] );
13    }
14  }
15
16  vidComp.addEventListener("ready", eready);
17  function ecomplete(e:Object):Void {
18    ++videoPlayerIndex;
19    if(videoPlayerIndex >= videoList.length) {
20      videoPlayerIndex = 0;
21    }
22
23    vidComp.activeVideoPlayerIndex = videoPlayerIndex;
24    vidComp.visibleVideoPlayerIndex = videoPlayerIndex;
25    vidComp.play();
26    vidName.text = e.target.contentPath;
27  }
28
29  vidComp.addEventListener("complete", ecomplete );
```

The first section of the code sets the initial values for the video list:

```
var videoLoaderIndex:Number = 0;
var videoPlayerIndex:Number = 0;
var videoList:Array = new Array("Warrior.flv","MAMMAAND.flv");
```

The first variable (videoLoaderIndex) will be used to hold the first value in the video list—which will then load the videos into the FLVPlayback component. The second variable does essentially the same thing, but its value will be used to tell the component which video to play. The third variable creates the list of videos. This is where you would enter the names of the FLV files to be played.

The next two lines of code are used to load the first video in the list into the component and to also add the file name to the dynamic text area on the Stage:

```
vidComp.contentPath = videoList[0];
vidName.text = vidComp.contentPath;
```

The two functions that follow are the workhorses. The first function creates an instance of the video player for each movie in the video list within your FLVPlayback component (the list is then used to load the video into the instance):

```
function eready(e:Object):Void {
  if ( videoLoaderIndex < videoList.length ) {
    videoLoaderIndex++;
    vidComp.activeVideoPlayerIndex = videoLoaderIndex;
    vidComp.load( videoList[videoLoaderIndex] );
  }
}
```

The first line ensures that the loading of each video is tied to the "ready" event that the component fires each time a video is loaded. Naturally, there are a finite number of videos and the conditional statement does the following:

- Checks to see if all of the videos have loaded. If they are all loaded, then we are done. If there are more videos, the code with the if (videoLoaderIndex < videoList.length) block is executed.

- Increments our index pointer to point to our next movie in our videoList array. (videoLoaderIndex++;)

The next two lines in the function tell Flash to set the activeVideoPlayerIndex by telling the FLVPlayback component (vidComp) which video player will be used to load the video:

```
vidComp.activeVideoPlayerIndex = videoLoaderIndex;
vidComp.load( videoList[videoLoaderIndex] );
```

After the video is identified, the next line simply loads it into the player but doesn't start the video.

The next line of code ties the function just created to the FLVPlayback component's event listeners:

```
vidComp.addEventListener("ready", eready);
```

Now that Flash knows which videos are in which instance of the component, it needs to be told what to do when a video has finished playing. That is the purpose of the second function. It will be triggered every time a video finishes.

The first line of code inside the function tells Flash to go to the next video:

```
++videoPlayerIndex;
```

The next line checks the list of values to see if you have exceeded the number of videos to be played; if so, it starts the process all over again by resetting the videoPlayerIndex value back to 0. This line is skipped if the value is lower.

The remaining code in the function is what makes it all happen on the screen:

```
vidComp.activeVideoPlayerIndex = videoPlayerIndex;
vidComp.visibleVideoPlayerIndex = videoPlayerIndex;
vidComp.play();
vidName.text = e.target.contentPath;
```

The activeVideoPlayerIndex is told which video in the list to currently use and to make that instance of the player the visibleVideoPlayerIndex. When the player becomes visible, the video starts to play and the video's name appears in the text box.

The last line of code simply attaches the function to the components by adding itself as an event listener (addEventListener) that executes when the video has finished playing:

```
vidComp.addEventListener("complete", ecomplete);
```

```
29  vidComp.addEventListener("complete", ecomplete );
```

Components handle events a lot differently from movie clips and buttons. Movie clips and buttons react to an event handler such as onPress .Components use listeners.

A listener-based event model is composed of two elements: a broadcaster and a listener. To understand the difference, think of a phone conversation. The event handler for the movie clip or button is like someone speaking into the phone. There are only two parties to the conversation, and only one of you is the recipient of the voice. A listener-based event is more like a radio broadcast. Instead of two people listening, there could be 200 people listening.

A listener offers you tremendous flexibility, including the following:

- **You can have an unlimited number of listeners per event.** You can trigger any number of event handlers in response to an important event. In this exercise, the event is the end of the video. The component listens for that event and essentially disappears.

- **When multiple events are broadcast, listeners can be written so they react only to some events.** If a radio station plays a song you like, you listen to it. If it is a song that doesn't appeal to you, you choose not to pay attention. It is the same way with listeners. In the case of our videos, only the component playing the video turns itself off when the video is finished. It couldn't care less that another one is loading up and getting ready to play.

- **A listener can respond to multiple events.** Think of a button; it responds only to an onPress event. A listener can respond to any broadcast event (the end of a video, for example) because all events are available to the listener.

7. Save the movie and test it.

The key thing to watch for here is how the two movies appear to play as if they were a single FLV file.

Using the TransitionManager Class to Fade in Video

In the previous exercise, you discovered how to use ActionScript to play a number of videos so they appear to be one big video. In this exercise, you build on what you have learned. But instead of creating the illusion of one big video, you create a movie that does the following:

- Plays a video when a button is clicked
- Uses a Fade transition when the button for a second video is clicked

What you see is that the video attached to the button you click appears to fade in over the currently playing movie, which is possible through the Transition class.

When you installed Flash Professional 8, you also installed two powerful classes: the Tween and Transition classes. These two classes allow you to add special effects to movie clips and components through ActionScript. In this exercise, you create three instances of the FLVPlayback component and use the Fade transition to fade the videos in and out—depending upon which button you click.

Flash Professional 8 comes with the following 10 transitions:

- **Iris:** Reveals the screen or a movie clip using a mask of a shape that zooms in.
- **Wipe:** Reveals the screen or movie clip using an animated mask of a shape that moves horizontally.
- **Pixel Dissolve:** The screen or the movie clip is masked using rectangles that appear or disappear.
- **Blinds:** Reveals the next screen or movie clip using rectangles that appear or disappear.
- **Fade:** The screen or movie clip fades in or fades out.
- **Fly:** The screen or movie clip slides in from a particular direction.
- **Zoom:** The screen or movie clip is zoomed in or out.
- **Squeeze:** The screen or movie clip is scaled either vertically or horizontally.
- **Rotate:** The screen or movie clip rotates.
- **Photo:** The screen or movie clip appears as though it was lit with a photo flash.

These transitions are all accessible through the TransitionManager class and it does exactly what its name says it does - it manages transitions. It allows you to apply, through ActionScript, one of the transitions to movie clips or components.

1. Open Flash Professional 8, create a new document, and set the Stage size in the property inspector to 320 × 280.

Even if the videos being used are 320 × 240, you need to leave room for the buttons on the Stage.

2. Add three layers to the Timeline and name them *actions*, *video*, and *buttons*.

By separating the elements, we can easily select them on the Stage.

3. Select the *buttons* layer, and select Window > Common Libraries > Buttons.

When the Button panel opens, open The classic buttons > Push Buttons folder and drag a copy of each of push button-yellow, push button-blue, and push button-red to the Stage.

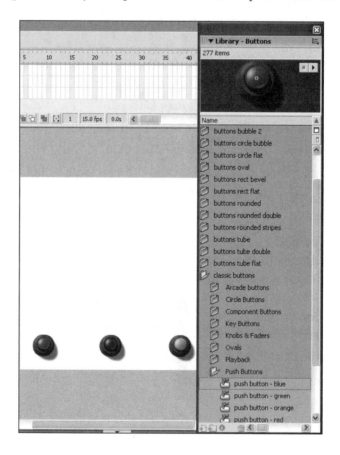

4. With the buttons on the Stage, select each one and give them the following instance names in the Property inspector:

- video1Button
- video2Button
- video3Button

5. Select the *video* layer and drag an instance of the **FLVPlayBack** component to the Stage.

With the component selected, add these values in the Property inspector:

- Width: 320
- Height: 240
- X: 0
- Y: 0
- Instance name: vidcomp

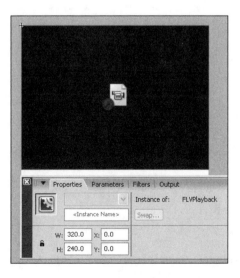

6. Save the file to the Lesson 8 folder.

Converge	Flash Video File	4,740 KB	
transitions	Flash Document	407 KB	
MAMMAAND	Flash Video File	4,137 KB	
Warrior	Flash Video File	2,215 KB	

7. Select the *actions* layer and press F9 to open the ActionScript panel.

When the panel opens, enter the following code:

```
import mx.transitions.*;
var videoLoadedCount:Number = 0;
var videoPlayerIndex:Number = 0;
var videoList:Array = new Array("Warrior.flv","Converge.flv", "MAMMAAND.flv");
for (var loaderLoop:Number = 1; loaderLoop <= videoList.length;
  loaderLoop++ ) {
  vidcomp.activeVideoPlayerIndex = loaderLoop;
  vidcomp.load( videoList[loaderLoop - 1] );
  }
function eready(e:Object):Void {
  ++videoLoadedCount;
  if ( videoLoadedCount == videoList.length ) {
  for (var playerLoop:Number = 1; playerLoop <= videoList.length;
    playerLoop++ ) {
    e.target.activeVideoPlayerIndex = playerLoop;
    e.target.play();
    }

  }
}

vidcomp.addEventListener("ready", eready);
function ecomplete(e:Object):Void {
  for (var playerLoop:Number = 1; playerLoop <= videoList.length;
    playerLoop++ ) {
    e.target.activeVideoPlayerIndex = playerLoop;
    e.target.play();
    }
  }
vidcomp.addEventListener("complete", ecomplete);
```

```
function transDone(e) {
  vidcomp.visibleVideoPlayerIndex = e.target.content._name;
  trace(e.target.content._name);
}

function buttonTransition(m:MovieClip, d:Number) {
  if (d != m.visibleVideoPlayer) {
    var other:MovieClip = m.getVideoPlayer(d);
    m.bringVideoPlayerToFront(d);
    var vp:MovieClip = other;
    TransitionManager.start(vp,{type:mx.transitions.Fade,
              direction:0,
              duration:4,
    easing:mx.transitions.easing.None.easeNone,
              param1:empty,
              param2:empty});
    vp.__transitionManager.addEventListener("allTransitionsInDone",transDone);
  }
}

video1Button.onPress = function() {
  buttonTransition(_level0.vidcomp, 1);
};

video2Button.onPress = function() {
  buttonTransition(_level0.vidcomp, 2);
};


video3Button.onPress = function() {
  buttonTransition(_level0.vidcomp, 3);
};
```

On the surface, this may seem to be an awful lot of code; in actual fact it is a variation on that used in the previous exercise. The major differences are the use of the `TransitionManager` class to trigger the `Fade` transition and the three buttons associated with the videos used in the exercise.

There are two other additions to the ActionScript from the previous exercise. The `eready` code waits until all videos have been loaded (using the counter) and then goes through each video instance and tells it to play its video. The `eComplete` code simply goes through all of the video instances and tells them to play their video as soon as one of them has completed.

Rather than go through the code in great detail, let's look at the major points of this script.

The first line of code tells Flash where to find the transitions. If it is used in your code, it is always the first line of ActionScript:

```
import mx.transitions.*;
```

The transitions are a class, and classes are organized much like the directory structure on your computer. In object-oriented terminology, the word *package* is used instead of the word *directory*. These packages are brought in using an `import` statement. In the case of this code, the statement says, "Import the transitions in the sub package named `transitions`, which is located in the package named `mx`." The asterisk is used to tell Flash to import all the classes found in the `transitions` sub package.

The first bit of code is a function whose sole purpose is to identify which instance is visible on the Stage:

```
function transDone(e) {
    vidcomp.visibleVideoPlayerIndex = e.target.content._name;
    trace(e.target.content._name);
}
```

The `trace` statement will also put the name of the currently visible FLVPlayback component into the Output panel on the Property inspector.

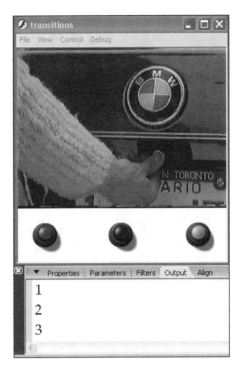

The second function is the actual transition and is triggered when one of the three buttons on the Stage is clicked.

```
49  function buttonTransition(m:MovieClip, d:Number) {
50      if (d != m.visibleVideoPlayerIndex) {
51          var other:MovieClip = m.getVideoPlayer(d);
52          m.bringVideoPlayerToFront(d);
53          var vp:MovieClip = other;
54          //this is a fade transition
55          TransitionManager.start(vp,{type:mx.transitions.Fade,
56                      direction:Transition.IN,
57                      duration:4,
58                      easing:mx.transitions.easing.None.easeNone,
59                      param1:empty,
60                      param2:empty});
61          vp.__transitionManager.addEventListener("allTransitionsInDone",transDone)
62      }
63  }
```

The first line names the function and names the FLVPlayback component, which is a movie clip, m, and the instance number—three were created earlier—is given the name of d.

```
function buttonTransition(m:MovieClip, d:Number) {
```

The next section of the function identifies the movie clip that is currently visible and the one that is associated, but not visible, with the button that was clicked. That movie clip is now placed in front of the one that is currently playing: bringVideoPlayerToFront(d);

```
if (d != m.visibleVideoPlayerIndex) {
  var other:MovieClip = m.getVideoPlayer(d);
  m.bringVideoPlayerToFront(d);
  var vp:MovieClip = other;
```

Now that the two instances have essentially been swapped, the one that is now sitting in the front needs to fade in. This is accomplished through the use of the TransitionManager class.

```
TransitionManager.start(vp,{type:mx.transitions.Fade,
            direction:Transition.IN,
            duration:4,
            easing:mx.transitions.easing.None.easeNone,
            param1:empty,
            param2:empty});
vp.__transitionManager.addEventListener("allTransitionsInDone",transDone);
  }
}
```

The first line of the code is a call to the TransitionManager.Start() method, which creates a new instance of the TransitionManager, designates the target object (vp), applies a transition (Fade) with an easing method (easing:mx.transitions.easing.None.easeNone,) and does the transition (vp.__transitionManager.addEventListener("allTransitionsInDone",transDone);)— all in one call.

What you can't do is simply load up a fade and expect it to work. This class can only used by specifying its full class name (mx.transitions.Fade) as a parameter for the TransitionManager class. After you have specified the fade, you set the value for the direction (use the Transition.IN constant for a fade-in effect) and the duration of the effect. In this case, the video fades in over the course of one half second.

The easing method is usually reserved for transitions that physically move the movie clip on the screen. In this case, you can specify where the easing will occur—the start, the end, or both—over the course of the transition. There are four easing methods:

- **easeIn**: The effect is triggered at the start of the transition.
- **easeOut**: The effect is triggered at the end of the transition.
- **easeInOut**: The effect is triggered at the start and the end of the transition.
- **easeNone**: No ease calculation is needed. Our example uses this method.

The final bit of code essentially says what happens when each of the buttons is pressed:

```
video1Button.onPress = function() {
    buttonTransition(_level0.vidcomp, 1);
};
```

The buttonTransition function is triggered by a button press; the FLVPlayback component is moved to the top of the stack on the main Timeline and is given the ID of 1.

```
49  function buttonTransition(m:MovieClip, d:Number) {
50      if (d != m.visibleVideoPlayerIndex) {
51          var other:MovieClip = m.getVideoPlayer(d);
52          m.bringVideoPlayerToFront(d);
53          var vp:MovieClip = other;
54          //this is a fade transition
55          TransitionManager.start(vp,{type:mx.transitions.Fade,
56                      direction:Transition.IN,
57                      duration:4,
58                      easing:mx.transitions.easing.None.easeNone,
59                      param1:empty,
60                      param2:empty});
61          vp.__transitionManager.addEventListener("allTransitionsInDone",transDone);
62      }
63  }
64
65  video1Button.onPress = function() {
66      buttonTransition(_level0.vidcomp, 1);
67  };
68
69  video2Button.onPress = function() {
70      buttonTransition(_level0.vidcomp, 2);
71  };
72
73  video3Button.onPress = function() {
74      buttonTransition(_level0.vidcomp, 3);
75  };
```

What You Have Learned

In this lesson you have:

- Used a Video object to contain a video (pages 290–292)
- Created NetConnection and NetStream objects to stream a video from a server (pages 292–295)
- Added controls to the Video object (pages 295–300)
- Used listeners to cue up sequential video playback (pages 301–308)
- Explored the TransitionManager class (pages 308–318)
- Added a fade transition to a video (pages 308–318)

9 Manipulating Video

The previous two lessons gave you a fairly solid grounding around the creation and use of video in Macromedia Flash Professional 8. This lesson builds upon what you have learned, but with a rather pleasant twist: You get to have fun with video.

One of the authors is rather fond of saying, "The amount of fun you can have with this application should be illegal." When it comes to video, the "fun" aspect should be regarded as a federal offense. For example, you learn how to use a video with an embedded alpha channel to create a series of rather interesting talking-head movies that use imaging, video—yes, you can now do video-on-video—and the filters in Flash Professional 8 to add a sense of playfulness to your work. You even create a video wall using a Web camera.

Along the way, you review how to add scripted cue points to a video that trigger events in Flash based upon where the playhead is located in the video. You learn how to mask video through a visit to Times Square in New York and even put yourself in the video through the use of a Web camera.

Let's have some fun.

Add cue points to an FLV and you can use one video to trigger events in a Flash movie...including playing other videos.

What You Will Learn

In this lesson you will:

- Create a FLV file containing an alpha channel
- Use the FLVPlayback component to play back a video containing an alpha channel
- Use cue points in a video to trigger events on the Flash Stage
- Use ActionScript to add cue points to a video
- Apply filters and blends to a video
- Connect a Web camera to a Flash movie
- Apply a video filter to a FLV file
- Apply advanced color effects to a video

Approximate Time

This lesson will require about 120 minutes to complete.

Lesson Files

Media Files:

betina.mov
betina.flv
Crockard.flv
tom1.flv
tom2.flv
crockard-low.flv

Starting Files:

Alpha.fla
Alpha2.fla.
CuePoint.fla
ScriptedCuePoints.fla
Effect.fla
StreetScene.fla
VideoOnVideo.fla

Completed Files:

Lesson09/Complete/Alpha.fla
Lesson09/Complete/Alpha2.fla
Lesson09/Complete/CuePoint.fla
Lesson09/Complete/ScriptedCuePoints.fla
Lesson09/Complete/Effect.fla
Lesson09/Complete/StreetScene.fla
Lesson09/Complete/VideoOnVideo.fla
Lesson09/Complete/VideoWall.fla

FLV Files and Video Alpha Channels

Prior to this release of Flash Professional 8, attempting to composite talking-head video over another video or even an image was a rather complicated procedure. If you have ever watched your local TV newscast and seen the meteorologist point out items of interest on a weather map, you have seen a talking-head video. The process of placing the meteorologist over the weather map is called *compositing* and what makes it all possible is the use of an alpha channel in a video.

An alpha channel in video is similar to a mask in Flash. Both hide areas of the screen and turn them transparent. In the case of video, this is usually accomplished by filming the subject against a blue or green backdrop in a studio and removing the background. This process is called *keying*, and is done in video compositing software such as Final Cut Pro (Mac) or Adobe AfterEffects 6.5 (Mac/PC). The final video is then output using the Animation (Millions) codec that retains the alpha channel embedded in the video.

Tip *Obviously, explaining how to key a background in a video is well out of the scope of this book. The software packages that allow you to do this have some excellent tutorials that walk you through this process.*

Tip *If you are incorporating video with an alpha channel into your Flash project, it is critical that you or your supplier create the video file using the Animation (Millions) codec. If the video uses a codec other than this one, the alpha channel will be lost.*

Note *The authors would like to thank Macromedia for permitting us to use the* betina.mov *file in this lesson and for making it available to you.*

1. Open the *Alpha.fla* file in your Lesson 9 folder.

In this exercise, you create a small movie in which a young woman walks across the screen and turns to look at the colored squares behind her. The purpose of this exercise is to simply make you familiar with an alpha channel and use it in Flash. As such, you embed the video directly into the SWF file. Although it was made clear in the previous lessons that this is not a best practice, it is quite useful for this particular task.

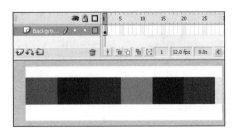

Tip *Embedding video into the SWF file is acceptable in situations in which the video length is small, such as 5 to 10 seconds. The issue is not playback but final file size and the Flash Timeline. Embedded video seriously increases the size of the SWF file, so there will be a significant wait for the SWF file to download. The other issue is the Timeline. Placing an embedded video on a Timeline increases the Timeline length to accommodate the video. If a video is set to play back at 30 frames per second (fps), it uses 30 frames on the main Timeline for each second of video. Considering that the maximum length of a Flash Timeline is about 13,000 frames, you can hit this limit rather easily when a video is embedded.*

2. Select File > Import > Import Video to open the Import Video dialog box.

The first screen asks you to locate the file to be imported. Click the Browse button and navigate to your Lesson 9 folder. Locate the file named betina.mov, select it, and click Open.

The path to the video appears in the dialog box. Click the Next button to open the Deployment screen. Select the Embed Video In SWF And Play In Timeline option and then click Next.

The Embedding screen that opens simply asks how you would like to embed the video into the movie. The first question—Symbol type—determines how the video appears in the library. Select Embedded video from the pop-down list. Select Place instance on stage to have the video placed on the Stage when it arrives in the library and then select Expand timeline if needed to have the Timeline expand to accommodate the frames in the video. You won't need to edit the video, so select Embed the entire video.

Click Next to open the Encoding screen.

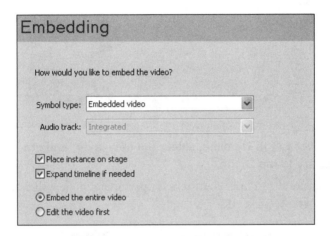

3. When the Encoding screen opens, click the Show Advanced Settings button.

This is the single most important screen in the entire process.

You can use an alpha channel only if you select the ON2VP6 codec and select Encode Alpha channel. Make the selections and click the Next button.

You are presented with a summary of your selections in the screen that appears. If you need to change anything at this point, click the Back button. If everything is OK, click the Finish button.

A dialog box appears, showing the progress of the encoding. When it finishes, the dialog box closes and the Betina video appears in your library.

The ON2VP6 codec and alpha channel encoding is restricted to use in Flash Player 8. If your Flash Player target is Flash Player, you will be restricted to using the Sorenson Spark codec and won't be able to encode the alpha channel.

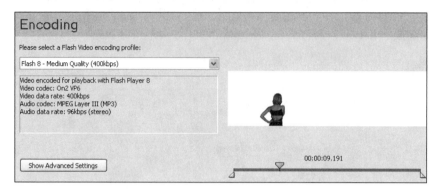

4. Add a new layer to the Timeline, select the new layer, and drag the *betina.mov* file from the library to the Stage.

As soon as you release the mouse, Flash asks for permission to lengthen the Timeline to accommodate the video. Click OK.

Scroll over to Frame 553 in the background layer and add a frame by selecting Insert > Timeline > Frame or by selecting the frame and pressing the F5 key.

5. Save the file to your Lesson 9 folder and test the movie.

Betina wanders across the screen and stops to contemplate the colored squares behind her.

Using the FLVPlayback Component

Knowing that you really shouldn't embed a video in a SWF file results in the following question: "So how do I do it?" The answer is simple: use the FLVPlayback component.

The advantage of using this component is that it automatically links to external content and pulls it into the SWF file upon playback. It is recommended the FLV file used by the component should be located in the same directory as the SWF file. This way the link between the component and the FLV file remain intact when you upload the file to your Web site.

1. Open the *Alpha2.fla* file located in your Lesson 9 folder.

When the file opens, add a new layer named video. Drag a copy of the FLVPlayback component from the FLVPlayback-Player 8 Components and place it in Frame 1 of the video layer.

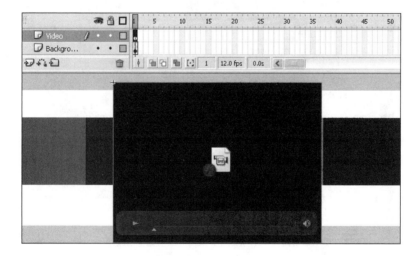

2. Select the component and select Window > Component inspector to open the Component inspector.

Double-click the contentPath value to open the Content Path dialog box. Click the Browse button and navigate to the betina.flv file located in your Lesson 9 folder. Select the Match source FLV dimensions radio button to ensure that the component expands to the dimensions of the FLV file.

Double-click the Skin value area to open the Skin dialog box. Select None from the Skin drop-down list and then click OK.

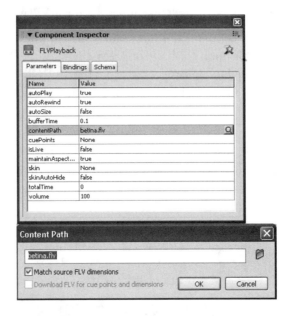

3. Close the Component Inspector, save the movie, and test it.

Tip	*When the FLVPlayback component is resized to accommodate a video it could, as in this example, expand to completely cover the Stage. The solution is to turn off the visibility of the component in the Timeline. Click the Show/Hide icon on the* video *layer, and the component will be hidden from view. If you test the movie with the component hidden, the video still plays.*

Tip	*You don't have to use a component to play the video. You can a video object along with* NetStream() *and* NetConnection() *to play the video.*

Using Cue Points in a Video to Trigger Events in Flash

When you regard video as a time-based medium, suddenly a whole word of possibility opens for you. In this exercise you use the Betina video in a rather interesting manner.

Notice that as she moves across the video, she stops to turn around and look at something. You can use the points where she does this to trigger such events as text on the Stage, an audio file or, in the case of this exercise, the playing of another video on the Stage. To create these triggers, you need to know the point in the video where she stops and turns and then add a cue point that ActionScript uses to start playing the video.

To find these points in the video, you use the QuickTime or Windows Media players to scrub through the video. As you learned in a previous lesson, *scrubbing* simply means to drag the playhead forward and backward through the video. When a point is identified, you need to write down the time when the event occurs. If you are looking for precise timing, you need to use a video editor such Final Cut Pro/Express or Motion (Mac), Adobe AfterEffects 6.5 (Mac/PC), or Adobe Premiere (PC). Video editors give you timing measured in milliseconds, ideal for close-captioning situations, whereas the players offer timing measured in seconds. Your choice depends upon your need for precision.

For this exercise, we used Final Cut Pro to identify our cue point times:

- **Cue Point 1**: 00:00:05.098
- **Cue Point 2**: 00:00:15.440
- **Cue Point 3**: 00:00:25.492

After you identify the cue points, they can be added in one of three ways:

- Using the FLVPlayback component
- Added to the FLV file when it is created
- Directly in ActionScript

The following two exercises explore these three options.

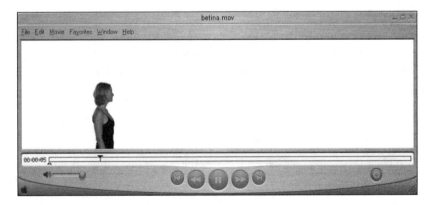

1. Open the *CuePoint.fla* file located in your Lesson 9 folder.

The interface has been constructed, and three video objects are located on the Stage. These objects start playing when Betina stops to look at them. The first is a very small one at the top of the Stage, just above the guy wearing the red shirt. The second video is located on the billboard with the graffiti, and the third one is located at the right edge of the Stage. Click the visibility icon for the walking girl layer. This makes the FLVPlayback component visible, and the Stage is covered by the component.

2. Select the FLVPlayback component on the Stage and click the Parameters tab in the Property inspector.

Double-click the Values area of the cuePoints item in the Parameters to open the Flash Video Cue Points dialog box.

Pay attention to the warning at the bottom of the dialog box: Event And Navigation Cue Points Are Not Editable. After the value is input, it is fixed in place and can't be changed. This is why it is so important to use accurate numbers. Cue points have three properties that are added in this dialog box. The have a name, a time, and a type—either Event or Disabled.

Click the plus sign (+) and in the Name area , enter Pause1.Click once in the time area and enter the location of the first cue point: 00:00:05.098. Select Event from the drop-down list. You need to add two more cue points. Click the plus sign to add a new cue point and enter the following:

- Pause2   00:00:15.440   Event
- Pause3   00:00:25.492   Event

Click OK to close the dialog box. When it closes the values just input appears in the component's parameters.

> **Tip** *Timing in video is quite precise. The values are hours:minutes:seconds:milliseconds. When precision is paramount, such as closed captions appearing or an animation or other event being triggered, milliseconds are the only unit of measurement you should be using.*

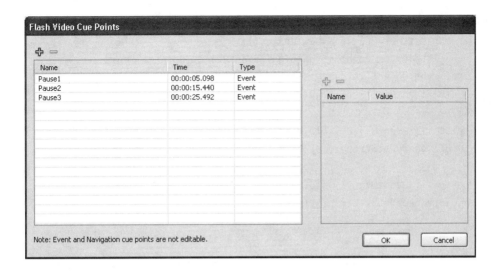

3. Turn off the visibility of the *walking girl* layer, select the first frame of the *actions* layer, and press F9 (PC) or Option-F9 (Mac) to open the Actions panel.

Part of the code has already been supplied. The first two lines create the `NetConnection()`, and lines 4,5, and 6 create a `NetStream` for each of the videos that play when triggered by a cue point.

Each of the videos will be placed in its own `NetStream` because only one video or audio file can play per stream. In the case of this exercise, each video plays when the cue point is reached. If they were not to have their own `NetStream`, the currently playing video would stop when the second video starts, and the second would stop when the third video starts.

```
1  var ourNetConnection:NetConnection = new NetConnection();
2  ourNetConnection.connect(null);
3
```

By attaching each video to its own `NetStream()`, they all play simultaneously.

Tip *Now that you know how to play multiple videos, approach this technique with a high degree of caution. The more videos that are playing, the bigger the hit on the bandwidth. The result is decreased performance. If you know your videos are small in dimension, adjust your data rate and dimensions as well to ease the burden on your bandwidth.*

4. Click once in Line 9 of the Script pane and enter the following code:

```
var ourListener:Object = new Object();
  ourListener.cuePoint = function( eventObject:Object ):Void {
  if( eventObject.info.name == "Pause1" ) {
    tomVideo1NetStream.play("tom1.flv");
  }
  else if( eventObject.info.name == "Pause2" ) {
    billboardNetStream.play("Crockard.flv");
  }
  else if( eventObject.info.name == "Pause3" ) {
    tomVideo2NetStream.play("tom2.flv");
  }
}
```

A cue point is an event. This code listens for the event, says what happens when the event is reached, and adds all this to an object called ourListener.

The if and else if conditional statements ensure that the videos are tied to a particular cue point. The use of == (Strict equality) ensures that the video plays only if a cue point named Pause1 is encountered. If a cue point named Pause 1 (note the space) is encountered, the cue point is ignored.

Each of the conditional statements looks first for a cue point, and if there is a match, streams the appropriate FLV file into the associated video object on the Stage. For example, the first statement looks for a cue point named Pause1. If it finds it, the tom1.flv file is streamed into the video object on the Stage with the instance name of tomVideo1.That object is the one at the top of the Stage that the cowboy is pointing to.

```
8  //————————Listeners Go Here————————————————————
9  var ourListener:Object = new Object();
10 ourListener.cuePoint = function( eventObject:Object ):Void {
11   if( eventObject.info.name == "Pause1" ) {
12     tomVideo1NetStream.play("tom1.flv");
13   }
14   else if( eventObject.info.name == "Pause2" ) {
15     billboardNetStream.play("Crockard.flv");
16   }
17   else if( eventObject.info.name == "Pause3" ) {
18     tomVideo2NetStream.play("tom2.flv");
19   }
20 }
```

5. Press Return/Enter and enter the following code:

```
walkingGirl.addEventListener( "cuePoint", ourListener );
billboardMovie.billboardVideo.attachVideo(billboardNetStream);
tomVideo1.attachVideo(tomVideo1NetStream);
tomVideo2.attachVideo(tomVideo2NetStream);
stop();
```

This code simply says that when a cue point is reached in the walkingGirl video, play the video associated with that cue point.

Click the Check Syntax button to make sure that you have not made any mistakes. Close the Actions panel.

```
22  walkingGirl.addEventListener( "cuePoint", ourListener );
23  billboardMovie.billboardVideo.attachVideo(billboardNetStream);
24  tomVideo1.attachVideo(tomVideo1NetStream);
25  tomVideo2.attachVideo(tomVideo2NetStream);
26  //——————————————————————————————————————
27  stop();
```

6. Save and test the movie.

As the girl walks across the screen, each of the videos starts to play based upon the cue point established in her video.

Adding Scripted Cue Points

In the previous exercise, the cue points were added using the FLVPlayback component. In this exercise, you add the cue points using ActionScript and then you add them when the FLV file is created.

Adding cue points in ActionScript uses the addASCuePoint() method. The arguments added to the method are the time and the name of the cue point. For example, to add the Pause1 cue point in ActionScript, you would enter the following:

```
walkingGirl.addASCuePoint( 5.098, "Pause1" );
```

1. Open the *ScriptedCuePoints.fla* file located in your Lesson 9 folder.

In this example, you still use the FLVPlayback component, but if you select the component on the Stage, the cue points are absent in the Parameters area of the Property inspector.

2. Select Frame 1 of the *actions* layer, open the Actions panel, and enter the following code into Line 25 in the Script pane:

```
walkingGirl.addASCuePoint( 5.098, "Pause1" );
walkingGirl.addASCuePoint( 15.440, "Pause2" );
walkingGirl.addASCuePoint( 25.492, "Pause3" );
```

The most interesting aspect of this code is that it is nothing more than an addition to the code entered in the previous exercise. In many respects those three lines are the code "written" by the component with cue points added in the component's parameters in the Property inspector..

```
24  // add Cue Points via actionscript
25  walkingGirl.addASCuePoint( 5.098, "Pause1" );
26  walkingGirl.addASCuePoint( 15.440, "Pause2" );
27  walkingGirl.addASCuePoint( 25.492, "Pause3" );
28
```

3. Save and test the movie.

The most important aspect of this SWF file is that there is no difference between this one and the one created in the previous exercise.

Adding Cue Points to a FLV File

The third method of adding cue points is to "hard-wire" them into the FLV file when it is created. Here's how:

1. Open the Flash 8 Video Encoder and import the *betina.mov* file located in your Lesson 9 folder.

When the video appears in the Encoder, click the Settings button to open the Flash Video Encoding Settings dialog box.

2. Click the Cue Points tab in the open dialog box.

The Cue Points area that opens is exactly the same as the one that opens when you add the cue points to the FLVPlayback component's parameters. The difference is the values can't be added directly into the dialog box.

Enter betinaCue into the Output filename text input box.

To add a cue point, drag the slider to the point in the video—somewhere between 4 and 5 seconds—and click the plus (+) sign in the Cue Points area. The time and the event will be added. Click the name and enter Pause1. Click inside the Cue Points area to accept the values.

Drag the preview slider to a point in the video between 15 and 16 seconds, click the + sign to add a new cue point, and name this one Pause2. Click inside the Cue Points area to accept the value and drag the preview slider to a point in the video between 25 and 26 seconds. Click the + sign again and name this one Pause3.

Click OK to close the Flash Video Encoding Settings dialog box.

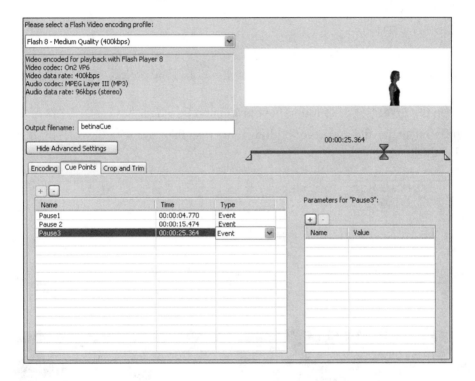

3. Click the Start Queue button to create the FLV file with embedded cue points.

Filters, Blends, and Flash Video

You have learned in previous lessons that filters and the blends are new to Flash Professional 8 and can be applied to text and movie clips. As you have discovered in this lesson, an alpha channel applied to a video functions in much the same manner as an alpha mask in Fireworks 8 or Photoshop CS2. The mask, in this case, follows the edges of the object, and anything outside of the mask's boundaries is essentially rendered transparent. Put those two concepts together and the creative possibilities in front of you are amazing.

In this exercise you will use the filters and blends to

- Apply a shadow behind the walking girl
- Give her a 3D look
- Turn her somewhat transparent
- Simulate the effect of having her stand in front of a slide projector

1. Open the *Effects.fla* file found in your Lesson 9 folder.

At the moment, the file consists of nothing more than the Stage with the colored squares used in the first exercise.

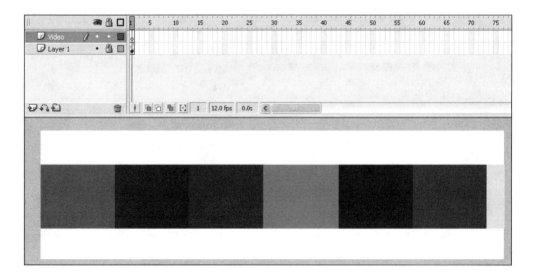

2. Select Insert › New Symbol.

When the New Symbol Dialog box opens, name the symbol **BetinaVid** and set the property to movie clip. Click OK to close the dialog box.

3. Double-click the BetinaVid symbol in the library to open the symbol editor.

Drag a copy of the FLVPlayback component to the Stage. Click the Parameters tab and use the following values:

- AutoPlay: True
- Skin: None.

4. Double-click the content path area to open the Content Path dialog box and navigate to the *betina.flv* file in your Lesson 9 folder.

Click the Match Source FLV dimensions box and click OK. The component will expand to match the dimensions of the FLV file linked to it. Select the component on the stage and set its *x* and *y* coordinates to 0 in the Property inspector.

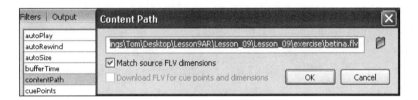

Click the Scene 1 link on the Timeline to return to the main Timeline.

5. Click once on the *video* layer and drag the BetinaVid symbol from the library to the Stage.

Set the *x* and *y* coordinates for the movie clip to 0,0 in the Property inspector.

This is the point where this technique gets rather interesting. If you were to simply drag a copy of the FLV component onto the Stage, the Property inspector would tell you the FLVPlayback component is a movie clip. It is and it isn't. Components, in very rudimentary terms, are movie clips that have a specific purpose and function quite a bit differently from traditional movie clips. As pointed out in Lesson 6, filters are applied to the "content" in a movie clip. This means even though the FLVPlayback component is in a movie clip named BetinaVid, the filter or the blend will be applied to the content of the movie clip which, in this case, is betina.flv.

In the case of a filter or a blend mode, the effect will be applied to the content inside the video's alpha channel.

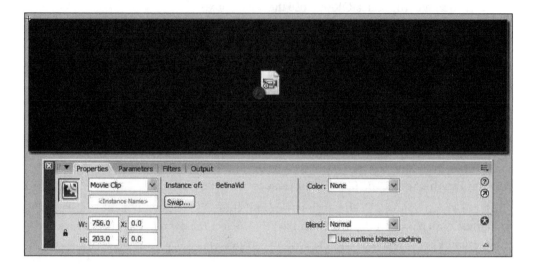

6. Select the movie clip on the Stage and click the Filters tab of the Property inspector.

Click the + sign and select Drop Shadow from the Filters menu. Use these settings:

- Blur X: 20
- Blur Y: 20
- Quality: High
- Distance: 10.

Save the movie and test it. She suddenly has a shadow that moves across the screen and matches her movement as she turns.

7. Close the SWF file. Select the movie clip on the Stage and select the Filters tab in the Property inspector.

Add the Bevel filter to the list. Use these Bevel filter settings:

- Blur X: 2
- Blur Y: 2
- Strength: 65%
- Quality: High
- Distance: 3

If you test the movie, the walking girl not only casts a shadow but also takes on a 3D appearance. Close the SWF file.

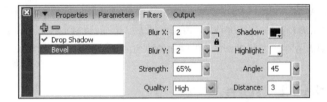

8. Select the movie clip on the Stage and click the properties tab to open the Property inspector.

Click the Filters tab, and click the minus (-) icon to remove the Drop Shadow and the Bevel from the movie clip.

With the movie clip still selected on the Stage, click the Properties tab and select Multiply from the Blend drop-down list. Test the movie. As Betina walks across the stage, the filter gives the effect of her walking in front of a projection of the colored squares behind her. The area of her body that appears over the square takes on the square's color while the area below the square remains unaffected.

Close the SWF file.

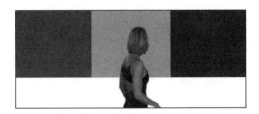

9. Change the blend effect from Multiply to Hard Light for the selected movie clip.

Click the Filters tab and apply a Drop Shadow filter. Test the movie. The effect is even more pronounced than that in the previous example.

10. Close the movie and don't save the changes.

Tip   *These techniques are pretty impressive. Don't forget, though, that you are dealing with video, and video does require bandwidth. The more effects and filters you load on, the bigger the bandwidth and CPU drain. If you do use these techniques, post the SWF file to a test site and have some people try them out for you.*

Other Video Filters

There will be occasions where the results of the FLV file conversion will be substandard. You can usually see this because the video appears to be pixilated. This effect is called *blocking* and is usually the result of a highly compressed video with a low data rate targeted at dial-up modems, for example.

The video deblocking filter can clean up the video but requires additional computing by Flash Player. You rarely have to apply deblocking to videos streamed through broadband because the data rate is high enough to maintain the integrity of the video.

New to Flash Professional 8 is a deranging filter that can be used only by the ON2VP6 codec. Ringing is similar to the effect you see in an overly compressed JPG image. There will be areas that lose their data and become a bright specular white color.

Removing deblocking uses the deblocking method found in the video class. The code that applies it is:

```
var myVideo :Video ;
myVideo.deblocking = value ;
```

The values are the following:

Auto deblocking:	0 (Let the Player determine the deblocking)
Deblocking off:	1 (Sorenson only)
Deblocking on:	2 (Sorenson only)
Deblocking and no deringing:	3 (ON2 only)
Deblocking and fast deranging:	4 (ON2 only)
Deblocking and better deranging:	5 (ON2 only)

If you have a video encoded using the Sorenson codec and you want to apply deblocking, the code would be as follows:

```
var myVideo :Video ;
myVideo.deblocking = 3;
```

To see how deblocking works, double-click the deblocking.fla file in your folder. The video that plays is highly compressed and has a low data rate. Let the video play for a few seconds, and you will see a bit of area in which the video is composed of blocks. Select an option from the menu, and you will see that the artifacts have somewhat disappeared.

Using Your Web Cam in Flash Professional 8

You have spent a lot of time creating and manipulating video for playback through Flash Player 8. There is another use for Flash Player: It can be used to control the input of audio and video while the move is playing. This is possible through two ActionScript classes that allow you to control the input and the output of streaming media: the Camera class and the Microphone class.

Even so, the use of a camera and a microphone is subject to Flash Player privacy policy. The user traditionally sets access to their microphone or camera in the Flash Player

Settings dialog box. This dialog box is accessed by a right-click (PC) or Control-click (Mac) on a SWF file and selecting Settings from the context menu.

The first item is the Privacy tab. It will ask for permission to access the microphone or the camera. You can choose to allow or deny the access, and you can even choose to remember your selection.

Privacy tab —

The next item is the Microphone tab. The user can choose which microphone to use, adjust the volume of the recording, suppress echo, and adjust the gain.

The final setting is the camera. Here, the user can choose which camera to use from the drop-down list.

Tip *Though DV cameras can be used they can be quite inconsistent in whether they play through the Flash Player or not. The most reliable cameras are Web cams such as a Logitech ball camera or an Apple iSight.*

After the permissions are in place, you can attach a camera to your computer and feed the video into the SWF file. This occurs through the use of the Camera class, which references the USB/Firewire cameras attached to your computer. You can also use the Camera class to control the encoder settings and the camera settings. The ActionScript syntax for referencing a camera is as follows:

```
var myCamera:Camera = Camera.get().
```

Tip *The Apple iSight is probably the coolest Webcam on the market today. Just be aware that the driver for this camera is Macintosh only and won't work on a PC.*

Tip *If you do have an iSight camera attached to your Mac, don't choose Apple iSight from the camera list. The quality of this selection is unacceptable. Instead, choose IIDC FireWire Video. This generic camera driver provides excellent quality.*

1. Open *StreetScene.fla* in your **Lesson 9** folder.

In this exercise, you will have your camera feed its signal into the three video objects in the video layer.

2. Turn off the visibility of the actions and framer layers.

You will see three images on the Stage; two of the images on the right have a video object placed over them.

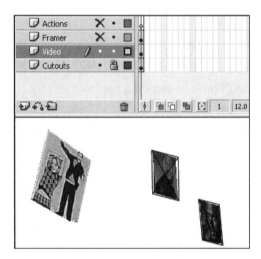

Drag a copy of the myVideo object to the Stage and align its lower-right corner with the lover-right corner of the image on the left. Select the Free Transform tool and move the center point, the white dot, to the lower-right corner of the video object. Rotate the select to match the image below it. Using the Free Transform tool's Scale and Skew tools to manipulate the shape of the video object to roughly match that of the image.

When you finish, select the Video object on the Stage and give it the instance name of myVid in the Property inspector. Turn on the visibility of the hidden layers.

Tip *Use the Zoom tool for precision, but just be aware that the best you can do is to approximate the shape. The interesting aspect of this is that an approximation does half of the job; your eyes will do the rest. The video will appear to take on the shape of the object because your eye will see the illusion.*

3. Select the first frame in the *actions* layer and press F9 (PC) or Option-F9 (Mac) to open the Actions editor. Enter the following:

```
var myCamera:Camera = Camera.get();
myVid.attachVideo(myCamera);
myVid2.attachVideo(myCamera);
myVid3.attachVideo(myCamera);
```

The second line of the code is the most important.

The first line of code creates the Camera object, gives it a name, and tells Flash to go get the video signal. The second line tells Flash to feed that video signal (attachVideo) into the Video object (myVid) on the Stage.

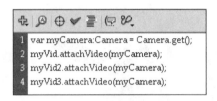

4. Click the Check Syntax button and if there are no mistakes, close the Actions panel and save and test the movie.

Wave to the people passing by on the street below.

Tip *To answer the obvious question, yes you can use the feed from a video camera attached to your computer and feed it–live–to the Web. This is done using the publish() method. The actual mechanics of doing this are out of the scope of this book.*

Playing Video on Video

As you saw in the cue points exercises, the ability to use video containing an alpha channel allows you play a video over a video. In this exercise, you return to Times Square and play a video over a video without the use of cue points.

1. Open the *VideoOnVideo.fla* file in the Lesson 9 folder.

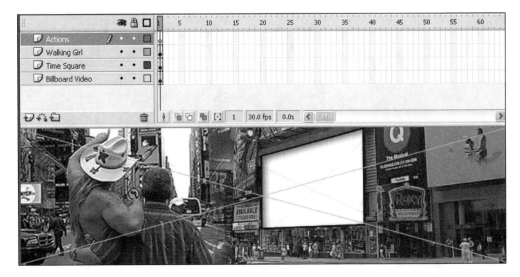

Pay attention to the two video objects on the Stage. One, the Girl video object from the library is above the Stage, and the other, Billboard Movie, is behind the image and carefully placed so it shows through the billboard.

The reason we placed the Billboard Movie under everything is to let the image frame the video. Although we could have just as easily placed the video object over the image, it would have been extremely difficult, thanks to the limitations of the Free Transform tool, to have that object precisely fit the perspective of the area into which it is being placed. By putting the video under the image, the "hole," it plays through acts as a sort of frame, and the video will take on the perspective angles in the hole in the image.

Tip *When preparing images for this technique, use a PNG image. This format allows you to bring images and their transparency into Flash Professional 8.*

2. Select the first frame in the actions layer, open the Actions panel, and enter the following:

```
var walkingGirl:Video;

var ourNetConnection:NetConnection = new NetConnection();

ourNetConnection.connect(null);
var walkingGirlNetStream:NetStream = new NetStream(ourNetConnection);
var billboardNetStream:NetStream = new NetStream(ourNetConnection);

walkingGirl.attachVideo(walkingGirlNetStream);
billboardMovie.billboardVideo.attachVideo(billboardNetStream);

billboardNetStream.play("Crockard.flv");
walkingGirlNetStream.play("betina.flv");
stop();
```

This code is no different from any of the code you have been using in this and the previous two lessons.

```
1   var walkingGirl:Video;
2
3   var ourNetConnection:NetConnection = new NetConnection();
4
5   ourNetConnection.connect(null);
6   var walkingGirlNetStream:NetStream = new NetStream(ourNetConnection);
7   var billboardNetStream:NetStream = new NetStream(ourNetConnection);
8
9   walkingGirl.attachVideo(walkingGirlNetStream);
10  billboardMovie.billboardVideo.attachVideo(billboardNetStream);
11
12  billboardNetStream.play("Crockard.flv");
13  walkingGirlNetStream.play("betina.flv");
14  stop();
```

The video object walkingGirl is created and the NetConnection() and NetStream() objects are created to accommodate the video streams. The streams are attached to their specific video objects, and the video associated with the object starts to play.

3. Save and test the movie.

The girl appears to stop and watch the guys on the bikes on the video screen.

Fun with the Flash Camera Object: A Video Wall

A very good friend of ours is Brendan Dawes, out of Manchester, England. We share a passion with Brendan which is "shredding the status quo" and for exploring the use of video in Flash.

A couple of years ago, Brendan posted a tutorial called Proximity Engine to his site (http://www.brendandawes.com/headshop/) that built upon a concept first developed by another friend of ours, Colin Moock. Brendan created a small Flash movie that scales an image and changes its opacity based on the closeness (Proximity) of the cursor to the object. Roll the cursor closer, and the object grows and its opacity increases to 100 percent. Move it away, and the object shrinks and fades.

We looked at it and thought, "That is really neat. What if we were to apply the same technique to live video from a Webcam instead of static images?" The result is a video wall.

Tip *This project uses multiple instances of the video feed. It is best run locally from your hard disk rather than through a browser.*

The exercise is actually rather uncomplicated. You need only the following:

- An embedded video
- A movie clip containing the embedded video
- Another movie clip containing the Proximity Engine

Preparing the Assets

This project will require a bit of computing power, so it is best to consider working with a small Stage size.

1. Open a new document in Flash 8. In the Property inspector, set the Stage size to 200 pixels wide by 150 pixels high. Set the Background color to black (#000000).

2. Open the library by pressing Ctrl+L (PC) or Cmd+L (Mac) and selecting New Video from the Library drop-down list. The Embedded Video symbol appears in your library.

The Embedded Video symbol is rather important. Adding this to a project tells Flash where to place the video stream from the camera connected to the computer. When you add the video , the Video properties dialog box will open and ask you whether the video is to be embedded in the timeline or controlled by ActionScript. Select the ActionScript option because you will use code to control it.

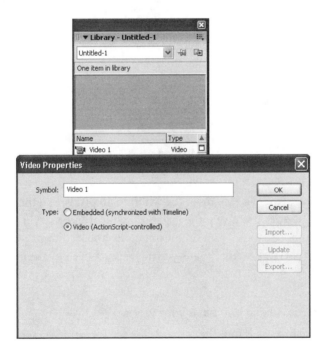

Having something to hold the video stream is important, but there really isn't much you can do with it. The only property of the object you can "play with" is its dimensions. This is where the power of the Flash movie clip becomes important. Movie clips are separate objects, and best of all, they have a load of properties that can be changed.

Tip *Although you will be using a video camera in this exercise, it works equally as well if you attach a FLV file to the video object.*

3. Create a new movie clip. When the New Symbol dialog box opens, name the symbol Vid and select Movie Clip as its property. Click OK.

The symbol appears in your library.

4. Double-click the Vid symbol in your Library to open the movie clip's Timeline.

Add two layers; the movie clip now has three layers. Starting at the top and working down, double-click each layer's name and enter the following layer names:

- engine
- actions
- video

5. Drag the Embedded Video symbol onto the *video* layer.

With the Embedded Symbol selected, set the width to 40 pixels, and the height to 30 pixels in the Property inspector. Also give it the instance name of "my_vid" in the Property inspector. The size chosen wasn't random: It maintains the traditional 4:3 aspect ratio of video. The name is also important because it will be referenced by the camera object you create later.

6. Close the Vid movie clip and save your work.

The next step in the process is to write the code for the Proximity Engine.

> **Note** *The code we are about to present was written by Brendan Dawes and is freely available if you download the Proximity source files from his site. Although many people think, "code is code," nothing is further from the truth. It is common courtesy to acknowledge the source, and Brendan does the same thing for Colin. The change we have made is to increase the scale value in the original code and to remove an unnecessary "debug" comment.*

7. Create a new movie clip named Engine.

Select Frame 1, press F9 to open the ActionScript Editor, and enter the following code:

```
var deltaX: Number = Math.round(_root._xmouse - _parent._x);
var deltaY: Number = Math.round(_root._ymouse - _parent._y);
var diff: Number  = Math.round(Math.sqrt((deltaX * deltaX) + (deltaY *
    deltaY)));

if (diff > 80) {
diff = 80;
};

// change alpha
_parent._alpha = (100 - diff);

// change scale
_parent._xscale = (150 - diff);
_parent._yscale = (150 - diff);
```

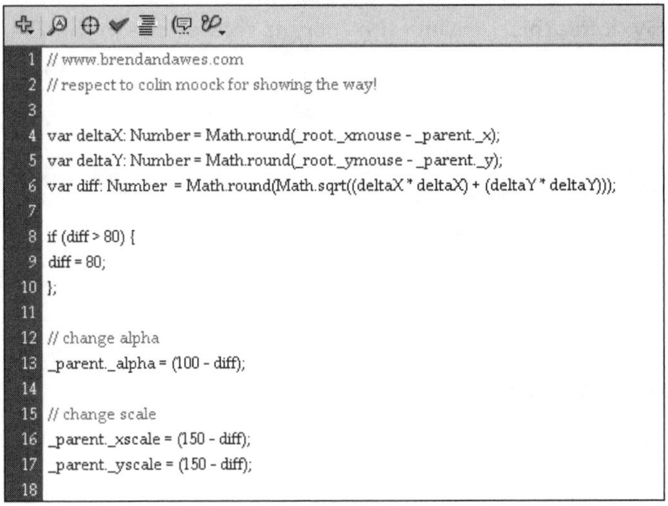

The code is broken into four distinct chunks. The first chunk determines the distance in pixels (deltaX,deltaY), between the mouse (_xmouse, _ymouse) and the Vid movie clip (_parent ._x , _parent._y) to which the engine is attached. These two values are then added together and multiplied and the square root of that value is determined. That number, if it contains decimal places, is rounded and given the name diff. This value drives the entire engine.

The next chunk basically keeps the value of `diff` to one that is manageable. In this case, the number is 80.

The third chunk sets the alpha (opacity) value of the Vid movie clip (_parent). If, for example, the cursor is a long way away from the clip, its alpha will be 20 percent (100 minus 80).

The last chunk sets the scale value for the Vid movie clip. If the cursor is, for example, 20 pixels away from the Video movie clip (`diff=20`) it will be scaled up to 130 percent, and its opacity will be increased to 80 percent.

The neat thing about this code is that all the instances of the Vid movie clip on the Stage will be reacting to the cursor's position. Those closest to the cursor will get larger and less opaque, and those further away will fade and get smaller.

Add a keyframe to Frame 2 of the Engine movie clip and add the following code in the ActionScript editor:

```
gotoAndPlay(1);
```

With the creation of the Vid and Engine movie clips, you can now begin to pull it all together.

8. **Open the Vid movie clip and drag an instance of the Engine movie clip into the *engine* layer. By doing this, you link the *_parent* references in the Engine code to the Vid movie clip.**

Click once in Frame 1 of the `actions` layer, open the Actions panel, and enter the following code to create the Camera object:

```
var my_cam:Camera = Camera.get();
my_vid.attachVideo(my_cam);
```

Click once on the Scene 1 link at the top of the Stage to return to the main Timeline and save your work.

Pulling It All Together

Having created the key movie clip, the time has arrived to assemble the video wall.

1. **Drag an instance of the Vid movie clip onto the Stage. Set its *x* and *y* coordinates to 0,0 in the Property Inspector.**

With the Option/Alt and Shift keys pressed, drag a copy of the instance to the right and snug the copy up against the first one. The position should be 40,0. Repeat this three more times until you have a row of five instances across the top of the Stage.

2. Select the entire top row of instances, press Option/Alt and Shift, and drag a copy of the row down until it sits snugly under the first row.

The position should be 0,30. Repeat this three more times until you have five rows of instances on the Stage.

3. Save the file, connect a Web camera, and test the file.

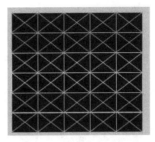

If you tested the project, you saw that the various objects change shape and opacity as you move the mouse around the screen. The cornerstone of this project is a movie clip. The great thing about movie clips is that they all have a number of properties that you can play with. This means you can dial up the cool factor with little or no extra effort.

4. Hold down Shift and click on each of the instances in the top row.

Select Advanced in the Color settings of the Property inspector and click the Settings button to open the Advanced Effect dialog box.

Each of the controls allows you to manage the saturation and hue of one of the colors as well as the selection's alpha. Set the red channel value to 100 percent and the green and blue values to 0 percent.

Select the instances in each of the remaining rows and play with their Advanced Effects as well.

Tip *You can apply the Advanced Effect controls to any movie clip on the Stage.*

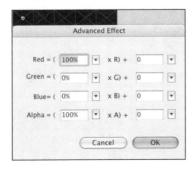

5. Save the movie and test it.

This exercise is a classic example of using the work of others to create your own variations of the technique. The Flash community is quite open with each other about sharing code, techniques, and examples. The unwritten rule is that the source should be acknowledged.

The other aspect of this exercise is a great lesson in how Flash techniques are developed. Colin Moock wonders what would happen when objects are in proximity to each other. Brendan Dawes wonders how that idea can be applied to images and we build upon the work of Brendan and Colin to apply the technique to create a video wall.

Tip If you want to have more fun with this technique, add a Microphone object to the project and tie the size of the video object to the gain level from the microphone.

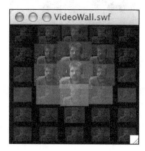

What You Have Learned

In this lesson you have:

- Created an FLV file containing an alpha channel (pages 321–326)
- Created a movie that uses cue points in a video to trigger events on the Flash Stage (pages 326–333)
- Applied a Flash filter effect to a video containing an alpha channel (pages 334–339)
- Created a movie that uses input from your Web camera (pages 339–344)
- Created a video-on-video effect (pages 345–346)
- Created a video wall that uses the Advanced Color effects (pages 346–352)

10 Communication Server: Audio and Video

In Lessons 7, 8, and 9 you learned how to create a video and have it play through a Web server using a progressive download. This lesson introduces you to the other method of delivering audio and video through Macromedia Flash Professional 8: streaming through Macromedia's Flash Communication Server MX, or (as it has become known in the developer community) *FlashComm Server*. When Flash Player 7 allowed for the reliable playback of longer video, and companies started realizing they could make extensive use of video on their sites, FlashComm Server moved from "curiosity" to "necessity" in a very short order.

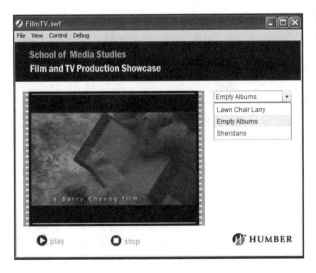

Using components and the Flash Communication Server, you can create "on demand" video experiences.

FlashComm Server is a real-time communication server that delivers audio and video to a Flash SWF file embedded in a Web page. The fundamental difference between a video delivered through FlashComm Server and one delivered from your Web server is that "Play means play." When video or audio is played back from a Web server, there is a slight delay while the SWF file loads up enough information to start playing the file. With FlashComm Server, there is no delay. The media—audio or video—starts playing immediately.

This lesson moves slowly through using FlashComm Server. You start with a rather simple streaming video—Lawn Chair Larry—that shows you how to prepare a Flash Professional 8 movie to stream through FlashComm Server and finishes with a rather interesting project: an MP3 player that can be added to a Web site.

To get started, you need to download and install the server onto your computer. A free trial is available at www.macromedia.com/cfusion/tdrc/index.cfm?product=flashcom. The other alternative is to actually purchase a FlashComm Server account from a service provider in your local area... or elsewhere. The beauty of the server is there is no need for it to be physically located where you live. As you learn in the following exercises, all you need to do is to point Flash to your FlashComm Server account, and Flash Player does the rest.

What You Will Learn

In this lesson you will:

- Tour the FlashComm Server
- Create a simple streaming video application
- Write the ASC file that is the link between the FlashComm Server and your SWF file
- Write the ActionScript that plays media located on your computer or through a remote FlashComm Server
- Control and play multiple videos from FlashComm Server
- Create an MP3 player to stream audio files from FlashComm Server

Approximate Time

This lesson will require about 120 minutes to complete.

Lesson Files

Media Files:

EmptyAlbums.flv
LawnChairLaryy.flv
Sheridans.flv
AppleSauce.mp3
DistantStorm.mp3
funkbeat.mp3

Starting Files:

FilmTV.fla
Larry.fla

Completed Files:

Lesson10/Complete/FilmTV.fla
Lesson10/Complete/Larry.fla
Lesson10/Complete/mp3.fla

Overview of the Flash Communication Server

As you move into the realm of rich media applications, you will inevitably bump up against the FlashComm Server. This relatively unheralded piece of Macromedia software allows you to put the "rich" in rich media. When you encounter sites that use lots of video and audio, the odds are good that you are seeing the FlashComm Server doing what it does best: providing video and audio content immediately and on demand.

If you have never used FlashComm Server, it is understandable to first regard it as a rather mysterious piece of software that can be rather intimidating. Toss into the mix the fact that Flash Professional 8 is the "tool of choice," and is it any wonder the average developer takes a look at those sites and says, "Whoa, dude. No way I can do that." Says who? It isn't difficult, nor is it mysterious. In fact, if you can input one line of code, you will be "good to go" sooner than you think.

Still, before you use the FlashComm Server, it is important that you understand how the tool works. In this exercise, you explore the major features of FlashComm Server.

The FlashComm Server is different from an ordinary Web server. This is important because the most common error made when first approaching its use is to think of it as just another Web server. It isn't. The purpose of FlashComm Server is, in very basic terms, to feed rich media content such as audio and video into a SWF file embedded in a Web page. Where a Web page uses the HTTP protocol to build the page, Flash SWF files sitting on that page connect to the FlashComm content on the FlashComm Server through Flash Player 8, using the *Real Time Messaging Protocol* (RTMP). RTMP is a bidirectional—Flash Player to FlashComm Server back to Flash Player—communication protocol. In many respects, think of FlashComm Server as being a hub. Flash Player connects to that hub using RTMP. What RTMP doesn't do is interact with HTTP. It interacts with Flash SWF files.

FlashComm Server uses its own ports when installed. For example, most Web servers run through ports 80, 81, and 8080, which are set up on a PC using the IIS Manager. FlashComm Server uses two default ports:

- **Admin (Port 1111):** This port is used by the FlashComm Server management consoles to monitor and control the server. This is why, if you want to access the FlashComm Server Management Console, you are asked for a username and password.
- **Server (Port 1935):** This is the port used by the FlashComm Server management consoles to maintain the communication link with Flash Player and other FlashComm Servers.

Finally, even the placement of files is different. In this lesson, you construct a number of projects, and their directories are located in two different locations. The FlashComm Server directory is located in the Macromedia program group and in Inetpub because the HTTP page will be run through Port 80 (Inetpub), but the files providing the communication with the SWF file in that HTTP page is located in the FlashComm Server applications folder running through Port 1935 (the Server default). This distinction is critical and becomes extremely important when the files are ready for upload to the Web.

Getting Started

Obviously, you need a local copy of the FlashComm Server. If you have taken advantage of the download, you should be aware that the FlashComm Server continues to function beyond the 30-day limit, provided that you installed a Developer Edition. The only major difference between the Developer Edition and the full commercial version, apart from the fact it is installed to your computer, is a reduced bandwidth allowance and the number of connections that can be made at any one time is limited. If you do download and install the FlashComm Server, also download the Updater 2, which you can obtain at www.macromedia.com/software/flashcom/.

After you have completed the installation, you need the Flash Communication Components, which are installed when you install the Flash Communication Server 1.5. If you don't have them, they can be downloaded from http://www.macromedia.com/support/flashcom/downloads_updaters.html. That is the good news. The bad news is they need to be updated to work with the FlashComm Server 1.5 and Flash Player 8. The updater is available at www.macromedia.com/software/flashcom/.

What we don't intend to do in this exercise is to get into the nitty-gritty details of actually using the FlashComm Server. You simply need to have it installed locally and running. We'll deal with using a remote FlashComm Server later in this lesson.

Tip *If you have the CommunicationComponents installed and updated in Flash MX Professional 2004, they can be used in Flash Professional 8. Locate the CommunicationComponents directory in C:\Program Files\Macromedia\Flash MX 2004\en\Configuration\Components\CommunicationComponents. Select the folder and copy it to C:\Program Files\Macromedia\Flash 8\en\Configuration\Components. When you launch Flash Professional 8, the Components appear in the library.*

Before you start in on the exercises, it is important you understand that working with FlashComm Server is quite a bit different from working locally—from using, for example, the Inetpub folder on a PC. When you install the Flash Communication Server, there are actually two paths created. One goes directly to FlashComm Server, and the other is to your Web server such as IIS or Apache. Both create a folder called applications, and it is important that you understand what files go where.

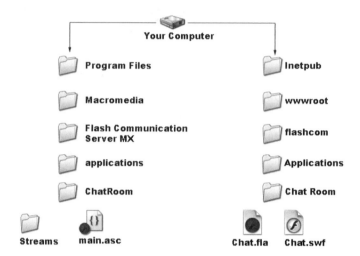

Notice that the FLA and SWF files you create sit in the Inetpub folder. You can also use this folder to hold any HTML pages you may create.

The files that make the application work—main.asc and a streams folder—are located in the FlashComm Server folder. This is fundamentally different from working with a regular HTML page that sits in the Inetpub folder. In this case, all the assets needed to run the HTML page are located in one place. In the case of a FlashComm Server application, the HTML files are located in Inetpub, but the server-side ActionScript that runs the Flash app in the Web page is located inside the applications directory of the Flash Communication Server. The folder that you place in this directory automatically creates the application.

The file that makes communication happen is an ActionScript Communication, (ASC) file, which can be created in Dreamweaver 8, Flash Professional 8, or even Notepad. When this file is created, it must be saved to the applications folder located in the FlashComm Server directory. The ASC file is server-side ActionScript and is based on the same ECMA standard as ActionScript. If you will use FlashComm Server to stream a FLV file, the FLV file would be placed in the streams folder.

Turning the FlashComm Server On and Off

When you install FlashComm Server, the server is always on and contentedly runs in the background. Although the FlashComm Server usually starts automatically when you start the computer, there will be the odd time, especially in the Windows environment, when the service fails to start. When this happens, perform the following steps.

1. Select Start > All Programs > Macromedia > Flash Communication Server MX.

The sub-menu that opens contains two menu items: Start Server and Stop Server. If you click the Start Server item, the Console briefly opens, starts up the server, and then closes. If you select the Stop Server item, you are asked if you really want to do this and if you want to shut down the Administration Console at the same time.

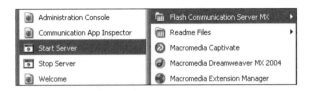

Assuming that everything went well, the FlashComm Server is installed and running. This would be a good time to visit the FlashComm Server Administration Console.

2. Select Start > All Programs > Macromedia > Flash Communication Server MX > Administration Console.

When the Administration Console opens. you are asked to log in. Enter the user name and password you set when you installed FlashComm Server. If you installed FlashComm Server on your computer, leave the host field at localhost. Click the Connect button. If everything has gone to plan, the connection light in the upper-right corner changes from red or orange to green, and the Administration Console then opens.

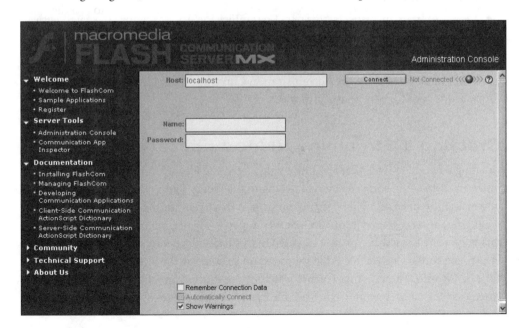

The Administration Console's purpose is to simply help you manage and monitor the server. When you log in, you enter as the Server Administrator. Note there are five tabs for various tasks and that the connection light is green. If you click the Ping button, you ask the server if it is in a responsive state. The server responds back with an acknowledgement. The time it takes between the request being made and the response is shown. A slow connection time, around 100 ms, might result in poor server performance, which usually is a symptom of a slow or congested network or server processor speed.

Along the top of the Console are a series of tabs, including the following:

- **Diagnostic:** This panel tells you how long the server has been running. Clicking the Ping button gives you an idea of performance. Clicking the Update button displays the history and current state of each application that has been loaded or unloaded.

- **Maintenance:** This area is designed to manage application instances, virtual hosts (Vhosts), and the server. For example, you can stop, pause, or restart the server by clicking the appropriate button.

- **Admin Users:** This is the area in which users and their access privileges are created and set.

- **Live Log:** This is available only if you are logged onto the server as an Administrator. The purpose of this panel is to watch connections, disconnections, and system errors that might occur. If FlashComm Server is installed on your local machine, you will rarely visit this panel.

- **License:** In many respects, this panel resembles the About menus associated with software applications. You see information such as the server version, license, and product being used.

Click the close box to close the Administration Console. Closing the Administration Console does not turn the FlashComm Server off.

Creating a Streaming Video Application

Creating a Flash SWF file that streams a video from the FlashComm Server is quite a bit different from using your Web server to stream the video. The SWF file and the HTML file in which it is embedded will be sitting on your Web server, but the video will be located on a different server: the FlashComm Server. A good way of understanding this is to visit this book's site to view the projects created in this lesson. When you open the page, the HTML file containing the SWF file is located on a server by the airport on the western edge of Toronto. The FLV files you are watching are located on a FlashComm Server in the Northeast corner of Toronto. The SWF file by the airport makes a "call" to the server on the other side of the city to play the video, and it happens instantly. When you work on your computer, it is the same process, but shorter distances. The HTML file and the SWF file are sitting in one directory, such as Inetpub, for example, whereas the FLV file is sitting in another directory within the FlashComm Server.

When you work with FlashComm Server you must keep in mind that there is a set path to the media. The path follows this syntax: `rtmp:/server/application/instance/ /` for a localhost (your computer) type call and `rtmp://server/application/instance/` for a remote call.

The `server` is the RTMP address that is usually expressed; for example, as a series of numbers such as 123.45.678.90 if you have an account or as `localhost` if you are working only on your computer. The application is the name of the folder where the files are stored on the FlashComm Server, and the instance is the name of the folder (inside the applications folder) containing the media files being streamed. It is becoming an increasingly common practice to name this folder __definst_. In the case of the example, the path to the video file would be `rtmp:/123.45.678.90/LawnchairLarry/_definst_`.

Where it gets a little complicated is that inside the application folder is another folder named streams, which is the __definst_ folder in which the audio and video files are located. You don't need to add this folder to the path because FlashComm Server knows to look for this folder when serving the files.

> **Tip** *RTMP is how data and messages are passed from the Flash Player 8 to the FlashComm Server. If you are using a FlashComm Server that is not installed locally you have to enter a hostname, IP address, or the machine name of the server being used. In this case there is a slight change: it is `rtmp://localhost/LawnChairLarry/_definst_`. Note the two forward slashes.*

1. Create a new folder named LawnchairLarry in the applications folder of the Flash Communication Server on your computer.

Create another folder named streams inside this folder and another named _definst_ inside the streams folder. Copy the `LawnChairLarry.flv` file from your Lesson 10 folder to the _definst_ folder. The video can be found in the FLV_files folder.

With the media in place, you can now turn your attention to the file that is the communicator between your SWF file and the FlashComm Server. This file uses the .asc extension.

2. Open Notepad and enter the following text:

```
load( "components.asc" );
application.onConnect = function( newClient, newUserName, test ) {
  gFrameworkFC.getClientGlobals(newClient).username =newUserName;
// set the user name for any UI component we may have
  application.acceptConnection(newClient);
// unconditionally accept our connection

  trace( "Hello: " + newUserName );
}
```

Save the file as main.asc and save it to the LawnchairLarry folder in the FlashComm Server applications directory on your computer.

The ASC file is a Flash ActionScript Communication file and (in very simple terms) is the ActionScript necessary to connect the SWF file and any components in the SWF file to the FLV file located in the streams folder. An ASC file can also load other ASC files. When working with FlashComm Server, there always has to be an ASC file and it must be in the applications directory.

The first line of code is standard for practically every ASC file you create. All it does is load any components that may be used in the application.

The function that follows, in many respects, is an insurance policy to ensure that you connect to the server. The first line inside the function gives the connection a name and allows the SWF file to connect to the server. The second line unconditionally accepts the connection between the SWF file and FlashComm Server. When the connection is made, it lets you know with a message to the Output panel in the Property inspector.

Although you can get away with only the first line of code, adding this function ensures that the connection to FlashComm Server is made.

> **Tip** You don't have to use a text editor to create an ASC file; it can be created in Dreamweaver 8 and in Flash Professional 8. When using Flash, select File > New, click the General tab, and select ActionScript Communication file in the New Document Dialog box. When you make the selection, the Script pane in the ActionScript panel opens.

> **Tip** If you want to edit an ASC file, simply double-click the file to open it in the ActionScript editor of Flash Professional 8.

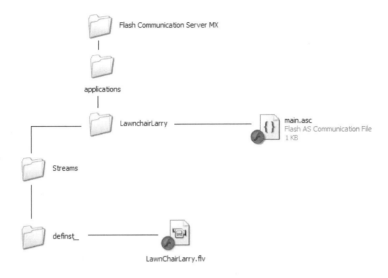

Flash Communication Server MX

applications

LawnchairLarry — main.asc
Flash AS Communication File
1 KB

Streams

definst_

LawnChairLarry.flv

3. Open the *Larry.fla* file located in your Lesson 10 folder.

This file requires you to add the actions that connect the SWF file to FlashComm Server.

This interface is fairly basic. The video plays in the video object named myVideo, and is controlled by the playButton and pauseButton buttons in the buttons layer. The interface is nothing more than a PNG file created in Fireworks 8.

Tip *Fireworks 8 is an amazing image editing and creation tool for Flash. Although you can follow standard operating procedure and import your Fireworks 8 documents into Flash using File > Import, a less convoluted route is to simply drag and drop the image from Fireworks 8 into Flash Professional 8.*

4. Select the actions layer and then press F9 to open the ActionScript Editor. Click once in the Script pane, and enter the following code:

```
var myVideo:Video;
var playButton:Button;
var pauseButton:Button;
var myNetConnection:NetConnection = new NetConnection();
```

The variables are all created and a new NetConnection is established.

5. Press Return/Enter and enter the following code:

```
myNetConnection.connect("rtmp://localhost/LawnChairLarry/_definst_");
```

This single line of code makes it all work. The FlashComm Server application is attached to the `NetConnection` using the `connect()` method.

The code is designed to work locally and you should note how it follows the `server/application/instance` syntax. You don't need to add the FLV file to the path because the `connect()` method is simply telling your SWF file which application and instance to connect to.

If you are connecting to a FlashComm Server account located at an ISP, the syntax would be slightly different:

```
myNetConnection.connect("rtmp:/123.45.678.90/LawnChairLarry/_definst_");
```

You need only a single forward slash (/) after `rtmp:`. And instead of `localhost`, you enter the IP address of the FlashComm Server. This address is supplied by the ISP when you arrange your FlashComm Server account.

The rest of the code simply attaches the video to the `myVideo` instance and establishes what the buttons do.

6. Press Return/Enter and enter the following code:

```
var myNetStream:NetStream = new NetStream(myNetConnection);
myVideo.attachVideo(myNetStream);
myNetStream.play("LawnChairLarry");

playButton.onPress = function() {
  myNetStream.pause(false);
}

pauseButton.onPress= function() {
  myNetStream.pause(true);
}
```

Click the Check Syntax button to ensure that there are no errors. If there are none, close the ActionScript editor.

```
 1  var myVideo:Video;
 2  var playButton:Button;
 3  var pauseButton:Button;
 4
 5  var myNetConnection:NetConnection = new NetConnection();
 6
 7  myNetConnection.connect("rtmp://localhost/LawnChairLarry/_definst_");
 8
 9  var myNetStream:NetStream = new NetStream(myNetConnection);
10  myVideo.attachVideo(myNetStream);
11  myNetStream.play("LawnChairLarry");
12
13  playButton.onPress = function() {
14      myNetStream.pause(false);
15  }
16
17  pauseButton.onPress= function() {
18      myNetStream.pause(true);
19  }
```

7. Save the file and then test it by pressing Ctrl+Enter (PC) or Cmd+Return (Mac).

The movie starts to play, and the Pause and Play buttons allow you to stop and start the video.

Controlling and Playing Multiple Movies with FlashComm Server

Now that you know how to get a single video to play, the next step is to allow the user to choose from a list of videos. When the user selects the video from the list, the video is immediately loaded and starts to play.

In this exercise, you construct a small showcase application for the film and television production students at the college at which one of the authors is an instructor. The faculty are somewhat new to showcasing student work on the Web and need to see how it could be done. This exercise is a Proof of Concept that shows them how they can use the Web as yet another medium to showcase the work of their students.

As you proceed through this exercise, you see that there is no difference between using FlashComm Server to play one video or three videos. The difference is in the use of a ComboBox component to list the videos and the use of Listeners to load and play the selected video.

1. Copy and paste the FilmTV folder in your Lesson 10 folder into the Flash Communication Server MX applications folder on your computer.

This folder contains the main.asc file as well as folders for streams and _definst_. Select the three videos from the FLV_files folder located in the Lesson 10 folder and copy and paste them into the _definst_ folder found in the FilmTV folder just added to FlashComm Server.

With the media in place, you can now construct the application that will be used to play the videos.

2. Open the *FilmTV.fla* file in your Lesson 10 folder.

When the file opens, notice that the interface is in place.

Note *The framer for the video is a simple 320 x 240 rectangle drawn in Fireworks 8. The rectangle is filled with a neutral gray, and the film sprocket holes were added using the Alien Skin Splat filters. The filter used is from the Frame series. It was a film frame and fit the bill quite nicely. The problem with filters is they stay within the dimension of the object to which they are applied. This means the video would have covered the entire graphic. To fix this problem, a blue square matching the dimensions of the video area was created, and the graphic was adjusted so that the gray display area matched the size of the blue rectangle. After that was done, the blue rectangle was deleted, and the framer was dragged from the Fireworks 8 canvas to the Flash Professional 8 Stage. Total design time from concept to placement in Flash was less than 10 minutes.*

Why is a Fireworks 8 lesson in a Flash Professional 8 lesson? Simple—the odds are good you have Fireworks 8 on your computer because it is included with the purchase of the Studio 8 products. Also, this demonstrates one of the fundamental truths of designing digital media: Let the software do the work. In this case, the Fireworks/Splat software combination did the job in a rather short time.

Tip *Although Flash Professional 8 ships with 14 blend modes, Fireworks 8 ships with 26 blend modes. If you apply a blend mode in Fireworks that is not found in Flash, the Fireworks blend still applies when the Fireworks 8 image is placed into Flash.*

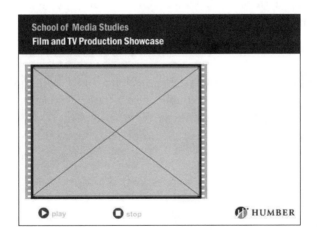

3. Select Window > Components to open the Components panel. Locate the ComboBox component in the User Interface components and drag a copy to the Stage.

The ComboBox component is one of the Flash components that have become somewhat indispensable because it functions both as a list component and as a drop-down list.

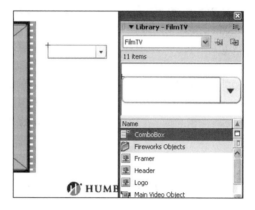

4. Select the ComboBox, open the Property inspector, and apply the following properties:

- Instance Name: myMovieChooser
- X: 382
- Y: 92

Now that the ComboBox has been given an instance name and precisely placed on the Stage, you can concentrate on having it function like a drop-down list.

5. Select the ComboBox component and then select Window > Component Inspector.

The Component inspector not only matches the items shown in the Parameters area of the property inspector but also has a couple of extra parameters—visible and minHeight, for example—that aren't found in the Property inspector. This is why many developers ignore the use of the Parameters area of the Property inspector and go right to the Component inspector.

Still the three parameters that most concern us—Data, Editable, and Labels—are found in both areas.

- **Data:** The values entered here are used by ActionScript and are associated with the labels that appear in the component. For example, you may have a list of URLs a user can visit. If one of them is Peachpit Press, the data associated with that menu item would be www.peachpit.com. In the case of our project, the data is the name of the FLV file to play.

- **Editable**: The values can either be True or False. If it is True, the user can enter text into the component.
- **Labels**: These are the menu names the user sees when the menu drops down during runtime.

6. Double-click the value area to open the Values dialog box, in which you enter the values associated with the labels in the menu.

To enter a value, click once in the first value input area and enter LawnChairLarry. To add a value, click the plus (+) sign. A new strip appears. Enter EmptyAlbums. Click the + sign again and enter Sheridans. Click OK to close the Value dialog box. The values you entered appear in the Component inspector.

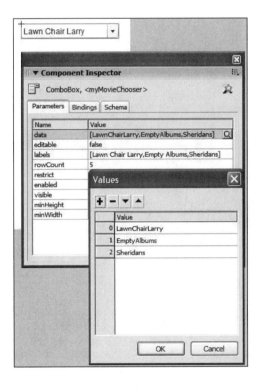

7. Click once in the editable area and select False from the drop-down menu. This ensures the ComboBox functions as a drop-down menu.

Double-click the Values area of the Labels strip to open the Values dialog box. The text you enter here appears in the menu. Keep in mind that the data you entered earlier is associated with the label you enter. Enter the following labels:

- `LawnChairLarry`
- `Empty Albums`
- `Sheridans`

Click OK to close the Values dialog box, and close the Component inspector.

8. Select the actions layer and then press F9 to open the ActionScript Editor. Click once in the Script pane, and enter the following code:

```
var playButton:Button;
var pauseButton:Button;

var myNetConnection:NetConnection = new NetConnection();

myNetConnection.connect("rtmp://localhost/FilmTV/_definst_");

var myNetStream:NetStream = new NetStream(myNetConnection);
myVideo.attachVideo(myNetStream);
```

The variables are all created, a new `NetConnection` is established, the FlashComm Server is connected to the `NetConnection` object, and the stream is established.

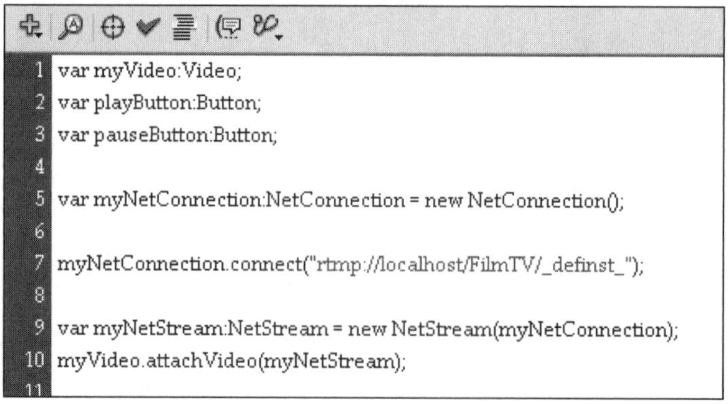

```
 1  var myVideo:Video;
 2  var playButton:Button;
 3  var pauseButton:Button;
 4
 5  var myNetConnection:NetConnection = new NetConnection();
 6
 7  myNetConnection.connect("rtmp://localhost/FilmTV/_definst_");
 8
 9  var myNetStream:NetStream = new NetStream(myNetConnection);
10  myVideo.attachVideo(myNetStream);
11
```

9. Press Return/Enter and then enter the following code:

```
function playMovie():Void {
myNetStream.play(myMovieChooser.data[myMovieChooser.selectedIndex]);
}
```

```
12  function playMovie():Void {
13      myNetStream.play(myMovieChooser.data[myMovieChooser.selectedIndex]);
14  }
```

This function simply pulls the data from the selected item in the ComboBox, which tells the SWF file which video to play.

When you entered each data value in the Value dialog box, there was a number associated with the data item. For example, the data item LawnChairLarry that you entered in the Value dialog box has the number 0 associated with it. This is the index value called by selectedIndex. The other important aspect of this line of code is the use of [ ]. These brackets indicate a list and that is exactly how Flash treats the data in a ComboBox component. The first item in any list has the Index value of 0. In this case the value would be the name of the FLV file named LawnChairLarry currently residing in the _definst_ folder.

The next thing to worry about is whether or not there is already a video playing. If there is, that video has to be closed and replaced with the one selected in the ComboBox.

10. Press Return/Enter and then enter this code:

```
var listenerObject:Object = new Object();
listenerObject.change = function(eventObject:Object):Void {
  myNetStream.close();     // unload our currently playing video
  playMovie();
}
```

In this code, you are creating a listenerobject that will wait for an item to be clicked—change—in the ComboBox. When the change event is detected the current stream playing the video is closed—myNetStream.close();—and the selected video is placed into the stream and starts playing—playMovie(); .

```
16  var listenerObject:Object = new Object();
17  listenerObject.change = function(eventObject:Object):Void {
18      myNetStream.close();  // unload our currently playing video
19      playMovie();
20  }
```

11. Press Return/Enter in the Script pane and then enter the following code:

```
playButton.onPress = function() {
  myNetStream.pause(false);
}
pauseButton.onPress= function() {
  myNetStream.pause(true);
}
```

Those two functions are the ones we have been using throughout this lesson to control the video that is currently playing. Press Return/Enter and add the final bit of code:

```
myMovieChooser.addEventListener( "change", listenerObject );
playMovie();
```

All these two lines do is to first tie the change and ListenerObject created earlier to the AddEventListener() method associated with the ComboBox component named myMovieChooser and start the video playing.

Click the Check Syntax button and, if everything is OK, close the ActionScript editor.

```
22  playButton.onPress = function() {
23      myNetStream.pause(false);
24  }
25
26  pauseButton.onPress= function() {
27      myNetStream.pause(true);
28  }
29
30  myMovieChooser.addEventListener( "change", listenerObject );
31  playMovie();
```

12. Save the movie to your **Lesson 10** folder and test the movie.

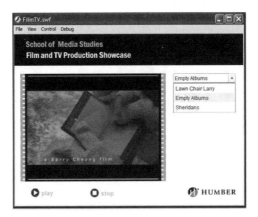

Streaming MP3 Files

In Lesson 5, you learned how to stream audio files through your Web server. FlashComm Server also does quite the job of streaming audio as well. The advantage offered you, the developer, of FlashComm Server over a Web server is the same one offered with video: Play means play.

In this exercise, you construct an MP3 player that allows the user to choose between three audio files and adjust the volume and pan levels for the selected song. Rather than hand you the file and show you how to wire it up with ActionScript, you build this project starting with a blank Stage.

Before you open Flash, copy the mp3Player folder from your Lesson 10 folder to your Flash Comm Server applications folder. This folder is the application you use in this exercise and contains the ASC file and the three MP3 files you use in this exercise.

1. Open Flash and create a new document.

When the Stage appears, click the Size button on the Property inspector to open the Document properties dialog box. Change the Stage size to 250 pixels wide by 150 pixels high. Click the OK button to accept the change and close the dialog box.

Add four new layers and name them, from the top down:

- Actions
- Controls
- Banner
- Gradient

2. Select the Gradient layer and draw a rectangle with the following properties:

- Width: 250
- Height: 150
- X: 0
- Y: 0
- Stroke: None
- Fill: Use the default.

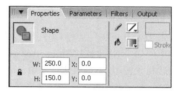

The fill color is about to change to a gradient, meaning you can use whatever color is being used in the toolbar. Right-click (PC) or Ctrl-click (Mac) on the box and then select Convert To Symbol from the context menu. When the New Symbol dialog box opens, name the symbol **Gradient** and select Movie clip as its property. Click OK. The blue line that now appears around the box tells you the selected object is a symbol.

3. Double-click the symbol on the Stage to open symbol-editing mode.

Select the rectangle, select Window > Color Picker, and select Linear as the color type. You will see the default White to Black gradient appear in the Color Mixer panel. Click the slider on the left of the gradient color bar to open the Color Picker which is the panel composed of color swatches used by Flash. Set the color to # FFFFCC, which is a very pale flesh tone. The gradient will be applied to the rectangle, and you can close the Color Mixer panel. Click the Scene 1 link at the top of the Timeline to return to the main Timeline. Lock the layer.

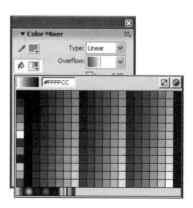

4. Select the Banner layer and draw a black rectangle that is 250 pixels wide by 40 pixels high.

Select the Text tool, click once on the black box, and enter **Pick A Tune**. Select the text and, in the Property inspector, apply the following properties:

- Text Style: Static Text
- Width: 104.2
- Height: 24.1
- X: 115
- Y: 5
- Font: Arial
- Size: 18
- Color: White, #FFFFFF
- Style: Bold
- Alignment: Left
- Anti-aliasing: Anti-alias for Readability

Select both the text and the box, and convert them to a movie clip named Banner. Return to the main Timeline and lock the banner layer.

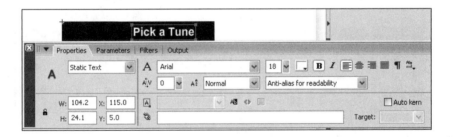

5. Select the Controls layer and add a fader-gain and knob-pan control from the Flash Buttons panel: Window > Libraries > Buttons > Knobs and Faders > fader-gain and knob-pan.

Select the fader-gain control on the Stage and, in the Property inspector, use the following values:

- Width: 35.9
- Height: 120.3
- X: 3.4
- Y: 17

These values serve to fit the slider onto the Stage and place the values box with this control in the Banner area, which makes them more noticeable. Select the knob-pan and set its *x* coordinate to 60 and its *y* coordinate to 78 in the Property inspector.

The next step creates the buttons for the music selections.

6. Select Insert › New symbol and then create a movie clip named Funk.

Select the Rectangle tool and draw a rectangle that is 90 pixels wide by 20 pixels high. Remove the stroke and fill the rectangle with a light gray: #999999. Select the Text tool, click once on the shape, and enter **Funkbeat**. Select the text and apply these properties in the Property inspector:

- Text Type: Static Text
- Font: Arial
- Size: 12 points
- Color: Black
- Style: Bold
- Alignment: Left
- Anti-aliasing: Anti-alias for Readability

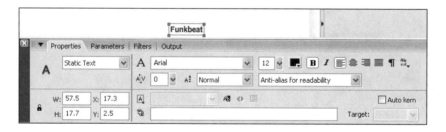

Return to the main Timeline, select the controls layer, and drag the movie clip onto the Stage. Set its *x* coordinate in the Property inspector to 130 and its *y* coordinate to 50.

7. Select the movie clip and click the Filters tab in the Property inspector. Add a Bevel filter to the movie clip and use these properties:

- Blur X: 5
- Blur Y: 5
- Strength: 100%
- Quality: High
- Angle: 45

- Distance 5:
- Type: Inner

The movie clip takes on a nice bevel effect.

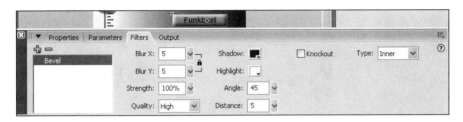

You need to create two more buttons just like the one just completed. Rather than repeating the process, you can actually let the software do the work for you.

8. Right-click (PC) or Ctrl-click (Mac) on the Funk movie clip in the library.

Select Duplicate from the drop-down list to open the Symbol dialog box. Rename the Symbol to **Applesauce** and then click OK. The symbol appears in the library. Double-click the symbol to open it and change the text to Applesauce. Repeat this step and name the next symbol **Storm**. Change its text to Dark Storm.

Drag both symbols to the controls layer and apply the Bevel filter to them using the values above.

9. Select each of the buttons just created and give them the following instance names:

- Funk: mcFunkBeat
- Applesauce: mcAppleSauce
- Distant Storm: mcDistantStorm

With the interface created, you can now turn your attention to the code that makes it work.

> **Tip** *Always choose High in the Quality area of a filter. Choosing Low or Medium, which are good for authoring but not playback, results in rather poor quality during playback.*

10. **Double-click the Volume control symbol to open the symbol's Timeline.**

Select the first frame of Layer 4 and press F9 (PC) or Option-F9 (Mac) to open the Actions panels. Scroll down to line 31 of the Script pane and replace that line of code with the following:

```
_root.dynamic_sound.setVolume(level);
```

```
29        }
30     }
31        _root.dynamic_sound.setVolume(level);
32   };
```

Close the Actions panel and click the Scene 1 link on the Timeline to return to the main Timeline. Double-click the pan knob, open its actions, and replace the code in Line 50 of the Script pane with this:

```
_root.dynamic_sound.setPan(level);
```

```
49     }
50        _root.dynamic_sound.setPan(level);
51   };
```

Those two lines connect the controls to a sound object you create in the next step.

> **Note** *A fuller explanation of how this code works can be found in the section "Controlling the Pan and Volume of a Sound Using the Flash Buttons" in Lesson 5.*

11. **Return to the main Timeline, select Frame 1 in the actions layer, open the Actions panel, and enter the following code:**

```
var dynamic_sound:Sound = new Sound();
var myNetConnection:NetConnection = new NetConnection();

myNetConnection.onStatus = function(info) {
   trace( "LEVEL: " + info.level + "  --  CODE: " + info.code    );
}

myNetConnection.connect("rtmp://localhost/mp3Player/_definst_");
```

The first two lines create the sound object dynamic_sound for the MP3 files and a new NetConnection() to accommodate the stream.

The function allows you to do a little troubleshooting if things don't work out during the test. The results appear in the Output dialog box in the Property inspector when you test the file and tell you if you have, indeed, connected to FlashComm Server.

```
1  var dynamic_sound:Sound = new Sound();
2  var myNetConnection:NetConnection = new NetConnection();
3
4  myNetConnection.onStatus = function(info) {
5      trace( "LEVEL: " + info.level + " — CODE: " + info.code );
6  }
7
8  myNetConnection.connect("rtmp://localhost/mp3Player/_definst_");
9
```

The final line of the code connects to the FlashComm Server; it is no different from that used for a video.

12. Press Return/Enter in the Script pane and then enter the following code:

```
var myNetStream:NetStream = new NetStream(myNetConnection);

gainSlider.attachAudio(myNetStream);
gainSlider.sound = new Sound(gainSlider);

mcFunkBeat.onRelease = function() {
    myNetStream.play("mp3:funkbeat");
};

mcAppleSauce.onRelease = function() {
    myNetStream.play("mp3:Applesauce");
};

mcDistantStorm.onRelease = function() {
    myNetStream.play("mp3:DistantStorm");
};
```

The first line creates the stream in the NetConnection(). The remaining functions are the instructions for the controls. The volume control—gainSlider—has the audio attached to it; the second line says, "Whatever sound is currently playing is attached to a sound object controlled by the slider." The functions for each of the buttons play the relevant MP3 file in the netStream.

Click the Check Syntax button to ensure that you have made no coding mistakes. If there are none, close the Actions editor.

```
11  var myNetStream:NetStream = new NetStream(myNetConnection);
12
13  gainSlider.attachAudio(myNetStream);
14  gainSlider.sound = new Sound(gainSlider);
15
16  mcFunkBeat.onRelease = function() {
17      myNetStream.play("mp3:funkbeat");
18  };
19
20  mcAppleSauce.onRelease = function() {
21      myNetStream.play("mp3:Applesauce");
22  };
23
24  mcDistantStorm.onRelease = function() {
25      myNetStream.play("mp3:DistantStorm");
26  };
```

13. Save the movie to your Lesson 10 folder and press Ctrl+Enter or Cmd+Return (Mac) to test the movie.

As soon as the movie starts playing, check the Output panel in your Property inspector to see the results of the trace statement. Click the various buttons to switch between audio files and use the volume slider.

What You Have Learned

In this lesson you have:

- Created an application for use on the Flash Communication server (pages 360–365)
- Created an ASC file that links the application to the SWF file (pages 360–365)
- Written the ActionScript that streams video and audio from the FlashComm Server (pages 360–365)
- Created a video player that plays multiple videos located on the FlashComm Server (pages 366–372)
- Used many features of the drawing and ActionScript features of Flash Professional 8 to create a streaming MP3 player (pages 373–380)

11 Using Dynamic Data

When data in a Macromedia Flash movie is constantly changing or updating, it is said to be *dynamic*. In Flash Professional 8, there are a number of ways to incorporate dynamic data into your movie. In fact, you have already used dynamic data in a previous lesson when you created a slide show that loaded the images into Flash using loadVars at runtime. However, there are a number of other methods that use dynamic data in Flash that provide you with a lot of control over what information is contained in the final SWF file and what the user views or reads when the movie is playing in a browser. This control is provided through a feature called *data binding*, which was introduced in Flash MX Professional. Data binding allows you to "connect" components to each other on the Stage. Essentially, a binding says, "When this data changes here, update

Twenty four images, one XML document and a blank stage are all you need to construct a rather interesting slide show in Flash Professional 8.

it over there." You can, for example, bind the data in an XML document to what you see in a ComboBox component being used as a menu. Some data components, such as the XML Connector, act as the conduit between the dynamic data source, such as an XML documents, and your Flash movie.

In this lesson, you explore how to work with XML data in Flash Professional 8. It starts with constructing a slide show using nothing more than ActionScript and a blank Stage. The next section constructs the same project, but uses an XMLConnector component to load the XML file that adds the images and text to the movie. The final part of the lesson introduces you to a shared object that allows users to leave the movie and pick up where they left off.

What You Will Learn

In this lesson you will:

- Learn the relationship between Flash and XML
- Parse an XML document to create a slide show
- Use the XMLConnector component
- Create a shared object

Approximate Time

This lesson will require about 90 minutes to complete.

Lesson Files

Media Files:

slideshow.xml
pix
thumbs

Starting Files:

Slideshow.fla
SlideshowXMLConnector.fla
Memoryslideshow.fla

Completed Files:

Lesson11/Complete/slideshow.fla
Lesson11/Complete/slideshowXMLConnector.fla
Lesson11/Complete/memoryslideshow.fla

Introduction to Dynamic Data

At its most basic level, dynamic data describes the process of sending data between the SWF file in a Web page and a Web server. What makes this process so appealing to developers is that it does not require changing the FLA file every time the data used by the SWF file changes. For example, it would be a tedious process to have a site that presents photographs with commentary that requires you to open the FLA file and change it to accommodate adding or deleting an image or a commentary.

Flash has a number of ways of incorporating dynamic data into a SWF file by using Web services, Flash Remoting, Flash Communication Server, XML, and loadVars. The ability to use Web services, XML, and the loadVars class was made available to you when you installed Flash Professional 8.

Note *This lesson focuses solely on one of the more common methods of communication between Flash and a Web server: through the use of XML. To help you understand Flash Remoting and Web services, we either need to explain databases or assume that you know how to create a dynamic Web site. We also have to assume that you use and understand Macromedia ColdFusion and a bunch of other technologies that are well out of the scope of this book.*

When you integrate a Flash application with data on a server, data is loaded into the movie or removed from the movie on the fly. In the case of the photographer's Web site, images and commentary can be changed hourly without having to open the FLA file. Other things you can do include sending e-mail, interacting with a database, and even loading charts and graphs into your SWF file. These types of applications are called rich Internet applications, and traditionally incorporate a dynamic data capability into their design.

To connect your SWF file to dynamic data on the server, you can either do it manually, through ActionScript, or use one of the data components found in the Data area of the Components panel. These components are drag-and-drop solutions that require you to add a couple of simple parameters to make them work.

Loading content into a SWF file also raises security issues because of the nature of Flash Player 8. If the data you are using is not hosted on the same domain as your SWF file, you need to create a cross-domain policy file. For example, if your SWF file is located at www.myslideshow.com/index.htm, the data, such as an XML file, should also be located in that domain. If it is located at www.myOtherSlideShow.com/index.htm, you need to create a cross-domain policy file and place it in that domain.

A cross-domain file is a simple XML file that includes information regarding which sites (www.myOtherSlideShow.com/index.htm) are permitted to access that data on the site looking for the data on another site (www.myslideshow.com/index.htm). You won't need to use this feature in this lesson, but if you need to create a cross-domain file, visit http://www.macromedia.com/cfusion/knowledgebase/index.cfm?id=tn_14213#return to review a TechNote regarding creating and loading cross-domain files.

XML and Flash

eXtensible Markup Language (XML) is now a standard for the sharing and exchanging of data on the Web. In Flash, XML is now being used for everything from news feeds to content management, and the odds are almost 100 percent that you will eventually create Flash documents that interact with a Web server. This means you need to parse and work with XML data.

If you are familiar with HTML, XML will be a familiar place. The major difference is that HTML uses predefined tags to mark up the page; XML lets you define the tags. By defining your own tags, you encounter the major difference between HTML and XML. In HTML, the tags are predefined and can't be added to. The language is not extensible. XML is extensible, so you invent the tags.

The purpose of an XML tag is to provide the data with a meaningful context. In HTML, the whole purpose of the tag is to define the presentation of the data. For example, an H1 tag in HTML doesn't really tell you much about the data between the tags:

```
<h1> Using XML Data in Flash </h1>
```

XML, on the other hand, uses semantic markup. In this case, the word *semantic* means to indicate the meaning of data. Thus, the XML version of that HTML is as follows:

```
<mainheader> Using XML Data in Flash </mainheader>
```

To create the Flash picture viewer for this lesson, you have to understand how the document you will be using is structured.

```xml
<?xml version="1.0" encoding="iso-8859-1" ?>
- <slideshow>
    <picture file="IMG_0408.jpg">We just got a new telephoto lens and were testing the range sitting
      in the Ponderosa across from the hotel we were staying in in Florida.</picture>
    <picture file="IMG_413.jpg">A shot of the mezzanine of our cruise ship from a few floors
      up.</picture>
    <picture file="IMG_0351.jpg">Top deck of the cruise ship also known as the Viking's
      Lounge.</picture>
    <picture file="IMG_451.jpg">A flock of pelicans... obviously an unknown rock band and not worth
      an autograph.</picture>
    <picture file="IMG_0422.jpg">Sunset at Cape Canaveral as we departed for The
      Bahamas.</picture>
    <picture file="IMG_0522.jpg">A colourful towel rack in Nassau... definitely called for a
      picture.</picture>
    <picture file="IMG_0545.jpg">A view of the ship from the dock.</picture>
    <picture file="IMG_0604.jpg">One of our many towel pets greeting us after a nice day.</picture>
    <picture file="IMG_0483.jpg">Nassau at dusk.</picture>
    <picture file="IMG_0525.jpg">Sunrise in the Bahamas. My wife got this shot while I was still
      asleep.</picture>
```

Notice that there are no HTML tags. Instead, the tags are <slideshow> and <picture>.
Those tags are called *elements*. Elements are composed of a start tag and an end tag, and
any information between those two tags is called contents.

Elements inside another element are said to be "children" of the element, and all XML
documents must have a root tag that must be the first element in the document. In the
case of our file, the root is the <slideshow></slideshow> tag.

Each complete tag in XML is called a *node*. For example, <picture file="IMG_413.jpg">A
shot of the mezzanine of our cruise ship from a few floors up.</picture> is a
node. Flash accesses XML data by looking for the nodes.

It is a common practice for XML documents to indent each layer of the document
hierarchy. Indents help you more easily recognize and understand the concepts of child
and sibling nodes.

When Flash accesses an XML file, it examines the relationship of the nodes to each other.
If we had a simple XML document, the code would look similar to this:

```xml
<photos>
  <photo>
    <caption>The British Columbia rain forest.</caption>
    <image>pic1.jpg</image>
  </photo>
</photos>
```

The root node is <photos> </photos>. The child node is <photo></photo>. The
<caption></caption> node is a child of the <photo></photo> node. In Flash, you
refer to <image></image> as a sibling of the photo node because it is the next node in the
same level of the structure and it is found between the <photo></photo> tags.

Finally, all XML documents should start with a prologue. In the case of this document, it is the following:

```
<?xml version="1.0" encoding="iso-8859-1"?>
```

All it does is identify the document as being formatted with XML and that the character encoding used is to the International Standards Organization (ISO) standard.

Nearly everything you do with XML in Flash involves the use of the XML class and involves one of the following:

- Formatting XML, with which you can create an XML document in Flash
- Parsing XML, which is a fancy term for breaking down the XML document into nodes
- Loading XML into Flash from an XML document
- Sending XML to a URL

Creating a New XML Object in Flash

The XML class in Flash has several methods you can utilize to create and format an XML document. There are 15 methods—ranging from `XML.addRequestHeader()` to `XML.toString()`—and, if you are new to Flash and XML you will quickly discover how difficult they are to use. There is a better way, according to Derek Franklin, author of *Flash MX 2004 ActionScript:Training from the Source.* He suggests creating a string and converting it to an XML object, which is a much easier and more common approach to the creation of XML objects.

An XML object in Flash is created using the following code:

```
var flashXML:XML = new XML();
```

In object-oriented programming (OOP), a class defines a category of an object. A class describes the properties (data) and the behavior (method) for an object. To use a class' methods and properties, you must first create an instance of the class. That is the purpose of the word new: It creates a new instance of the class. That instance is referred to as an *object.*

To hand the new XML object the XML-formatted data when it is created, you can put the name of the XML data between the empty brackets. You can also use the `parseXML()` method to parse an XML document/string into an existing XML object.

Let's assume you want to create the following XML document in Flash:

```
<MyAuthors>
  <Name Title= "First">Tom Green</name>
  <Name Title= "Second">Jordan Chilcott </name>
</MyAuthors>
```

To accomplish this, you would first create the document as a string and then convert that string into an XML object by placing it in new XML(). Here's the code that accomplishes that task:

```
var myString: String = <MyAuthors>
  <Name Title= \"First\">Tom Green</name>
  <Name Title=\"Second\">Jordan Chilcott </name>
</MyAuthors>;
var myXML: XML = new(myAuthors);
```

All the code does is create the string and convert it to an XML object called myXML. This object can then be sent to a server using the send() method, which is explained later in this lesson. This example is terribly inefficient and is for illustration purposes only. A cleaner way is to simply send the string in the first place.

Now that you know how to create an XML file, the next skill is learning how to access the data contained in an existing XML file.

Do you remember your high school or grade school English classes, in which you had to identify the parts of a sentence such as subject, predicate, conjunction, and phrase? What you were doing was parsing a sentence by breaking it down into its parts. When someone tells you they are writing a script that parses an XML document, all they are really saying is that the script will extract information from the XML document and somehow use it in Flash.

When you parse an XML document, you are converting it from a string—a collection of words—into a logical grouping of nodes. After the XML document has been parsed, you can then access its various elements using the XML node properties that Flash generates during the parsing process (such as nextSibling, nodeValue, and so on). In many respects, you can think of the parsing process as skipping along the parsed XML object to access or manipulate the data in the nodes.

When you call the XML load() method, it automatically downloads the XML file you specify.

There are 18 properties used by the XML load() method and rather than get into each one, we will deal with a few of the most common using the XML document that identifies the authors:

- **firstChild**: This property points to the first node in the tree structure. For example, the following:

  ```
  myXML.firstChild.firstChild
  ```

  would return this:

  ```
  <name Title= "First">Tom Green</name>
  ```

  The first child node of the XML document is the root node <MyAuthors>, and the first child of that node is name.

- **childNodes:** This property returns a list (array) of the child nodes at any point in the XML document. An example is as follows:

```
var myArray: Array = myXML.firstChild.childNodes.
```

- **nextSibling:** This property points to the next node in the same level of the XML tree structure. For example, the following:

```
myXML.firstChild.nextSibling
```

would return this:

```
<name Title= "Second">Jordan Chilcott </name>
```

- **attributes:** This property hands off an associative array of attribute names. For example, the following:

```
myXML.firstChild.firstChild.nextSibling.attributes. Title
```

would return this:

```
First
```

When you first start working with XML data in Flash, you mostly work with it when you are loading or sending out the XML. To load XML from a remote source, such as your site, follow these steps:

1. Create the XML object.

2. Load the XML, using the *load()* method, into the SWF file.

The code to do this is the following:

```
var myXML:XML = new XML();
myXML.load("http://mySite.ca/authors.xml");
```

You can create your own XML document right in Flash. The really interesting thing about the XML class is that you send and load the document *almost* simultaneously.

We use the word *almost* because technically Flash never simultaneously sends and loads an XML document. If you think about that you can grasp this concept. The time between Flash starting to send the XML document and loading the server's response will take time. The amount of time is totally dependent upon the amount of XML data that's being sent/received. Add to that time your connection speed/lag to the server—and back— as well as the amount of time it takes the server to receive the data, parse it, process it, reformat its own XML response, and transmit that back, and there will be a delay. In most cases, all this can happen in the course of a second or two; in some cases, it can take several seconds.

Sending the data uses the `send()` method and a destination URL. It would look similar to this:

```
var myXML:XML= new XML("<Greeting><Text>Hello World!</text></Greeting>");
myXML.send ("http://mySite.ca/apage.asp");
```

Parsing XML: Creating a Slide Show

When Ken Burns created the Civil War series for PBS a few years back, he didn't have much video footage to work with. He did have thousands of photographs, and through the clever use of panning, zooming, music, and narration, kept viewers glued to their sets while the series ran. This exercise mimics that effect by panning and zooming a series of images while providing a text-based commentary for the user.

This exercise is different from all of the others in this book because you will be working with a completely blank Stage. The images reside in a folder outside of the SWF file and are called into movie clips in the library. These movie clips are loaded onto the Stage when the movie plays. The navigation at the bottom of the movie is composed of a series of movie clips containing thumbnail images that are lined up beside each other, and the text is used as a buffer between the image and the navigation.

In many respects, this is a completely dynamic movie. The movie is compiled when it opens in Flash Player, and the content is loaded into the movie, from an XML document, at the same time.

The entire movie is dependent upon an XML document that contains the image name and the text. The Flash movie accesses the XML document and puts the images in their appropriate locations. It also accesses the text node in the XML document and places the text associated with the image in a dynamic text box.

```
<picture file="IMG_0422.jpg">Sunset at Cape Canaveral as we departed for The
  Bahamas.</picture>
```

This lesson also explores "depth" in a Flash movie.

If you were to put three different colored boxes in the same layer on the Flash Stage, they would overlap each other. What you are looking at is the concept of depth in Flash. Movie clips occupy space in three dimensions on the Flash Stage: x, y, and z. The z axis is the depth, and if one movie clip sits above another, on the Stage it has a higher depth value. The depth value for the Stage is 0,which means a movie clip sitting above the Stage has depth value of 1, and a movie clip above that one will have a depth value of 2 or higher. Flash developers use this property of a movie clip to great effect. There are many Flash sites that contain objects that move in front of each other, at runtime, by simply changing the depth value through ActionScript.

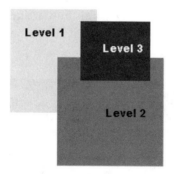

Finally, this exercise actually involves three variations on the theme:

- **Variation One:** Use ActionScript to parse the XML document and build the movie
- **Variation Two:** Use the XMLConnector data component to access the XML document
- **Variation Three:** Create a function that remembers where the user was in the slide show and returns to that point when the user opens the slide show

1. Open *Slideshow.fla* in your Lesson 11 folder.

Notice that the Stage is blank and there are only two layers: content and actions. The only layer you will be using is the actions layer. The movie clips in the library are the building blocks of this application. They will be used to hold text, display images for navigation, and hold and animate the images being viewed.

Up until now, you have been hard-coding your data into your Flash applications. This application is different because the data for the movie will be received from the slideshow.xml file. The most interesting aspect of this application is that Flash has no idea how many pictures are used in the slide show. This means the code will be written so that it can handle any number of images.

Aside from being able to handle any number of pictures, you need to keep the viewer engaged in the presentation, which is why you will be using the "Ken Burns Effect" to apply motion to a still image. The effect is surprisingly simple to implement in Flash and brings your images to life. For the best results, make your images larger than the area in which you are presenting them. For the purposes of this lesson, the dimensions of the images are 720 × 480. We are also including thumbnails whose dimensions are 60 × 40 each.

The raw material for this lesson is located in your Lesson 11 folder. Other than the SWF file you will create, it contains the contents of the folder that will be uploaded to the Web server. The pix folder contains the large images that will be the focus of the show. The thumbs folder contains the images used to construct the navigation at the bottom of the screen. The slideshow.xml document tells Flash which images to use and the text associated with the image.

Tip *If you check the filenames for the smaller thumbnail images and the larger images contained in the pix folder, you will notice that the filenames are identical. This is a little trick to use when you are reusing content. In this case, the thumbnails will be used for navigation. Click the thumbnail, and the larger image appears. Keeping the filenames the same keeps the XML document manageable and only requires you to tell Flash where each folder is rather than parsing XML code to use different filenames.*

thumbs

pix

slideshow
XML Document
3 KB

2. Select the keyframe in Frame 1 of the *actions* layer, open the Actions panel, and enter the following code into the Script pane:

```
var kbEffect:MovieClip;
var kbEffectOld:MovieClip;

var kbEffectCounter:Number = 0;
var kbPictureIndex:Number = 0;

var slideShowXML:XML = new XML();
var slideShow:Array;
```

The first two variables are used to name the movie clips used to hold the large images. The first one holds the image being viewed; the second one is used when the current image is replaced with another. When there are two images on the Stage, the image being replaced appears to fade out, and this occurs in the clip named kbEffectOld.

The next two variables keep track of the number of images in the show.

The final variables create an XML object named slideShowXML which are used to hold the XML file with the data, and the second variable puts that data in a list named slideshow.

```
1   var kbEffect:MovieClip;
2   var kbEffectOld:MovieClip;
3
4   var kbEffectCounter:Number = 0;
5   var kbPictureIndex:Number = 0;
6
7   var slideShowXML:XML = new XML();
8   var slideShow:Array;
```

3. Press Return/Enter and enter the following code into Line 10 of the Script pane:

```
function getNextPicture() {
  var kbMovie:String = "kb" + (Math.floor( Math.random() * 4 ) + 1);

  var kbPictureNode:XMLNode = slideShow[kbPictureIndex++];
  var kbPicture:String = kbPictureNode.attributes.file;

  var kbTextNode:XMLNode = kbPictureNode.firstChild;
  _root.pictureDescription.pictureDescription.text = kbTextNode.nodeValue;
```

This is the function that loads the pictures and their descriptions into the movie when it starts. To understand how this works, let's start with the broad picture.

When the movie starts playing, the image name and the description of the image has to be pulled out of the XML document. The image eventually winds up in the Picture Container movie clip in the library, and the text is placed in the Picture Description movie clip.

To do this, you need to work with the data contained in each node of the XML file. Using the first bit of data in the XML file, which is the first node, you see the following:

```
<picture file= "IMG_0408.jpg">We just got a new telephoto lens
    and were testing the range sitting in the Ponderosa across
    from the hotel we were staying in in Florida.</picture>
```

Everything between the `<picture></picture>` tags is a node.

`file= "IMG_0408.jpg"` is an attribute of the node and, as you can see, is used to contain the filename of the image, which is actually the value of the attribute named `file`.

The text description is first "chunk" of data in the node, meaning it is the `firstChild` of the node.

The first thing this code does is to choose one of the movie clips named `kb1`, `kb2`, `kb3`, or `kb4`. To do this, the first task is to construct the name of the movie clip and put it in a string named `kbMovie`. This is accomplished by using the `math.random()` method, which picks a random number between 0 and 1. This always results in a decimal value. That value is then multiplied by 4, and 1 is added to the result. For example, assume that the random value picked is .547. The number chosen would be 3.188. Obviously, you don't have a movie clip with that name, so you need to "trim off" the decimal value. This is the purpose of the `math.floor();` method. Thus, the value for the kbMovie string is kb3.

Tip *This is a rather clever method of choosing a random value. If you do the math using a variety of numbers, you will always obtain a value between 1 and 4.*

Now you know that the movie clip named kb3 in the library will be used to hold the chosen image. The rest of the function chooses the image for the movie clip and the description text associated with that image from the XML document.

The first step is to identify the nodes. Each node is contained in the `slideShow` array variable created earlier. This list, if you could see it, would be a series of numbers starting at 0 and ending at 23. Zero is always the first index number in a list and, in this case, is also the starting value for the variable kbPictureIndex. If you count the nodes in the XML document, you find there are 24 of them. The number 24 takes into account that the first node value is 0.

Even though there is a list with 23 values, each of those values must be accessed. This is the purpose of the ++ operator in the following line:

```
kbPictureNode:XMLNode = slideShow[kbPictureIndex++];
```

The operator is a postincremental operator, meaning the value of `kbPictureNode` starts at 0, but increments by 1 with each iteration of this function after you have accessed the value. The first iteration, therefore, says start with the node that has the value 0 in the XML document and then set the next iteration of the value to 1.

Now that the node has been identified, you need to separate the data in the node. The data is the image name contained in the file attribute and the description. The next line in the function does that:

```
var kbPicture:String = kbPictureNode.attributes.file;
```

It essentially says, "The value of `kbPicture` is a string. This value is found in the `attribute` named file in the current node named `kBPictureNode`."

With the image identified, the next step is to access the text associated with the picture. The first step in this process is to tell Flash where the text is located. In this case, the code tells Flash the next bit of data you need is the firstChild of the node you are currently examining:

```
var kbTextNode:XMLNode = kbPictureNode.firstChild;
```

It is given the name kbTextNode to ensure that there is absolutely no confusion between what is a picture and what is text in the node.

Tip *Notice that the variables all use the name of the item being used. This is to ensure that you know exactly what the variables refer to. You can use any name for your variables but one named kbHuggyBearNode doesn't give you much of an idea of what it is referring to. When naming variables, always assume that someone other than you will be examining the code. Also, if you are wondering about the kb prefix used in our* variables, *it is Ken Burns' initials.*

Knowing where the data is located, you can pull it out and place it in the movie clip named Picture Description. The line of code that accomplishes this is the following:

```
_root.pictureDescription.pictureDescription.text = kbTextNode.nodeValue;
```

Note *The text is placed into the movie clip due to its Linkage identifier. If you right-click on the Picture Description movie clip in the library and select Linkage, you see that name has been used as the ActionScript identifier.*

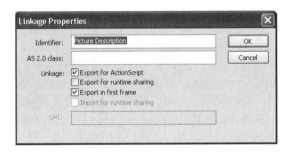

4. Press Return/Enter twice and then enter the following code:

```
kbEffectOld = kbEffect;
  kbEffectOld.swapDepths( 100 );
kbEffect = _root.attachMovie( kbMovie, "kbEffect" + kbEffectCounter++,
  101, {_x:0, _y:0, _alpha:0} );
kbEffect.pictureContainer.loadMovie( "pix/" + kbPicture );
kbEffect.onEnterFrame = function() {
  this._alpha += 5;
  if( this._alpha > 95 ) {
    this.onEnterFrame = null;
  }
};
if( kbPictureIndex >= slideShow.length ) {
  kbPictureIndex = 0;
  }
}
```

With the data identified, you can start using it. This section of code is how the "Ken Burns Effect" is created programmatically. As each large picture is brought onto the Stage it is animated on the Stage, and the picture replacing it fades in above the current image.

The process starts by giving the current image the name of kbEffectOld and ensuring that it is always at the below the image that is being added to the Stage. This is the purpose of the swapDepths(); method. When the new image comes in, it will always be above the image currently on the Stage. When it is time to get rid of the image and make room for the new one, the image is renamed and moved to a depth level of 100, which lets us know exactly where it is located in the stack.

The image will have to be placed in a movie clip and the next line of code identifies the movie clip to be used and some of its properties:

```
kbEffect = _root.attachMovie( kbMovie, "kbEffect" +
  kbEffectCounter++, 101, {_x:0, _y:0, _alpha:0} );
```

The new image, named kbEffect, is to be loaded into the kbMovie movie clip identified in the previous code section. This procedure is accomplished by using the attachMovie(); method. This method takes a symbol from the library—in this case, one of the kb movie clips—and attaches it to the main Timeline (_root). It is also given an instance name that is a combination of the string "kbEffect" and the current incremental value of the kBEffectCounter variable. The movie clip, without the image, is placed above the old movie clip at a depth of 101, and it is also precisely placed on the Stage and the content made invisible by setting the movie clip's alpha value to 0.

> **Note** *You might be wondering why we didn't use the duplicateMovieClip(); method instead of attachMovie();. Although they do essentially the same thing, there is a fundamental difference between them: duplicateMovieClip() copies from a Timeline, whereas attachMovieClip() copies from the library.*

> **Note** *With 24 images, you might be thinking that the Stage will become awfully crowded with a stack of images in quite a few copies of kb movie clips. In actual fact, there will be a maximum of only two of them on the Stage at any one time. The attachMovie() method brings a movie clip from the library to the Stage. The removeMovieClip(); method gets it off of the Stage. Double-click the kb1 movie clip and open its ActionScript. You'll see that the removeMovieClip() method is used.*

Having created the movie clip to hold the image, the next line of code identifies the image that will appear in the movie clip:

```
kbEffect.pictureContainer.loadMovie( "pix/" + kbPicture );
```

The loadMovie() method is used to go to the pix folder, in which the images are located and get the images used in the movie. It then uses the the file attribute value kbPicture from the XML file to load the image into the pictureContainer movie clip., This movie clip is nested inside of the current kb movie clip. The kb movie clip is sitting at the depth of 101—above the one the viewer currently sees. With the image waiting to come in, the next bit of codes fades it in.

The following function is what causes the image to fade in:

```
kbEffect.onEnterFrame = function() {
  this._alpha += 5;
  if( this._alpha > 95 ) {
    this.onEnterFrame = null;
  }
};
```

Using an onEnterFrame event, the movie clip's alpha value is increased by 5 percent every time the playhead enters the frame until its alpha value is greater than 95 percent. When this value is reached, the null value stops the process.

Here's a little-known alpha trick. You can set the alpha value to a number– 1000, for example–that is seriously higher than 100, which is the "official" maximum value for alpha. What this does is to provide a high-contrast effect if the graphics are composed of gradient and radial fills that have varying alpha values. Can you have an alpha value that is less than 0, such as -5? No. Any value less than 0 renders the graphic as if it were at 0 percent alpha.

The final two lines of code check to make sure that you haven't run out of nodes. If the next value needed is 23, the movie resets at the first image and starts to process all over again.

```
21   kbEffectOld = kbEffect;
22   kbEffectOld.swapDepths( 100 );   // move us down a level below for the next picture transition to occur
23
24   kbEffect = _root.attachMovie( kbMovie, "kbEffect" + kbEffectCounter++, 101, {_x:0, _y:0, _alpha:0} );
25
26   kbEffect.pictureContainer.loadMovie( "pix/" + kbPicture );
27
28   kbEffect.onEnterFrame = function() {
29     this._alpha += 5;
30     if( this._alpha > 95 ) {
31       this.onEnterFrame = null;
32     }
33   };
34
35   if( kbPictureIndex >= slideShow.length ) {
36     kbPictureIndex = 0;
37   }
38 }
```

5. Press Return/Enter twice and then enter the following code:

```
function showThumbs() {
  var thumbLevel:Number = 200;
  for( var thumbLoopIndex:Number = 0;
    thumbLoopIndex < slideShow.length;
    thumbLoopIndex++ ) {
    var kbPictureNode:XMLNode = slideShow[thumbLoopIndex];
    var kbPicture:String = kbPictureNode.attributes.file;

    var thumbPic:MovieClip = _root.createEmptyMovieClip( "thumb" +
      thumbLoopIndex, thumbLevel + thumbLoopIndex );
    thumbPic._y = (Math.floor(thumbLoopIndex / 8) * 40) + 320;
    thumbPic._x = ((thumbLoopIndex % 8) * 60);thumbPic._alpha = 100;

    thumbPic.loadMovie( "thumbs/" + kbPicture );
  }
}
```

Having identified the image to show and its corresponding text, the next step is to construct the grid of thumbnails at the bottom of the Stage using a function named showThumbs().

The function starts by creating a separate level or depth value that will be used when the grid is constructed.

The actual grid is constructed by first iterating, using the for loop, through the slideShow array created earlier and then relating the index value in the array with the name of an image contained in each XML node.

Each image is then placed into a movie clip named thumbPic. This movie clip is an emptyMovieClip that is created at runtime. The syntax for createEmptyMovieClip is as follows:

```
createEmptyMovieClip( instance,level);
```

If you look at the following code, you will see this syntax is actually adhered to:

```
_root.createEmptyMovieClip("thumb" + thumbLoopIndex, thumbLevel +
    thumbLoopIndex );
```

The emptyMovieClip is placed on the main Timeline—root. The instance name parameter combines the string "thumb" with the node's location in the thumbLoopIndex array. Thus, each emptyMovieClip receives a unique instance name. The second parameter puts each of these movie clips on a separate level. Again, each level is unique because it is the sum of the thumbLevel and its position in the thumbLoopIndex array.

Having created the movie clip, the next three lines in the code construct the grid:

```
thumbPic._y = (Math.floor(thumbLoopIndex / 8) * 40) + 320;
thumbPic._x = ((thumbLoopIndex % 8) * 60);
thumbPic._alpha = 100;
```

The first line places 8 pictures that are 40 pixels high in a row. The second line determines that each picture is 60 pixels wide.

The rows are constructed by placing eight pictures in a line and creating three rows.

```
40  function showThumbs() {
41      var thumbLevel:Number = 200;
42      for( var thumbLoopIndex:Number = 0; thumbLoopIndex < slideShow.length; thumbLoopIndex++ ) {
43          var kbPictureNode:XMLNode = slideShow[thumbLoopIndex];
44          var kbPicture:String = kbPictureNode.attributes.file;
45
46          var thumbPic:MovieClip = _root.createEmptyMovieClip( "thumb" + thumbLoopIndex, thumbLevel + thumbLoopIndex );
47          thumbPic._y = (Math.floor(thumbLoopIndex / 8) * 40) + 320; // 8 pictures are in a row 40 pixels high
48          thumbPic._x = ((thumbLoopIndex % 8) * 60); // each picture is 60 pixels wide
49          thumbPic._alpha = 100;
50
51          thumbPic.loadMovie( "thumbs/" + kbPicture );
52      }
53  }
```

You can see how this happens by following how the first picture in each row is placed onscreen. The thumbloopIndex is the list. There are 24 pictures, so the list is composed of numbers, separated by commas, that starts with 0 and ends with the number 23. If you count the thumbnails starting with 0, the three images that start each row are the numbers 0, 8, and 16 in the list.

The first image will be placed 320 pixels from the top of the Stage. The calculation is (Math.floor(0/8)* 40 +320. Multiply 0 by 40, and the result is 0. Add that to 320, and you get the result.

The second image will be placed lower. Remember that the images are 40 pixels high, so it needs to be placed 369 pixels from the top of the Stage. This is exactly the result you will obtain from the calculation. It is a similar situation for the picture that is number 16 in the array. It is 400 pixels from the top of the Stage. This is all accomplished through the Math.floor() method that strips out any decimals from a calculation. All the items in the top row always result in a value of 0. Those in the middle row always have a value of 1, and those in the bottom row always have a value of 2.

Placing the images across the Stage is a bit different. Their ._x value is the result of a "modulo" calculation. Modulo is one of those odd calculations that has extremely powerful results. What a modulo calculation does is use the remainder of a division calculation as its result, and the result is always a whole number. There are no decimals. The operator symbol for a modulo calculation in Actionscript is %. For example, the modulo calculation of 12%5 would have a result of 2. When the numerator value of the modulo is less than the value of the denominator, the result is always the value of the numerator.

For example, the calculation for the first image is (0%8)*60. The result is 0*60, which means that the first image is placed against the left edge of the stage at coordinates 0,320. The calculation for the second image is (1%8)*60. The result is (1)*60. If you do the calculation for each of the 24 images, you see that the images are always placed at 0,60,120,180,240,300 and 360 on the *x* axis.

The final line of code simply ensures that each image has an alpha value of 100%.

6. **Press Enter/Return twice and then enter the following code:**

```
slideShowXML.onLoad = function( success:Boolean ):Void {
  var slideShowRoot:XMLNode = slideShowXML.firstChild;
  slideShow = slideShowRoot.childNodes;

  showThumbs();
  getNextPicture();
}

_root.attachMovie( "Picture Description", "pictureDescription",  1000,
    { _x:0, _y:280 } );

slideShowXML.ignoreWhite = true;
slideShowXML.load( "slideshow.xml" );

stop();
```

In many respects, this function is the end game of the process. So far, you have:

- Created the variables used by the movie
- Separated the data in the XML document into lists containing the image name and the description
- Created the effect that fades the images in as they are added to the movie
- Constructed the grid of images at the bottom of the interface

What you haven't done is:

- Tell the movie which XML document to access
- Tell the movie where to place the `pictureDescription` movie clip in the library on the Stage

The code just entered does just that.

The function starts with the `XML.onLoad` event for the XML object created earlier. This event can have only two results, indicating whether or not the load of the XML document was successful. The only two Boolean values, therefore, are `true` or `false`.

If the XML document loaded successfully each node in the XML document is given the name `slideShowRoot`, and each child node is given the name `slideShow`. The function finishes by executing the `showThumbs()` and `getNextPicture()` functions.

The next line of code deals with the placement of the `pictureDescription` movie clip located in the library.

The next two lines tell Flash to ignore any white space in the XML document and identify the XML document to be used in the movie.

The first line is rather important:

```
slideShowXML.ignoreWhite = true;
```

If the Boolean value is set to `true`, Flash will ignore white spaces in the document. White spaces can be spaces before words, the result of pressing Return/Enter, or even tab stops. If Flash reads these spaces—`ignoreWhite=false`—all spaces will be treated as nodes, making it extremely difficult to parse the XML document.

The following line loads the `slideshow.xml` document used in this exercise from a specific location:

```
slideShowXML.load( "slideshow.xml" );
```

Tip The `XML.load();` method is the heart and soul of using XML in Flash. It is the one that identifies the XML document to be used and the code falls apart if it is missing.

The last line stops the playhead from moving to Frame 2.

```
55  slideShowXML.onLoad = function( success:Boolean ):Void {
56      var slideShowRoot:XMLNode = slideShowXML.firstChild;
57      slideShow = slideShowRoot.childNodes;
58
59      showThumbs();
60      getNextPicture();
61  }
62
63  _root.attachMovie( "Picture Description", "pictureDescription", 1000, {_x:0, _y:280} );
64
65  slideShowXML.ignoreWhite = true;
66  slideShowXML.load( "slideshow.xml" );
67
68  stop();
```

7. Save the movie and test it.

What you have done is a bit of magic. You have created something from nothing through the use of ActionScript, a few lines of XML code, and images located in two separate folders. In the next exercise, you'll reduce the amount of code in this exercise through the use of the XMLConnector component.

Using the XMLConnector Component

This exercise shows you how connect the slideshow.xml document to the Flash movie using the XML Connector component to load the XML data.

The XMLConnector component makes connecting XML data in Flash easy to accomplish. Rather than manually inputting the location of the XML document, you use the Property inspector for this purpose and because a component is being used, you have to create a listener to detect the loading of the XML data.

1. Open *slideshowXMLConnector.fla* in your Lesson 11 folder.

2. Open the Components panel and drag a copy of the XMLConnector component, located in the Data components, from the panel to a location just above the Stage.

This component really serves no function other than as a connection between the XML document and the Flash movie. As such, it won't be seen by the user, so placing it off the Stage or on the Stage does not affect its functionality.

With the component selected, open the Property inspector and give it the instance name of ourXMLConnector. Click the Parameters tab in the Property inspector, and set the URL to slideshow.xml and the direction to receive. Finally, ensure that ignoreWhite is set to true.

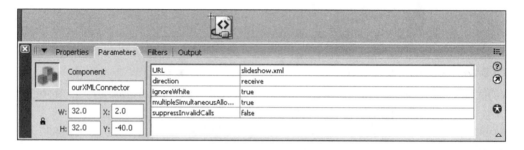

What you have done is to give the component a name that can be used by ActionScript. You have also identified the name of the XML document to be used by the component, set the data flow between Flash and the XML document to be one way (data will only move from the XML document into Flash), and told the component to ignore any white space that is found in the XML document.

3. Select the keyframe in the *actions* layer and press F9 (PC) or Option-F9 (Mac) to open the Actions panel. You will see a lot of the code, which matches that used in the previous exercise, has already been included.

Identify the XMLConnector in the code by clicking once in Line 9 of the Script pane and entering the following:

```
var ourXMLConnector:XMLConnector;
```

4. Scroll down to Line 56 of the Script pane, click once, and enter the following code between the comments:

```
var xmlListener:Object = new Object();
xmlListener.result = function(evt:Object) {
  trace( evt.target.results );
  slideShowXML = evt.target.results;
```

The first line creates a new object named xmlListener. The next three lines in the function determine what triggers the Listener. The first line creates the function that tells the Listener object to listen for the XMLConnector starting up. The second line simply prints all the XML data to the screen when you test the movie. This line is optional, but it is a good way of seeing whether everything is working. The final line is the key. When the XMLConnector starts—evt—the XML data from the XML document targeted in the Property inspector is loaded into the XMLConnector–target—is pulled into the Flash movie and stored—results—in the variable named slideShowXML.

```
55  //add the XMLConnector component listener code here
56  var xmlListener:Object = new Object();
57    xmlListener.result = function(evt:Object) {
58      trace( evt.target.results );
59      slideShowXML = evt.target.results;
```

5. Scroll down to Line 72 of the Script pane, click once, and enter the following code between the comments:

```
ourXMLConnector.addEventListener( "result", xmlListener );
ourXMLConnector.trigger();
```

These two lines of code are easy to understand.

The first line creates the listener for the XMLConnector component. The second line is what makes the XMLConnectror component turn on.

```
71  //XMLConnector methods
72  ourXMLConnector.addEventListener( "result", xmlListener );
73  ourXMLConnector.trigger();
74  //
75  stop();
```

If you can't remember how to "trigger" a data source through ActionScript, the necessary code is always available. Select Window > to open the behaviors panel. Click the plus (+) sign and select Data > Trigger Data Source.

This opens the Trigger Data Source window. Select the XMLConnector component and click OK. The "trigger" code is added automatically.

6. Save the movie and test it.

Notice that it functions no differently from the first slide show.

Using a Local Shared Object

A shared object is much like a suitcase: It stores data, and the data in the suitcase becomes available when the suitcase is opened. In Flash, there are two types of shared objects: Local and Remote.

A Local shared object is much like the ubiquitous cookie you receive on the World Wide Web (although in Flash it is a bit more intuitive). What it does is enable data to be stored on your user's computer. In the case of this exercise you will create a Local shared object that remembers which picture users were looking at when they left the site. When they come back to the site, the slide show will start, not at the beginning but with the last picture they were viewing before they moved on to eBay or quit browsing to check their e-mail.

A Remote shared object, which we won't be examining, is commonly used on the Flash Communication Server. What it doesn't do is store data on a computer. A Remote shared object stores data on the server or shares data, in real time, with all the users connected to the application. A good example is the ability to instantly update a chat running through the server. When the text is posted, everybody who is connected to the chat sees the text.

1. Open *memorySlideShow.fla* located in your Lesson 11 folder.

When the movie opens, select the first frame of the actions layer and open the Actions panel. The code is no different from that created in the first part of this exercise. What is different is that we indicated where the code for the shared object will be placed.

```
10  // Create the Shared Object
11
12  //
13
14  function getNextPicture() {
15      var kbMovie:String = "kb" + (Math.floor( Math.random() * 4 ) + 1);
16
17      // first remember where we left off
18
19      //
```

2. Click once in Line 11 of the Script pane and then enter the following code:

```
var ourSharedObject:SharedObject = SharedObject.getLocal("slideShow", "/" );
var ourPictureIndex:String = ourSharedObject.data.pictureIndex;
if( ourPictureIndex != undefined ) {
  kbPictureIndex = parseInt( ourPictureIndex );
}
```

The first line of code creates a variable named ourSharedObject that uses the SharedObject class. It then uses the getLocal() method of the SharedObject class identify the name of the shared object—"sideshow"—and uses the "/" to indicate the local path to the object. This is the syntax for a the getLocal() method: SharedObject.getLocal(objectName, localPath.);.

The next line retrieves the index of the picture we last left off at—pictureIndex—which is stored in the data property used by the variable named ourSharedObject. Note that all data stored in a shared object must be strings.

The final two lines deals with the issue of what happens if the string named ourPictureIndex contains a valid index. Of course, at this point, there is no index, so the second line which tells Flash that the data in ourPictureIndex will be converted to an integer–parseInt–and be used as our starting picture index in kbPictureIndex, will not be executed:

```
kbPictureIndex = parseInt( ourPictureIndex );
```

After you have run your slide show, you then have a valid index in your shared object to be used the next time you start your application.

Now that you have created the shared object, the next step is to put it to use. The first thing this sharedObject will need to do is to remember where the user was in the slide show when they left.

```
10  // Create the Shared Object
11  var ourSharedObject:SharedObject = SharedObject.getLocal("slideShow", "/" );
12  var ourPictureIndex:String = ourSharedObject.data.pictureIndex;
13  if( ourPictureIndex != undefined ) {
14      kbPictureIndex = parseInt( ourPictureIndex );// Pick up where we left off
15  }
16  //
```

3. Click once in Line 22 in the Script pane and enter the following code:

```
ourSharedObject.data.pictureIndex = kbPictureIndex.toString();

ourSharedObject.flush();
```

These two lines are all you need.

Shared objects can't work with binary data, so the first line ensures that the array (list) named kbPictureIndex is converted to a string.

The second line is the workhorse that remembers where you left off. The flush() method of the SharedObject class immediately writes the text file containing all the data in the object. If you don't use it, Flash will create the file when the user closes the SWF file in the

Web page. The best way to imagine how the flush() method works is to think of a document containing 24 numbers that start with zero. As soon at the SWF file is opened, the text document is created, and the first number in line is 0. When the next image is visible, the flush() method overwrites the existing document and creates a new one. Only this time the first number is 1.

What happens if there is a huge amount of data that is contained in the SharedObject? Won't this result in a very large file being added to the user's computer? That is the purpose of the parameter in the flush() method. The syntax is ourSharedObject.flush(minimum disk space).

We have left the parameter empty simply because the file is rather small. If you think the shared object will grow to a size of 750K, you would put that number between the brackets. What would happen, in this case, is that when the user starts the movie, Flash will ask for permission to set that amount of space aside on the user's hard drive for the file.

```
21    // first remember where we left off
22    ourSharedObject.data.pictureIndex = kbPictureIndex.toString();  // data must be in string format - no binaries
23    ourSharedObject.flush();
24    //
```

4. Save and test the movie.

What You Have Learned

In this lesson you have:

- Learned about the relationship between Flash and XML (pages 383–388)
- Parsed XML to create a slide show (pages 389–403)
- Used an instance of the XMLConnector component (pages 403–406)
- Created a local shared object (pages 407–409)

12 Going Mobile with Flash Professional 8

It should come as no surprise that Macromedia Flash has gone mobile. The ubiquity of cell phones and handheld devices has driven the demand for rich content that goes well beyond the text-based solutions that were common with these devices only a couple of years ago. Flash was a natural choice to meet this demand simply because the files are so small and load so quickly.

At the time of this writing, Flash is a de facto standard for rich content delivery through cell phones throughout Asia and is quickly approaching a similar critical mass in Europe. We are also starting to see Flash establish itself in North America and the predictions are that it, too, will become a North American standard by 2008.

To catch a glimpse of what is in store, you need do nothing more than ride a train or a subway in Japan. The riders all use their cell phones to play games, get the latest news and weather, and check flight schedules.

The completed site is viewed on a cell phone.

In North America, the interest in delivering content through cell phones and Personal Digital Assistants (PDAs) is being driven not only by corporations in the public sector. Educational institutions, both K-12 and post-secondary, are seriously looking at how these devices can be used to facilitate learning. Other applications range from traffic reports in New York City to language training—and this technology is still in its infancy. To get a sense of what you can do and what can be done with mobile content a good starting point is Macromedia's Mobile and Devices Center at `http://www.macomedia.com/mobile`.

In this lesson, you create two applications. The first is a tour of a local college designed for cell phone delivery. The purpose is to give visitors the same access to the college as those who would visit the college's Web page using a PC.

The second exercise is an interactive map on a PDA. The purpose is to show the user a map of where they are located, which can then be dragged around the screen. This project is created for delivery through a Windows Mobile browser on a PDA.

What You Will Learn

In this lesson you will:

- Learn how Flash Professional 8 is used on cell phones and PDAs
- Learn how handheld devices and cell phones create unique design and production challenges
- Choose a cell phone and use the Emulator to test a small movie
- Create an interactive Flash movie for use on a cell phone
- Use keypress events navigation on a cell phone
- Create an interactive movie for use on a PDA

Approximate Time

This lesson will require about 90 minutes to complete.

Lesson Files

Media Files:

none

Starting Files:

Humber.fla
Whereameye.fla

Completed Files:

Lesson12/Complete/MobileTest.fla
Lesson12/Complete/Humber.fla
Lesson12/Complete/WhereamEye.fla

Flash and Devices

The first thing you have to understand about developing for mobile content is that you can't use Flash Professional 8; you have to use Flash Lite 1.1, which is equivalent to Flash Player 4.0. This, however, does not mean you have to purchase another version of Flash. When you create a mobile application you will probably use one of the templates included with Flash Professional 8. These templates are all designed to play through the Flash Lite Player, and this is set in the Publish Settings options. When it comes to using ActionScript, you can also choose the Flash Lite version right in the Actions panel. This means that should you attempt to apply a Drop Shadow filter to an object on the Stage, Flash displays an Alert box that essentially says the feature is unavailable for the Player version being targeted.

Tip *If you are at all serious about developing content for mobile devices, obtain a free copy of the Flash Lite 1.1 CDK (Content Developer Kit) that is available for download at* http://www.macromedia.com/software/flashlite/.

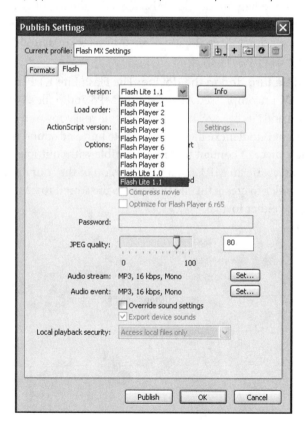

Before you start on this exercise, it is important that you understand there are some fundamental differences between the projects in the lesson and all the projects that have preceded it in this book. Some of the more important differences include the following:

- **Navigation and key events:** There is no mouse for user input on a cell phone. The methods for user input are limited to the Up, Down, and Select keys on the handset and the number and "*", "#" on the handset.

- **Fonts are limited:** A cell phone screen is smaller than that on a PDA, so the fonts you use must be legible and readable. You can use both device and embedded fonts. The problem with embedded fonts is that they do maintain continuity of design, but they also add to the file size. Device fonts are a good alternative and if used properly, tend to be both legible and readable on a small screen.

- **Keep it really small:** Keep code to a minimum and use compressed bitmaps to keep things small. Creating images to the exact screen size in either Photoshop CS2 or Fireworks 8 is a good habit to develop. Also consider the use of GIF or JPG images that use a quality compression of between 65 and 80 percent. Although Flash loves vectors, cell phones don't. Keep the use of vector images to a minimum and substitute JPG images where appropriate.

- **Sound should be targeted to the device:** The Flash Lite 1.1 Player supports MIDI, MFi, SMAF, WAV, uncompressed ADPCM, and MP3 audio files. No matter how you look at it, sound adds to file size. If you have obtained a copy of the Flash Lite 1.1 CDK, the FlashLiteBundler.exe file lets you create bundled sound files that allow you to create a single piece of content that is compatible with multiple devices. For example, you can create an MP3 and a WAV version of the sound file and run them through the bundler to create the file that allows the sound to be played on handsets that only support either format.

- **Keep an eye on the device:** ActionScript allows you to access a host of specific device capabilities and variables. For example, you can use ActionScript to visually represent features on the handset such as battery life, signal strength, e-mail sent, and so on.

- **Use templates:** If you are developing for a particular handset, consider the creation of a template. Flash Professional 8 installs a few that are accessible from the Start page or through File > New. It is also a good idea to periodically check the Macromedia Mobile and Devices Developer Center—http://www.macromedia.com/devnet/devices—for any new templates available for download.

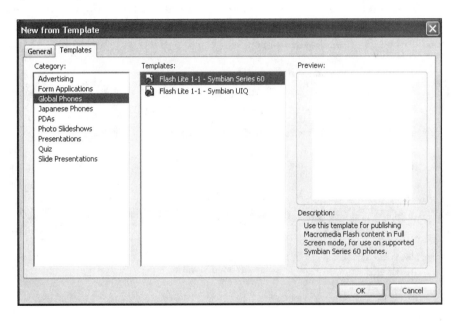

- **Test, test, test:** New to Flash Professional 8 is an emulator for your device that is launched when you test your movie by selecting Ctrl > Enter (PC) or Cmd > Return (Mac). If the movie works as expected in the emulator, test the movie on the handset you will be using.

Creating a Movie for a Device

In this exercise, you create a very basic movie that will get you comfortable working with a device template and testing the movie. This movie consists of a small animation and a button that replays the animation when it finishes.

1. Open Flash and on the Start page, select Create from Template > Global Phones.

This opens the New From Template dialog box. Select Flash Lite1-1 - Symbian Series 60. Click OK.

When the Flash interface opens, notice the small Stage size and that two layers—Actions and Content—are created on the Timeline. Add a new layer named buttons. The Stage size matches the size of the device's screen, which is 176 pixels wide by 208 pixels high.

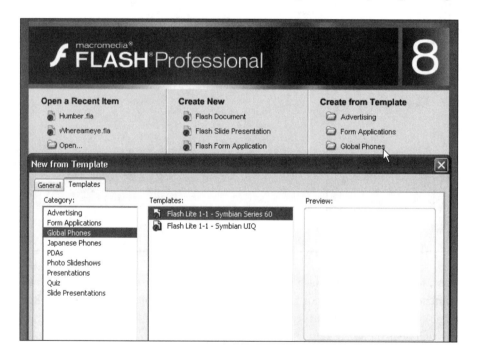

2. In the Property inspector, click the Settings button in the Device area.

The Device Settings dialog box opens, in which you can select the device you want to target. The Manufacturer section on the right of the dialog box lets you select a manufacturer, and the Test Device section on the right enables you to select a specific model of the target phone.

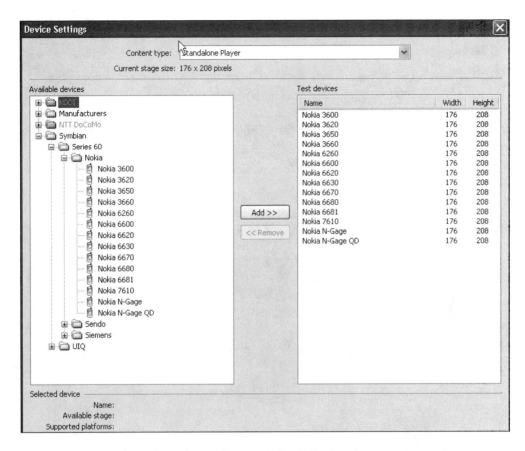

The Content type drop-down list at the top of the dialog box lets you choose the content type you want to create. If you select one of these content types, the devices that don't support it will be dimmed in the Test Device section list.

At the bottom of the dialog box is a Check For New Devices link. Click this link to go to the Macromedia site; any new devices will be listed and available for download.

In the Device Settings dialog box, make the following selections:

- **Content Type:** Standalone Player
- **Manufacturer:** Nokia
- **Test Device:** Nokia 6620

Click OK. The dialog box closes and you are returned to the main Timeline.

3. Select the Text tool, click once on the Stage in the Content layer, and enter the words "Hello World".

Right-click the text, and select Convert To Symbol from the context menu. Convert the selection to a graphic symbol named Text.

Drag the symbol to the bottom of the Stage and add a keyframe in Frame 10. Drag the symbol to the top of the Stage and add a motion tween.

4. Add a new layer named "buttons" and add a keyframe to Frame 10 of the *buttons* layer.

Draw a small box and fill it with grey—#666666. Select the Text tool and enter the word **Again**. Select both the box and the text, and group them by selecting Modify > Group. Select the grouped object and convert it to a button symbol named Button.

5. Select the button on the Stage and then open the Actions panel by selecting **Window › Actions.**

Enter the following script into the script pane:

```
on(Press) {
   gotoAndPlay(1);
}
```

Add a keyframe at Frame 10 of the Actions layer, and add the following script:

```
stop();
```

Save the movie and name it **MobileTest**.

6. Press Ctrl-Enter (PC) or Cmd-Return (Mac) to test the movie.

The test window that opens is the Device Emulator built into Flash Professional 8. This emulator works only with devices and is not launched at any other time other than when a device is being used.

The emulator mimics the keys on a cell phone that one would press to play or interact with the movie.

In the Test Device drop-down list, select the Nokia 6620 device.

Roll the cursor over the controls on the device. When you roll over a control it highlights. Click the Folder icon above the Input button. When you click the folder, you see the button highlighted in yellow. Click the input button, and the movie plays.

Tip *Selecting the Trace, Information, or Output selections results in messages, if any, appearing in the Flash Output panel.*

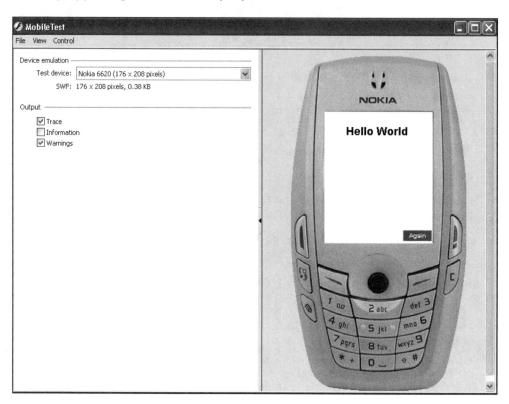

Building an Application for a Cell Phone

In this exercise, you confront and resolve an all-too-common request. The client wants to make the site available to cell phone users. The problem is that HTML-based Web sites don't easily transition from the big screen to the small screen. You can put a lot of information in a large space, but as that space shrinks there is a corresponding shrinkage of the information that can appear in that area. In the case of a cell phone, anything more than two bits of information would be a bit much.

The site we use for this exercise is one that actually exists. It is the home page for the college at which one of the authors teaches.

Attempting to put all of that information into a space that is 176 pixels wide by 208 pixels high simply doesn't work. Yet when you take a close look at the information hierarchy in that page, the design becomes somewhat self-evident. The large image on the page can be used as the entry screen for the Flash movie. The images along the bottom of the screen are the entry points into the site. The text area on the right side of the screen contains information that could be used elsewhere, and the same applies to the buttons along the top of the page.

The plan, therefore, is to use the large image as a sort of splash screen for the application. If the user wants to contact the college, there will be a button to accommodate a "speed dial" call to the college directly from the application. There will also be a button that allows the user to obtain more information about the college. When the button is clicked, the images appear as a scrolling graphic that provides a bit more information regarding the various areas of the college, and the user can scroll through these areas by using the left and right buttons on the cell phone to navigate. When an image appears, there will be a short description of that area of the college.

Note *The authors want to thank William Hanna, Dean of the School of Media Studies at the Humber Institute of Technology and Advanced Learning, for his assistance in this project and Robert Gordon, President, for allowing us to use the Institute's images and branding for this exercise.*

Obviously, that is a lot of work. In this exercise, you construct two major pieces of the project: the intro screen and the navigation with descriptions.

1. Open *Humber.fla*, located in your Lesson 12 folder.

Add the test devices for this project. In the previous exercise, you worked with only one device. In this one, you use one of the more common models on the market: the Nokia Series 60 phone.

2. Open the Property inspector and click the Device Settings button to open the Device Settings dialog box.

If there are any devices shown, select all of them and click the Remove button to clear the Test Devices area. This procedure does not delete the devices; it merely clears them from the list.

In the Available Devices area, select Symbian > Series 60 > Nokia. Click the Add button, and all the devices in that folder are added to the Test devices area. Click OK to close the Add devices dialog box. Save the file.

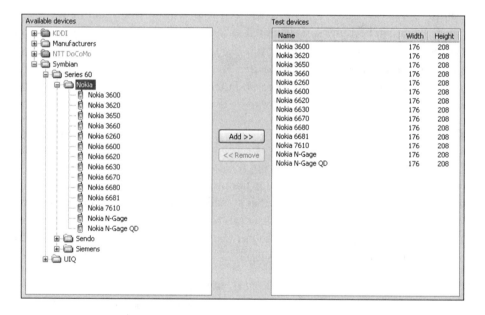

3. Select Frame 1 of the *Menu* layer and drag a copy of the Tour and the Contact buttons from the library to the Stage.

These buttons are the main navigation buttons for this application. Clicking the Tour button moves the user elsewhere in the movie, and clicking the Contact button calls the college.

Select the Tour button and then open the Actions panel by selecting Window > Actions. Although not necessary, a good habit to develop when working with devices is to change the ActionScript version in the drop-down list in the upper left of the Actions panel to **Flash Lite 1.1 ActionScript**.

Tip Keep in mind that the Flash Lite 1.1 Player uses ActionScript, so practically every line of code in this book, to this point, simply won't work on a device. If you are a long-time Flash user, you might want to consider reviewing the Actions, Methods, and Properties contained in the various Flash Lite books in the Actions panel. This includes reviewing the FSCommands in the Flash Lite Actions book.

Click once in the Script pane and then enter the following code:

```
on(press) {
   gotoAndPlay("Tour");
}
```

All this code does is send the playhead to the Tour label on the main Timeline.

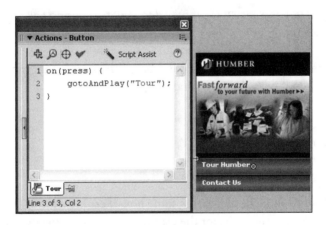

4. Click the Contact button on the Stage and add the following script:

```
on(press) {
   getURL("tel:1-234-567-8910");
}
```

This function is actually quite powerful. Throughout this book, you have been using the getURL(); method to navigate to Web sites. What you are seeing here is that it can also be used to dial a cell phone.

Tip *When you use the* getURL(); *method to initiate a phone call, the user is prompted by Flash Lite to allow or deny the placing of the call.*

5. Select Frame 1 of the *actions* layer and delete any code that may be found in this frame. Replace it with the following:

```
stop();
_focusRect = false;
fscommand2("resetsoftkeys");
fscommand2("setquality", "high");
fscommand2("fullscreen", "true");
```

These five lines can be thought of as being some housekeeping chores. The first line stops the playhead on Frame 1 and waits for the user the select one of the two buttons.

The second line turns off the yellow box that appears around any selection. The term *focus* simply means that the selected item is visible or accessible to the user.

The next three lines use fscommands to perform a variety of functions. fscommands were a feature of Flash 4 that allowed Flash to communicate with the host device or operating system. In this case, the communication is between Flash and the cell phone.

The third line resets the softkeys—the ones used on the cell phone to navigate through the interface—to their default states. Later on in this exercise, you'll write the code that tells the softkeys what to do.

The fourth line determines the quality of the graphics the users see on their cell phone screen. The default for Flash Lite is medium-quality. The high parameter changes the image quality to the best possible.

The fifth line simply expands the movie to fill the screen of the cell phone.

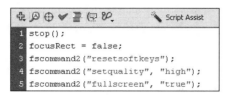

```
1 stop();
2 focusRect = false;
3 fscommand2("resetsoftkeys");
4 fscommand2("setquality", "high");
5 fscommand2("fullscreen", "true");
```

6. Save and test the movie.

When the emulator opens, click the phone and instead of using the mouse, press the Up and Down arrow keys on your keyboard. The two buttons and the soft keys used will be selected. Another interesting trick is to use the keyboard to change the phone displayed in the emulator. Select a phone from the Test device drop-down list, and the phone changes. Now press the Up and Down arrows on your keyboard. As you press the arrows, you will navigate through the devices and can see how the interface will appear on each device in the list.

Tip   *If you do use the keyboard to switch between devices, click the phone in the emulator to either test the movie using your mouse or to use the keyboard to navigate through the movie on the phone.*

Creating the Navigation Screen

In this part of the exercise, you create the user interface that gives the user a bit more information about the various aspects of the college. This area contains the following:

- Animations that present each of the main areas from the college's home page
- A dynamic text area that gives the user a bit more information about the selection
- Buttons that move the user through the navigation or return the user back to the first frame of the movie

1. Select Frame 10 of the *NavStrip* layer, add a keyframe, and then drag the NavStrip movie clip from the library to the keyframe.

Select the movie clip on the Stage; in the Property inspector, set the x coordinate to 32 and the y coordinate to 36. This aligns the strip with the H in the logo.

The problem you now confront is that the strip is entirely visible. The plan is to have only one image visible at any one time and the text describing that image to appear in the text box under it. This is easily solved by masking the strip and having the strip move upward when the user clicks a button.

2. Add keyframes at Frames 15, 20, 25, and 30 of the *NavStrip* layer. To move the strip upward, select each keyframe and use the following value in the *y* coordinate area of the Property inspector:

- Keyframe 15 = -43
- Keyframe 20 = -122
- Keyframe 25 = -200
- Keyframe 30 = -278

Tip   *Those numbers were determined by selecting View > Rulers and adding a horizontal guide that aligned with the top of the image. When each key frame was created, the Up arrow key was used to move the next image in the sequence to align with the ruler guide. The strip was selected and the y value in the Property inspector was noted. When we finished, the Horizontal guide was dragged back onto the horizontal ruler to remove the guide from the Stage.*

With the strip aligned, click once between the keyframes and add a motion tween.

With the animation created, you can now turn your attention to ensuring that only the image to be seen is visible—not the entire strip.

3. Drag the playhead to the keyframe at Frame 10. Select the *NavStrip* layer and add a layer. When the layer appears, add a keyframe in Frame 10 of this new layer.

Select the Rectangle tool and draw a rectangle that matches the dimensions of the first image in the strip. Don't be concerned with fill color or even stroke. Right-click (PC) or Ctrl-click (Mac) on this new layer and select Mask from the context menu. The strip is masked, and only the first image is visible.

4. Select the text box on the Stage; in the *var* area of the Property inspector, enter *description*.

This where Flash Lite ActionScript 1.1 shows its age. You can't use Strict Data typing with this version of ActionScript, and variable names are assigned to text boxes through the var area of the Property inspector.

Select the text in the text box and delete it.

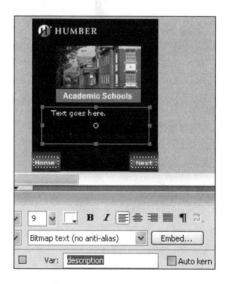

5. Add a keyframe to Frame 10 of the *KeyCatcher* layer. Drag a copy of the KeyCatcher button and place on the pasteboard in the keyframe just created.

If your application must handle several different keypress events, you could either create a single button for each keypress event or use a single button, with ActionScript, to handle all keypress events. This type of button is commonly called a *keycatcher* (or key listener) button.

Instead of creating buttons that move the strip up and down, you will use the Up and Down softkeys on the cell phone for this purpose. This explains why you are using an all-purpose keycatcher. The other aspect of this is that the button will catch key events and perform various functions, designated by the program. It isn't necessary that the user see it so this explains why it is sitting on the pasteboard.

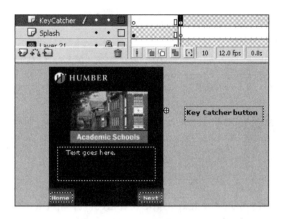

6. Select the button on the Stage and press the F9 (PC) or Option-F9 (Mac) key to open the Actions panel. Click once in the Script pane and enter the following code:

```
on (keyPress "<PageUp>") {
  gotoAndStop("Home");
}

on (keyPress "<PageDown>") {
  play();
}
```

The first handler "catches" when the user presses the left key on the device, which executes a PageUp event and sends the playhead back to the Home marker. The second handler "catches" the press of the right key on the devices sending a Pagedown event, which moves the playhead to the next frame. This initiates the animation of the image moving up.

The obvious question is, "What are the PageUp and PageDown keys." If you look at the interface, you will notice two graphic symbols named Next and Home. These are essentially blank buttons- buttons that contain only a hot spot, but they are placed directly over the PageUp and PageDown keys on the device.

Save the movie.

```
1  on (keyPress "<PageUp>") {
2      gotoAndStop("Home");
3  }
4
5  on (keyPress "<PageDown>") {
6      play();
7  }
```

7. Select the keyframe in Frame 10 of the *actions* layer, open the Actions panel and enter the following code:

```
description = "There are eight major schools on two campuses in  Toronto.";
fscommand2("SetSoftKeys", left, right);
stop();
```

```
1  description = "There are  eight major schools on two campuses in Toronto.";
2  fscommand2 ("SetSoftKeys", left, right);
3  stop();
```

These three lines of code place the text in the text area, remap the left and right softkeys and stop the playhead on the frame until the correct softkey is pressed.

SetSoftKeys remaps the left and right softkeys of the device, provided that they can be accessed and remapped. After this command is executed, pressing the left key generates a PageUp keypress event, and pressing the right key generates a PageDown keypress event. In the case of this exercise, the ActionScript associated with the PageUp and PageDown keypress events is executed by the *KeyCatcher* when the respective key is pressed.

Tip *There are 38 events that can be accessed through the SetSoftKey command. To review these events, you can double-click the SetSoftKey command in the fscommand2 book to add it to the Script pane. This results in a tooltip that allows you to scroll through the various iterations of this command.*

Tip *You don't have to use the keywords left and right as parameters in this command. These parameters are either names of variables or constant string values such as Home and Next. Thus the second code line could just as easily be written as fscommand2("SetSoftKeys","Home,Next");*

8. Select the keyframe in Frame 15 of the *actions* layer and enter the following code:

```
stop();
description = "Part time and full time employment opportunities at Humber."
```

9. Select the keyframe in Frame 20 of the *actions* layer and enter the following code:

```
stop();
description = "When we teach the best, shouldn't you hire the best.";
```

10. Select the keyframe in Frame 25 of the *actions* layer and enter the following code:

```
stop();
description = "Quality education is more than words at Humber.";
```

11. Select the keyframe in Frame 30 of the *actions* layer and enter the following code:

```
stop();
description = "Press releases, news and announcements regarding the
   Humber community.";
```

12. Select the keyframe in Frame 35 of the *actions* layer and enter the following code:

```
gotoAndPlay("Tour");
```

13. Save the movie and test it.

This has been a fairly simple exercise designed to expose you to creating an application for a cell phone. The key to this exercise is understanding the navigation through the movie is done through the use of the keys on the hand set. This is why keyPress and SetSoftKeys are important to understand.

As you test the movie, change to a variety of different models in the emulator to examine how the movie looks in the new device as well as the keys that must be pressed to allow the user to navigate through the movie.

Tip *There are several movies that demonstrate the various techniques you can use to further explore creating Flash Lite movies for devices. On the PC they are located in* `C:\Program Files\Macromedia\Flash 8\Samples and Tutorials\Samples\FlashLite`*. On the Mac they can be found in* `Macintosh HD\Applications\Macromedia\Macromedia Flash 8\Samples and Tutorials\ Samples\Flash Lite`*.*

Tip *If you have a cell phone you want to use for testing, the easiest way of loading the file into the phone for this purpose is to connect using Bluetooth. Before testing with a cell phone, make sure your model is Flash-enabled by visiting* `http://www.macromedia.com/mobile/supported_devices/handsets.html`*. A full list of handsets and the features they support are located on this page.*

Creating a Windows Mobile Application

The other type of device you will inevitably encounter will be a wireless PDA. Although the sales of cell phones are far outstripping the sales of PDAs, they are relatively common and are being used in hospitals, by the military, and in education. Business is making extensive use of this technology for sales, training, and communications purposes.

What is driving the popularity of these devices is the inclusion of wireless features—either built-in or through a separate card—that allows users to access the Web through a browser. The other interesting aspect of developing for Windows Mobile is the capability to bypass the Web and simply load the application—the Flash SWF you create—directly onto the device.

In this exercise, you create a small application that allows a user to interact with a map and also provide the user with a Help screen.

Tip *The Palm OS is not covered in this exercise. Although Palm essentially launched the PDA market, the browsers contained in the Palm OS are still unable to use the Flash Player because of licensing issues. If you have a Palm device you can still follow this exercise, but the final SWF file will have to be loaded directly onto your device. Also be aware that certain Palm OS PDA models, such as the Sony Clie, only support Flash Player 5. This lesson uses Flash Player 6, which is the current player used by Windows Mobile.*

1. Open Flash Professional 8. On the Start page, select Create From Template > PDAs to open the New From Template dialog box.

In this dialog box, you find list of templates for Motorola, Nokia, Sony Clie, and Windows Mobile devices. The three choices for Windows Mobile are as follows:

- **Windows Mobile - Browser:** This choice results in a smaller Stage (240 × 268) to accommodate the browser menu bars at the top and bottom of the PDA screen.

- **Windows Mobile - Full Screen:** This choice gives you the largest Stage (240 × 320) because only the Windows Mobile menu bars at the top and the bottom of the device's screen need to be accommodated.

- **Windows Mobile - SIP Open:** This choice gives you the smallest screen real estate (240 × 175). The reason the Stage is so small is that it is reduced to accommodate the Stylus Input Panel used to add text to an open window on a PDA.

Select Windows Mobile - Full Screen.

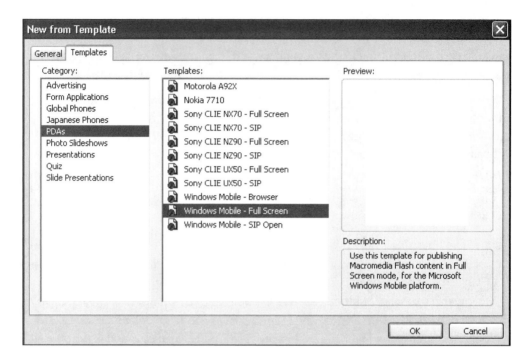

2. When the movie opens, open the library by pressing Ctrl-L (PC) or Cmd-L (Mac).

Inside the library is a graphic named HP5400.gif. This graphic is an image of an HP iPaq 5400. It is similar to the cell phone images from the previous exercise to give you an idea of how your movie will look in a PDA.

Drag the image to the screen and position the screen area of the iPaq so that the Flash Stage is visible.

You should also note there are two layers that are a part of the template: ActionScript and Content. The ActionScript layer contains the following line of code:

```
fscommand("FullScreen", true);
```

This line uses an `fscommand` to tell the Windows Mobile OS to display the movie in `Fullscreen` mode. If you choose not to use this mode, set the value to `false`. Finally, if you examine the Property inspector, notice that the player is Flash Player 6 and the ActionScript used is version 1.

Now that you know how to open a PDA template and use the various elements, it's time to create a small PDA-based application. Close the movie and don't save the changes.

Tip *Don't pay too much attention to the layers in the template. You can add as many layers as you want to a Flash movie destined for PDA playback.*

Tip *It is up to you whether you choose to use the PDA graphic from the library. If you do add the graphic, position it to accommodate the Stage and then lock the layer. All subsequent layers can go under the layer containing the PDA. When you get ready to publish the document, unlock the layer and delete it.*

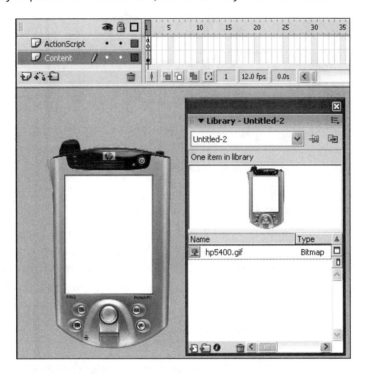

3. Open *Whereameye.fla*, located in your Lesson 12 folder.

We have included the opening animation and not much else. All the remaining assets you will require can be found in the library.

The plan for this project is to start with the opening animation and, when it finishes, to lead right into the interactive map. If you move the playhead to Frame 6, you see that we have included an interactive menu and the WhereamEye logo is at the top of the Stage.

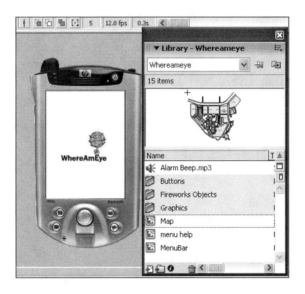

4. Add keyframes to Frame 6 of the *mask* and *map* layers.

Select the keyframe in the map layer and drag a copy of the Map movie clip to the Stage. The map is quite large and covers quite a bit of the Stage and the pasteboard. The user will be dragging this map around the Stage, which means you don't have to be concerned with its positioning. When you have the map on the Stage, select it and give it the instance name Map.

To confine the user's view of the map to the Stage, you need to mask it.

5. Select the keyframe in Frame 6 of the *mask* layer. Select the Rectangle tool and draw a square that covers the stage in the visible area. Right-click (PC) or Ctrl-click (Mac) on the layer name and select Mask from the context menu. The edges of the map outside the mask area are now hidden.

With the assets in place on the Stage, you can now concentrate on writing the code.

Throughout this book, we have been using mask *layers. You can also create a mask using ActionScript. In this exercise, you could give the rectangle the instance name of* Mask *and use the* setMask(); *method in the* actions *layer to create the mask, which would require the following line of code to accomplish:*

Map.setMask(Mask);

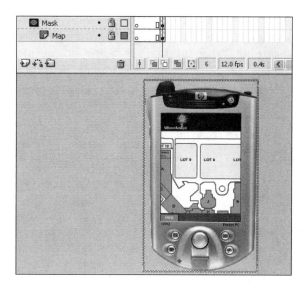

6. Select Frame 1 of the *actions* layer, open the Actions panel, and enter the following code into line 2 of the Script pane:

```
navSound = new Sound();
navSound.attachSound("BeepSound");
```

Note the Help menu in Frame 6. These two lines code create a Sound object named navSound and attach the sound to that Sound object. This allows you to play the BeepSound in the library when the menu is selected and when the menu is closed.

The sound called in the Sound object does not match that for the sound's name in the library. Right-click (PC) or Cmd-click (Mac) on the sound in the library and select Linkage from the context menu. The sound name is in the Linkage dialog box, and Export for ActionScript *is selected. Full details regarding linking sound can be found in Lesson 5.*

7. Double-click the menu help movie clip in the library to open the Symbol editor.

If you need to add a menu it is best to use a movie clip rather than use a component such as the ComboBox component because components add more weight to a movie than a movie clip. In the case of a PDA with limited memory and a wireless connection to the Internet, the added file size will slow down the process.

Regarding the Help menu, notice that it is a simple two-frame movie with the actual Help dialog box, with a close button, located in Frame 2 of the movie clip. When the user taps the Help button with the stylus, the sound plays, and the playhead moves to Frame 2 and opens the Help dialog box. When users finish reading the information, they tap the Close button, a sound plays, and the playhead returns to Frame 1. To start, select the button in Frame 1 of the buttons layer and give it the instance name of btnHelp in the Property inspector.

Select Frame 1 of the Actions layer , open the Actions panel and then enter the following code:

```
stop();
btnHelp.onPress = function() {
  gotoAndStop(2);
   _root.navSound.start();
}
```

This code is fairly self-explanatory. The most important feature of the code is the onPress event. When you are adding buttons to a PDA-based movie, buttons can have only two events attached to them: onPress and onRelease. What you can't have is a button that uses the onRollOver event. On a PDA, buttons can only have two states: Up or Down. The same rule applies to Button symbols. Create the Up and the Down states in the Button symbol editor.

Move the playhead to Frame 2 of the movie clip and click once on the Close button. Give it the instance name of btnClose in the Property inspector. Now that the instance has been created, you can write the code that moves the playhead back to Frame 1 when the Close box is tapped with the stylus.

Select the keyframe in Frame 2 of the actions layer and enter the following code into the Script pane:

```
btnClose.onRelease = function() {
  gotoAndStop(1);
 _ root.navSound.start();
};
```

Close the open movie clip by clicking the Scene 1 link on the main Timeline.

> **Tip** *Note that the menu is sitting above the 0,0 point because the button symbol is sitting at the point in Frame 1 of the movie clip. Placing the menu above the button gives the illusion of a pop-up dialog box.*

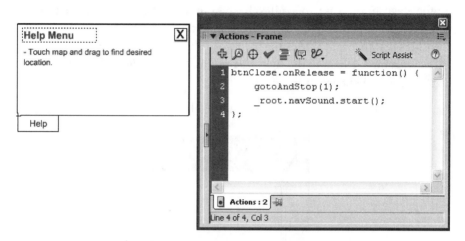

8. Select Frame 6 of the *actions* layer, open the Actions panel, and enter the following code into the Script pane:

```
stop();
var xmax = 0;
var ymax = 0;
var xmin = (xmax - Map._width) + 225;
var ymin = (ymax - Map._height) + 225;
```

The first action stops the playhead on Frame 6. The variables establish the boundaries in which the map can be dragged. By doing this, you ensure that the user doesn't drag the map image well beyond its visible area on the Stage.

Think of the Stage as being a box. The first two values—xmax and ymax—set values for how far the image can be dragged up and to the left. The next two values—xmin and ymin—set how far the map can be dragged (to the right and the left) beyond those two values and still leave some of the image visible on the Stage. That is the purpose of the number 225. The Stage is actually 240 pixels wide. By using this number, you ensure that there is always some of the of the picture showing.

Follow the math. The map image is 768 pixels wide. You have the upper-left corner of the image sitting at the 0,0 point. If you were to drag the map to the left until the left edge of the image was on the left edge of the Stage, its *y* value in the Property inspector would be -768. If you were to permit this, and if the user lifted the stylus from the screen, there would be no way of tapping on the image because it would be sitting flush with the left edge of the Stage. In this case, the ymin value becomes important. That value is (0-768) + 225. This means the farther to the left that the map can be dragged is to a *y* value of -583, which ensures that the right side of the map stops about 15 pixels from the left edge of the Stage. Dragging the map to the right ensures that the left edge of the image can't be dragged beyond the left edge of the Stage.

Having established the boundaries, you can now code the Drag actions.

9. Press the return key twice and then enter the following three functions:

```
Map.onPress = function() {
    Map.startDrag(false, xmin, ymin, xmax, ymax);
};

Map.onRelease = function() {
    Map.stopDrag();
};

Map.onReleaseOutside = function() {
    Map.stopDrag();
};
```

The first function is the one that is in play when the user is dragging the map on the Stage. It uses the startDrag(); method to allow it to be dragged. The parameters for this function establish the sides of the "box" in which it can be dragged. The syntax for this method is startDrag(lockCenter, Left,Top,Right,Bottom). The lockCenter parameter, which is optional, is tied to where the mouse clicks the image to start the drag. If the value is false, the *x* and *y* values for the image's center point are where the mouse is clicked. If the value is false, the calculation uses the physical location of the center point.

To understand this, again follow the math. The map is 768 pixels wide and 768 pixels high, so its center point is located at 384,384. If the value is set to false and the user clicks and drags the map in the center of the Stage, the center point for the image sifts to 120,160.

The remaining two functions stop the drag option if the user lifts the stylus or releases the mouse.

```
1  stop();
2  var xmax = 0;
3  var ymax = 0;
4  var xmin = (xmax - Map._width) + 225;
5  var ymin = (ymax - Map._height) + 225;
6
7  // Drag actions for Map
8  Map.onPress = function() {
9      Map.startDrag(false, xmin, ymin, xmax, ymax);
10 };
11
12 Map.onRelease = function() {
13     Map.stopDrag();
14 };
15
16 Map.onReleaseOutside = function() {
17     Map.stopDrag();
18 };
```

Script Assist

10. Save the movie and press the Ctrl-Enter (PC) or Cmd-Return (Mac) keys to test the movie.

Drag the map around the screen. Notice that you can't drag it beyond the edges of the Stage? Click the Help button, and you hear the sound and open the menu. Click the Close button on the menu, and you hear the sound and the menu closes.

What You Have Learned

In this lesson you have:

- Learned how to design a Flash Professional 8 movie for a cell phone (pages 416–432)
- Written scripts targeted for a Flash Lite 1.1 Player (pages 416–432)
- Used the new Device Emulator in Flash Professional 8 to test a movie destined for a cell phone (pages 424–425)
- Learned how to create a Flash Professional 8 movie for a PDA (pages 433–442)
- Learned how to code for stylus used on a PDA (pages 433–442)

13 Publishing a Flash Movie

The first thing you have to understand about publishing a Macromedia Flash document to the Web is that the SWF file isn't a Web document. When people tell you they have created a Flash site, that statement is not exactly correct. The SWF file can appear in your Web site only if it is embedded into an HTML page. Thus a "Flash site" is composed of your SWF file, any media—audio, video, images, text, XML documents—it might use from external sources, and the HTML page that "holds" the SWF file. You do not necessarily have to upload the file to a Web server to complete this lesson. You can create the HTML page, create the SWF file, and even try player detection without going online.

Publishing a movie involves a lot more than clicking the Publish button.

In this lesson, you create the HTML page containing the slide show from Lesson 3. You create the HTML document in Flash, publish a profile, learn more about the publishing settings, add Flash player detection, and even add the SWF file and post it to the Web using Macromedia Dreamweaver 8.

What You Will Learn

In this lesson you will:

- Create a publish profile
- Change the publish settings
- Detect a visitor's Flash Player and redirect the visitor as necessary
- Embed a SWF file into an HTML page
- Upload the slide show to a server and view it online

Approximate Time

This lesson will require about 90 minutes to complete.

Lesson Files

Media Files:

Image01.jpg
Image02.jpg
Image03.jpg
Image04.jpg
Image05.jpg

Starting Files:

SlideShow_AS.fla

Completed Files:

Lesson13/Complete/SlideShow_AS.fla

Publishing a SWF file

A Flash file must be converted to a SWF file before it can appear in a Web site. Throughout this book, you actually published a number of SWF files because when you test the file by pressing Ctrl-Enter (PC) or Cmd-Return (Mac) you created a SWF file that you previewed. However, to view any Flash movie in a browser, the SWF file must be embedded into an HTML page. The process of creating the SWF file is also called "publishing" and uses the Flash Publish Settings dialog box to control what gets published, compatibility, and other variables that affect playback through a Web page.

In this lesson you publish the SlideShow_AS file and embed that file into an HTML document.

1. Open the *SlideShow_AS* file in the Lesson 13 folder. To open the publish settings, choose File > Publish Settings when the file opens in Flash.

When the Publish Settings dialog box opens, you see two tabs that allow you to control how the files are generated in Flash.

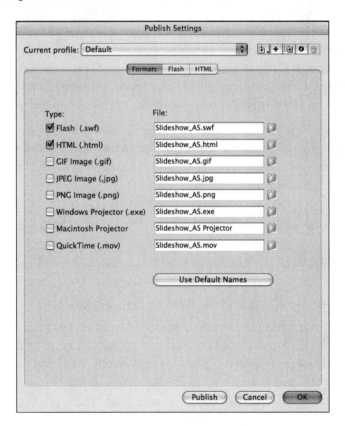

The Formats tab allows you to publish a variety of formats, simultaneously, which range from the SWF file to an EXE file that is a Flash projector file. Projector files are ideal for creating interactive CD-ROMs, computer-based presentations, and kiosks. Flash Player is embedded right into the projector, meaning that users do not need to worry if they have installed Flash Player 8. Other formats available include animated GIF files, images, and even video.

Tip *If you publish the Flash movie in the MOV format, you lose all interactivity. One of the more common uses for this format is for animations created for broadcast purposes.*

2. **Click the New Profile button at the top of the Publish Settings dialog box. Enter a name for the publish profile and then click OK.**

The Publish Profile is a handy way of saving your publish settings to your hard drive. The advantage of this feature is the ability to save the same profile and use it for a variety of different SWF documents you might subsequently create. Although you really don't need to create a profile for this relatively simple document, it is a skill you will use at a later date.

When you click the New Profile, the Create New profile dialog box opens. Enter **MyProfile** into the text input area and click the OK button. The name will be added to the Current Profile drop-down menu whenever you return to the Publish Settings, and you can modify these settings at any time.

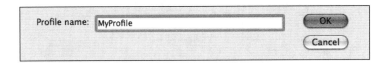

3. **Make sure that the HTML and the SWF formats are selected.**

You will create a project that can be viewed in your browser, and you will need the HTML format to create the HTML document you will be opening in your browser. If this project were being placed in a Dreamweaver 8 page, you wouldn't need to select the HTML option.

4. Click the Flash tab and select the Flash Player 8 from the Version drop-down list. Set the load order to Bottom up and the ActionScript version to ActionScript 2.0. Deselect Omit Trace Actions and make sure the Compress Movie check box is selected.

The Flash area of Publish Settings is where you determine the changes to the Flash Player you will be publishing to. All the Players are listed in the Version drop-down list, and ActionScript 2.0 works fine in Flash Player 6, but the Strict Data Typing introduced to Flash Player 7 doesn't work in Flash Player 6. If you are publishing to a device, you need to select Flash Lite 1.0 or Flash Lite 1.1 from the list.

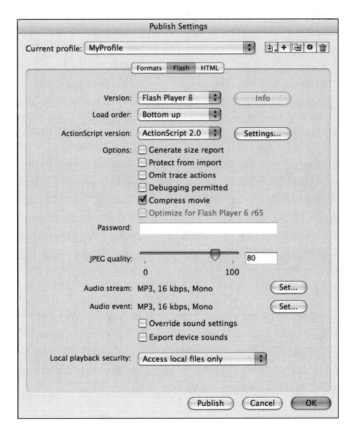

Tip   *If you are unsure of the Flash Player or ActionScript version needed for the selected player, test the SWF file and view the results in the Player. If you don't see the feature or results you were expecting, you know you have to choose an older player version.*

Tip *The Flash Player you select is also used in the authoring environment. For example, if you choose to use Flash Player 7 and add a drop shadow filter, a dialog box appears, telling you this feature is not available in Flash 7.*

Flash 8

This feature is not supported by Flash Player 7. To use this feature, you must target Flash Player 8.

Publish Settings...   OK

Load order controls the way the layers in your Flash movie load into the Player. The default setting is Bottom up, which means the layers load from the lowest layer to the highest. This is noticeable when someone accesses your Flash movie using a dial-up connection. It can also have an impact on your ActionScript because actions pointing to lower layers are available before those on the higher layers. The good news is that this affects only the first frame of the movie.

There are also a number of other options in this panel. Generate Size Report shows the data contained in the final SWF file in the Output panel. You see the frames, symbols, text characters, actions, and bitmaps listed. Selecting Omit Trace Actions should be done before the movie is published. Throughout this book you have written a number of little trace actions in ActionScript and seen the results in the Output panel. This is a great method of ensuring that everything works when you are building the movie. When you publish the movie, this isn't necessary and selecting it does not affect the movie's performance, other than to slightly improve it.

The Protect From Import option stops viewers from adding the SWF file to their FLA files. Keep in mind that even if you do protect your SWF file from import, there are tools that will undo this action. There are also tools that permit people to open the SWF file and access your ActionScript. It is vitally important that you do not place sensitive company information or passwords in a SWF file.

Selecting Debugging Permitted allows you to remotely debug your SWF file. You would access the file online and enter a password when prompted, which also helps add a layer of security to the file. If someone downloads the SWF file, a password is needed when it is imported into Flash.

The Compress Movie option allows it to compress the SWF file to the smallest possible size. This works only for Flash Player 6 and higher.

5. Set the JPEG quality to 85 and select the Override Sound Settings check box. Leave the Audio Stream and Audio Event settings at their default values.

The JPEG compression slider functions just like the ones in Photoshop and Fireworks 8. Higher values mean better quality because there is not as much compression applied. A good rule of thumb is to use a value between 80 percent and 100 percent. Lower quality does result in a smaller SWF file, but there is a real risk of the image quality degrading.

The Override Sound Settings check box override any settings you set for Audio files in the library. Clicking this check box also applies the settings for all sound used in the SWF file. The result is a lower file size for the SWF file when it is published. To change the Audio settings, click the Set button to open the Sound Settings dialog box. In this dialog box you can change the compression, sample rate, and quality. Clicking the Set button beside the Audio Event area also opens the Sound Settings dialog box.

6. Click the Publish button to publish the SWF file; then click the Import/Export profile button, and choose Export to export your profile.

When you click the Publish button at the bottom of the Publish Options panel, the SlideShow_AS.fla file is converted to SlideShow_AS.swf. The new file and the HTML file are placed into the folder containing the original FLA file. If you want to save the SWF file and the HTML file to a different folder, click the Browse button to open the Select Publish Destination dialog box and navigate to a different folder.

> **Tip** It is common for developers to save the FLA file to one folder and to save the SWF and HTML files, if needed, to the directory that eventually is uploaded to the Web.

Selecting the Export option in the Publish profiles allows you to create a profile that can be used for other Flash files. The profile will be saved as an XML document located in `<path to Flash 8 Directory>/Flash 8/en/Configuration/Flash Profiles`. This XML file contains all the settings that can then be used when you create another FLA file. Profiles placed into the Flash Profiles folder appear in the Profiles drop-down list.

7. Click OK to close the Publish Settings dialog box. Save the changes you have made by selecting File > Save.

At this point, you can minimize the application and either double-click the SWF file to play it or double-click the HTML file to view the SWF file in a browser.

Bandwidth Profiler

A very useful tool to use when you are testing a movie, prior to publishing, is the Bandwidth Profiler, which gives you a graphic representation of the bandwidth used during playback.

1. With the *Slideshow_AS.fla* file open, test the movie.

When the movie appears, select View > Bandwidth Profiler or press Ctrl-B (PC) or Cmd-B (Mac) to open the Bandwidth Profiler.

The Bandwidth Profiler actually gives you quite a bit of very useful information: the Stage dimensions, frame rate, SWF file size, and even how long it will take for the movie to start playing.

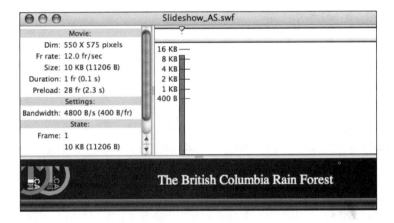

The graph shows you how much bandwidth is required by each frame of the movie, which can help you optimize your SWF file. If a frame has lots of content and a rather tall spike, consider moving some of that content to another frame in the movie. Another interesting feature of the Bandwidth Profiler is the ability to simulate download times from within the Flash authoring environment. You do this by selecting View > Simulate Download. When you select this menu item, the SWF file simulates playback on slower Internet connections and tells you, roughly, how long the user will have to wait. You can change the connection speed for the simulation by selecting View > Download Settings and choosing from the menu.

Get into the habit of testing the movie at a variety of speeds, including any custom speeds, which range from a 14.4 modem to a T1 connection used by many institutions. Testing at a variety of speeds gives you a generally good idea of how long a user will have to wait for the content to download before they start using your movie. If there is an overly long wait, you can be sure that your visitors will leave your site.

Detecting the Flash Player

When a visitor arrives to view your movie, you have no idea whether they have the correct Flash player installed or even if they have a Flash Player at all. Flash detection is a "black art," and many Flash developers and coders have created their own Flash detection scripts. However, you can let Flash do all the heavy lifting for you and create the Flash detection script for you when you publish your movie.

If you have used earlier versions of Flash, such as Flash MX Professional 2004, the creation of a Flash detection script was a rather cumbersome process that involved the creation of a number of files ranging from GIF to HTML. Flash Professional 8 streamlines this process and removes a lot of the guesswork involved in previous version of the application. Here's how:

1. Open *Slideshow_AS.fla* and open the Publish Settings dialog box by selecting File > Publish Settings.

Select the HTML option in the formats panel, which adds the HTML tab to the panel. This also ensures that both the Flash SWF file and the HTML page into which it will be embedded are created when you click the Publish button.

2. Select the Flash Tab and ensure that Flash Player 8 is the Player version to be used and that ActionScript 2.0 is the ActionScript version.

This is the first step in the process. Always choose your target player and ActionScript version before creating a Flash Detector.

> **Tip** You don't always have to select File > Publish Settings. Click the Settings button in the Publish area of the Property inspector to open the Publish Settings dialog box.

3. Click the HTML tab and select Detect Flash Version.

The Player version chosen in the previous step is selected. The two input boxes allow you to enter in the decimals used for subsequent releases that fix bugs or improve functionality. These are usually referred to as "dot releases" and you can enter those numbers into the version area as well.

4. Click the Template drop-down list and select Flash HTTPS.

The templates are HTML templates that are used for everything from setting up a Pocket PC page for the file to embedding a Flash movie that has been converted to a QuickTime movie. When you make your choice, click the Inform button to find out what each one does.

The HTTPS selection redirects the user to a secure server in which they can obtain the Flash Player if it is not detected.

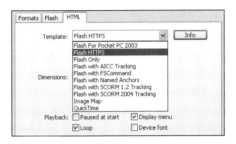

The other settings on this page don't need to be modified, but here is a list that discusses what each one does:

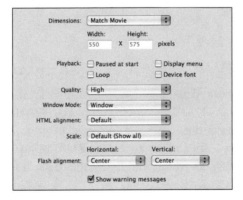

- **Dimensions:** You can set the dimensions for the Flash SWF file that will be embedded into the HTML document. The default is Match Movie, but you can also change the size using either pixels or percentages as your measurement unit.
- **Playback:** These selections determine how the movie plays at runtime. Paused At Start means the user will have to click something to move out of Frame 1. The Loop option means the SWF file plays and returns to Frame 1 after it finishes. Display Menu allows users to display a context menu when they right-click (PC) or Cmd-click (Mac) the SWF file while it is playing. Select the Device Font option to use device fonts in static text boxes. Only the static text boxes in the movie that use device fonts will be affected.

- **Quality:** The quality settings in this drop-down list range from Low to Best. Low doesn't use anti-aliasing, but the Auto Low selection attempts to use a better quality on playback and plays the movie quickly. The default is High.

- **Window Mode:** Use this setting to control the wmode attribute in the HTML document. Window is the default, and the Flash SWF file appears in a normal browser window. Opaque Windowless leaves the background in the Flash document but removes the browser from around it. If you do choose this mode, be sure to give the user a button that closes the SWF file when it is finished. Transparent Windowless sets the background of the Flash movie to transparent and removes the browser window, including the title bar, as well. This is how Flash movies appear to "float" over an HTML page.

- **HTML Alignment:** Positions the SWF file in the browser window.

- **Scale:** Select this option if you changed the dimensions of the SWF file. Default maintains the aspect ratio of the file. Exact Fit displays the SWF file without keeping the aspect ratio while still maintaining the values entered in the Dimensions area. No Border scales the SWF file, but keeps the aspect ratio but crops the Stage if necessary. No Scales keeps the SWF file at its original dimensions, even if the user resizes the browser window.

- **Flash Alignment:** Aligns the SWF file in the browser window and determines cropping, if necessary.

Embedding a SWF File in a Dreamweaver 8 Page

When you create the SWF file and you have a graphical HTML editor such as Dreamweaver 8, you don't need to create an HTML file. When you place a SWF file into a Dreamweaver 8 page, Dreamweaver generates the <object> and <embed> tags necessary to display the SWF file on a Web page. One other advantage to using Dreamweaver 8 is the ability to test the animation from within Dreamweaver and to test the page containing the SWF file from within a browser right in Dreamweaver.

> **Note** Although we are using Macromedia Dreamweaver 8, this section can be completed if you own Dreamweaver MX or Dreamweaver MX 2004.

Before launching Dreamweaver, you need to create the directory where the SWF file, the HTML page, and any other documents such as a CSS document and images will reside. We have included a folder—BCSlideShow—in the Lesson 11 exercises that you can use for this purpose. The images used in the slide show are contained in this folder. If you use IIS on a PC you can copy this folder from the CD to the directory you use for Web pages. On the Mac, copy this folder to Macintosh HD/name/Sites. If you use neither, feel free to work from your desktop.

1. Open *Slideshow_AS.fla* in Flash and open the **Publish Settings** dialog box.

In the Formats pane deselect the HTML option. Click the Browse button in the Flash (SWF) area to open the Select Publish destination dialog box and navigate to the BCSlideShow folder. Click the Save button to save this path. Click the Publish button, and the SWF file is published to the folder just selected. When the Progress dialog box closes, save the Flash file and quit Flash.

Tip *You might hear Flash developers tell you that they just "compiled a SWF file." All that means is they just published the SWF file.*

Tip *The Publish Destination will include the path to the SWF on your computer. If you want to avoid this set the Publish Destination then click the "Use Default Names" button. This will remove the path.*

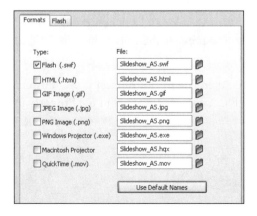

2. Open Dreamweaver 8 and open a new HTML page by selecting File > New and selecting Basic Page from the Category area and by selecting HTML in the Basic Page area and clicking the Create button.

A basic page in Dreamweaver 8 is essentially blank. You'll deal with that next. When the new page opens, enter **BC_SlideShow** in the Title area of the toolbar and select File > Save As to save the page to your folder containing the SWF file.

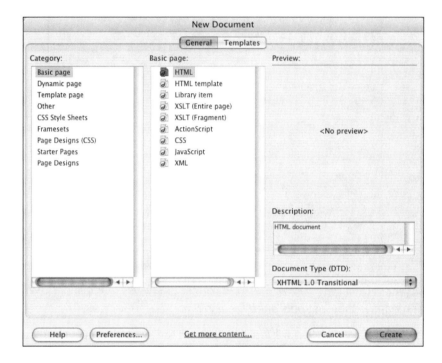

3. Select Modify > Page Properties to open the Page Properties dialog box.

Select black—#000000—as the text color and a light grey—#CCCCCC—as the background color. Click the Apply button to preview the color. Click the OK button, and the page fills with the background color.

Click once on the page and enter **The BC Rainforest Presentation**. Select the text and select Heading 1 from the Format drop-down list in the Property inspector. Press Return/Enter twice.

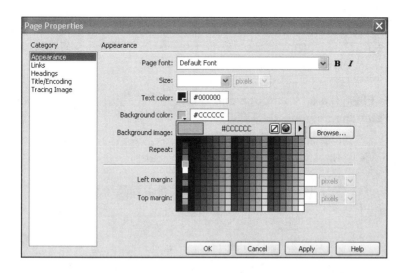

4. Select Insert > Media > Flash to open the Select File dialog box.

Dreamweaver can manage a wide range of media types, which is the purpose of the menu and the Select File dialog box. When the dialog box opens, be sure to select File System in the Select File Name From area. The Data Source selection is reserved for dynamic sites that use server technologies such as ColdFusion MX 7. Navigate to the folder in which the SWF file is located and select it by clicking it once. Select Document from the Relative To: area and click OK. The SWF file appears on the page as a gray box with a Flash symbol in the middle.

5. Select the Flash file on your page and click the Play button in the Property inspector to play the movie.

Selecting the Flash movie also changes the Property inspector to reflect your choice. To stop the movie from playing, simply click the Stop button.

Another useful feature of Dreamweaver 8 is the Round Trip editing feature. If you find a problem with the file, you can edit the Flash movie in Flash, compile the SWF file, and return to Dreamweaver 8 where the updated SWF file appears.

To prepare for a round trip, click the Browse button in the SRC area of the Property inspector, locate your FLA file, and select it. When you close the dialog box you will be prompted to move the file to the same directory as the SWF file. Click OK.

The next step is to click the Edit button in the Property inspector, which launches Flash and opens the source file for the SWF file. You can now make your changes, compile the movie, and save the FLA file. Instead of quitting Flash, click the Done button just above the Flash Timeline, which closes Flash and returns you to Dreamweaver.

6. To preview the Dreamweaver 8 page containing the Flash SWF file, select File > Preview in Browser or press F12 (PC) or Option-F12 (Mac).

The browser opens, and you can review how the SWF file will work in the browser. Close the Browser to return to Dreamweaver.

At this stage of the game, you can either choose to upload the files to your Web server or simply save the page and quit Dreamweaver. If you do decide to upload the files to your site, you can choose to use a third-party FTP application such as WS_FTP Pro on the PC or Transmit on the Mac. You can also use Dreamweaver's internal FTP application for a similar purpose.

Note *The following instructions require you to have defined a site in Dreamweaver. Defining a site is out of the scope of this book and will not be covered.*

7. If the Files panel isn't open, select Window > Files or press F8 to open it.

This panel gives you a view of all the folders and files used in the current site. If the folder isn't visible, check to see whether you have opened the correct site. If you haven't, select it from the list in the Site drop-down list.

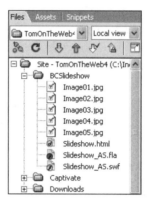

8. Click once on the folder to be uploaded and click the Put button in the Files panel.

The Background File Activity dialog box opens, which shows you the progress of the upload. New to Dreamweaver 8 is the FTP in the background feature. In previous versions of the application, when you were uploading folders and files to a server, you were essentially stopped from doing anything else on you computer until this process had finished. Dreamweaver 8 changes this. Now you can click on the page or open another page to work on while the file is uploading. When the process is completed, quit Dreamweaver.

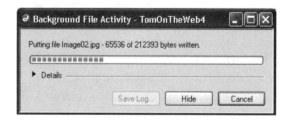

Wrapping it all up

Congratulations! You have completed the exercises in the book and been taken on a journey through Flash Professional 8. So what do you do next? We suggest you go make yourself a cup of coffee, pour yourself a soft drink or a juice, and just sit back and smile.

What you have done is journey through one of the most intriguing Web development applications available and completed a number of projects ranging from the relatively simple to the complex. Think about what you knew about working with Flash when you first opened the cover of this book and now think about how you have created movies with animations and an MP3 Player. You have created Flash movies with text and movies with video. You have created Flash projects that are destined for playback on cell phones and PDAs, and movies that contain one frame and a blank Stage. You have come a long way and, we hope, have had a huge amount of fun.

So what's the next step in the journey? As one of the authors is fond of saying, "You know the basics; now drive a truck through it." Take what you have learned and expand your knowledge. We have included a number of Flash sites in Appendix B that will help you with that process. There are also a number of companion volumes in this series that are designed to further your ActionScript knowledge and the whole field of using Flash to build applications.

We want to conclude this book with a small bit of advice. Approach Flash expecting to have fun. Talk to any Flash developer or listen to any of the Flash names that speak at conferences around the world and you will discover they are having fun with Flash. It is this sense of wonder and fun that drives the Flash community forward. The bit of advice?

The amount of fun you can have with Flash should be illegal. We will see you in jail!

What You Have Learned

In this lesson you have:

- Created a Publish profile (pages 445–450)
- Changed the publish settings (pages 445–450)
- Detected the Flash version (pages 452–454)
- Created an HTML page in Dreamweaver 8 for the project (pages 454–461)
- Explored the Round Trip feature between Flash Professional 8 and Dreamweaver 8 (pages 454–461)
- Uploaded a file to Web server (pages 454–461)

A KEYBOARD SHORTCUTS

File Menu

Command	Windows Shortcut	Macintosh Shortcut
New	Ctrl+N	Cmd+N
Open	Ctrl+O	Cmd+N
Close	Ctrl+W	Cmd+W
Close All	Ctrl+Alt+W	Cmd+Option+W
Save	Ctrl+S	Cmd+S
Save As	Ctrl+Shift+S	Cmd+Shift+S
Import To Stage	Ctrl+R	Cmd+R
Open External Library	Ctrl+Shift+O	Cmd+Shift+O
Export Movie	Ctrl+Alt+Shift+S	Cmd+Option+Shift+S
Publish Settings	Ctrl+Shift+F12	Option+Shift+F12
Default Publish Preview (HTML)	F12	Cmd+F12
Publish	Shift+F12	Shift+F12
Print	Ctrl+P	Cmd+P
Exit	Ctrl+Q	Cmd+Q

Edit Menu

Command	Windows Shortcut	Macintosh Shortcut
Undo	Ctrl+Z	Cmd+Z
Redo	Ctrl+Y	Cmd+Y
Cut	Ctrl+X	Cmd+X
Copy	Ctrl+C	Cmd+C
Paste In Center	Ctrl+V	Cmd+V
Paste In Place	Ctrl+Shift+V	Cmd+Shift+V
Clear	Backspace	Delete

Edit Menu *(continued)*

Command	Windows Shortcut	Macintosh Shortcut
Duplicate	Ctrl+D	Cmd+D
Select All	Ctrl+A	Cmd+A
Deselect All	Ctrl+Shift+A	Cmd+Shift+A
Find And Replace	Ctrl+F	Cmd+F
Find Next	F3	F3
Cut Frames	Ctrl+Alt+X	Cmd+Option+X
Copy Frames	Ctrl+Alt+C	Cmd+Option+C
Paste Frames	Ctrl+Alt+V	Cmd+Option+V
Clear Frames	Alt+Backspace	Option+Delete
Remove Frames	Shift+F5	Shift+F5
Select All Frames	Ctrl+Alt+A	Cmd+Option+A
Edit Symbols	Ctrl+E	Cmd+E
Preferences	Ctrl+U	Flash Professional > Preferences

View Menu

Command	Windows Shortcut	Macintosh Shortcut
Go To First	Home	Home
Go To Previous	Page Up	Page Up
Go To Next	Page Down	Page Down
Go To Last	End	End
Zoom In	Ctrl+=	Cmd+=
Zoom Out	Ctrl+-	Cmd+-
Magnification: 100%	Ctrl+1	Cmd+1
Magnification: 400%	Ctrl+4	Cmd+4
Magnification: 800%	Ctrl+8	Cmd+8
Show Frame	Ctrl+2	Cmd+2
Show All	Ctrl+3	Cmd+3
Outline	Ctrl+Alt+Shift+O	Cmd+Option+Shift+O
Fast Preview	Ctrl+Alt+Shift+F	Cmd+Option+Shift+F
Anti+Alias	Ctrl+Alt+Shift+A	Cmd+Option+Shift+A
Anti+Alias Text	Ctrl+Alt+Shift+T	Cmd+Option+Shift+T
Work Area	Ctrl+Shift+W	Cmd+Shift+W
Rulers	Ctrl+Alt+Shift+R	Cmd+Option+Shift+R
Show Grid	Ctrl+'	Cmd+'

View Menu (continued)

Command	Windows Shortcut	Macintosh Shortcut
Edit Grid	Ctrl+Alt+G	Cmd+Option+G
Show Guides	Ctrl+;	Cmd+;
Lock Guides	Ctrl+Alt+;	Cmd+Option+;
Edit Guides	Ctrl+Alt+Shift+G	Cmd+Option+Shift+G
Snap To Grid	Ctrl+Shift+'	Cmd+Shift+'
Snap To Guides	Ctrl+Shift+;	Cmd+Shift+;
Snap To Objects	Ctrl+Shift+/	Cmd+Shift+/
Edit Snapping	Ctrl+/	Cmd+/
Hide Edges	Ctrl+H	Cmd+Shift+E
Show Shape Hints	Ctrl+Alt+H	Cmd+Option+H

Insert Menu

Command	Windows Shortcut	Macintosh Shortcut
New Symbol	Ctrl+F8	Cmd+F8
Frame	F5	F5

Modify Menu

Command	Windows Shortcut	Macintosh Shortcut
Document	Ctrl+J	Cmd+J
Convert To Symbol	F8	F8
Break Apart	Ctrl+B	Cmd+B
Optimize	Ctrl+Alt+Shift+C	Cmd+Option+Shift+C
Add Shape Hints	Ctrl+Shift+H	Cmd+Shift+H
Distribute To Layers	Ctrl+Shift+D	Cmd+Shift+D
Convert to Keyframes	F6	F6
Clear Keyframe	Shift+F6	Shift+F6
Convert To Blank Keyframe	F7	F7
Scale And Rotate	Ctrl+Alt+S	Cmd+Option+S
Rotate 90 Degrees Clockwise	Ctrl+Shift+9	Cmd+Shift+9
Rotate 90 Degrees Counter-Clockwise	Ctrl+Shift+7	Cmd+Shift+7
Remove Transform	Ctrl+Shift+Z	Cmd+Shift+Z
Bring To Front	Ctrl+Shift+Up	Cmd+Shift+Up
Bring Forward	Ctrl+Up	Cmd+Up

Modify Menu *(continued)*

Command	Windows Shortcut	Macintosh Shortcut
Send Backward	Ctrl+Down	Cmd+Down
Send To Back	Ctrl+Shift+Down	Option+Shift+Down
Lock	Ctrl+Alt+L	Cmd+Option+L
Unlock All	Ctrl+Alt+Shift+L	Cmd+Option+Shift+L
Align Left	Ctrl+Alt+1	Cmd+Option+1
Align Horizontal Center	Ctrl+Alt+2	Cmd+Option+2
Align Right	Ctrl+Alt+3	Cmd+Option+3
Align Top	Ctrl+Alt+4	Cmd+Option+4
Align Vertical Center	Ctrl+Alt+5	Cmd+Option+5
Align Bottom	Ctrl+Alt+6	Cmd+Option+6
Distribute Widths	Ctrl+Alt+7	Cmd+Option+7
Distribute Heights	Ctrl+Alt+9	Cmd+Option+9
Make Same Width	Ctrl+Alt+Shift+7	Cmd+Option+Shift+7
Make Same Height	Ctrl+Alt+Shift+9	Cmd+Option+Shift+9
To Stage	Ctrl+Alt+8	Cmd+Option+8
Group	Ctrl+G	Cmd+G
Ungroup	Ctrl+Shift+G	Cmd+Shift+G

Text Menu

Command	Windows Shortcut	Macintosh Shortcut
Plain	Ctrl+Shift+P	Cmd+Shift+P
Bold	Ctrl+Shift+B	Cmd+Shift+B
Italic	Ctrl+Shift+I	Cmd+Shift+I
Align Left	Ctrl+Shift+L	Cmd+Shift+L
Align Center	Ctrl+Shift+C	Cmd+Shift+C
Align Right	Ctrl+Shift+R	Cmd+Shift+R
Justify	Ctrl+Shift+J	Cmd+Shift+J
Letter Spacing Increase	Ctrl+Alt+Right	Cmd+Option+Right
Letter Spacing Decrease	Ctrl+Alt+Left	Cmd+Option+Left
Letter Spacing Reset	Ctrl+Alt+Up	Cmd+Option+Up

Control (Ctrl) Menu

Command	Windows Shortcut	Macintosh Shortcut
Play	Enter	Return
Rewind	Ctrl+Alt+R	Cmd+Option+R
Test Movie	Ctrl+Enter	Cmd+Return
Debug Movie	Ctrl+Shift+Enter	Cmd+Shift+Return
Test Scene	Ctrl+Alt+Enter	Cmd+Option+Return
Test Project	Ctrl+Alt+P	Cmd+Option+P
Enable Simple Frame Actions	Ctrl+Alt+F	Cmd+Option+F
Enable Simple Buttons	Ctrl+Alt+B	Cmd+Option+B
Mute Sounds	Ctrl+Alt+M	Cmd+Option+M

Window Menu

Command	Windows Shortcut	Macintosh Shortcut
Duplicate Window	Ctrl+Alt+K	Cmd+Option+K
Timeline	Ctrl+Alt+T	Cmd+Option+T
Tools	Ctrl+F2	Cmd+F2
Properties	Ctrl+F3	Cmd+F3
Library	Ctrl+L	Cmd+L
Actions	F9	Option+F9
Behaviors	Shift+F3	Shift+F3
Debugger	Shift+F4	Shift+F4
Movie Explorer	Alt+F3	Option+F3
Output	F2	F2
Project	Shift+F8	Shift+F8
Align	Ctrl+K	Cmd+K
Color Mixer	Shift+F9	Shift+F9
Color Swatches	Ctrl+F9	Cmd+F9
Info	Ctrl+I	Cmd+I
Transform	Ctrl+T	Cmd+T
Components	Ctrl+F7	Cmd+F7
Component Inspector	Alt+F7	Option+F7
Accessibility	Alt+F2	Option+F2
History	Ctrl+F10	Cmd+F10
Scene	Shift+F2	Shift+F2
Strings	Ctrl+F11	Cmd+F11
Web Services	Ctrl+Shift+F10	Cmd+Shift+F10
Hide Panels	F4	F4

Actions Panel

Command	Windows Shortcut	Macintosh Shortcut
Pin Script	Ctrl+=	Cmd+=
Close Script	Ctrl+-	Cmd+-
Close All Scripts	Ctrl+Shift+-	Cmd+Shift+-
Go To Line	Ctrl+G	Cmd+,
Find And Replace	Ctrl+F	Cmd+F
Find Again	F3	Cmd+G
Auto Format	Ctrl+Shift+F	Cmd+Shift+F
Check Syntax	Ctrl+T	Cmd+T
Show Code Hint	Ctrl+Spacebar	Cmd+Spacebar
Import Script	Ctrl+Shift+I	Cmd+Shift+I
Export Script	Ctrl+Shift+X	Cmd+Shift+X
Script Assist	Ctrl+Shift+E	Cmd+Shift+E
Hidden Characters	Cmd+Shift+8	Ctrl+Shift 8
Line Numbers	Ctrl+Shift+L	Cmd+Shift+L
Word Wrap	Ctrl+Shift+W	Cmd+Shift+W
ActionScript Preferences	Ctrl+U	Cmd+U (Only in the Actions Panel)

Debugger Panel

Command	Windows Shortcut	Macintosh Shortcut
Word Wrap	Ctrl+Shift+W	Cmd+Shift+W
Continue	F10	Option+F10
Stop Debugging	F11	Option+F11
Step In	F6	F6
Step Over	F7	F7
Step Out	F8	F8

Output Panel

Command	Windows Shortcut	Macintosh Shortcut
Word Wrap	Ctrl+Shift+W	Cmd+Shift+W
Copy	Ctrl+C	Cmd+C
Clear	Backspace	Delete
Find	Ctrl+F	Cmd+F
Find Again	F3	Cmd+G

B Getting Help: The Flash Community

It will happen to you eventually. You need to do something that is specific to your movie and you just can't find out how to do it. There is a huge support community out there just waiting to help you solve problems, learn new techniques, and even share your knowledge. In recent years, the number of blogs, tutorial sites, and even mailing lists has grown in direct relation to the rise of Flash. The fascinating aspect of the Flash community is that it is an "open" community. We are all learning something new every day, and everyone from superstars to those just learning Flash are encouraged to share what you have learned with the rest of the community.

In the following pages, we list some of the more useful resources available to you. This list is in no way to be regarded as definitive, but it is a great place to start.

Macromedia Flash Professional 8: Training From The Source

A lot of work has gone into this book and we encourage you to contact us if you have any questions or get stuck. Although there are two of us, we don't guarantee an immediate reply—but you will get a response.

Book Site: www.tomontheweb3.ca

This book's Web site. We have the exercise files for each chapter available for download, as well as contact information and a lot more.

Tutorial and Resource Sites

There are a ton of these out there on the Internet. A simple Google search for "Flash Tutorials" returned more than 15 million results. Obviously, you can't visit all of them, so the key to finding the site that works for you is to simply "surf" and find the site that is most tuned to your need. Here is a short list of some of the more popular sites that will help you expand your Flash skills:

CommunityMX: www.communityMX.com

This subscription-based site is devoted to all things Macromedia and has a large number of tutorials—both free and for sale—that range from the basic to the advanced. The site also contains a Forum for subscribers where they can get their problems dealt with in short order.

Brendan Dawes: www.brendandawes.com

Artist, thinker, tinkerer, and film fan, Brendan Dawes' site is a worth a bookmark because it will take time to review the Flash tutorials, projects, and other eclectic musings on this site.

Flash MX: www.flash-mx.com

A Flash site devoted to news, tutorials, book and software reviews, and anything else to do with Flash.

FlashKit: www.flashkit.com

One of the older, more established sites out there. The site is a bit difficult to navigate, but the range of tutorials and so on is extensive.

Were-Here: www.were-here.com

A rather comprehensive site with a full range of resources and tutorials aimed at all levels of expertise.

Macromedia Developer Center: www.macromedia.com/devnet/

The Developer Center (also known as the Dev Center) is a great jumping-off point for learning how to use all Macromedia's products. Each product has its own area.

Ultrashock: www.ultrashock.com/

An online community run by many of the "names" in the Flash business.

Quantumwave: quantumwave.com/flash/

Dave Yang has posted one of the more comprehensive listings of Flash resources and blogs available.

InformIT: www.informit.com

A large bookstore resource. There is an extensive listing of Flash books and articles in the Design and Creative Media area.

Flash Zone: www.flzone.com

Flash resources, extensions, and tutorials.

FlaZoom: www.flazoom.com

This site is more a portal to interesting Flash work than anything else.

FlashColdFusion: www.flashcfm.com

Everything you ever needed to know about how Flash and ColdFusion work together.

FlashMagazine: www.flashmagazine.com

An online magazine that deals with all things Flash.

Flash Devices: www.flashdevices.net

Bill Perry, who is involved in Macromedia's move into devices, runs this site.

Flash Enabled: www.flashenabled.com

Flash on devices and device galore can be found on Phil Torrone's site.

Levitated: www.levitated.net

Jarred Tarbell proves that math and Flash can create some stunning art. Most of the pieces are available for download and subsequent code deconstruction.

Yugop: www.yugop.com

Yugo Nakamura never ceases to amaze the Flash community with his works that stretches what anybody ever thought was possible in Flash.

Josh Davis: www.joshuadavis.com

The biggest name in the Flash industry regularly posts experiments, tutorials, and source code to the community.

Actionscript.org: www.actionscript.org/

A great resource for learning the language.

Actionscript.com: www.actionscript.com

A rather well-put-together Flash reference and online community.

Person13: www.person13.com

Joey Lott's compilation of articles and tutorials dealing with Flash Remoting and ActionScript.

Colin Moock: www.moock.org

If Josh Davis is the biggest name in Flash design, Toronto-based Colin Moock is his ActionScript counterpart.

FlashGuru: www.flashguru.co.uk

Guy Watson's site has an extensive collection of tutorials and links regarding Flash.

Forums and Lists

Think of the Flash forums as being a level 1 trauma center. They are a great place to ask questions, look for solutions, and even share your knowledge. The fascinating thing about the forums is this: Don't be terribly surprised if one of the "names" in the business answers your question.

CommunityMX: `www.communitymx.com`

Quite a few topic-specific forums in its Flash area.

Macromedia Web Forums: `http://webforums.macromedia.com/flash/`

If you have a problem, a comment or need help, this site is Ground Zero. The forum is also available as a newsfeed at `news://forums.macromedia.com`.

Were Here: `www.were-here.com`

One of the busier ones around.

Flashkit: `www.flashkit.com`

The oldest and biggest Flash forum on the Web.

E-mail lists are also becoming quite popular. They provide a sense of community and immediacy generally not found in the forums. A lot of the lists range from high-traffic to sporadic, and from highly visible to obscure. Here are some of the more common (public) ones out there:

Figleaf Software: `http://chattyfig.figleaf.com`

Hit this site and you can subscribe to a number of Flash lists sponsored by this training company. The lists cater to skill levels ranging from the advanced (Flashcoders) to the beginner (Flashnewbies).

Flasher: `http://www.chinwag.com/flasher/`

General discussion of all things Flash-related.

FlashPro: `http://flash-list.com/`

A mailing list for professional Flash designers and ActionScript coders.

Macromedia.com

This is one of those sites that every Flash user has bookmarked in the browser. It is deep, indulgent and just loaded with goodies. In fact this site will help you work through this book and will be invaluable when you finish it.

Software Download: `www.macromedia.com/downloads`

All of Macromedia's software is available for purchase or as a 30-day trial.

Macromedia Developer Center: `www.macromedia.com/devnet/`

The Developer Center (also known as the Dev Center) is a great jumping-off point for learning how to use all of Macromedia's products. Each product has its own area and new articles, written by the pros, appear almost daily. Whether it be a tutorial, a presentation, or an article, you are sure to find something that will catch your interest.

Tech Notes (Flash): `http://www.macromedia.com/support/flash/technotes.html`

The tech notes, in many respects, are a rather extensive collection of FAQs that cover a variety of issues identified both by Macromedia and the Developer Community with Flash.

Site of the Day: `http://www.macromedia.com/cfusion/showcase/index.cfm`

Sometimes you just need some inspiration or an answer to the question, "What are other people doing with Flash?" While you are there, a visit to the Site of the Day Archive is invaluable.

Extending Flash: `http://www.macromedia.com/exchange/`

The Macromedia Exchange is a great place to search for free components or extensions, or to purchase components and extensions created for Flash by the Developer community. The Exchange does cover just Flash. You can find something for every application in the Studio 8 collection at this location.

User Groups:
`http://www.macromedia.com/cfusion/usergroups/index.cfm`

If there is one aspect of Macromedia that separates it from the rest of the software developers it is its User Group program. The odds are that there is an extremely active Macromedia User Group where you live or close by. This page provides a comprehensive listing of the User Groups.

Macromedia Blogs: `http://weblogs.macromedia.com/mxna/`

The MX News Aggregator for Macromedia and the Macromedia community in general. Some of the more popular Macromedia posters are John Dowdell, who can always be counted on for an eclectic but dead-on view of the Web development business and Mike Chambers who is among the Macromedia "point men" in all matters relating to Flash.

Macromedia Press Books

Here's a listing of other Macromedia Press books that will help you to expand your Flash knowledge:

Macromedia Flash 8: A Tutorial Guide

0-321-39414-3
Written by Jay Armstrong and Jen deHaan

Learning ActionScript 2.0 for Macromedia Flash 8

0-321-39415-1
Written by Jen and Peter deHaan

Using ActionScript 2.0 Components with Macromedia Flash 8

0-321-39539-5
Written by Bob Berry, Jen deHaan, Peter deHaan, David Jacowitz and Wade Pickett

Developing Extensions for Macromedia Flash 8

0-321-39416-X
Written by Barbara Snyder

Macromedia Flash 8 ActionScript: Training from the Source

0-321-33619-4
Written by Derek Franklin and Jobe Makar

Macromedia Flash 8: Training from the Source

0-321-33629-1
Written by James English

ActionScript 2.0 Language Reference for Macromedia Flash 8

0-321-38404-0
Written by Francis Cheng, Jen deHaan, Robert L. Dixon and Shimul Rahim

Index

C

caching bitmaps, 237–238
call() method (NetConnection class), 293
Camera class, 339
CDK (Content Developer Kit), 413
cell phone applications, 411–442
    building, 420–432
    creating a movie, 416–420
    Flash and devices, 413–415
CELP (Code Excited Linear Prediction), audio
        codecs, 166
Character Embedding dialog box, 30
Check Spelling command (Text menu), 138
Check Spelling dialog box, 138
Check Syntax button, 50–51, 343
childNodes property, load() method, 388
classes, 43
    ActionScript, 59–61
    Camera, 339
    Connection, ActionScript, 289
    custom, 61
    LoadVars(), accessing external data, 65–71
    Microphone, 339
    NetConnection, 289, 293–295
    NetStream, 289
    strict data typing, 57
    TransitionManager, customizing Flash Video
        Player, 308–317
    User Interface, ActionScript, 289
    Video, 294
close() method (NetConnection class), 293
Code Excited Linear Prediction (CELP), audio
        codecs, 166
codes
    hinting, 58–59
    writing to external files, 43
Color Chip, 21
Color Mixer command (Window menu), 92
Color Mixer panel, 92, 374
Color Picker, 19, 93
Color Picker command (Window menu), 374
Color Swatches panel, 93
colors
    animation, 228–232
    graphics, slide shows, 90–93
    hexadecimal, 90
    palette, 90
    sampling, 91
    selection, 19

Combine Objects command (Modify menu), 85
ComboBox component, 368
commands
    Control menu, Loop Playback, 204
    Edit menu
        Copy, 95
        Cut, 104
        Paste, 95
        Paste In Place, 140
        Paste in Place, 104
        Preferences, 4, 8
        Undo, 84
    File menu
        Edit Sites, 39
        Import, 17, 95, 257
        Import to Library, 168
        New, 278
        Open, 37
        Preview in Browser, 459
        Publish Settings, 9, 34, 36, 98
        Revert, 142
        Save, 450
    Flash menu, Preferences, 8
    Global Functions menu, Timeline Control, 53
    Help menu, Flash Help, 46
    Insert menu
        Media, 457
        New Symbol, 91, 335
        Timeline, 109, 324
    Modify menu
        Break Apart, 144
        Combine Objects, 85
        Convert to Symbol, 9, 103
        Document, 7, 73
        Group, 418
        Page Properties, 456
        Shape, 81
        Timeline, 144
        Transform, 84
    Select menu, All, 95
    Template menu, Global Phones, 416
    Text menu
        Check Spelling, 138
        Spelling Setup, 136
    View menu
        Bandwidth Profiler, 451
        Grid, 104, 105
        Guides, 21, 105
        Magnification, 15
        Rulers, 20, 105, 130, 427

E

Ease In/Ease Out, tweening, 207–211
Ease slider, 208
easing methods, 317
ECMA-252 scripting standards, 43
edges, feathering, 82
Edit Envelope dialog box, 196
Edit Format Options button, 28, 125
Edit Grid command (View menu), 104
Edit Grid dialog box, 104–105, 105
Edit Guides command (View menu), 21, 105
Edit Guides dialog box, 105
Edit menu commands
  Copy, 95
  Cut, 104
  keyboard shortcuts, 463–464
  Paste, 95
  Paste In Place, 140
  Paste in Place, 104
  Preferences, 4, 8, 458
  Undo, 84
Edit Sites command (File menu), 39
editable parameter, 150
Editable parameter (Component Inspector), 369
Editor (ActionScript), 363
effects, text, 138–139
  animating letters, 143–144
  drop shadow with filter, 139–142
  masks, 142–143
elements, XML (eXtensible Markup Language), 385
Embed button, 30
<embed> tag, 35
embedded fonts, 26
Embedded Video symbol, 347, 348
Embedding screen (Import Video dialog box), 323
enabled parameter, 151
Encode Audio radio button (Flash 8 Video
    Encoder), 269
Encoder dialog box, 270
Encoding page (Video Import wizard), 258
Encoding Settings window (Flash 8 Video
    Encoder), 264
Encoding tab (Flash 8 Video Encoder), 265
Envelope command (Modify menu), 85
errors, Check Syntax button, 51
events, 43
  ActionScript, 71–75
  sounds, 169–171
  triggers, 326–333

Expert mode, 51
Export for ActionScript button, 247
eXtensible Markup Language (XML), 384
eXtensible Media Platform (XMP), metadata, 7
external data, accessing with LoadVars() class,
    65–71
external files, write code to, 43
Eyedropper tool, 91
eyedroppers, 21

F

Fade transition, 309
fading in video, TransitionManager class, 308–317
feathering edges, 82
Figleaf Software Web site, 473
File menu commands
  Edit Sites, 39
  Import, 17, 95, 257, 322
  Import to Library, 168
  keyboard shortcuts, 463
  New, 278
  Open, 37
  Preview in Browser, 459
  Publish Settings, 9, 34, 36
  Revert, 142
  Save, 450
files
  ActionScript, 3
  external, write code to, 43
  JavaScript, 3
  Project, creating, 37–38
  sizes, image resizing, 25
Files command (Window menu), 460
fills, vectors, 81–84
filters
  adding drop shadows to text, 139–142
  animation
    blending, 232–238
    Blur filter, 212–216
    drop shadows, 216–222
    tweening, 222–228
    Flash installed, 217–218
    manipulation of video, 334–339
Finish Video Import page (Video Import wizard),
    259
Fireworks 8, creating bitmaps, 79
firstChild property, load() method, 387
Flash 8 Video Encoder. *See* Video Encoder
Flash 8 Video Encoder dialog box, 270

M

Training from the Source

cromedia's *Training from the Source* series is one of the best-selling series on the market.
s series offers you a unique self-paced approach that introduces you to the major features
the software and guides you step by step through the development of real-world projects.

h book is divided into a series of lessons. Each lesson begins with an overview of the lesson's
ntent and learning objectives and is divided into short tasks that break the skills into bite-size
ts. All the files you need for the lessons are included on the CD that comes with the book.

cromedia Flash 8:
ning from the Source
N 0-321-33629-1

Macromedia Flash
Professional 8: Training
from the Source
ISBN 0-321-38403-2

Macromedia Flash 8
ActionScript: Training
from the Source
ISBN 0-321-33619-4

Macromedia Studio 8:
Training from the Source
ISBN 0-321-33620-8

cromedia Dreamweaver 8:
ning from the Source
N 0-321-33626-7

Macromedia Dreamweaver 8
with ASP, PHP and ColdFusion:
Training from the Source
ISBN 0-321-33625-9

Macromedia Fireworks 8:
Training from the Source
ISBN 0-321-33591-0

macromedia®
PRESS

Macromedia Tech Support: http://www.macromedia.com/support

Licensing Agreement

The information in this book is for informational use only and is subject to change without notice. Macromedia, Inc., and Macromedia Press assume no responsibility for errors or inaccuracies that may appear in this book. The software described in the book is furnished under license and may be used or copied only in accordance with terms of the license.

The software files on the CD-ROM included here are copyrighted by Macromedia, Inc. You have the non-exclusive right to use these programs and files. You may use them on one computer at a time. You may not transfer the files from one computer to another over a network. You may transfer the files onto a single hard disk so long as you can prove ownership of the original CD-ROM.

You may not reverse engineer, decompile, or disassemble the software. You may not modify or translate the software or distribute copies of the software without the written consent of Macromedia, Inc.

Opening the disc package means you accept the licensing agreement. For installation instructions, see the ReadMe file on the CD-ROM.